SERIES 24

EXAM STUDY GUIDE 2021
+ TEST BANK

SECURITIES INSTITUTE
SECURITIES LICENSING SERIES

The Securities Institute of America proudly publishes world class textbooks, test banks and video training classes for the following Financial Services exams:

Securities Industry Essentials exam / SIE exam
Series 3 exam
Series 4 exam
Series 6 exam
Series 7 exam
Series 9 exam
Series 10 exam
Series 22 exam
Series 24 exam
Series 26 exam
Series 39 exam
Series 57 exam
Series 63 exam
Series 65 exam
Series 66 exam
Series 99 exam

SERIES 24
EXAM STUDY GUIDE 2021 + TEST BANK

The General Securities Principal Examination

The Securities Institute of America, Inc.

Published by The Securities Institute of America, Inc.

ISBN: 978-1-937841-17-1(Paperback)

ISBN 978-1-937841-18-8 (ePub)

Printed in the United States of America.

10 9 8 7 6 5 4 3 2 1

Contents

CHAPTER 5

CHAPTER 6

CHAPTER 9

INVESTMENT COMPANIES AND OTHER PRODUCTS 261

About the Series 24 Exam

Congratulations! You are on your way to becoming a registered principal, licensed to supervise a broker dealer's general securities business. The Series 24 exam will be presented in a 150-question multiple-choice format. Each candidate will have 3 hours and 30 minutes to complete the exam. A score of 70% or higher is required to pass.

The Series 24 is as much a knowledge test as it is a reading test. The writers and instructors at The Securities Institute have developed the Series 24 textbook, exam prep software, and videos to ensure that you have the knowledge required to pass the test and to make sure that you are confident in the application of that knowledge during the exam.

IMPORTANT EXAM NOTE

The Series 24 exam may use the terms Nasdaq, Nasdaq market center execution system, or NMCES to describe the Nasdaq workstation, or market test takers are advised to be aware of this and to treat the terms as interchangeable.

TAKING THE SERIES 24 EXAM

The Series 24 exam is presented in multiple-choice format on a touchscreen computer known as the PROCTOR system. No computer skills are required, and candidates will find that the test screen works in the same way as an ordinary ATM machine. Each test is made up of 150 questions that are randomly chosen from a test bank of several thousand questions. The test has a time limit of 3 hours and 30 minutes, which is designed to provide enough time for all candidates to complete the exam. The Series 24 exam is composed of questions that focus on the following areas:

Function 1: Supervision of Registration of the Broker Dealer and Personnel Management Activities	9 questions	6%
Function 2: Supervision of General Broker Dealer Activities	45 questions	30%
Function 3: Supervision of Retail and Institutional Customer-Related Activities	32 questions	21%
Function 4: Supervision of Trading and Market Making Activities	32 questions	21%
Function 5: Supervision of Investment Banking and Research	32 questions	21%
TOTAL	**150 Questions**	**100%**

HOW TO PREPARE FOR THE SERIES 24 EXAM

For most candidates, the combination of the textbook, exam prep software, and video class instruction proves to be enough to successfully complete the exam. It is recommended that the candidate spend at least 60 to 70 hours preparing for the exam by reading the textbook, underlining key points; watching the video class; and completing as many practice questions as possible. We recommend that a candidate schedule the exam no more than one week after completing the Series 24 exam prep.

Test-Taking Tips

- ❑ Read the full question before answering.
- ❑ Identify what the question is asking.
- ❑ Identify key words and phrases.
- ❑ Watch out for hedge clauses, such as *except* and *not.*
- ❑ Eliminate wrong answers.
- ❑ Identify synonymous terms.
- ❑ Be wary of changing answers.

WHAT TYPE OF POSITIONS MAY A SERIES 24 REGISTERED PRINCIPAL HOLD?

A Series 24 registered principal may supervise and manage a firm and its agents, and conduct a general securities business.

WHAT SCORE IS REQUIRED TO PASS THE EXAM?

A score of 70% or higher is needed to pass the Series 24 exam.

ARE THERE ANY PREREQUISITES FOR THE SERIES 24?

A general securities principal must have passed the SIE and one of the following series 7, 16, 57, 79, 82, 86 or 87 exams.

HOW DO I SCHEDULE AN EXAM?

Ask your firm's compliance department to schedule the exam for you or to provide a list of test centers in your area. You must be sponsored by a FINRA member firm prior to making an appointment. The Series 24 exam may be taken any day that the exam center is open.

WHAT MUST I TAKE TO THE EXAM CENTER?

A picture ID is required. All other materials will be provided, including a calculator and scratch paper.

HOW SOON WILL I RECEIVE RESULTS OF THE EXAM?

The exam will be graded as soon as you answer your final question and hit the Submit for Grading button. It will take only a few minutes to get your results. Your grade will appear on the computer screen, and you will be given a paper copy at the exam center.

If you do not pass the test, you will need to wait 30 days before taking it again. If you do not pass on the second try, you will need to wait another 30 days. If you fail a third time, you must wait six months to take the test again.

About This Book

The writers and instructors at The Securities Institute have developed the Series 24 textbook, exam prep software, and videos to ensure that you have the knowledge required to pass the test and to make sure that you are confident in the application of that knowledge during the exam. The writers and instructors at The Securities Institute are subject-matter experts as well as Series 24 test experts. We understand how the test is written, and our proven test-taking techniques can dramatically improve your results.

Each chapter includes notes, tips, examples, and case studies with key information; hints for taking the exam; and additional insight into the topics. Each chapter ends with a practice test to ensure that you have mastered the concepts before moving on to the next topic.

About the Test Bank

This book is accompanied by a test bank of hundreds of questions to further reinforce the concepts and information presented here. The test bank is provided to help students who have purchased our book from a traditional bookstore or from an online retailer such as Amazon. If you have purchased this textbook as part of a package from our website containing the full version of the software, you are all set and simply need to use the login instructions that were emailed to you at the time of purchase. Otherwise to access the test bank please email your purchase receipt to sales@securitiesce.com and we will activate your account. This test bank provides a small sample of the questions and features that are contained in the full version of the exam prep software.

If you have not purchased the full version of the exam prep software with this book, we highly recommend it to ensure that you have mastered the knowledge required for your exam. To purchase the exam prep software for this exam, visit The Securities Institute of America online at: www.securitiesce.com or call 877-218-1776.

About The Greenlight Guarantee

Quite simply the Greenlight guarantee is as follows:
Pass our Greenlight exam within 5 days of your actual exam, and if you do not pass we will refund the money you paid to The Securities Institute. If you only have access to the Limited Test Bank through the purchase of this textbook, you may upgrade your online account for a small fee to include the Greenlight exam and receive the full benefits of our greenlight money back pass guarantee.

About The Securities Institute of America

The Securities Institute of America, Inc. Helps thousands of securities and insurance professionals build successful careers in the financial services industry every year. In more than 25 years we have helped students pass more than 250,000 exams. Our securities training options include:

- Classroom training
- Private tutoring
- Interactive online video training classes
- State-of-the-art exam prep test banks
- Printed textbooks
- ebooks
- Real-time tracking and reporting for managers and training directors

As a result, you can choose a securities training solution that matches your skill level, learning style, and schedule. Regardless of the format you choose, you can be sure that our securities training courses are relevant, tested, and designed to help you succeed. It is the experience of our instructors and the quality of our materials that make our courses requested by name at some of the largest financial services firms in the world.

To contact The Securities Institute of America, visit us on the Web at: www.securitiesce.com or call 877-218-1776.

CHAPTER 1

Brokerage Office Procedures

INTRODUCTION

Guidelines for the practices that a brokerage firm uses to conduct the operation of its daily business are regulated by industry, state, and federal regulators. These guidelines are the foundation for the way that the firm handles all business, from hiring a new agent to executing a customer's order. All Series 24 candidates must have a full understanding of a brokerage firm's operations and procedures to successfully complete the exam.

HIRING NEW EMPLOYEES

A registered principal of a firm will be the individual who interviews and screens potential new employees. The principal will be required to make a thorough investigation into the candidate's professional and personal backgrounds. With few exceptions, other than clerical personnel, all new employees will be required to become registered as an associated person with the firm. The new employee will begin the registration process by filling out and submitting a Uniform Application for Securities Industry Registration, also known as Form U4. Form U4 is used to collect the applicant's personal and professional history, including:

- 10-year employment history
- Five-year resident history
- Legal name and any aliases used
- Any legal or regulatory actions

The principal of the firm is required to verify the employment information for the last three years and must attest to the character of the applicant by signing Form U4 prior to its submission to FINRA. All U4 forms will be sent to the Central Registration Depository (CRD) along with a fingerprint card for processing and recording. The employing firm must maintain written procedures to verify the accuracy of the information on the new hire's U4 form. A comprehensive review of the information must take place within 30 days of the form being submitted to FINRA. Fingerprint cards may be submitted in hard copy or electronically. The candidate's fingerprints will be submitted to the FBI for review. If after three good faith attempts to submit fingerprints the FBI determines that the fingerprints are ineligible or cannot be read the candidate will not be asked to submit a fourth set of fingerprints and the FBI will conduct a name check to search the candidate's history. Any applicant who has answered yes to any of the questions on the form regarding his or her background must give a detailed explanation in the DRP pages attached to the form. The applicant is not required to provide information regarding:

- Marital status
- Educational background
- Income or net worth

Information regarding the employee's finances will be disclosed on Form U4 if the associated person has ever declared bankruptcy, if the employee has any unsatisfied judgements or liens, or entered into a compromise with creditors. For example, if a registered person entered into a short sale in a real estate transaction, and the bank forgave any portion of the loan, this must be reported on the employee's form U4. Interestingly, if the representative is in the process of being foreclosed upon for their primary residence, this action need not be reported by the employee. Any development that would cause an answer on the associated person's U4 to change requires that the member update the U4 within 30 days of when the member becomes informed of the event. In the case of an event that could cause the individual to become statutorily disqualified, such as a felony conviction or misdemeanor involving cash or securities, the member must update the associated person's U4 within 10 business days of learning of the event. Additionally, broker dealers are required to perform independent background checks on its employees every 5 years to ensure that no judgements, liens or disclosable events have gone unreported by the registered person. Registered persons who fail to disclose any unsatisfied judgements or liens are subject to significant regulatory action that could result in the person being barred from the industry in extreme cases. If a member firm conducts employee drug testing, and a registered person fails the drug test, this is neither reportable on form u4 nor a reason for statutory disqualification.

RESIGNATION OF A REGISTERED REPRESENTATIVE

If a registered representative voluntarily resigns or has his or her association with a member firm terminated for any reason, the member must fill out and submit a Uniform Termination Notice for Securities Industry Registration, which is known as Form U5. The member must submit the form to FINRA within 30 days of the termination. The member firm is also required to give a copy of the form to the representative upon termination. The member must also state the reason for the termination, either voluntary or for cause. Voluntary terminations cover all terminations that were not the result of the agent being fired for violations of industry or company regulations, such as staff reductions. An associated person's registration is nontransferable. A representative may not simply move his or her registration from one firm to another. The employing firm that the representative is leaving must fill out and submit a Form U5 to FINRA, which terminates the representative's registration. The new employing firm must fill out and submit a new Form U4 to begin a new registration for the associated person with the new employer. The new employer is required to obtain a copy of the U5 form filed by the old employing member either from the employee or directly from FINRA within 60 days of submitting the new U4. The previous employer is not required to provide a copy to the new member firm. If the new employing member asks the associated person for a copy of the U5, the member has two business days to provide it. If the member requests a copy of the U5 from the agent who has not received a copy of his or her U5 from the old employer, the agent must promptly request it from the old employer and provide it to the new employer within two business days of receipt. Should an agent's previous employer discover facts that would alter the information on Form U5, the previous employer must file an amended Form U5 within 30 days and provide a copy to the former employee. A representative who leaves the industry for more than 24 months is required to requalify by exam. During a period of absence from the industry of two years or less, FINRA retains jurisdiction over the representative in cases involving customer complaints and violations.

 TAKE**NOTE!**

A firm may not allow an inactive agent to "park" his or her license with the firm and may not maintain an inactive agent's license on the books simply to ensure that the agent does not have to requalify by exam. The one exception to the rule is for agents in the military who are called to active duty. While on active duty, the agent's registration and continuing education requirements will be "tolled" until he or she returns. While on active duty the agent may not conduct business but may receive commissions generated from his or her book of business. Once the agent returns from active duty he or she has 90 days to reenter the securities industry. If after 90 days the agent does not reenter the business, the 24-month window begins. An agent who has already left the industry upon joining the military will have his or her 24-month window tolled as of the date active-duty begins. Upon return, if the individual has not re-entered the industry on the 91st day, the 24-month window will pick up where it was tolled.

REGISTRATION EXEMPTIONS

The following individuals are exempt from registration:

- Clerical
- Nonsupervising officers and managers not dealing with customers
- Non-U.S. citizens working abroad
- Floor personnel

PERSONS INELIGIBLE TO REGISTER

Individuals applying for registration must meet the association's requirements in the following areas:

- Training
- Competence
- Experience
- Character

Anyone who fails to meet the association's requirements in any of the above listed areas may not become registered. An individual may also be disqualified by statute or through rules for any of the following:

- Expulsion, suspension, or disciplinary actions by the Securities and Exchange Commission (SEC) or any foreign or domestic self-regulatory organization (SRO).
- The individual caused the expulsion or suspension of a broker dealer or principal.
- The individual made false or misleading statements on the application for registration on Form U4 or Form B-D.
- Felony conviction or misdemeanor involving securities, bribery, falsification of reports, perjury, or any other felony within the last 10 years.
- Court injunction or order barring the individual.

A member firm may seek to maintain the employment of or to initially hire a person who has been statutorily disqualified by filing an appeal to FINRA's registration and disclosure (RAD) department. The appeal may be decided by the department or referred to the National Adjudicatory Counsel (NAC). A hearing may be held by the Statutory Disqualification Committee and appealed to the NAC. The position being applied for under the appeal may only be clerical in nature and may not entail duties of a registered agent. A person who has been convicted of a felony that occurred less than 10 years ago may apply for a waiver to FINRA or the broker dealer's self-regulatory organization. If a waiver is granted the SRO must notify the SEC of the granting of such waiver. The SEC may overturn or object to the waiver being granted. If the waiver is granted the person covered by the waiver will be subject to heightened supervisory procedures. The heightened supervisory procedures should be designed in writing for the specific individual based on their past or pending violations. As part of the supervisory requirements, the individual subject to statutory disqualification must be assigned to a designated principal.

TAKENOTE!

A person who was convicted of a felony more than 10 years ago is always required to disclose it on Form U4.

DISCIPLINARY ACTIONS AGAINST A REGISTERED REPRESENTATIVE

If another industry regulator takes disciplinary action against a representative, the employing member firm must notify FINRA. Actions by any of the following should be immediately disclosed to the association:

- SEC
- An exchange or association
- State regulator
- Clearing firm
- Commodity regulatory body

Also immediately reportable to FINRA are any of the following:

- A customer complaint alleging theft, forgery, or misappropriation of customer assets
- Indictment, conviction, or plea of guilty or no contest to a criminal matter
- If the agent becomes a respondent or defendant in a matter in excess of $15,000 or if the firm becomes a respondent or defendant in a matter in excess of $25,000
- An agent is disciplined by the employing member firm or commissions are withheld from an agent, or the agent is fined in either case in amounts in excess of $2,500

FINRA defines immediate notification for the above listed matters as being within 10 days. All disclosures must include the type of action brought as well as the name of the party bringing the actions and the name of the representative involved. The firm will make the disclosure on Form U4. FINRA will submit disciplinary actions that are taken by FINRA on Form U6 and they will be recorded on the employee's record. All disciplinary actions as well as final arbitration awards, along with a record of the agent's registrations and employment history, are available through FINRA's BrokerCheck program. FINRA members are required to regulate the activities of its associated people and must disclose to the association any action that the member takes against a registered representative. Should a registered representative feel that the information disclosed through the BrokerCheck program is inaccurate the representative may request an amendment to the disclosure by filling out and submitting a BrokerCheck comment form. Additionally, should the CRD contain information that is deemed to be inaccurate, factually impossible or otherwise false, that information may be expunged and permanently removed from the agent's record.

TERMINATION FOR CAUSE

A member may terminate a registered representative for cause if the representative has:

- Violated firm policy.
- Violated the rules of the New York Stock Exchange (NYSE), FINRA, the SEC, or any other industry regulator.
- Violated state or federal securities laws.

A firm may not terminate a representative who is the subject of investigation by any securities industry regulator until the investigation is completed.

OUTSIDE EMPLOYMENT

If a registered representative wants to obtain employment outside of his or her position with a member firm, the registered representative must first provide written notification to the employing member firm. The member firm may reject or limit the representative's outside employment. Exceptions to this rule are if the registered representative is a passive investor in a business, is a board member of a nonprofit organization or if the representative owns rental property. Neither the rental property nor the income received is required to be reported. However, if a registered representative obtains a real estate license or acts as a property manager for a large rental property, these would qualify as outside business activities and must be disclosed to the employer as well as on Form U4. Note that the representative need not inform his/her employer regarding outside employment of a spouse or other family members.

PRIVATE SECURITIES TRANSACTIONS

A registered representative may not engage in any private securities transactions without first obtaining the broker dealer's prior written approval. The registered representative must provide the employing firm with all documentation regarding the investment and the proposed transaction. An example of a private securities transaction would be if a representative helped a startup business raise money through a private placement. If the representative is going to receive compensation, the employing member firm must supervise the transaction as if the firm itself executed the transaction. If a representative sells investment products that the employing member does not conduct business in without the member's knowledge, then the representative has committed a violation known as selling away. An exception to this is if the representative is helping an immediate family member raise money and the representative receives no compensation for his or her role in the private transaction. In this case, the notification and permission of the member is not required.

GIFT RULE

Broker dealers may not pay compensation to employees of other broker dealers. If a broker dealer wants to give a gift to an employee of another broker dealer, the gift must:

- Be valued at less than $100 per person per year.
- Be given directly to the employing member firm for distribution to the employee.
- Have the employing member's prior approval for the gift.

The employing member must obtain a record of the gift, including the name of the giver, the name of the recipient, and the nature of the gift. These rules have been established to ensure that broker dealers do not try to influence the employees of other broker dealers. An exception to this rule would be in cases where an employee of one broker dealer performs services for another broker dealer under an employment contract. The following are also excluded from the $100 limit:

- Occasional meals
- Business-related travel
- Lucite prospectus and awards
- Occasional tickets to sporting events

A key to determine if tickets are a gift or entertainment is if the person providing the tickets attends the event. If the person attends, it is considered entertainment. Records of gifts and employment contracts must be retained for three years. Prior FINRA approval is not required for employment contracts between members. The gift rule also applies to gifts given to or received from customers of the firm or agent. In the case of a mutual fund holding a seminar, the mutual fund may pay for a registered representative's travel-related expenses and the seminar must be held at a "reasonable" location. Spouses of agents are allowed to attend; however, the mutual fund may only pay for the travel expenses of the agent. The agent's expenses may not be paid for by the fund in exchange for past sales or the promise of sales in the future.

 TAKE**NOTE!**

Firms and agents also may not give a gift to influence any report or dissemination of information designed to influence the price of a security.

SHARING IN A CUSTOMER'S ACCOUNT

It is permissible for a representative to maintain a joint account with a customer as long as the firm approves it in advance. The representative may share in the profit and loss of the account only in direct relation to his or her contribution to the account. A registered representative is precluded from sharing in the profit and loss of an account without making any financial contribution to the account. The one exception to this rule is when a registered representative establishes a joint account with an immediate family member. A registered representative may share disproportionately in the profits and losses of an account when the joint account is established with an immediate family member.

BORROWING AND LENDING MONEY

Borrowing and lending of money between registered persons and customers is strictly regulated. If the member firm allows borrowing and lending between representatives and customers the firm must have policies in place that will allow for the loans to be made. Loans may be made between an agent and a customer if the customer is a bank or other lending institution, where there is a personal or outside business relationship and that relationship is the basis for the loan, or between two agents registered with the same firm. The firm must provide the agent with written preapproval for the loan unless the loan is being made between the agent and an immediate family member or a bank. The approval documentation must be maintained for 3 years from the date when the loan was repaid or 3 years from the rep's termination from the firm.

ORDER TICKETS

Prior to executing a customer's order the representative must fill out the appropriate order ticket and present it to the trading department or wire room for execution. All order tickets will include:

- Buy or sell.
- Name of security.
- Number of shares or bonds.
- Account name and number.
- Account type (i.e., cash or margin).
- Price and time limits, if any.
- Solicited or unsolicited.
- Discretionary authority exercised or discretionary authority not exercised, if applicable.
- Time stamp when entered, executed, changed, or canceled.

EXECUTING AN ORDER

An important part of executing a customer's order lies in the operational procedures that route the order to the markets and handle trade input functions for the order once it has been executed. The brokerage firm assigns specific departments to handle all of the important functions of trade execution and input. The departments are:

- Order room/wire room
- Purchase and sales department
- Margin department
- Cashiering department

ORDER ROOM/WIRE ROOM

Once a representative has received an order from a client, the representative must present the order for execution to the order room. The order room will promptly route the order to the appropriate market for execution. Once the order has been executed, the order room will forward a confirmation of the execution to the registered representative and to the purchase and sales department.

PURCHASE AND SALES DEPARTMENT

Once the order has been executed the purchase and sales department inputs the transaction to the customer's account. The purchase and sales department, sometimes called "P&S," is also responsible for mailing confirmations to the customer and for all billing.

MARGIN DEPARTMENT

All transactions, regardless of the type of account, are sent through the margin department. The margin or credit department calculates the amount of money owed by the customer and the date when the money is due. The margin department will also calculate any amount due to a customer.

CASHIERING DEPARTMENT

The cashiering department handles all receipts and distributions of cash and securities. All securities and payments delivered from clients to the firm are processed by the cashiering department. The cashiering department will also issue checks to customers and, at the request of the margin department, will forward certificates to the transfer agent.

BECOMING A STOCKHOLDER

Although some people purchase the shares directly from the corporation when the stock is offered to the public directly, most investors purchase the shares from other investors. These investor-to-investor transactions take place in the secondary market on the exchange or in the over-the-counter market. Although the transaction in many cases only takes seconds to execute, trades actually take several days to fully complete. Let us review the important dates regarding transactions for a "regular-way" settlement.

TRADE DATE

The trade date is the day when the order is actually executed. Although an order has been placed with a broker, it may not be executed on the same day. Certain types of orders may take several days or even longer to execute. A market order, however, will be executed as soon as it is presented to the market, making the trade date the same day the order was entered.

SETTLEMENT DATE

The buyer of a security actually becomes the owner of record on the settlement date. When an investor buys a security from another investor, the selling investor's name is removed from the security and the buyer's name is recorded as the new owner. The settlement date is two business days after the trade date. This is known as T + 2 for all regular-way transactions in common stock, preferred stock, corporate bonds, and municipal bonds. Government bonds and options all settle the next business day following the trade date. Any trade done on a cash basis settles on the same day regardless of the security involved in the transaction. Settlement dates are set by the Uniform Practice Code.

PAYMENT DATE

The payment date is the day when the buyer of the security has to have the money to the brokerage firm to pay for the purchase. The payment date for securities under the industry rules is four business days after the trade date, or T + 4. Payment dates are regulated by the Federal Reserve Board under Regulation T of the Securities Exchange Act of 1934. Although many brokerage firms require their customers to pay for their purchases sooner than the rules state, the customer has up to four business days to pay for the trade.

VIOLATION

If the customer fails to pay for the purchase within the four business days allowed, the customer is in violation of Regulation T. As a result, the brokerage firm will "sell out" and freeze the customer's account. On the fifth business day following the trade date, the brokerage firm will sell out the securities that the customer failed to pay for. The customer is responsible for any loss that may occur as a result of the sell out and the brokerage firm may sell out shares of another security in the investor's account in order to cover the loss. The brokerage firm will then freeze the customer's account, which means that the customer must deposit money upfront for any purchases in the next 90 days. After the 90 days have expired, the customer is considered to have reestablished good credit and may then conduct business in the "regular way" and take up to four business days to pay for trades. A customer may get an additional four business days to pay for the trade by requesting an extension. An extension request must be submitted to the NYSE or FINRA before the expiration of the fourth business day. A broker dealer may ignore a call for cash of $1,000 or less.

CLEARLY ERRONEOUS REPORTS

If a registered representative reports the execution of a trade to a customer and that report is clearly an error, then that report is not binding on the agent or the firm. The customer must accept the trade as it actually occurred, not as it was erroneously reported, so long as the transaction was in line with the terms of the order.

EXECUTION ERRORS

If a transaction is executed away from a customer's limit price or is executed for too many shares of stock, the customer in not obligated to accept the transaction. A registered representative who is informed of an execution error should immediately inform the principal of the error.

If the firm has executed an order at the wrong price, size, or side of the market or in the wrong security, the trade should promptly be moved into the firm's error account and offset as soon as possible. Neither the firm nor the agent may solicit trades to resolve the error and remove it from the error account. However, should the firm receive an unsolicited customer order during the time the trade is in the error account, the firm may use those shares to satisfy the unsolicited order. If the error involved a customer order, the order as it was executed will be journaled into the error account and subsequently posted to the customer's account in line with the customer's instructions. Execution errors for too many shares or away from a customer's limit price are examples of trades that will be moved to the error account. The traders or representatives who move trades to the error account must fully document the error for review by the principal.

If a customer makes an error entering the terms of an order over an online trading platform, the customer is obligated to accept the execution in line with the terms entered, not as intended. The customer in this case should be advised to execute an order to reverse the trade over the online trading portal.

EXAMPLE

A customer who maintains an account with a broker dealer enjoys working with his agent when making investment decisions. Virtually all of the customer's orders are executed by his registered rep once a trading decision has been made. The customer has owned 500 shares of ABC Microchips for some time and his rep is on vacation in the week just prior to ABC releasing its earnings. Concerned about how the report will be received, the customer logs on to his account to sell his 500 shares of ABC. Not being familiar with the online trading platform the customer enters the order to buy 500 shares of ABC instead of entering an order to sell 500 shares. The customer, who is now long 1,000 shares of ABC, should be advised to enter an offsetting order to sell 1,000 shares of ABC. Any losses as a result of the customer's error will be absorbed by the customer and are not the responsibility of the firm.

CORPORATE AND MUNICIPAL SECURITIES SETTLEMENT OPTIONS

Regular-way transactions in corporate stocks and bonds, Americans depository receipts/ADRs, and municipal bonds settle on the third business day, or T + 3. However, occasionally either party to the transaction may request an alternative settlement. Other settlement options include:

- Cash
- Next day
- Seller's option
- Buyer's option
- RVP/DVP/COD

CASH

A transaction done on a cash basis settles the same day. A cash trade requires that the buyer have the funds available for payment and the seller to have the securities available for delivery on the day the trade is executed. Cash trades executed prior to 2:00 p.m. EST settle by 2:30 p.m. EST. Trades executed after 2:00 p.m. EST settle within 30 minutes.

NEXT DAY

A transaction executed for a next day settlement requires that the buyer has the cash available for payment and the seller has the securities available for delivery on the next business day.

SELLER'S OPTION

A seller who wishes to lock in a sale price for the securities but who, for some reason, is not able to deliver the securities, may elect to specify a seller's option settlement. The seller may specify the date on which the securities will be delivered but may not deliver the securities any sooner than the third business day. If the seller wants to deliver the securities earlier then specified in the contract, the seller must give the buyer one day written notice of his or her intention to settle the trade early.

BUYER'S OPTION

Buyers may specify the date when they will make payment for the securities and accept delivery of the securities, much the same as a seller's option.

RVP/DVP/COD

Many trusts and other fiduciaries will not allow cash to be paid out until the securities they purchased are delivered. Alternatively, in the case of a sale, they will not allow the securities to be delivered until payment is received. A bona fide RVP/DVP account will allow the transaction to settle no sooner than the regular way of T + 2 but no later than 35 calendar days. The account is given up to 35 days to settle the transaction. In the case of a purchase, the securities have to be registered in the buyer's name by the transfer agent and delivered. It is the responsibility of the party entering the order for a RVP/DVP account to assure the member executing the order that the bank is aware of the purchase and will make prompt payment when the certificates are presented. When entering an order to sell securities from an RVP/DVP account delivery must be made within two business days.

WHEN-ISSUED SECURITIES

When a corporate issuer declares a stock split, the stock will trade in the marketplace on a when-issued basis, prior to the distribution of the new shares. Sellers of the stock during this time may sell the stock on a when-issued basis or may deliver the old securities with a due bill attached for the new shares. Corporate securities sold on a when-issued basis will normally settle two business days after the securities are issued. Municipal securities that are sold prior to the certificate being available for delivery are sold on a when-issued basis. The purchaser will receive a when-issued confirmation and a final confirmation two days prior to the certificate's delivery. If for some reason FINRA's Uniform Practice Committee does not determine the settlement date for when issued securities, the transaction will settle when determined by the seller provided that at least 1 business day notice has been provided to the buyer.

GOVERNMENT SECURITIES SETTLEMENT OPTIONS

Regular-way transactions in government securities settle on the next business day, or T + 1. There are, however, times when either party to the transaction may request an alternative settlement. Other settlement options include:

- Cash
- Seller's option

- Buyer's option
- RVP/DVP/COD

The settlement options available to investors in government securities are similar to those for corporate and municipal securities. However, government securities that are traded on a when-issued basis settle the day after the securities are available for delivery.

TAKE**NOTE!**

All foreign internal securities traded (not ADRs) will require the exchange of currency and will settle and clear through the rules and procedures of the foreign market where the security is principally traded.

ACCRUED INTEREST

Most bonds pay interest semiannually based on their maturity date. An investor who wishes to sell a bond between the interest payment dates will be owed the interest that has become due or that has accrued during the holding period. Investors who purchase the bonds between interest payment dates will receive the full semiannual interest payment on the bond's next interest payment date. As a result, the purchaser of the bonds must pay the seller the portion of the earned interest, which is known as accrued interest. Most bonds trade with accrued interest, also known as "and interest." There are only two dates during the month that a bond may pay interest: the 1st and the 15th of the month. Interest on a new issue of bonds begins to accrue on the dated date. It is not unusual for an investor who purchases a new issue of debt securities to owe accrued interest to the issuer for bonds that are delivered after the dated date. Semiannual interest payments may be made on the 1st or 15th of the following months:

January & July
February & August
March & September
April & October
May & November
June & December

CALCULATING ACCRUED INTEREST

Interest on all bonds accrues from the last interest payment date up to, but not including, the settlement date. Accrued interest calculations for corporate and municipal securities use a 360-day year in which all months contain 30 days. To determine the amount of accrued interest due or owed for corporate and municipal issues, use the following formula:

principal × rate × time

(principal × interest rate) × (number of days/360) = accrued interest

To calculate the accrued interest for a government issue, use the actual number of calendar days in the month and a 365-day year.

CLOSE OUTS

In the case where the selling broker dealer fails to deliver the securities to the buying broker dealer, the buying broker dealer may close out the trade by purchasing the securities in the open market. This is known as a buy in, and the selling broker dealer will be responsible for any loss as a result of the buy in. Notice of the buying broker dealer's intention to buy in the selling broker dealer may be done no sooner than one business day past the settlement or trade date plus three business days. The broker dealer executing the buy in must send notice to the contra party no later than 12 noon, two business days prior to buying the broker dealer in. The failing broker has until 3PM EST on the notice date to deliver the subject securities. The first day that a broker dealer may buy in a security is trade date plus five business days. If a selling broker dealer delivers securities in good form to the buying broker dealer and the securities are rejected, the selling broker dealer may sell out the securities immediately. FINRA rules require the mandatory close out of certain naked short positions. If a firm or a customer has a naked short position and fails to deliver the subject securities 10 business days after the settlement date, the position is subject to a mandatory buy in. A special notation next to their symbol on the Nasdaq workstation identifies securities subject to the mandatory buy in. Subject securities must have a net short position of at least 10,000 shares and the net short position must be at least 1/2% of the issuer's outstanding stock. A full list of all subject securities, known as threshold securities, is available online. The mandatory close out does not apply to short positions established as a result of bona fide market making, fully hedged, or arbitrage positions.

CUSTOMER CONFIRMATIONS

All customers must be sent a confirmation at or before the completion of the transaction. Industry rules consider the completion of the transaction to be the settlement date. For buyers of the security, it is the time when the payment is made. If the customer has the funds available in the account, it is the time when the funds are moved through a book-keeping entry. For the seller, it is the time when the security is delivered. If the security is delivered prior to its due date, completion will occur when the payment is credited into the account. It is unlawful to settle a transaction without having sent a confirmation of the transaction to the customer. All customer confirmations must include:

- Customer's name and account number.
- Description of the transaction, such as buy or sell.
- Trade date and settlement date.
- Number of shares, bonds, or units.
- Price.
- CUSIP number.
- Amount due or owed.
- Commission charged for agency transactions.
- Markup charged for riskless principal transactions.
- Markup charged for principal transactions in Nasdaq Global Market and third-market trades ("reported securities"), as required under SEC Rule 10b-10.
- Markup charged for Nasdaq Capital Market securities stocks under FINRA rules.
- Yield information for bonds.
- If bonds or preferred stock is callable.
- Whether the firm acted as an agent or principal.
- Whether the firm acted as agent for the other side of the transaction—known as "dual agency."
- Amount of commission or markup or markdown.
- If the firm makes a market in the security.
- If there is a control relationship between the firm and the issuer of the security.
- Information regarding where the transaction was executed.
- If the firm received payment for executing the order with another firm.

- The time of execution or a statement that the time will be furnished upon request.

If the customer requests additional information within 30 days of the transaction, as detailed on the confirmation, the firm has five business days to provide it. If the customer's request is made after 30 days, the firm may take up to 15 days to provide the information. If the firm receives payment for executing orders with other firms (payment for order flow), the firm must disclose this at the time the customer opens the account and annually thereafter.

RULES FOR GOOD DELIVERY

All securities delivered by a customer or another broker dealer must be in good condition and must:

- Be signed by all owners, and all owners must be alive.
- Be in the correct denominations, such as number of shares or par value of bonds.
- Have all attachments.
- Be accompanied by a uniform delivery ticket.

The owner of a security must endorse the certificate at the time of sale to ensure its negotiability or sign a stock or bond power, also known as a power of substitution. The stock power, when attached to the certificate, will make it negotiable and includes an irrevocable power of attorney. All signatures must be accepted by the transfer agent. To ensure that the transfer agent accepts the signatures on certificates delivered by NYSE member firms, the NYSE started the Medallion Signature Guarantee Program, which allows NYSE members to stamp the certificates with a medallion rather than sign them. This stamp ensures that the transfer agent will accept the certificates for transfer and provides indemnification insurance for fraud. A member firm may also use the medallion seal to effect the change of ownership for an account, the gifting of shares and for estate matters for the account of a deceased client. The Medallion Program members pay to participate in the program.

Examples of invalid signatures are:

- The signature of a minor.
- The signature of a deceased person.
- The signature of only one owner if jointly registered.
- A forged signature.

REJECTION OF DELIVERY

The buying firm may reject the delivery of securities from the selling member if:

- The certificates are mutilated.
- The certificates are not in the proper denominations.
- All attachments are not present.
- The signatures are invalid.
- The signatures have not been guaranteed.
- The securities are delivered prior to settlement.
- The wrong securities are delivered.
- If the specific bond being delivered has been called and was not identified as being called at the time of the trade.

DELIVERY OF ROUND LOTS

Stock certificates must be delivered in denominations that are in round lots or in lots that easily add up to create round lots. Stock certificates for odd lots are cleared separately.

EXAMPLE

A customer sells 200 shares of XYZ. The following certificates are considered good delivery:

One certificate for 200 shares

Two certificates for 100 shares

Two certificates for 60 shares and two certificates for 40 shares

Twenty certificates for 10 shares

The following is not good delivery:

Five certificates for 40 shares

One certificate for 130 shares

Certificates that cannot be easily added up to 100 shares are not good delivery. If the selling broker dealer delivers a certificate for a portion of the trade and the remaining shares will add up to one round lot or multiples of round lots, then the buying broker dealer must accept the partial delivery.

DELIVERY OF BOND CERTIFICATES

Bond certificates delivered between broker dealers must be in par values of $1,000 or $5,000 and must be in bearer form unless clearly identified as otherwise at the time of the trade. Partially called bonds are not considered to be good delivery between broker dealers. However, bonds subject to a total call are good delivery. If a bond is delivered with a coupon missing, the buying broker dealer will deduct the value of the coupon payment from the amount delivered to the seller. Municipal bonds delivered without the legal opinion attached must be identified as being traded ex legal in order to be considered good delivery.

RECLAMATION

A broker dealer may return or demand the return of securities previously accepted for delivery through a process known as reclamation. A broker dealer using the reclamation process must make the demand by submitting a Uniform Reclamation Form to the contra broker dealer. The reasons for rejecting delivery listed above are also valid reasons for instituting the reclamation process.

MARKING TO THE MARKET

A broker dealer who has an open contractual commitment to another broker dealer will monitor the market value of the securities involved relative to the contract or trade price. This process is known as marking to the market. A broker dealer who is partially unsecured can issue a call or demand for more collateral. If a firm sends a mark to the market demand to another broker dealer, the demand must be met promptly.

EXAMPLE

If a broker dealer borrows $20,000 worth of securities for a customer who is executing a short sale for $20,000 worth of ABC, the borrowing broker dealer would have to deposit $20,000 with the lending broker dealer as collateral for the securities. If the market value of ABC increases to $25,000, the broker dealer who loaned the securities may demand that the borrowing broker dealer deposit an additional $5,000 as collateral. Alternatively, if the market value of ABC had fallen to $15,000, the borrowing broker dealer may demand a return of $5,000.

CUSTOMER ACCOUNT STATEMENTS

A customer must receive a statement every month in which there is activity in the account. All customers must receive account statements at least quarterly when there has been no activity in the account. Examples of activity include:

- Purchases and sales.
- Dividend and interest received.
- Interest charged.
- Addition or withdrawal of cash or securities.

Customer account statements must show:

- All positions in the account.
- All activity since the last statement.
- All credit and debit balances.

TAKENOTE!

Customers who have accounts containing penny stocks must receive monthly statements showing the value of the penny stock position.

Brokerage firms that hold customer cash and securities are required to disclose their financial condition to their clients by sending them a balance sheet every six months or on the request of a customer with cash or securities on deposit.

CARRYING OF CUSTOMER ACCOUNTS

Not all brokerage firms maintain the physical possession of the customers' cash and securities. A brokerage firm that maintains the account of its customers and holds their cash and securities is known as a carrying firm, or a self-clearing member. A broker dealer may find it easier to have another member provide the clearing and custodial functions for its customers' accounts. This type of broker dealer is known as an introducing broker dealer or correspondent. Anytime a clearing agreement is executed or amended it must be sent to FINRA for review. The clearing member must notify the introducing member of the reports it offers correspondent broker dealers to monitor customer accounts when it executes the agreement and at least annually no later than July 1. Additionally, the introducing member must notify the clearing member of the reports it needs to supervise customer accounts. The introducing member forwards all cash and securities to the carrying or clearing member for deposit into the customers' accounts. The clearing firm sends the customers' statements and confirmations to the introducing firm's customers. If a firm clears all of their transactions on a fully disclosed basis, all customers of the introducing firm must be notified of the fact in writing when the account is opened. Since customers of the introducing firm receive confirmations and statements with the name of both the introducing member and the clearing firm it is not unusual for the clearing firm to receive a customer complaint from a customer of an introducing firm. In this case, the clearing firm must notify the customer that the complaint was received and immediately forward the complaint to the introducing firm and to FINRA. If the introducing broker is also a market maker, the clearing firm must stand behind all of the introducing firm's trades. An introducing member may also choose to clear its trades through an omnibus account maintained at the clearing firm. In this case, all transactions are cleared through one account, and the clearing member does not know for whom the trade was executed. The introducing member is required to send customer confirmations if they clear through an omnibus account. Omnibus accounts are not allowed to purchase securities on margin for customers. All securities must be paid for in full. The clearing agreement must detail the responsibility of each party relating to:

- The preparation and maintenance of records
- The opening, approving, and supervision of customer accounts
- Extension of credit receipt and delivery of cash and securities
- Acceptance and execution of orders
- Preparation and mailing of statements and confirmations

DIVIDEND DISTRIBUTION

If a corporation decides to pay a dividend to its common stockholders, it may not discriminate as to who receives the dividend. The dividend must be paid to all common stockholders of record. Existing stockholders do not need to notify the company that they are entitled to receive the pending dividend—it will be sent to them automatically. However, new purchasers of the stock may or may not be entitled to receive the dividend, depending on when they purchased the stock relative to when the dividend is going to be distributed. Let's now examine the dividend distribution process.

DECLARATION DATE

The declaration date is the day that the board of directors decides to pay a dividend to common stockholders of record. The declaration date is the starting point for the entire dividend process. The company must notify the regulators at the exchange or FINRA, depending on where the stock trades, at least 10 business days prior to the record date.

EX DIVIDEND DATE

The ex dividend date, or the ex date, is the first day when purchasers of the security are no longer entitled to receive the dividend that the company has declared for payment. Stated another way, the ex date is the first day when the stock trades without (ex) the dividend attached. The exchange or FINRA sets the ex date for the stock based on the record date determined and announced by the corporation's board of directors. Because it takes two business days for a trade to settle, the ex date is always one business day prior to the record date.

RECORD DATE

The record date is the day when investors must have their names recorded on the stock certificates in order to be entitled to receive the dividend that was declared by the board of directors. Stockholders whose names are on the stock certificates (owners of record) will be entitled to receive the dividend. The investor must have purchased the stock before the ex dividend date in order to be an owner of record on the record date. The record date is determined by the corporation's board of directors and is used to determine which shareholders will receive the dividend.

PAYMENT DATE

This is the day when the corporation actually distributes the dividend to shareholders, which completes the dividend process. The payment date is controlled and set by the board of directors of the corporation and is usually four weeks following the record date.

STOCK PRICE AND THE EX DIVIDEND DATE

It is important to note that the value of the stock prior to the ex dividend date reflects the value of the stock with the dividend. On the ex dividend date, the stock is now trading without the dividend attached, and new purchasers will not receive the dividend that had been declared for payment. As a result, the stock price will be adjusted down on the ex dividend date in an amount equal to the dividend.

EXAMPLE

TRY declares a $.20 dividend payable to shareholders of record as of Thursday, August 22. The ex dividend date will be one business day prior to the record date. In this case, the ex date will be Wednesday, August 21. If TRY closed on Tuesday, August 20, at $24 per share, the stock would open at $23.80 on Wednesday.

Sunday	Monday	Tuesday	Wednesday	Thursday	Friday	Saturday
				1	2	3
4	5	6	7	8	9	10
11	12	13	14	15	16	17
18	19	20	21	22	23	24
25	26	27	28	29	30	31

DIVIDEND DISBURSEMENT PROCESS

The corporation's dividend disbursement agent is responsible for the distribution of dividends and will send the dividends to the shareholders of record on the record date. Most investors, for convenience, have their securities held in the name of the broker dealer, also known as the street name. As a result, the dividend disbursement agent will send the dividends directly to the broker dealer. The broker dealer's dividend department will collect the dividends and distribute them to the beneficial owners. The dividend department also handles:

- Stock dividends
- Stock splits
- Bond interest payments
- Rights distributions
- Warrant distributions

It is fair and reasonable for a brokerage firm to charge a fee for the collection of dividends and other services as long as the fee is not excessive and is in line with the fees charged by similar firms.

DUE BILLS

Should the wrong party receive a dividend or any other type of distribution, the buying broker dealer whose customer is owed the dividend will send a due bill to the selling broker for the amount of the dividend owed. In most cases, this would happen when the buyer purchased the stock just prior to the ex date and the security was delivered late to the buyer.

PROXIES

Common stockholders have the right to vote on major corporate issues. Most stockholders, however, do not have the time to attend the meetings and must therefore vote using an absentee ballot, known as a proxy. The Securities Exchange Act of 1934 requires that all corporations that distribute proxies solicit votes from their shareholders. The corporation will send proxies to the shareholders of record. Stockholders who have their securities held in street name will have the proxies forwarded to them by the brokerage firm. The brokerage firm will then cast the beneficial shareholder's votes as indicated on the proxy as the shareholder of record. Proxies that have been signed and returned without indicating how to vote must be voted in accordance with the issuer's management's recommendation. If a shareholder fails to return the proxy to the member at least 10 days prior to the annual meeting, the member may vote the shares as it sees fit, as long as the matter is not of major importance. If the vote concerns a major issue, such as a merger, the member may never cast the votes. Member firms are required to forward proxies and other corporate communications, such as annual and quarterly reports, to the beneficial owner and the issuer is required to reimburse the member for reasonable expenses.

CHAPTER **1**

Pretest

BROKERAGE OFFICE PROCEDURES

1. When hiring a new employee, the principal is responsible for all of the following, EXCEPT:
   - **a.** confirming the agent's employment for the last three years.
   - **b.** obtaining a U5 directly from the employee.
   - **c.** attesting to the character of the employee.
   - **d.** signing the U4 form prior to submission.

2. As it relates to influencing the employees of member firms, which of the following are true?
   - **I.** The gift may be given to the employee.
   - **II.** A record of the gift must be maintained by the employing firm.
   - **III.** The gift must be given to the employer for distribution.
   - **IV.** A contractual relationship is excluded from the rule.
     - **a.** I and IV
     - **b.** II and III
     - **c.** II, III, and IV
     - **d.** I, II, and IV

3. All of the following personnel are exempt from the registration requirement, EXCEPT:
   a. a manager who acts as a liaison between the firm and the board of directors.
   b. a clerical employee.
   c. the firm's Web designer, who posts information about the market conditions on the firm's website.
   d. a sales assistant who occasionally accepts a customer's order.

4. As it relates to securities held in street name, which of the following are true?
   I. The corporation will send proxies to the broker dealer.
   II. The corporation will not reimburse the broker dealer for forwarding the proxies.
   III. The broker dealer may vote blank proxies any way it wishes.
   IV. A shareholder who attends the annual meeting will have his or her proxies voided.
   a. I and III
   b. II and III
   c. I and IV
   d. II and IV

5. A broker dealer that does not carry customer accounts is required to do all of the following, EXCEPT:
   a. clear all trades on an omnibus basis.
   b. forward all securities to the carrying firm.
   c. forward all checks to the carrying firm.
   d. in the case of market making, have the carrying firm stand behind all trades.

6. All of the following are reasons to reject delivery, EXCEPT:
   a. the signatures are not guaranteed.
   b. the customer has determined that the investment is unsuitable.
   c. the certificate is unclear.
   d. a bond is missing a coupon.

7. A security has been delivered late to the buying member after the record date for a dividend distribution. Which of the following is true?

   I. The seller will keep the dividend.

   II. The buyer will be owed the dividend.

   III. The buying member will send a due bill.

   IV. The selling member will receive the dividend.

   a. I and II

   b. II and III

   c. I only

   d. II, III, and IV

8. A customer who purchased 1,000 shares of XYZ on margin two months ago and has not executed any order since:

   a. must receive a statement this month.

   b. does not need to receive a statement this month.

   c. must receive a statement for the last two months only.

   d. should have received a statement for the last two months and must receive one this month as well.

9. A brokerage firm may charge a fee for which of the following?

   I. The safekeeping of securities.

   II. The collection of dividends.

   III. Lack of activity in the account.

   IV. The clipping of coupons.

   a. I and II

   b. II and III

   c. I, II, and IV

   d. I, II, III, and IV

10. A wealthy customer has just made a purchase in a margin account. The account has substantial assets. The brokerage firm, as a courtesy to the client, may ignore a call for cash for up to:

    a. $1,000.

    b. $10,000.

    c. $5,000.

    d. $500.

CHAPTER 2

Record Keeping, Financial Requirements, and Reporting

INTRODUCTION

All broker dealers are required to prepare and maintain reports and records according to industry regulations. The content and timing of the reports depend on the nature of the report. SEC Rule 17a-3 sets forth the requirements for broker dealer reporting, timing, and content. SEC Rule 17a-4 sets the retention requirements for those records. Records subject to these rules must be maintained anywhere from three years to the life of the firm. Records that are required to be maintained must be readily accessible for the first two years.

Under SEC Rule 17a-3, a significant number of records must be filed and maintained by broker dealers. The following is a list of those records and their definitions:

BLOTTERS

Blotters are records of original entry and must reflect transactions as of the trade date. Blotters must be prepared no later than the following business day, or T + 1. This would include a historical account of all the daily transactions, such as:

- Purchases and sales of securities
- Receipts and disbursements of cash
- Receipts and deliveries of securities

GENERAL LEDGER

The general ledger reflects the firm's assets, liabilities, income and expenses, and capital accounts. The firm's trial balance and other financial reports can be prepared from this to show the broker dealer's financial condition. It must be prepared monthly.

CUSTOMER ACCOUNTS

Customer accounts are itemized records of each cash and margin account for each customer. This reflects all purchases, sales, receipts, and deliveries of cash and securities for each customer as well as the new account form and margin agreement, if applicable.

SUBSIDIARY (SECONDARY) RECORDS

Subsidiary records are prepared from the blotter. They include:

- Securities in transfer: Securities in the process of being transferred into a customer's name.
- Dividends and interest received: A record of all dividends and interest due to the customer (long) or payable by the customer (short).
- Securities borrowed and loaned: Records of the broker dealer's borrowing or loaning of securities to complete its transactions.
- Monies borrowed, monies loaned: This also includes any collateral used in connection with the loan.
- Securities failed to receive or deliver: These records must show the date due as well as the date received or delivered.

SECURITIES POSITION BOOK (LEDGER) STOCK RECORD

A securities position book or stock record is a record of the long and short position in each security, whether carried for the account of the broker dealer or for the account of a customer. The location of these securities must also be maintained.

ORDER TICKETS

An order ticket, also known as an order memorandum, is a record detailing the terms and conditions of an order to purchase or sell a security. Records must be maintained whether or not the order is executed.

CONFIRMATIONS AND NOTICES

A confirmation is a notice of the terms and conditions of an executed order. Copies of all confirmations and notices of other debits and credits must be maintained.

MONTHLY TRIAL BALANCES AND NET CAPITAL COMPUTATIONS

Monthly trial balances and net capital computations serve as a check on the current status and accuracy of the firm's ledger account and financial condition. Firms are required to file their net capital computations with regulators via the FOCUS form.

EMPLOYMENT APPLICATIONS

A copy of the registration application or U4 form will suffice as an employment application. Applications must be approved in writing by an authorized representative of the member.

RECORDS REQUIRED TO BE MAINTAINED FOR THREE YEARS

The following is a list of records that must be maintained by the firm for three years:

- Retail communication (formerly advertising and sales literature)
- Institutional communications
- All changes to the text and content on the firm's website
- Order tickets
- Confirmations

- Option records
- FOCUS reports
- Monthly trial balances
- Subsidiary ledgers
- Long and short securities differences
- Compliance and policy and procedure manuals (kept after changes)
- U4, U5, fingerprints, and employment applications for terminated employees

RECORDS REQUIRED TO BE MAINTAINED FOR SIX YEARS

The following is a list of records that must be maintained by the firm for six years:

- Blotters
- General ledgers
- Customer ledgers
- Customer account records
- Customer ledgers
- Stock records/position records

RECORDS REQUIRED TO BE MAINTAINED FOR THE LIFE OF THE FIRM

The following records must be maintained for the life of the firm:

- Articles of incorporation
- Corporate stock certificate books
- Minute books from meetings of the board of directors
- Partnership records
- Form BD

OTHER RECORD RETENTION REQUIREMENTS

In addition to the standard 3-year, 6-year, and lifetime record retention requirements, certain other records have their own requirements. The various records and requirements are as follows:

- Exception reports from clearing firms—18 months
- Written customer complaints under FINRA rules—4 years
- Written customer complaints under MSRB rules—6 years
- Suspicious Activity Reports (SAR)—5 years
- Information collected to verify customer identity—5 years
- Currency transaction reports CTR Form 112—5 years

The following chart outlines SEC Rule 17a-3 (records that must be kept), and SEC Rule 17a-4, which details how long records must be kept:

SEC Rule 17a-3 Records That Must Be Kept Current by Broker Dealers	SEC Rule 17a-4 Time Period Records Must Be Preserved	SEC Rule 17a-4 Time Period Records Must Be Kept in a Readily Accessible Place
Subsidiary records	3 years	First 2 years
Trial balance	3 years	First 2 years
Employment applications for associated persons	Until 3 years after person has terminated employment	Until 3 years after person has terminated employment
Order tickets	3 years	First 2 years
Checkbooks, bank statements	3 years	First 2 years
Blotters (records of original entry)	6 years	First 2 years
General ledger	6 years	First 2 years
Security position records (each long and short position)	6 years	First 2 years
Customer ledgers	6 years	First 2 years
Director's minutes	Life of enterprise	First 2 years
Stock certificate books	Life of enterprise	First 2 years
Partnership articles and articles of incorporation	Life of enterprise	First 2 years

SEC Rule 17a-3 requires that the records of a broker dealer be kept current. The following chart summarizes guidelines for what SEC defines as current:

Records	Definition of Current
General ledger	Posted at least monthly no later than 10 business days after month end
Blotter or other original entry records	Prepared no later than business day after trade date
Securities position record	Posted no later than business day after settlement date
Customer purchase and sale transaction	Recorded in customer accounts no later than settlement date
Trial balance and capital computation	Prepared no later than 10 business days after month end
Securities failed to deliver or receive ledger	Posted no later than second business day after settlement date
Money borrowed and loaned ledger	Posted no later than second business day after securities are forwarded to transfer agent
Securities transfer ledger	Posted no later than second business day after securities are forwarded to transfer agent
Long and short security differences	Recorded in ledger account no later than seven business days after discovery
Securities borrowed and loaned	Posted no later than two business days after movement of securities
Order tickets	Prepared prior to order execution
Option records	No later than the business day after the option position is open
Confirmations	No later than the business day after the trade date

REQUIREMENT TO PREPARE AND MAINTAIN RECORDS UNDER SEC 17A-3 AND 17A-4

A broker dealer that introduces all of its transactions on a fully disclosed basis is exempt from the preparation and maintenance requirement for most records. The carrying or clearing broker dealer is required to prepare and maintain the records relating customer accounts and securities. If the broker dealer clears its transactions through a bank, the bank must provide the introducing broker with a statement that the records relating to the customers' accounts are the property of the broker dealer. The clearing bank must also provide written notice to the SEC that the records are available to be inspected. If a broker dealer clears its transactions on an omnibus basis, the introducing member will be responsible for the preparation and maintenance of most records. Broker dealers may store records in electronic format provided that they inform their designated examining authority (DEA) 90 days prior to implementing the electronic system.

FINANCIAL REQUIREMENTS

All broker dealers are required to maintain a minimum level of financial solvency known as net capital. Net capital can best be described as the broker dealer's liquid net worth found as follows:

liquid assets – total liabilities = net capital

A broker dealer's net capital requirement is contingent upon the type of securities business the firm is engaged in. The SEC sets forth the rules regarding net capital for broker dealers and sets requirements for:

- Determining a firm's net capital
- Minimum net capital
- Subordinated loans
- Maximum aggregate indebtedness
- Allowable aggregate indebtedness relative to net capital

General securities broker dealers carrying customer accounts have a financial responsibility or minimum net capital of $250,000. A broker dealer who carries customer accounts is known as a clearing broker dealer. Clearing broker dealers must be members of both the Depository Trust & Clearing Corp/DTCC and the National Securities Clearing Corp/NSCC, and are qualified to:

- Settle transactions for customer accounts.
- Hold funds and securities.
- Handle variable annuity or mutual fund transactions by wire order or through application.
- Act as market makers for corporate securities.
- Be members of syndicates for any type of underwriting.

TAKENOTE!

A large general securities broker dealer may be subject to an alternative minimum net capital requirement. A broker dealer who is subject to the alternative minimum net capital must have net capital equal to the greater of $250,000 or 2 percent of its aggregate debit items computed in accordance with the Formula for Determination of Reserve Requirement.

Broker dealers who generally do not carry customer accounts have a financial responsibility or minimum net capital of $50,000. These are known as fully disclosed or introducing broker dealers. These broker dealers:

- May not carry customer accounts or hold customer cash or securities.
- Can only deal in underwritings on a best efforts or all-or-none basis. If involved in a firm commitment underwriting, the net capital must increase to $100,000.
- All customers' securities and funds must be forwarded to a carrying broker dealer, with checks made payable to the carrying broker dealer or escrow agent.
- May handle variable annuity or mutual fund transactions by wire order or through application.
- May not act as a market maker.
- May execute up to 10 transactions per year for the firm's proprietary account.

Broker dealers who engage solely in the sale of redeemable shares of registered investment companies and variable contracts, or who do not receive customer cash and securities, or who engage only in transactions relating to a merger or acquisition or direct participation programs, have a financial responsibility of $5,000. These broker dealers:

- May not carry customer accounts or hold customer cash or securities.
- May not receive customer cash or securities.
- May sell variable annuities and mutual funds by application only. No wire orders.
- May not participate in any underwriting.

TAKE**NOTE!**

A broker dealer who handles mutual fund orders on a wire basis must have minimum net capital of $25,000.

The net capital requirement for broker dealers who engage in the sale of options outside of a registered national securities exchange or association is $250,000.

Market makers in over-the-counter (OTC) securities must maintain net capital in an amount equal to the greater of the following two requirements:

- $100,000, up to a maximum of $1,000,000

or

- $2,500 for each security it makes a market in with a bid price more than $5, and $1,000 for each such security with a bid price $5 or less.

EXAMPLE

Market Maker A is quoting 50 stocks with a bid price of less than $5 and 100 stocks with a bid price greater than $5. Based on these market making activities the firm's net capital would be found as follows:

$$50 \times \$1{,}000 = \$\ 50{,}000$$
$$+\ 100 \times \$2{,}500 = \$250{,}000$$
$$\$300{,}000$$

The following chart summarizes the minimum dollar amount of net capital for broker dealers:

Type of Broker Dealer	Minimum Net Capital
Mergers and acquisitions or direct participation programs	$ 5,000
Investment companies on a subscription basis only	$ 5,000
Introducing firm that does not receive customer funds or securities	$ 5,000

(Continued)

Type of Broker Dealer	Minimum Net Capital
Purchases investment company securities on a wire basis or sells stock for customers whose proceeds are immediately invested in open end investment companies	$ 25,000
Introducing firm receiving customer funds or securities for immediate delivery to clearing firm	$ 50,000
Participating in best efforts or all or none underwritings only	$ 50,000
Introducing dealer executing more than 10 proprietary trades per year	$ 100,000
Participating in firm commitment underwritings	$ 100,000
Carries customer accounts but does not retain custody of customer funds or securities (k)(2)(i) firms	$ 100,000
Market makers	$ 100,000
General securities broker dealer carrying customer accounts (carrying firm)	$ 250,000
Acts as a CQS market maker in listed securities	$ 500,000
Acts as a central clearing agent for customers who execute orders through various broker dealers (prime broker)	$ 1,500,000
Acts as an executing broker for prime brokerage transactions or as a block positioner	$ 1,000,000
Maintains a joint back office between two or more broker dealers for carrying or clearing accounts	$ 25,000,000

AGGREGATE INDEBTEDNESS

Aggregate indebtedness includes money owed to customers, customer-related debts, accounts, and taxes payable. The relationship of a broker dealer's aggregate indebtedness to net capital determines a broker dealer's financial condition. Aggregate indebtedness includes:

- Money owed to customers (customers' credit balances)
- Customer securities loaned to other broker dealers
- Loans payable, collateralized by customer securities

TAKENOTE!

Aggregate indebtedness only includes debt related to customers. Other debt incurred by the broker dealer is not included. As the level of aggregate indebtedness increases, a firm's net capital requirement increases.

In order for a broker dealer to remain in business, the ratio of aggregate indebtedness to net capital (AI/NC) cannot exceed:

- 8:1 for firms in their first year of business.
- 15:1 for firms older than one year.

HAIRCUTS

A haircut is a deduction taken from the market value of securities in inventory for the purpose of determining net capital. A haircut is taken to allow for the volatility in securities prices and to reflect the fact that positions held in inventory may be offset at prices that are somewhat different from current market prices. Haircut deductions are 15 percent of the net long or short positions for securities that are:

- Traded on a national exchange.
- Listed on Nasdaq.
- Regulation T-listed OTC margin stock.
- OTC stocks with three or more independent market makers, excluding the broker dealer, computing net capital.
- Redeemable shares of investment companies registered under the Investment Company Act of 1940 (mutual funds).
- Convertible debt selling at or above par.

Haircut deductions on other stocks with a limited market (one or two independent market makers) are 40 percent on both the long and short positions. Unregistered securities under the Securities Act of 1933 or those with no ready market receive a 100 percent haircut (no value given in computation of firm's net capital). An additional haircut of 15 percent is applied to proprietary positions of a broker dealer on the market value of a stock in excess of 10 percent of its tentative net capital if the concentration limit is held for more than 11 business days. This is known as undue concentration. Tentative net capital is the broker dealer's net capital prior to haircut deductions. The additional 15 percent haircut is applied only to the amount of securities in excess of 10 percent of the tentative net capital. In the case of equity securities, the undue concentration rule only applies to the greater of the amount of the position in excess of $10,000 or the market value of 500 shares. For debt securities, the undue concentration rule only applies to the amount in excess of $25,000.

Undue concentration haircuts are not applied to exempt securities, such as U.S. government securities. An open contractual commitment (underwriting commitment or delayed delivery contract) requires a 30 percent haircut for figuring net capital. The 30 percent reduction is increased by any unrealized loss on the position and decreased by any unrealized gain. A fail-to-deliver contract is money receivable to a broker dealer and can count in the net capital computation, provided it is not outstanding five business days or longer past the settlement date. The haircut on the aged fail-to-deliver contracts (more than five business days) is 15 percent for listed stocks and 40 percent otherwise. These haircuts on aged fail-to-deliver contracts encourage prompt settlement of securities transactions. A broker dealer who has a fail-to-deliver contract outstanding for more than 60 days may not sell nonexempt securities for its own account or for the account of a customer if the security in question is a domestic, Canadian, or ADR security. A broker dealer who fails to deliver a foreign security after 90 days will be subject to the same restriction. A broker dealer may apply to FINRA in writing for an exception to this rule. A fail-to-receive contract is a stock receivable to a broker dealer. If the securities have not been sold, there is no change to aggregate indebtedness. If the securities have been sold, aggregate indebtedness would be increased.

BOX COUNTS

All broker dealers that maintain custody of securities must conduct a quarterly count of the securities it has in its possession or control. Securities that are considered to be in a broker dealer's control are securities in transfer or transit. The quarterly count must be made no less than two months apart and not more than four months apart. If a broker dealer's physical count reveals fewer certificates than are recorded on its books, the firm has a short securities difference. A short securities difference will result in a deduction from the broker dealer's net capital if not resolved in seven business days from the time of discovery. On the eighth day from discovery the broker dealer will have to take a haircut equal to 25 percent of the current market value of the security. After 15 days, the position will be subject to a 50% haircut, after 21 days the position will be subject to a 75% haircut, and after 28 days the position will be subject to a 100% haircut. If the short securities difference is not resolved within 45 days the short securities difference must be bought in. If the broker dealer's physical count reveals more certificates than it has on its records the broker dealer has a long securities difference. A long securities difference has no effect on a broker dealer's net capital.

MISSING AND LOST SECURITIES

The Securities Information Center (SIC) is in charge of keeping reports for all lost and stolen securities. SEC Rule 17f-1 outlines the requirements for reporting an inquiry with respect to missing, lost, counterfeit, or stolen securities. When it is believed criminal activity was involved, the theft must be reported within one business day of discovery to the SIC, the registered transfer agent for the issue, and the Federal Bureau of Investigation (FBI). When criminal activity is not believed to be involved and securities have been missing or lost for at least two business days, a report must be made on the third business day to the SIC and the registered transfer agent for the issue. When securities are found to be counterfeit, a report must be made within one business day of discovery to the SIC, the registered transfer agent for the issue, and the FBI. If securities are discovered to be missing after an internal audit or box count and no criminal activity is suspected, a report must be filed with the SIC within 10 business days of discovery or as soon as the securities can be identified by certificate number. When stolen, missing, lost, or counterfeit securities have been recovered, the appropriate authority must be notified within one business day of the recovery. Required inquiries must be made by the SIC whenever securities come into the possession of a reporting institution, unless:

- The institution compares the securities against bondholder or stockholder lists as part of its business.
- The securities certificate came directly from the issuer or the issuer's agent.
- The securities certificate is received from another reporting institution and is registered in the name of the customer or was previously sold to the customer and verified through internal records.
- The transaction did not exceed a face value of $10,000 for bonds or a market value of $10,000 for stocks.
- The securities certificate is received as part of a normal drop by the reporting institution.

The SIC will accept reports on securities not listed above.
The following securities are not subject to the above provisions:

- Securities without Committee on Uniform Securities Identification Procedures (CUSIP) numbers.
- Bond coupons.
- Uncertified securities.

- A securities issue that is represented by a single master certificate registered in the name of the clearing agency (a global securities issue).
- Securities that do not provide negotiable securities certificates.

THE CUSTOMER PROTECTION RULE

The customer protection rule ensures that customer funds held by a broker dealer are maintained in safe areas of the business related to servicing its customers or are deposited in a special reserve bank account. The broker dealer must make the following monthly computation to determine the amount required to be on deposit in its special reserve bank account for the exclusive benefit of the customers:

(credit items – debit items) × 105 percent = the amount to be deposited in the special reserve account

If the broker dealer computes weekly rather than monthly, only 100 percent of the credit excess must be deposited in the reserve account. A broker dealer must compute weekly if at any time its aggregate indebtedness exceeds 800 percent of its net capital or if its aggregate funds owed to customers exceeds $1,000,000. Weekly reporting must continue until neither condition occurs for four successive weeks. The required deposit into the special reserve account must be made by 10 a.m. Tuesday, two business days after the weekly calculation is made. Money placed in the special reserve account is deducted from the broker dealer's aggregate indebtedness. The special reserve bank account may not be used for any of the following purposes:

- To secure a loan to the broker dealer.
- Be subject to a lien by a bank against the broker dealer.
- Be used to allow bank-offset privileges against other accounts of the broker dealer.

Also note the following relating to the special reserve account:

- It may only contain cash or U.S. government securities.
- If debit items exceed credit items, no deposit need be made.
- The funds contained in the account reduce the amount of the broker dealer's aggregate indebtedness.
- A broker dealer may withdraw excess beyond the required deposit in the special reserve account.

 TAKE**NOTE!**

A broker dealer must obtain notification from the bank that it is informed of these restrictions and that money is being held for the exclusive benefit of customers of the broker dealer.

Exemptions from SEC Rule 15c3-3 are listed under Subsections (k)(2)(A) and (k)(2)(B) and are referred to by those section names in the trade. A (k)(2)(A) broker dealer exemption is available if the broker dealer:

- Does not carry margin accounts.
- Promptly transmits all customer funds and delivers all securities received in trade.
- Does not hold funds or securities for clients.

A (k)(2)(B) broker dealer exemption is available if the broker dealer:

- Clears all transactions with a clearing broker dealer.
- Promptly transmits all client funds and securities to a clearing broker dealer who carries the accounts and maintains the books.

Form X-17a-5 is the fundamental reporting form used by broker dealers to report financial conditions to the regulatory agencies. Also known as the FOCUS report, it is filed electronically and has the following parts:

- FOCUS Part I is a summary of key financial ratios and numbers that is filed monthly within 10 business days after the end of the month by broker dealers who carry customer accounts.
- FOCUS Part II is a balance sheet, income statement, and net capital computation that is filed quarterly. Any broker dealers who clear or carry customer accounts must file Part II within 17 business days from the end of each calendar quarter.
- FOCUS Part II-A is a less comprehensive version than Part II that is filed quarterly. Any broker dealer who does not carry or clear customer accounts must only file FOCUS Part IIA within 17 business days after the end of each calendar quarter.
- Supplemental Statement of Income (SSOI). FINRA may require certain firms to file a statement of income to provide FINRA with a better

understanding of the broker dealer's revenue and expenses. These designated firms will be required to file the SSOI within 20 days of the end of each quarter.

Rule 17a-5 also requires broker dealers who carry customer accounts to furnish customers with financial statements twice a year. One will be an audited financial statement, which must also be filed with the SEC not more than 60 days after the date of the financial statements. This report must be sent to customers within 45 days of when the report was sent to the SEC. The other report will be an unaudited statement sent approximately six months later. Current balance sheets must also be made available to bona fide customers at their request. Broker dealers must also furnish customers with the following information within 105 days after the date of the audited report:

- An unconsolidated balance sheet with appropriate notes prepared in accordance with generally accepted accounting principles.
- A statement of the amount of the firm's net capital and its required net capital.
- A statement indicating the existence of any material inadequacies in the accounting system, the internal accounting control, or the procedures for safeguarding securities.
- A statement indicating that Part I of Form X-17a-5 is available for copying at the principal office of the broker dealer and at the regional office of the SEC.

Reports explaining any of following situations (within 15 days of occurrence) must be sent to the SEC and FINRA:

- The services of an accountant/auditor are contracted.
- The services of an accountant/auditor are terminated.
- A change in the firm's fiscal year. The reason for the change must be supplied and the request must be approved.
- An extension of time is needed to file an annual report.

 TAKE**NOTE!**

All firms are required to file an audited FOCUS report II or IIA within 60 days of its year end in hard copy. The firm must submit two copies to the principal office of the SEC, one copy to the SEC regional office, and one copy to FINRA. A firm may request a maximum extension of 30 days to file the annual report. Under no conditions may the report be filed more than 90 days after year end.

All accountants providing audit services to broker dealers must be independent from and not under the control of the broker dealer.

THE EARLY WARNING RULE

The early warning rule is intended to give the SEC early notice of impending financial difficulty of a broker dealer by requiring any broker dealer subject to Rule 15c-3-1 (Uniform Net Capital Rule) to notify the SEC and the examining authority of the broker dealer (FINRA or stock exchange) within 24 hours. If any net capital computation shows a firm's ratio of aggregate indebtedness to net capital to be in excess of 12:1 or its net capital is less than 120 percent of its required net capital, or if net capital is less than 5% of debit items for firms who use the alternative computation method, a violation of the early warning rule has occurred. As a result, a FOCUS report Part II or II-A must be filed within 15 calendar days after month's end and filing must continue until three successive months have elapsed in which neither of the above conditions have occurred. The following situations require notification:

- If a broker dealer's net capital is less than the minimum required or its principal amount of satisfactory subordination agreements exceeds 70 percent of its debt plus equity total for a period in excess of 90 days, the broker dealer must give immediate telegraphic notice of the violation and within 24 hours of such a net capital rule violation the following additional reports must be filed with the SEC:
  - FOCUS report Part II or Part II-A (whichever is required).
  - Details of certain other accounts as required by the SEC.
- If the broker dealer fails to make and keep current books and records, pursuant to Rule 17a-3, it must give immediate (same day) telegraphic notice of the situation to the SEC and its DEA and a report stating corrective

measures taken must be subsequently filed within 48 hours of the telegraphic notice.

- If a broker dealer discovers or is informed by an independent public accountant that a material inadequacy exists in its books, it must give telegraphic notice within 24 hours of the discovery and a report stating corrective measures taken must be subsequently filed within 48 hours of the telegraphic notice.

Any telegraphic notice or report required under Rule 17a-11 must be given or filed with the following agencies:

- SEC principal office in Washington, D.C.
- Regional office of the SEC where the broker dealer's main office is located.
- Examining authority for the broker dealer (FINRA or the appropriate stock exchange).

TAKE**NOTE!**

A broker dealer must immediately cease doing business with the public if the broker dealer's net capital falls below its required net capital.

FINRA FINANCIAL REQUIREMENTS

FINRA monitors the financial condition of member firms very closely. If FINRA feels that the financial or operational condition of a firm is compromised or is experiencing difficulty, FINRA may take action by restricting or reducing the firm's business. FINRA may require the firm to stop expanding its business if the following conditions persist for more than 15 business days: if its net capital is less than 150 percent of its minimum required net capital or if AI:NC is greater than 10:1. FINRA may also require the member to reduce its business if the following conditions exist for more than 15 business days: the firm's net capital is less than 125 percent of its minimum required net capital or AI:NC is greater than 12:1. Indications that the firm is experiencing financial difficulty would include:

- The firm cannot settle transactions in a timely manner.
- The firm cannot demonstrate that it is in compliance with the net capital or customer protection requirements.

- The firm fails to maintain its books and records.
- The firm's excess net capital has fallen 25 percent in the last 2 months or 30 percent in the last three months.

FINRA may require the firm to:

- File special financial reports.
- Close out or reduce inventory positions.
- Deliver free credit balances and fully paid securities to customers.
- Not open new customer accounts.
- Close branch offices.
- Execute unsolicited orders only.
- Execute liquidating transaction only.
- Restrict payments to officers.
- Require an independent audit.
- Eliminate or discontinue unsecured loans.

SUBORDINATED LOANS

Satisfactory subordination agreements are instruments that allow an individual to loan cash or securities to a broker dealer in return for interest paid to the lender (this is debt for the broker dealer). Subordinated lenders are not considered to be customers of the broker dealer and are not provided SIPC coverage in the event of the broker dealer's failure. Under SEC Rule 17a-11, a violation is deemed to occur if the principal amount of satisfactory subordination agreements exceeds 70 percent of the broker dealer's debt plus equity total for a period in excess of 90 days. This means that subordinated debt can be considered part of the broker dealer's net capital but only if it is through satisfactory subordination agreements. In order for the loan to be satisfactory, it must meet the following requirements:

- The agreement must be in writing.
- The agreement must be for a specific dollar amount, even if securities are pledged.
- The agreement must subordinate any right of the lender to receive payment to the claims of all present and future creditors of the broker dealer.

- The proceeds of the loan may be used by the broker dealer for any general business purpose.
- The agreement must have a maturity of at least one year.
- The agreement may not be subject to cancellation by either party.

There are two forms of subordination agreements:

- Subordinated loan agreements for cash contributions only.
- Secured demand notes, which are used when securities are pledged.

With a secured demand note, a 30 percent haircut provision is applied for all securities normally subject to a 15 percent haircut. Limited market securities are subject to the standard haircut. The loan is carried at the value after the haircut. The securities that are pledged must be fully paid for, freely transferable (not subject to Rule 144), and must be in bearer form, registered in the name of the broker dealer or custodian for the broker dealer. Any dividends received on the shares will be paid to the lender of the stock. If the loan meets these requirements, the amount of the agreement is considered part of the broker dealer's net capital. If the initial agreement is for a term exceeding one year, a prepayment clause may be written into the agreement. However, no prepayment may be made during the first year. Prepayments (before maturity) are permitted as long as the prepayment does not force the ratio of aggregate indebtedness (AI) to net capital (NC) to exceed 10:1 (1,000 percent) or the NC to fall below 120 percent of its minimum. The repayment obligation of a broker dealer under any subordination agreement at maturity is suspended if, after paying the debt, the broker dealer's AI exceeds 1,200 percent of its NC or if the resulting NC is less than 120 percent of the minimum required NC of the broker dealer (5 percent of debits for firms using the alternative method). A broker dealer may prepay its subordinated loan so long as the agreement has been in force for at least a year and the firm's IA:NC is not greater than 10:1. The filing requirements for any proposed subordination agreement include:

- Two copies of the proposed agreement to be filed with the regional office of the SEC in which the broker dealer maintains its principal place of business, at least 10 days prior to the proposed effective date of the agreement.
- Copies of the agreement must also be filed with the examining authority for the broker dealer (usually FINRA or stock exchange) 30 days prior to its effective date.

An officer, partner, parent company, or subsidiary of a member may not withdraw capital contributions from the member if it would cause the member's net capital to fall below 120 percent of its required net capital or cause its AI:NC to exceed 10:1. If the withdrawal of capital by any of the above is more than 30 percent of the firm's excess net capital in a 30 day period, the member must notify the SEC two business days prior to the withdrawal. The SEC has the right to limit or restrict the withdrawal.

TEMPORARY SUBORDINATION AGREEMENTS

A temporary subordination agreement may be entered into with a duration of less than one year. These would be used for fully disclosed firms ($50,000) that wish to enter into a firm commitment underwriting. The haircut for firm commitment underwritings is 30 percent of the firm's participation for IPOs and 15 percent for additional offerings. The temporary subordinated loan is used to restore the firm's net capital after the haircuts are taken into consideration. The maximum duration is 45 days. No more than three of these temporary agreements may be used in any 12-month period, and they cannot be entered into to rectify an early warning violation.

CALCULATING NET CAPITAL

All net capital computations must be conducted in line with generally accepted accounting principles (GAAP). The calculation starts by determining the broker dealer's total available capital as follows:

net worth + subordinated loans = total available capital

When calculating net capital, a broker dealer is required to then subtract illiquid/nonallowable assets such as buildings, equipment, exchange memberships, prepaid expenses, and intangibles from its total available capital to determine its tentative net capital as follows:

total available capital – non allowable assets = tentative net capital

The final step in the calculation is to subtract haircuts from the firm's tentative net capital to determine the firm's allowable net capital:

tentative net capital – haircuts = net capital

It is unlikely that you will have to perform a net capital computation on the exam. It is, however, important that you understand how, when, and why net capital computations are calculated.

FIDELITY BONDS

FINRA member firms are required to obtain a fidelity bond that covers the firm's officers and employees. The purpose of the fidelity bond is to protect the firm's customers from:

- Fraudulent acts
- Loss of securities
- Check forgery
- Securities forgery

The fidelity bond does not cover broker dealer bankruptcy or losses incurred as a result of errors or omissions. The required amount of the fidelity bond is based on the firm's net capital. The minimum required fidelity bond coverage is 120 percent of the firm's net capital for firms whose required net capital is less than $600,000 with a $25,000 minimum. The minimum fidelity bond requirement is based on 120 percent of the firm's highest net capital requirement during the preceding 12 months. All firms must review their fidelity bond coverage annually and must make any required changes to the coverage within 60 days of the anniversary date of the bond's issuance. For firms whose minimum required net capital is greater than $600,000, the minimum required fidelity bond coverage is $750,000. The minimum required coverage increases to a maximum of $5,000,000 for a firm whose minimum required net capital is greater than $12,000,000. If a broker-dealer makes a substantial change to its blanket fidelity bond or if the coverage is terminated, the broker-dealer must immediately notify FINRA.

CHAPTER 2

Pretest

RECORD KEEPING, FINANCIAL REQUIREMENTS, AND REPORTING

1. A broker dealer executing customer orders must post activity to the blotter by the end of the:
   a. trade date.
   b. settlement date.
   c. following business day.
   d. payment date.

2. All of the following records must be maintained for three years, EXCEPT:
   a. order tickets.
   b. general ledgers.
   c. U4 forms.
   d. FOCUS reports.

3. Trial balances must be prepared no later than:
   a. one business day after the week's end.
   b. one business day after the month's end.
   c. 10 business days after the quarter's end.
   d. 10 business days after the month's end.

4. A new broker dealer may not have an aggregate indebtedness in excess of which of the following?
   a. 7:1
   b. 5:1
   c. 8:1
   d. 15:1

5. A clearing broker dealer whose net capital falls below the required minimum under Rule 15c3-1 must do which of the following?
   I. Cease doing business with the public.
   II. Send immediate telegraphic notice to the SEC and the examining authority.
   III. File FOCUS Part II within 24 hours.
   IV. File a report within 48 hours specifying the steps taken to correct the deficiency.
   a. I only
   b. II and III
   c. I, II, and III
   d. II and IV

6. The haircut on an aged fail-to-deliver contract for a broker dealer is:
   a. 15 percent for listed securities; 40 percent otherwise.
   b. 30 percent for listed securities; 60 percent otherwise.
   c. 40 percent for listed securities; 70 percent otherwise.
   d. There is no haircut for failing to deliver.

7. A broker dealer that does business exclusively in open-end mutual fund shares and transmits customers' orders on a wire basis must have net capital of:
   a. $5,000.
   b. $25,000.
   c. $30,000.
   d. $50,000.

8. Which of the following are true regarding FOCUS Part I reports?
   - I. They are filed electronically.
   - II. They must be filed within 17 business days of the quarter's end.
   - III. The must be filed within 10 days of the end of the month.
   - IV. They must be filed by both carrying and introducing firms.
     - a. II and IV
     - b. I and III
     - c. I, II, and IV
     - d. I, III, and IV

9. With regard to subordinated loan agreements, which of the following are true?
   - I. They must be filed with the SEC and the firm's DEA.
   - II. They may be added to the broker dealer's net worth.
   - III. They must be filed 30 days prior to becoming effective.
   - IV. They must be for a minimum of two years.
     - a. III and IV
     - b. I and II
     - c. I, II, and, III
     - d. I, II, III, and IV

10. A newly formed broker dealer is introducing all of its accounts on a fully disclosed basis to a general securities firm. The firm is receiving customers' cash and securities and is promptly forwarding them to the general securities firm carrying its accounts. What is the new member's minimum net capital requirement?
    - a. $5,000
    - b. $50,000
    - c. $100,000
    - d. Not less than 1/8 of aggregate indebtedness

11. When calculating net capital, a broker dealer will subtract haircuts from its:
    - a. net worth.
    - b. nonallowable assets.
    - c. total available capital.
    - d. tentative net capital.

12. All of the following are nonallowable assets when calculating net capital, EXCEPT:

a. the company's main office owned outright by the firm.

b. the company's membership with the NYSE.

c. OTC securities with two independent market makers.

d. an unsecured receivable.

13. The customer protection rule requires broker dealers to deposit how much in a special reserve account?

a. 105 percent of customer credit balances

b. 105 percent of customer fails-to-receive

c. 115 percent of customer credit balances

d. 115 percent of customer fails-to-receive

14. A broker dealer that executes customer mutual fund orders on a wire basis only may execute how many transactions for its own account and not be subject to an increase in its net capital requirement?

a. 15 in any 12-month period

b. 10 in any 12-month period

c. 6 in any 12-month period

d. 3 in any 12-month period

15. All of the following are required to be kept for six years, EXCEPT:

a. blotters.

b. customer ledgers.

c. general ledgers.

d. broker dealer bank records.

16. A general securities firm that carries customer accounts and has been in business for 11 years has net capital of $800,000. What is its maximum aggregate indebtedness?

a. $12,000,000

b. $1,200,000

c. $6,400,000

d. $640,000

17. A broker dealer that handles investment company orders and is subject to a net capital requirement of $25,000 may do which of the following?

a. Participate in a firm commitment underwriting

b. Make markets in up to 10 securities

c. Execute a customer's sell order for a listed security and invest the proceeds in a mutual fund

d. None of the above

18. A firm's aggregate indebtedness has just reached 12:1. Which of the following are true?

I. The firm must file an early warning report.

II. The firm only needs to file an early warning report if it is a first-year firm.

III. The report may be made electronically or by fax.

IV. The report must be made to the firm's DEA and the SEC within 48 hours.

a. I and III

b. II and III

c. I and IV

d. II and IV

19. The minutes of the board of directors meetings must be kept for:

a. three years, two years readily accessible.

b. six years, two years readily accessible.

c. the life of the firm, two years readily accessible.

d. the life of the firm, six years readily accessible.

20. A member firm has uncovered a material problem with its accounting. What must the firm do?

a. It must notify the SEC and FINRA within 24 hours of the discovery.

b. It must notify only the SEC within 24 hours.

c. It must notify the SEC and FINRA within 24 hours and detail its corrective action within 48 hours.

d. It must notify the SEC and FINRA within 48 hours and detail the corrective action within 72 hours.

CHAPTER 3

Issuing Corporate Securities

INTRODUCTION

The Securities Act of 1933 was the first major piece of securities industry regulation that was brought about largely as a result of the stock market crash of 1929. Other major laws were also enacted to help prevent another meltdown of the nation's financial system, such as the Securities Exchange Act of 1934, but we will start our review with the Securities Act of 1933 because it regulates the issuance of corporate securities.

The Securities Act of 1933 was the first major piece of securities industry legislation, and it regulates the primary market. The primary market consists exclusively of transactions between issuers of securities and investors. In a primary market transaction, the issuer of the securities receives the proceeds from the sale of the securities. The Securities Act of 1933 requires nonexempt issuers (typically corporate issuers) to file a registration statement with the Securities and Exchange Commission (SEC). The registration statement, formerly known as an S-1, is the issuer's full-disclosure document for the government. The registration statement must contain detailed information relating to the issuer's operations and financial condition and must include:

- A balance sheet dated within 90 days of the filing of the registration statement.
- Profit and loss statements for the last 3 years.
- The company's capitalization.
- The use of proceeds.
- Shareholders owning more than 10 percent of the company's securities.
- Biographical information on the officers and directors.

The registration statement will be under review by the SEC for a minimum of 20 days. During this time, known as the cooling-off period, no sales of securities may take place. If the SEC requires additional information regarding the offering, the SEC may issue a deficiency letter or a stop order that will extend the cooling-off period beyond the original 20 days. If the SEC has issued a stop order, the 20-day cooling-off period will begin again once the resubmission of the registration statement has been completed. A registered representative may only begin to discuss the potential offering with customers after the filing date.

THE PROSPECTUS

While the SEC is reviewing the securities' registration statement, registered representatives are very limited as to what they may do with regard to the new issue. During the cooling-off period, the only thing that a registered representative may do is obtain indications of interest from clients by providing them with a preliminary prospectus, also known as a red herring. The term "red herring" originated from the fact that a preliminary prospectus must have a statement printed in red ink on the front cover stating: "these securities have not yet become registered with the SEC and therefore may not be sold." An indication of interest is an investor's or broker dealer's statement that it might be interested in purchasing the securities being offered. The preliminary prospectus contains most of the same information that will be contained in the final prospectus, except for the offering price, the effective date, and the proceeds to the issuer. The preliminary prospectus will usually contain a price range for the security to be offered. If the securities are ultimately sold at a price outside of the range contained in the preliminary prospectus and the adjusted offering price is disclosed in the final prospectus, the issuer will not be required to file an amendment unless the maximum aggregate price deviates from the range by more than 20%. If the issuer fails to file the final prospectus within 15 days of the effective date, It must file a post effective amendment to disclose the change All information contained in a preliminary prospectus is subject to change or revision. The preliminary prospectus must be given in hard copy to expected purchasers at least 48 hours before the sale is confirmed if the company has not been a reporting company under the Securities Exchange Act of 1934. This is done to ensure that the final prospectus is not the first piece of information forwarded to the purchaser.

THE FINAL PROSPECTUS

All purchasers of new issues must be given a final prospectus before any sales may be allowed. The final prospectus serves as the issuer's full-disclosure document for the purchaser of the securities. If the issuer has filed a prospectus with the SEC and the final prospectus can be viewed on the SEC's website, a prospectus will be deemed to have been provided to the investor through the access equals delivery rule. The access equals delivery rule only applies to the final prospectus during the offering and during any aftermarket delivery requirements. A preliminary prospectus must be physically sent to potential purchasers. Once the issuer's registration statement becomes effective, the final prospectus must include:

- Type and description of the securities.
- Price of the security.
- Use of the proceeds.
- Underwriter's discount.
- Date of the offering.
- Type and description of underwriting.
- Business history of issuer.
- Biographical data for company officers and directors.
- Information regarding large stockholders.
- Company financial data.
- Risks to purchaser.
- Legal matters concerning the company.
- SEC disclaimer.

FREE WRITING PROSPECTUS

A free writing prospectus is any form of written communication published or broadcast by an issuer which contains information about the securities offered for sale that does not meet the definition of a statutory prospectus. Common examples of a free writing prospectus include:

- Marketing materials
- Graphs
- Term sheets
- Emails
- Press releases

The free writing prospectus should include a legend recommending that the individual read the statutory prospectus to obtain more information relating the securities being offered. A hyperlink will be used in many cases to direct the reader to the statutory prospectus. An issuer who meets the definition of a well-known seasoned issuer may use an FWP at any time before or after the filing of a registration statement. A seasoned issuer may only use an FWP after the filing of the registration statement with the SEC. An unseasoned or non-reporting issuer may use a free writing prospectus only after a registration statement is filed with the SEC and must either send a statutory prospectus with FWP or must include a hyperlink to a statutory prospectus. Issuers who use free writing prospectuses will file them with the SEC over the SEC's website.

PROVIDING THE PROSPECTUS TO AFTERMARKET PURCHASERS

Certain investors who purchase securities in the secondary market just after a distribution must also be provided with the final prospectus. The term for which a prospectus must be provided depends largely on the type of offering and where the issue will be traded in the aftermarket. If the security has an aftermarket delivery requirement, a prospectus must be provided by all firms that execute a purchase order for the security during the term. The after market prospectus delivery requirements may be met electronically and are as follows:

- For IPOs: 90 days after being issued for securities quoted on the OTCBB or in the Pink OTC Market (formerly pink sheets), 25 days for listed or Nasdaq securities.
- Additional offerings: 40 days for securities quoted on the OTCBB or in the Pink OTC Market (formerly pink sheets). No aftermarket requirement for listed or Nasdaq securities.

SEC DISCLAIMER

The SEC reviews the issuer's registration statement and the prospectus but does not guarantee the accuracy or adequacy of the information. The SEC disclaimer must appear on the cover of all prospectuses and states: "These securities have not been approved or disapproved by the SEC nor have any representations been made about the accuracy or the adequacy of the information."

MISREPRESENTATIONS

Financial relief for misrepresentations made under the Securities Act of 1933 is available for purchasers of any security that is sold under a prospectus that is found to contain false or misleading statements. Purchasers of the security may be entitled to seek financial relief from any or all of the following:

- The issuer.
- The underwriters.
- Officers and directors.
- All parties who signed the registration statement.

- Accountants and attorneys who helped prepare the registration statement.

A due diligence meeting will be held during the cooling-off period to ensure that the information contained in the prospectus is accurate.

TOMBSTONE ADS

SEC Rule 134 allows certain types of advertisements to be run relating to a new issue. Tombstone ads are the only form of advertising that is allowed during the cooling-off period. A tombstone ad is an announcement and description of the securities to be offered. A tombstone ad lists the names of the underwriters, where a prospectus may be obtained, and a statement that the tombstone ad does not constitute an offer to sell the securities and that the offer may only be made by a prospectus. Tombstone ads are traditionally run to announce the new issue, but they are not required and do not need to be filed with the SEC. Tombstone ads may also include:

- The amount of the security to be offered
- The date of sale
- A general description of the issuer's business
- The price of the security

FREE RIDING AND WITHHOLDING/FINRA RULE 5130

A broker dealer underwriting a new issue must make a complete and bona fide offering of all securities being issued to the public and may not withhold any of the securities for:

- The underwriters.
- Another broker dealer.
- A firm employee or a person who is financially dependent on the employee.
- An employee of another FINRA member.

TAKENOTE!

An exception to FINRA Rule 5130 applies to employees of limited broker dealers who engage solely in the purchase and sale of investment company products or direct participation programs (DPPs). Employees of limited broker dealers may purchase new issues. This exemption applies only to the employees of the limited broker dealer, not to the firm itself.

These rules are in effect for initial public offering, but they are especially prevalent when dealing with a hot issue. A hot issue is one that trades at an immediate premium to its offering price in the secondary market. A broker dealer may not free ride by withholding securities for its own account or for the accounts of those listed above. FINRA Rule 5130 covers initial offerings of common stock only. Exempt from the rule are offerings of additional issues, bonds, and preferred shares. These offerings may be purchased by registered persons. FINRA Rule 5130 requires that a broker dealer (not the Rep) obtain an eligibility statement from all account owners who purchase a new issue of stock within 12 months prior to the purchase. Some people may purchase hot issues so long as the amount is not substantial and they have a history of purchasing new issues. These conditionally approved people are:

- Officers and employees of financial institutions.
- Nonsupported family members.
- Accountants, attorneys, and finders associated with the underwriting.
- Accounts where the restricted persons' interest is limited to 10 percent or less or where a maximum of 10 percent of the allocation of new issue is for the benefit of such persons. This is known as the carve out procedure.

The agreement among the underwriters must clearly state how the syndicate will handle the repurchase of shares trading at a premium. If a client "flips" the hot issue in the secondary market and the shares are repurchased by the book running lead underwriter, those shares must be used to cover any syndicate short position. If no syndicate short position exists, the shares may be used to cover unfilled qualified customer orders at the offering price. Any account to receive these shares must receive the shares through a random allocation process. In the extremely unlikely event that no unfilled orders exist, the syndicate may sell the shares in the market and anonymously donate the profits to an unaffiliated charity. If a purchaser sells the stock (flips) within 30 days of the offering the syndicate may not seek to reclaim any sales credit earned by the agent or member unless the stock was sold back to the syndicate's penalty bid. Issuers who are going public are allowed to direct stock to the officers, directors, and employees of the company. The number of shares directed to the employees of the issuer are part of and are not in addition to the number of shares being underwritten.

 TAKE**NOTE!**

Syndicate members may not allocate shares of hot issue to the accounts of individuals who are in a position to direct business to the firm. This includes portfolio managers who may direct execution business to the member as well as officers and directors of companies who have been an investment banking client in the last 12 months or when the company is an anticipated investment banking client. Doing so is a violation known as spinning.

UNDERWRITING CORPORATE SECURITIES

Once a business has decided that it needs to raise capital to meet its organizational objectives, it must determine how to raise the needed capital. Most corporations at this point will hire an investment banker, also known as an underwriter, to advise them. Investment-banking is the broad umbrella term used to describe a variety of investment banking services provided by FINRA members. Included in the definition of investment banking services are acting as an underwriter, syndicate or selling group member, financial adviser to an issuer regarding an m&a transaction, placement agent in a private transaction, providing capital or lines of credit. The underwriter works for the issuer, and it is the underwriter's job to advise the client about what type of securities to offer. The issuer and the underwriter together determine whether stocks or bonds should be issued and what the terms will be. The underwriter is responsible for trying to obtain the financing at the best possible terms for the issuer. The underwriter will:

- Market the issue to investors.
- Assist in the determination of the terms of the offering.
- Purchase the securities directly from the issuer to resell to investors.

The issuer is responsible for:

- Filing a registration statement with the SEC.
- Registering the securities in the states in which it will be sold, also known as blue-skying the issue.
- Negotiating the underwriter's compensation and obligations to the issuer.

TYPES OF UNDERWRITING COMMITMENTS

The agreement between the issuer and the underwriter spells out the underwriter's responsibilities to the issuer. The agreement may take a variety of forms and may include:

- Firm commitment
- Best efforts
- Mini-maxi
- All or none
- Standby

FIRM COMMITMENT

In a firm commitment underwriting, the underwriter guarantees to purchase all of the securities being offered for sale by the issuer regardless of whether it can sell them to investors. A firm commitment underwriting agreement is the most desirable for the issuer because it guarantees the issuer all of the money right away. The more in demand the offering is, the more likely it is that it will be done on a firm commitment basis. If the issue is in extremely high demand and is oversubscribed, the underwriter may exercise its greenshoe provision to cover overallotments. This will allow the underwriter to purchase an additional 15 percent of the issue from the issuer. In a firm commitment, the underwriter puts its own money at risk if it can't sell the securities to investors.

MARKET-OUT CLAUSE

An underwriter offering securities for an issuer on a firm commitment basis is assuming a substantial amount of risk. As a result, the underwriter will insist on having a market-out clause in the underwriting agreement. A market-out clause would free the underwriter from its obligation to purchase all of the securities in the event of a development that impairs the quality of the securities or that adversely affects the issuer. If a syndicate was underwriting a new issue for a biotech company with a drug in clinical trials and the FDA rejected the drug for use, the underwriters could invoke the market-out clause. Poor market conditions are not a reason to invoke the market-out clause.

BEST EFFORTS

In a best efforts underwriting, the underwriter will do its best to sell all of the securities that are being offered by the issuer but in no way is the underwriter obligated to purchase the securities for its own account. The lower the demand for an issue, the greater likelihood that it will be done on a best efforts basis. Any shares or bonds in a best efforts underwriting that have not been sold will be returned to the issuer.

MINI-MAXI

A mini-maxi is a type of best efforts underwriting that does not become effective until a minimum amount of the securities have been sold. Once the minimum has been met, the underwriter may then sell the securities up to the maximum amount specified under the terms of the offering. All funds collected from investors will be held in escrow until the underwriting is completed. If the minimum amount of securities specified by the offering cannot be reached, the offering will be canceled and the investors' funds that were collected will be returned to them.

ALL OR NONE (AON)

With an all-or-none underwriting, the issuer has determined that it must receive the proceeds from the sale of all of the securities. Investors' funds are held in escrow until all of the securities are sold. If all of the securities are sold, the proceeds will be released to the issuer. If all of the securities are not sold, the issue is cancelled and the investors' funds will be returned to them. All contingent offerings must have a qualified financial institute QFI to act as an escrow agent for the offering. A general securities broker dealer, bank, or trust company may all act as an escrow agent.

STANDBY

A standby underwriting agreement will be used in conjunction with a preemptive rights offering. All standby underwritings are done on a firm commitment basis. The standby underwriter agrees to purchase any shares that current shareholders do not purchase. The standby underwriter will then resell the securities to the public.

TYPES OF OFFERINGS

Securities that are being sold under a prospectus may include securities that are part of different types of offerings. The different types of offerings include initial public offerings, subsequent primary offerings, and registered secondary offerings.

INITIAL PUBLIC OFFERING (IPO)/NEW ISSUE

An initial public offering is the first time that a company has sold its stock to the public. The issuing company receives the proceeds from the sale minus the underwriter's compensation.

SUBSEQUENT PRIMARY/ADDITIONAL ISSUES

In a subsequent primary offering, the corporation is already publicly owned and the company is selling additional shares to raise new financing. The shares being sold under a subsequent primary distribution may be offered at a stated price or the shares may be sold at the market once the issue is effective. If the issue is an at-the-market offering, the shares may be sold at different prices in the marketplace.

PRIMARY OFFERING VS. SECONDARY OFFERING

In a primary offering, the issuing company receives the proceeds from the sale minus the underwriter's compensation. In a secondary offering, a group of selling shareholders receives the proceeds from the sale minus the underwriter's compensation. A combined offering has elements of both the primary offering and the secondary offering or split. Part of the proceeds go to the company and part of the proceeds go to a group of selling shareholders.

AWARDING THE ISSUE

There are two ways in which the corporation may select an underwriter. A corporation may elect to have multiple underwriters submit bids and then choose the underwriter with the best bid. This is known as a competitive bid underwriting. Or, a company may elect to select one firm to sell the issue and negotiate the terms of the offering with it. This is known as a negotiated underwriting. Most corporate offerings are awarded on a negotiated basis, whereas municipal bond offerings are usually awarded through competitive bidding.

THE UNDERWRITING SYNDICATE

Because most corporate offerings involve a large number of shares and a very large dollar amount, they will be offered through several underwriters known as the underwriting syndicate. The syndicate is a group of investment banks that have agreed to share the responsibility of marketing the issue. The managing underwriter, also known as the lead underwriter or book running manager, leads the syndicate. If the syndicate plans to stabilize the issue in the aftermarket to allow for an orderly distribution of the shares, only one bid may be placed, and the stabilizing bid must be entered at or below the offering price. Most underwriting agreements will have an over-allotment or green shoe provision that allows the syndicate to purchase additional shares from the issuer at the original price The green shoe provision will allow the syndicate to purchase additional shares equal to 15 percent of the offering.

SELLING GROUP

The syndicate may form a selling group in an effort to help market the issue. Members of the selling group have no underwriting responsibility and may only sell the shares to investors for a fee known as the selling concession.

Occasionally the employees of the issuer may assist in selling the securities of the issuer. This is allowed with the permission of the managing underwriter so long as the employees are not paid based on the sales and are not disqualified from or registered as agents of any broker dealer.

UNDERWRITER'S COMPENSATION

The group of broker dealers that make up the underwriting syndicate will be compensated based upon their role as a syndicate member. The only syndicate member that may earn the entire spread is the lead or managing underwriter.

MANAGEMENT FEE

The lead or managing underwriter will receive a fee known as a management fee for every share that is sold. In most cases, the managing underwriter is the firm that negotiated the terms of the offering with the issuer and formed the syndicate.

UNDERWRITER'S FEE

The underwriter's fee is the cost of bringing the issue to market and is a fee assessed for each share that is sold by the syndicate. If there is any money remaining after all expenses are paid, the syndicate members will split it based upon their commitment level in the underwriting.

SELLING CONCESSION

The selling concession will be paid to any syndicate member or selling group member who sells the shares to the investors. The selling concession is the only fee that the selling group members may earn.

TAKENOTE!

With the approval of the syndicate manager, a member of the syndicate or selling group may sell the shares to a FINRA member firm who is not participating in the offering. The FINRA member will receive part of the selling concession known as the reallowance.

UNDERWRITING SPREAD

The total amount of the management fee, the underwriting fee, and the selling concession make up the total underwriting spread. This is the difference between the gross proceeds of the offering and the net proceeds to the issuer.

PUBLIC OFFERING PRICE: $12

SELLING CONCESSION $1.50
UNDERWRITING FEE $.75
MANAGEMENT FEE $.25

PROCEEDS TO ISSUER: $9.50 PER SHARE

In this example the underwriting spread is $2.50 per share.

FACTORS THAT DETERMINE THE SIZE OF THE UNDERWRITING SPREAD

Many factors determine the amount of the underwriter's compensation for offering the securities on behalf of the issuer. Some of these factors are:

- The type of securities to be offered.
- The size of the issue.
- The quality of the securities to be issued.
- The perceived demand for the securities.
- The type of underwriting agreement.
- The quality of the issuer's business.

REVIEW OF UNDERWRITING AGREEMENTS BY FINRA

With certain exceptions, underwriting agreements must be submitted to FINRA's Corporate Finance Department for review no later than three days after the filing of any registration with the SEC or with any state regulator. If the offering is not required to be filed at either the federal or state level, as is the case with private placements, the agreement must be filed with FINRA at least 15 business days prior to the anticipated offering date. In most cases, the agreement is submitted by the managing underwriter. FINRA will review the maximum total compensation to the underwriters to ensure that the underwriter's compensation is fair and reasonable in light of the size and complexity of the offering. Documents relating to common stock, convertible bonds, preferred stock, non-investment grade bonds, Regulation A, Rule 147, DPPs, rights, warrants, and closed-end funds must be filed. The submission must include:

- The maximum offering price.
- The maximum underwriter's discount.
- The maximum estimated reimbursement for the underwriter's expenses.

UNDERWRITER'S COMPENSATION

The largest percentage of the underwriter's compensation will come in the form of the underwriter's discount. Other items received by the syndicate will also be considered compensation and are reported to the corporate finance department, such as:

- Reimbursement of costs not usually borne by the issuer.
- Options, rights, or warrants.
- Shares of the issuer.
- Finder's fees reimbursed by the issuer.
- The amount of any non-accountable expense allowance.
- Overallotment provisions (green shoe).
- Right of first refusal on future offerings.

UNREASONABLE COMPENSATION

FINRA's Corporate Finance Department will review all of the compensation received by the underwriter and determine if the total amount of compensation is reasonable. One of the main focuses of the CFD is to ensure that underwriters do not take advantage of issuers by demanding fees that are excessive. The Corporate Finance Department considers all of the following to be excessive and unreasonable:

- A non-accountable expense allowance greater than 3 percent of the underwriting spread.
- A greenshoe provision in excess of 15 percent of the offering.
- Freely transferable shares amounting to greater than 1 percent of the offering, which are not subject to a 6-month lock up.
- Warrants, rights, or options exercisable below the public offering price or with a duration greater than 5 years, or that total more than 10 percent of the number of shares offered.
- Right of first refusal to additional offerings greater than 3 years.
- A termination or trail fee greater than 2 years requiring payment to be made to the underwriter if the issuer cancels the offering or switches underwriters.

If the CFD notifies the lead underwriter that the compensation is excessive the lead underwriter must inform the syndicate and adjust the compensation. Once the CFD is satisfied that the compensation is reasonable the offering may proceed. Expenses that are not considered when looking at the underwriter's compensation would be:

- Printing costs
- Accounting fees
- Blue-sky fees

TAKENOTE!

When determining the total amount of compensation received by the underwriter, FINRA's Corporate Finance Department will look back 180 days (6 months) and assume that any compensation received from the issuer was received as compensation for the offering.

The following are all exempt from the filing of the underwriting agreement with the Corporate Finance Department:

- U.S. government securities
- Municipal securities
- Redeemable investment company shares
- Variable contracts

- Private placements

OFFERING OF SECURITIES BY FINRA MEMBERS

When a FINRA member firm wishes to raise money by offering securities for sale to investors special rules apply to the offering. When a FINRA member firm goes public it may not underwrite its own securities. The member wishing to go public must engage the services of a qualified independent lead underwriter. A qualified independent lead underwriter is a FINRA member who has been the book running lead underwriter in at least 3 offerings in the last 3 years. The member's participation in those offerings must have been for at least 50 percent of the shares being sold. The proceeds of member offerings must be placed in escrow and may not be released for use by the member until the member has completed a net capital computation and submitted it to FINRA. The computation must show that the member's AI:NC that does not exceed 10:1 or that its net capital is greater than 120 percent of its required net capital. When calculating the net capital the member may use the funds being held in escrow as part of the calculation. If the net capital computation shows AI:NC of greater than 10:1 or if its net capital is less than 120 percent of its required net capital the offering will be canceled and the funds returned to investors. If the member calculates net capital using the alternative method the offering will be canceled if the member's net capital is less than 7 percent of aggregate debit items. When a FINRA member is offering securities for sale the member who is issuing the securities must file the underwriting agreement with FINRA's Corporate Finance Department. If the member is raising money for itself (or for an entity it controls defined as having at least a 50% ownership stake) through a member private offering (MPO) the member must file the private placement memorandum or term sheet with FINRA's CFD within 15 calendar days of the first sale. If no offering documents are to be used FINRA must be notified of that fact.

EXEMPT SECURITIES

Certain securities are exempt from the registration provisions of the Securities Act of 1933 because of the issuer or the nature of the security. Although the securities may be exempt from the registration and prospectus requirements of the act, none are exempt from the antifraud provisions of the act. Examples of exempt securities are:

- Debt securities with maturities of less than 270 days and sold in denominations of $50,000 or more.
- Employee benefit plans.
- Option contracts, both puts and calls on stocks and indexes.

Examples of exempt issuers are:

- U.S. government
- State and municipal governments
- Foreign national governments
- Canadian federal and municipal governments
- Insurance companies
- Banks and trusts
- Credit unions and savings and loans
- Religious and charitable organizations

TAKE**NOTE!**

Insurance and bank holding companies are not exempt issuers.

EXEMPT TRANSACTIONS

Sometimes a security that would otherwise have to register is exempt from the registration requirements of the Securities Act of 1933 because of the type of transaction that is involved. Issuers who are seeking to raise money through an exempt transaction may test the waters by soliciting interest from potential investors and by holding "demo days" prior to selecting the type of transaction. The following are all exempt transactions:

- Private placements/Regulation D offerings
- Rule 144
- Regulation S offerings
- Regulation A offerings
- Rule 145
- Rule 147 intrastate offerings

PRIVATE PLACEMENTS/ REGULATION D OFFERINGS

A private placement is a sale of securities that is made to a group of accredited investors where the securities are not offered to the general public. Accredited investors include institutional investors and individuals who:

- Earn at least $200,000 per year if single,

  or

- Earn at least $300,000 jointly with a spouse,

  or

- Have a net worth of at least $1,000,000 without the primary residence.

The SEC has recently added a new category that will allow an individual to qualify as an accredited investor. Individuals who meet certain educational or certification requirements can now meet the definition of accredited investor. Included in this category are individuals who have an active Series 7, 65 or 82 license. Reasonable efforts must be made to ensure purchasers meet the definition of an accredited investor. Brokerage accounts, bank accounts credit reports and tax documents may be used for verification purposes. An existing partnership which consists of both accredited and non-accredited investors will be seen as one purchaser under regulation D and allowed to purchase the shares. Partnerships formed specifically to purchase shares of the offering would have all of the partners' financial status reviewed independently to determine the eligibility of each partner.

Sales to nonaccredited investors for private placements are limited to 35 in any 12-month period. No commission may be paid to representatives who sell a private placement to a nonaccredited investor. If the issuer is not going to allow offers to be made to non accredited investors no disclosure documents are required to be provided. For private placements being offered to both accredited and non-accredited investors, all investors must be provided with an offering memorandum. All investors in private placements must hold the securities fully paid for at least six months and sign a letter stating that they are purchasing the securities for investment purposes. Stock purchased though a private placement is known as lettered stock, legend stock, or restricted stock, because there is a legend on the stock certificate that limits the ability of the owner to transfer or sell the securities. There is no limit as to how many accredited investors may purchase the securities. The limits on the amount of money that may be raised under the various regulation D offerings are as follows:

- Regulation 504 D allows issuers to raise up to $10 million.
- Regulation 506 D allows issuers to raise an unlimited amount of capital.

PURCHASER'S REPRESENTATIVE

A purchaser's representative is an individual designated in writing by the prospective purchaser to represent the purchaser when evaluating the suitability of a private placement. A purchaser's representative may not:

- Receive a blanket appointment to represent the investor for all private placements.
- Own more than 10 percent of the issuer's stock.
- Be an officer, director, employee, or affiliate of the issuer, unless he or she is a close relative of the prospective purchaser.

For private placements exceeding $5 million, the offering will be limited to institutional, accredited, and nonaccredited investors who together with their purchaser's representative have the financial and business knowledge to evaluate the offering. The issuer in a private placement may not advertise the issue or hold a seminar open to the general public. However, a seminar held exclusively for qualified potential purchasers would be allowed. The JOBS Act now allows investors to view private placement documents online so long as the website requires an investor to submit a questionnaire documenting assets, income, and investment experience. This questionnaire must be reviewed and if qualified for participation the issuer or broker dealer may assign the investor a username and password granting them access to view the details of the offerings. The JOBS Act also allows offerings conducted under regulation 506 D to advertise and generally solicit investors to participate in the offering.

RULE 144

Regulates how control or restricted securities may be sold. Rule 144 designates:

- The holding period for the security.
- The amount of the security that may be sold.
- Filing procedures.
- Method of sale.

Control securities are owned by officers, directors, and owners of 10 percent or more of the company's outstanding stock. Control stock may be obtained by insiders through open-market purchases or through the exercise of company stock options. There is no holding period for control securities. However, insiders are not allowed to earn a short swing profit through the purchase and sale of control stock in the open market. If the securities were held less than six months, the insider must return any profit to the company.

Restricted securities may be purchased by both insiders and investors though a private placement or be obtained through an offering other than a public sale. Securities obtained through a private placement or other non-public means need to be sold under Rule 144 in order to allow the transfer of ownership. For reporting companies, restricted stock must be held fully paid for, for six months. After six months the securities may be sold freely by noninsiders so long as the seller has not been affiliated with the issuer in the last three months. It's important to note that rule 144 imposes a 12 month holding period for the restricted stock of non reporting issuers who fail to meet the requirements of adequate publicly available information. Rule 144 sets the following volume limits for both restricted and control stock during any 90-day period. The seller must file Form 144 at the time the order is entered and is limited to the greater of:

- The average weekly trading volume for the preceding four weeks,

  or

- 1 percent of the issuer's total outstanding stock.

Securities may be sold under Rule 144 four times per year. Restricted securities sold under Rule 144 become part of the public float and the seller, not the issuer, receives the proceeds of the sale. For orders for 5,000 shares or less and that do not exceed $50,000, Form 144 does not need to be filed. If the owner of restricted stock dies, his or her estate may sell the shares freely without regard to the holding period or volume limitations of Rule 144 so long as the decedent was not an affiliate of the issuer.

If the purchaser of restricted stock gifts the shares, to another person or to a trust, the holding period transfers to the recipient of the shares. Additionally, shares that have been pledged as collateral for a loan and subsequently surrendered will have the holding period transfer to the recipient.

TAKENOTE!

There is a six-month holding period for control stock acquired through a private placement, and control stock is always subject to the volume limitations.

BROKER TRANSACTIONS UNDER RULE 144

A firm handling a customer's sale under Rule 144, except for in very limited circumstances, must execute the orders on an agency basis for the customer. The broker dealer may execute the order with a market maker or may inquire with customers who have expressed an unsolicited interest in the securities in the last 10 days or with a broker dealer who has expressed interest in the securities in the last 60 days. Firms that are classified as bona fide block positioners are allowed to purchase the stock on a principal basis.

RULE 144A

Rule 144A permits the resale of restricted stock to qualified institutional buyers (QIBs). A QIB is defined as a company that owns investments worth at least $100 million and includes:

- Corporations
- Partnerships
- Insurance companies
- Investment companies
- Banks
- Trust funds
- Pension plans
- Registered investment advisers
- Small business development companies

The broker dealer must verify that the customer meets the definition of a QIB, When determining the eligibility for a buyer to participate in a 144a transaction, the broker dealer may use any of the following:

- The purchaser's most recent, publicly available financial statements
- The purchaser's most recent publicly available information appearing in documents filed in an SRO
- The purchaser's most recent publicly available information appearing in a recognized securities manual or filed with a foreign regulator

- A certification by the purchaser's chief financial officer or other executive

The broker dealer may not rely on the information on the customer's account card.

 TAKE**NOTE!**

A broker dealer will be considered a QIB if it owns $10 million worth of securities or if it engages in riskless principal transactions for other QIBs.

To qualify for the exemption provided under Rule 144A, the QIB must be purchasing the securities for its own account or for the account of other QIBs. Not all securities will be eligible for an exemption under Rule 144A. Ineligible securities include:

- Securities of registered investment companies.
- Securities of the same class as those listed on an exchange or Nasdaq.
- Certain warrants and convertible securities.

All purchasers of securities under Rule 144A must be informed that the seller is relying on the exemption provided under Rule 144A, and the issuer of the securities must be willing to provide financial information to owners and prospective purchasers. The PORTAL Market has been developed to help ensure compliance with Rule 144A and to help facilitate Rule 144A transactions. Transactions that qualify under Rule 144A may be executed without regard to any holding period otherwise imposed so long as the buyer is a QIB. However, the QIB is still subject to the holding period of the original purchaser.

PRIVATE INVESTMENT IN A PUBLIC EQUITY (PIPE)

Public companies that wish to obtain additional financing without selling securities to the general public may sell securities to a group of accredited investors through a private placement. The accredited investors in most cases will be institutional investors who wish to invest a large amount of capital. Common stock, convertible or nonconvertible debt, rights, and warrants may all be sold to investors through a PIPE transaction. Obtaining capital through a PIPE transaction benefits the public company in a number of ways:

- Reduced transaction cost.
- Term disclosure only upon completion of the transaction.
- Increased institutional ownership.
- Quick closing.

Securities sold through a PIPE transaction are subject to Rule 144. If the issuer files a registration statement after the closing of the offering sales may begin immediately upon the effective date.

REVERSE MERGER

A reverse merger, sometimes called an alternative public offering or APO, can be used by a private company as a cost-effective alternative to a traditional public offering. In an APO transaction, a private company acquires or merges with a company that is already public as a means of taking itself public. Once completed, the private company will be publicly traded at a significantly lower cost and with less dilution than in a traditional offering. The details of the transaction will be reported upon completion on Form 8K.

REGULATION S OFFERINGS

Domestic issuers who make a distribution of securities exclusively to offshore investors do not have to file a registration statement for the securities under the Securities Act of 1933. In order to qualify for the exemption offered under Regulation S, the issuer may make no offerings of the securities within the United States and may not announce or distribute literature relating to the securities within the United States. Securities distributed under Regulation S are subject to a distribution compliance period, during which the securities may not be resold to domestic investors. The distribution compliance period is 6 months for equities if the issuer is a reporting company and files 10-Qs, 10-Ks and 8-Ks, and one year for non reporting companies. The distribution compliance period is 40 days for debt. Sales of the securities may take place in off-shore markets anytime after the initial sale. Issuers must report the sale of securities under Regulation S by filing form 8K.

REGULATION A OFFERINGS

Regulation A allows US and Canadian issuers to raise up to $75 million in any 12 month period. A Regulation A offering provides issuers with an exemption from the standard registration process. This exemption from full registration allows smaller companies access to the capital markets without having to go through the expense of filing a full registration statement with the SEC. The issuer will instead file an abbreviated notice of sale or offering circular known as an S1-A with the SEC. Issuers are required to file 2 years of audited financial statements with the SEC and purchasers of the issue will be given a copy of the offering circular rather than a final prospectus. Purchasers of the issue must have the preliminary or final offering circular mailed to them 48 hours before mailing the confirmation. The same 20-day cooling-off period also applies to Regulation A offerings. Regulation A has two tiers, with Regulation A now sometimes being referred to as Regulation A plus. Tier 1 allows issuers to raise up to $20 million. Of this $20 million, no more than $6 million may be offered by selling shareholders. Tier 2 allows issuers to raise up to $75 million, of which no more than $22.5 million may be offered by selling shareholders. When determining the total amount of money raised through a regulation A offering, the look-back period includes money raised in the past 12 months.

CROWDFUNDING

Crowdfunding has become a popular way for issuers to raise capital from small investors. Issuers may offer securities to investors for purchase through a broker dealer or through a registered crowdfunding portal. The portal must be registered with the SEC and must also be a FINRA member firm. Issuers who raise capital through crowdfunding may not engage directly in crowdfunding as a way to sell shares to investors. Issuers who sell shares through crowdfunding must register the securities with the SEC by filing form C. Because most of the securities are speculative in nature, broker dealers and crowdfunding portals must offer educational material to investors who are considering purchasing securities offered through crowdfunding. The material must detail the risks involved in making investments in companies through the crowdfunding process as well as the fact that the securities have a limited amount of liquidity. Investors who purchase shares through crowdfunding may not sell the shares for 12 months. Shares however may be transferred earlier to a relative or to a trust controlled by the investor or as a result of death or divorce. Early transfer will also be allowed if the purchaser is an accredited investor or if the securities are part of an SEC registered offering. Investors who purchase shares are limited to the amount of securities they may purchase through the crowdfunding process in any 12 month period. Investors who have an annual income or a net worth of less than $100,000 are limited to purchasing the greater of $2,000 worth of securities or 5% of their annual income or net worth. If the investor uses the 5% calculation to determine their purchase limit the amount the person may purchase will be the lesser of the two amounts. Investors who have an annual income or a net worth greater than $100,000 may invest the lesser of 10% of their annual income or net worth up to a maximum of $100,000. Investment limits have been removed for accredited investors and issuers may raise up to $5 million through the crowdfunding process.

TAKENOTE!

If any covered person, such as an officer or director of an issuer, has been the subject of a disqualifying event, such as being convicted for securities fraud or having been barred by a regulator, the exemption from registration offered through Regulation A, Regulation D, and Regulation crowdfunding may not be used by the issuer.

RULE 145

Rule 145 requires that shareholders approve any merger or reorganization of the company's ownership. Any merger or acquisition will be reported to the SEC on form S-4. Stockholders must be given full disclosure of the proposed transaction or reclassification and must be sent proxies to vote on the proposal. Rule 145 covers:

- Mergers involving a stock swap or offer of another company's securities in exchange for a company's current stock.
- Reclassification involving the exchange of one class of the company's securities for another.
- Asset transfers involving the dissolution of the company or the distribution or sale of a major portion of the company's assets. In the case of a spin-off, the shareholder will retain the securities of the issuer and will receive shares of the newly independent company that was the subject of the spin off.

Rule 145 does not cover:

- Stock splits
- Reverse splits
- Changes in par value

RULE 147 INTRASTATE OFFERING

Rule 147 allows an issuer to raise an unlimited amount of capital within one state. Because the offering is being made only in one state, it is exempt from registration with the SEC and is subject to the jurisdiction of the state securities administrator. In order to qualify for an exemption from SEC registration, the issue must be organized and have its principal place of business in the state and meet at least one of the following business criteria:

- 80% of the issuer's income must be received in that state.
- 80% of the offering's proceeds must be used in that state.
- 80% of the issuer's assets must be located in that state.
- A majority of the issuer's employees are based in-state.

All purchasers must be located within the state and must agree not to resell the securities to an out-of-state resident for 6 months.

If the issuer is using an underwriter, the broker dealer must have an office in that state.

The SEC has also adopted Rule 147A, which is largely identical to Rule 147. However, Rule 147A allows companies that are incorporated out of state to utilize the Rule 147 exemption so long as the company's principal place of business is in that state. Rule 147 A also allows issuers to use the internet and to advertise securities being offered through Rule 147. Offers may be made to residents while out of state. However, all sales are still limited to investors residing in the state where the offering is being conducted. Interestingly, an existing domestic partnership made up of partners from both in-state and out-of-state would be allowed to purchase these shares being issued under Rule 147.

RULE 137 NONPARTICIPANTS

Firms that are not participating in a distribution of securities may issue recommendations, information, or opinions relating to the securities that are in registration, if the issuer is a reporting company, as required by the Securities and Exchange Act of 1934. So long as the broker dealer did not receive compensation for issuing the report from the issuer, a selling shareholder, or a participant in the distribution, it will not constitute an offer of the securities.

RULE 138 NONEQUIVALENT SECURITIES

If a registration statement has been filed for a nonconvertible bond or a nonconvertible preferred stock, a broker dealer, who is a participant in a distribution of the securities, may in the normal course of business issue recommendations, information, or opinions relating to the issuer's common stock or convertible securities. If the registration statement covers common stock or a convertible security of the issuer, a broker dealer may only issue recommendations, information, or opinions relating to the issuer's nonconvertible debt or preferred stock.

RULE 139 ISSUING RESEARCH REPORTS

A broker dealer who is participating in a distribution of an additional issue may continue to issue research reports relating to the issuer if the issuer is a large reporting company under the Securities and Exchange Act of 1934 and:

- The company is followed by analysts.
- The information, opinion, or recommendation appears in a regularly published report.
- Information, opinions, or recommendations that are at least as favorable as the current report must have been contained in the previous report.
- The company that is subject to the offering is not highlighted or featured more prominently than other companies in the report.

If the broker dealer is not currently covering the company, the report is not considered to be issued with sufficient regularity. Any projections relating to the company's earnings may not extend past the current fiscal year. Broker dealers may issue reports for smaller issuers if the report contains information relating to a substantial number of issuers in the same industry as the issuer, or a list of securities currently recommended by the broker dealer, so long as the information relating to the registrant is not displayed more prominently than other information in the same report.

If the conditions for continuing to publish research reports are not met, managers, co-managers, and syndicate members participating in the underwritings of IPOs may not issue research reports relating to the IPO until 10 days have passed from the offering's effective date. The quiet period for managers and co-managers is reduced for secondary and follow-on offerings to 3 days from the effective date. Syndicate and selling group members have no quiet period for follow-on offerings. It is important to note that these rules are not in effect for the underwriting of debt securities. If the company is classified as an emerging growth company with annual revenue of less than $1 billion research reports may be distributed any time after the IPO. Additionally, the standard prohibition against a research analyst attending a pitch meeting to win the underwriting business is waived in the case of an emerging growth company so long as their involvement is limited to winning the underwriting or investment banking deal. One additional exception to the quiet period occurs in the event of a material development at the company. Should a material change take place (requiring the filing of an 8K) such as the approval of a new drug, research reports may be published and analyst appearances may take place with the approval of the firm's legal or compliance department.

RULE 415 SHELF REGISTRATION

Rule 415 allows an issuer to register securities that may be sold for its own benefit, for the benefit of a subsidiary, or in connection with business plans in an amount that may be reasonably sold by the issuer within a two-year period. The two-year window starts from the registration date and allows the issuer and the underwriters flexibility in the timing of the offering. Issuers who qualify as well-known seasoned issuers (WKSI, as defined on page 85) and who qualify for automatic registration may sell securities for up to three years. Rule 415 also allows the issuer to register to sell securities on a continuous basis in connection with an employee benefit plan or upon the conversion of other securities.

TAKENOTE!

An issuer who loses its status as a well-known seasoned issuer may continue to sell the securities under Rule 415 until it files its next 10K.

SECURITIES OFFERING REFORM RULES

The SEC has adopted the securities offering reform rules, which are designed to modify and streamline the filing and communication requirements of issuers under the Securities Act of 1933. The rules focus on the following areas:

- The communications related to registered securities offerings.
- Registration and other procedures in the offering and capital-formation processes.
- The delivery of information to investors, including the timeliness of that delivery.

The rules adopted have placed an increased importance on the value of electronic communications and filing and have helped eliminate cumbersome and outdated filing requirements.

SEC RULE 405

SEC Rule 405 defines certain classes of issuers who may be entitled to use a streamlined registration process depending on how the issuer is classified. Well-known seasoned issuers and seasoned issuers may take advantage of automatically effective shelf registration of securities by filing Form S-3 or F-3. The registration of the securities covered under the filing of Form S-3 or F-3 is effective immediately upon filing.

WELL-KNOWN SEASONED ISSUER (WKSI)

An issuer that within 60 days of its eligibility determination has at least $700 million worth of voting and nonvoting common equity held by nonaffiliates or that has issued within the last three years at least $1 billion in nonconvertible securities for cash (excluding common equity). A WKSI also includes a company that is a majority-owned subsidiary of a WKSI. If during the course of an offering the WKSI sees the value of its securities fall below the required levels to be considered a WKSI, the issuer may continue to sell the securities until it files its next 10-K.

SEASONED ISSUER (PRIMARY S-3 ELIGIBLE)

An issuer that has a public float of $75 million meets the requirements of Form S-3 to register a primary offering of securities.

UNSEASONED REPORTING ISSUER (NOT PRIMARY S-3 ELIGIBLE)

An issuer that is required to report under the Exchange Act but that does not qualify with the requirements of Form S-3 or F-3 to file a primary offering of securities.

INELIGIBLE ISSUER

A reporting issuer that is not current with the filing of reports required under the Securities Exchange Act. Ineligible issuers also include:

- Companies who have filed for bankruptcy within the last three years.
- Blank check companies.
- Shell companies.
- Issuers of penny stock.
- Issuers that are limited partnerships that don't have a firm commitment underwriting agreement to sell securities.
- Issuers that have been subject to a stop order or have been convicted of a felony or misdemeanor under the Exchange Act directly or indirectly through a subsidiary within the last three years.

ADDITIONAL COMMUNICATION RULES

An issuer who is a reporting company may continue to release regular business communications with forward-looking statements prior to the effective date of an additional offering of securities. A forward-looking statement is one that contains information about what may possibly happen in the future, such as projected sales or new products. If the securities being offered are the subject of an IPO for a non-reporting issuer, only standard factual business communications may be released by the company. Standard factual information contains information relating to products or services and is not intended to be used by potential investors to make an investment decision. These two safe harbors allow the companies to continue to communicate without violating the gun jumping provisions of the communications rules. The gun jumping rules are designed to limit communications during the time an issue is in registration and to prevent companies from trying to create more favorable market conditions for the securities than otherwise would exist. If the company is a reporting company under the Securities Exchange Act of 1934, the issuer may use forward looking statements in both their prospectus and annual reports provided that the statements are clearly identified as forward looking. Key words such as expect, predict, potential, and anticipate are all used to inform the reader that the statements are not facts but projections based on management's beliefs. If the company uses a third party to review the projections it must disclose the nature of any relationship, the qualifications of the reviewer, and the extent of the review. The company is under no obligation to have the projections reviewed.

Road shows are designed to help the company communicate the details of the offering to broker dealers and representatives. Road shows have been traditionally held at large hotels in financial centers across the country. More and more these road shows are being conducted over the Internet via webinars and are known as electronic road shows. These road shows may be broadcast live and recorded for playback and may be available on demand. If the recorded road show is for an IPO of equity securities, the recorded road show must be filed with the SEC unless at least one version is made available to the public in addition to the financial community. Recorded road shows for additional issues do not have to be filed with the SEC.

Certain conference calls and meetings attended by research analysts can be a cause for concern when an analyst is speaking with customers or potential customers regarding an M-A transaction or investment banking deal. Specifically prohibited are three-way communication involving the analyst, customers and any representative of investment banking, or the issuer. Analysts who attend in-person meetings should ensure that they do not speak to customers or potential customers in the presence of investment-banking agents or individuals representing an issuer. It's important to note that a research analyst may attend a meeting with an issuer who is an investment banking client to discuss the prospects of a merger or acquisition involving the issuer. However, the transaction must have been reported to the media and no members of investment-banking may attend.

DPP ROLL-UP TRANSACTIONS

From time to time one or more limited partnerships may wish to combine their operations and assets to achieve better returns and economies of scale. By combing the partnerships investors may be able to achieve better returns and realize greater liquidity for their partnership interests. Member firms who solicit votes from investors may receive a fee for their services so long as the fee is payable in equal installments regardless of the outcome, and the fee to be received does not exceed 2 percent of the value of the securities to be received upon exchange of the interests. Investors must receive full disclosure of all the related risk factors and be provided with a statement from the general partner as to its opinion regarding the fairness of the transaction. If an investment bank or investment adviser has issued a negative opinion regarding the transaction it must be disclosed to the investors. Failure to disclose a negative option in connection with a roll-up transaction constitutes fraud.

CHAPTER 3

Pretest

ISSUING CORPORATE SECURITIES

1. A syndicate has published a tombstone ad prior to the issue becoming effective. Which of the following must appear in the tombstone?
   I. A statement that the registration has not yet become effective
   II. A statement that the ad is not an offer to sell the securities
   III. Contact information
   IV. No commitment statement
   a. III and IV
   b. II and III
   c. I and II
   d. I, II, III, and IV

2. During a new issue registration, false information is included in the prospectus to buyers. Which of the following may be held liable to investors?
   I. Officers of the issuer
   II. Accountants
   III. Syndicate members
   IV. People who signed the registration statement
   a. I and III
   b. I, II, III, and IV
   c. I, II, and III
   d. I, II, III, and IV

3. A syndicate may enter a stabilizing bid:
   a. whenever the price begins to decline.
   b. at or below the offering price.
   c. to ensure an increase from the offering price.
   d. to cover overallotments only.

4. Corporations may do all of the following, EXCEPT:
   a. issue preferred stock only.
   b. issue nonvoting common stock.
   c. sell stock out of the treasury.
   d. repurchase its own shares.

5. A corporation in your state wants to sell 1,000,000 shares of stock at $5 per share to investors. Which of the following is NOT a business requirement under Rule 147?
   a. 80 percent of corporate assets must be located in the state.
   b. 80 percent of proceeds must be used in the state.
   c. 80 percent of the income must be derived from activity within the state.
   d. 80 percent of the purchasers must be in the state.

6. During an underwriting of a hot issue, the syndicate exercises its greenshoe provision. This will allow the syndicate to buy an additional _________ of the offering.
   a. 20 percent
   b. 25 percent
   c. 15 percent
   d. 10 percent

7. Which of the following is NOT a type of offering?
   a. Rule 149 offering
   b. Subsequent primary offering
   c. Secondary offering
   d. Combined offering

8. Once a company decides to raise long-term capital to meet its needs, it will do which of the following?

a. Approach the money market to determine how much capital can be raised.
b. Hire an underwriter to advise the issuer about the type of securities to issue.
c. Hire a dealer to issue stock for public purchase.
d. Hire a broker to issue stock for public purchase.

9. A firm participating in the offering of a private placement may sell the private placement to no more than ________ nonaccredited investors in any 12-month period.
   a. 12
   b. 6
   c. 35
   d. 15

10. A company doing a preemptive rights offering would most likely use what type of underwriting agreement?
    a. Best efforts
    b. Firm commitment
    c. All or none
    d. Standby

11. A Regulation A offering as amended by the Jobs Act pertains to an:
    a. intrastate offering of securities.
    b. offering of bonds.
    c. offering of $50,000,000 or less.
    d. offering of $3,000,000 or less.

12. Rule 145 covers which of the following?
    a. Stock splits
    b. Stock swaps
    c. Reverse splits
    d. Changes in par value

13. The SEC has been reviewing a company's registration statement and would like clarification on a few items. The SEC would most likely:

a. call the company.
b. issue a stop order.
c. issue a deficiency letter.
d. call the lead underwriter.

14. Which of the following is NOT a type of underwriting commitment?
a. Primary commitment
b. Standby commitment
c. Best efforts commitment
d. Firm commitment

15. XYZ has just gone public and is quoted on the Nasdaq Capital Market securities market. Any investor who buys XYZ must get a prospectus for how long?
a. 30 days
b. 25 days
c. 60 days
d. 45 days

16. A red herring given to a client during the cooling-off period will contain all of the following, EXCEPT:
a. proceeds to the company.
b. use of proceeds.
c. biographies of officers and directors.
d. a notice that all the information is subject to change.

17. For an insider to sell unregistered stock under an exemption from registration with the SEC, Form 144, Notice of Offering, which contains certain information, must be filed with the SEC. The insider can sell securities during the period of time in which the notice of offering is effective, which is:
a. 60 days.
b. 6 months.
c. 90 days.
d. 12 months.

CHAPTER 4

Trading Securities

INTRODUCTION

Investors who do not purchase their stocks and bonds directly from the issuer must purchase them from another investor. Investor-to-investor transactions are known as secondary market transactions. In a secondary market transaction, the selling security owner receives the proceeds from the sale. Secondary market transactions may take place on an exchange or in the over-the-counter (OTC) market. Although both facilitate the trading of securities, they operate in a very different manner. We will begin by looking at the types of orders that an investor may enter and the reasons for entering the various types of orders.

TYPES OF ORDERS

Investors can enter various types of orders to buy or sell securities. Some orders guarantee that the investor's order will be executed immediately. Other types of orders may state a specific price or condition under which the investor wants the order to be executed. All orders are considered day orders unless otherwise specified. All day orders will be canceled at the end of the trading day if they are not executed. An investor may also specify that an order remain active until canceled. This type of order is known as *good 'til cancel* or *GTC*.

MARKET ORDERS

A market order will guarantee that the investor's order is executed as soon as the order is presented to the market. A market order to either buy or sell guarantees the execution but not the price at which the order will be executed. When a market order is presented for execution, the market for the security may be very different from the market that was displayed when the order was entered. As a result, the investor does not know the exact price that the order will be executed at.

BUY LIMIT ORDERS

A buy limit order sets the maximum price that the investor will pay for the security. The order may never be executed at a price higher than the investor's limit price. Although a buy limit order guarantees that the investor will not pay over a certain price, it does not guarantee an execution. If the stock continues to trade higher away from the investor's limit price, the investor will not purchase the stock and may miss a chance to realize a profit.

SELL LIMIT ORDERS

A sell limit order sets the minimum price that the investor will accept for the security. The order may never be executed at a price lower than the investor's limit price. Although a sell limit order guarantees that the investor will not receive less than a certain price, it does not guarantee an execution. If the stock continues to trade lower away from the investor's limit price, the investor will not sell the stock and may miss a chance to realize a profit or may realize a loss as a result.

TAKENOTE!

It is important to remember that even if an investor sees stock trading at its limit price, it does not mean that the investor's order was executed, because there could have been stock ahead of the investor at that limit price.

STOP ORDERS/STOP LOSS ORDERS

A stop order, or stop loss order, can be used by investors to limit or guard against a loss or to protect a profit. A stop order will be placed away from the market in case the stock starts to move against the investor. A stop order may be entered at a fixed price or as a trailing stop order that follows the price of the stock and maintains a set relationship to the current price of the stock, such as 2 percent or $1 away from the current price. A stop order is not a live order; it has to be elected. A stop order is elected and becomes a live order when the stock trades at or through the stop price. The stop price is also known as the trigger price. Once the stock has traded at or though the stop price the order becomes a market order to either buy or sell the stock, depending on the type of order that was placed.

BUY STOP ORDERS

A buy stop order is placed above the market and is used to protect against a loss or to protect a profit on a short sale of stock. A buy stop order could also be used by a technical analyst to get long the stock after the stock breaks through resistance.

EXAMPLE

An investor has sold 100 shares of ABC short at $40 per share. ABC has declined to $30 per share. The investor is concerned that if ABC goes past $32 it may return to $40. To protect its profit, the investor enters an order to buy 100 ABC at 32 stop. If ABC trades at or through $32, the order will become a market order to buy 100 shares, and the investor will cover the short at the next available price.

SELL STOP ORDERS

A sell stop order is placed below the market and is used to protect against a loss or to protect a profit on the purchase of a stock. A sell stop order could also be used by a technical analyst to get short the stock after the stock breaks through support.

EXAMPLE

An investor has purchased 100 shares of ABC at $30 per share. ABC has risen to $40 per share. The investor is concerned that if ABC falls past $38 it may return to $30. To protect its profit, the investor enters an order to sell 100 ABC at 38 stop. If ABC trades at or through $38, the order will become a market order to sell 100 shares, and the investor will sell its stock at the next available price.

If in the same example the order to sell 100 ABC at 38 stop was entered GTC, we could have a situation such as this:

ABC closes at 39.40. The following morning ABC announces that it lost a major contract and opens at 35.30. The opening price of 35.30 elected the order, and the stock would be sold on the opening or as close to the opening as practical.

STOP LIMIT ORDERS

An investor would enter a stop limit order for the same reasons it would enter a stop order. The only difference is that once the order has been elected the order becomes a limit order instead of a market order. The same risks that apply to traditional limit orders apply to stop limit orders. If the stock continues to trade away from the investor's limit, the investor could give back all of its profits or suffer large losses.

VWAP ORDERS

Large institutions will often place orders to be executed at a volume-weighted average price (VWAP). When looking at the VWAP for a security, one must take into consideration the number of shares that are traded at each price and not just the prices themselves. As a result, trades that are executed for more shares have a larger impact on the VWAP. If ABC trades 100 shares at 50 and 1,000 shares at 51, the average price of the two trades would be 50.50. But when you take the volume of the trades at the respective prices into consideration, the VWAP is 50.91. To determine the VWAP, the total dollar value of the trades must be added together and divided by the total number of shares purchased. This is found as follows:

(100 shares × $50) = $5,000 + (1,000 shares × $51) = $51,000 = $56,000,
$56,000 / 1,100 shares = 50.91

OTHER TYPES OF ORDERS

An investor may enter several other types of orders:

- All or none (AON)
- Immediate or cancel (IOC)
- Fill or kill (FOK)
- Not held (NH)
- Market on open (MOO)/market on close (MOC)

AON orders: May be entered as day orders or GTC. AON orders, as the name implies, indicate that the investor wants to buy or sell all of the securities or none of them. AON orders are not displayed in the market because of the required special handling and the investor will not accept a partial execution.

IOC orders: The investor wants to buy or sell whatever it can immediately and whatever is not filled is canceled.

FOK orders: The investor wants the entire order executed immediately or the entire order canceled.

NH orders: The investor gives discretion to the floor broker as to the time and price of execution.

MOO or MOC orders: The investor wants its order executed on the opening or closing of the market, or as reasonably close to the opening or closing as practical. If the order is not executed, it is canceled. Partial executions are allowed.

TAKE**NOTE!**

Market on close orders on the NYSE must be entered by 3:45 p.m. No MOC orders may be entered after 3:45 p.m. unless there is an order imbalance on the opposite side of the the market that is 50,000 shares or greater.

THE EXCHANGES

The most recognized stock exchange in the world is the New York Stock Exchange (NYSE). There are, however, many exchanges throughout the United States that all operate in a similar manner. Exchanges are dual-auction markets. They provide a central marketplace where buyers and sellers come together in one centralized location to compete with one another. Buyers compete with other buyers to be the highest price anyone is willing to pay for the security, and sellers compete with other sellers to be the lowest price at which anyone is willing to sell a security. All transactions in an exchange-listed security that are executed on the exchange have to take place in front of the designated market maker (DMM) for that security. The DMM is an exchange member who is the designated market maker in that security and is responsible for maintaining a fair and orderly market for the stock in which he or she specializes. The DMM stands at the so-called trading post where all the buyers and sellers must go to conduct business in the security. This is the reason for the crowd that you see on the news and financial reports when they show the floor of the exchange. All securities that trade on an exchange are known as listed securities.

PRIORITY OF EXCHANGE ORDERS

Orders that are routed to the trading post for execution are prioritized according to price and time. If the price of more than one order is the same, orders will be filled as follows:

- **Priority:** The order that was received first gets filled first.
- **Precedence:** If the time and price are the same, the larger order gets filled.
- **Parity:** If all conditions are the same, the orders are matched in the crowd and the shares are split among the orders.

THE ROLE OF THE DESIGNATED MARKET MAKER

The DMM, formerly known as a specialist, is an independent exchange member who has been assigned a stock or group of stocks for which he or she is the DMM. DMMs are responsible for:

- Maintaining a fair and orderly market for the securities.
- Buying for their own accounts in the absence of public buy orders.
- Selling from their own accounts in the absence of public sell orders.
- Acting as agents by executing public orders left with them.
- Displaying quotes for their own account at the inside market a certain percentage of the time.
- Determining the opening and closing prices for securities and providing price discovery.

A large amount of capital is required in order to fulfill the requirements of a DMM. As a result, most DMMs are employees of DMM firms. Although the DMM is not required to participate in every transaction, every transaction for that security that is executed on the exchange must take place in front of the DMM. The DMM may act as either an agent or as a principal if he or she plays a role in the transaction.

THE DMM ACTING AS A PRINCIPAL

In the absence of public orders, the DMMs are required to provide liquidity and price improvement for the stocks in which they, as the DMMs, are required to trade against the market, and may now trade for their own account at prices that would compete with public orders.

EXAMPLE

If the public market for XYZ is quoted as follows:

	Bid	Offer
10 × 10	**20.45**	**20.55**

There is a 20.45 bid for 1,000 shares and 1,000 shares offered at 20.55.

If a public sell order came in to sell the stock, the DMM could purchase the stock for their own account at 20.45 because they are on parity with the public. The DMM could also purchase the stock for his or her own account at 20.50 and would be improving the price that the seller would be receiving. This is known as price improvement. Alternatively, if a public buy order came in, the DMM could sell the stock from his or her own account at 20.55 because he or she is now allowed to compete with the public. He or she could also sell the stock to the customer at 20.50 because, once again, that would be providing price improvement for the order.

THE DMM ACTING AS AN AGENT

DMMs are also required to execute orders that have been left with them. Orders that have been left with the DMM for execution are said to be "left or dropped on the DMM's book." The DMM is required to maintain a book of public orders and to execute them when market conditions permit. The types of orders that may be left with the DMM are:

- Buy and sell limit orders
- Stop orders
- Stop limit orders
- Both day and GTC orders
- AON orders

Market on close/limit on close and limit on close orders may be entered or canceled up until 3:45 on the NYSE. After 3:45 p.m., market and limit on close orders may only be entered if there is an order imbalance of 50,000 shares or more on the opposite side of the market. A market on close or limit on close order that had been entered in error may be cancelled up until 3:58 p.m.

The DMMs will execute the orders if and when they are able to and will send a commission bill to the member who left the order with them for execution. The fee commission charged by the DMM is usually only a cent or a fraction of a cent per share. The DMM is also required to quote the best market for the security to any party that asks. The best or inside market is composed of the highest bid and the lowest offer. This is made up from bids and offers contained in the DMM's book and in the trading crowd. The inside market is also the market that is displayed to broker dealers and agents on their quote systes.

When quoting the inside market, the DMM will add all of the shares bid for at the highest price and all of the shares offered at the lowest price to determine the size of the market. Certain types of orders are not included when determining the inside market; they are:

- Stop orders
- AON orders

A DMM may not accept the following types of orders:

- Market orders
- Immediately executable limit orders
- NH orders
- IOC orders
- FOK orders

Market orders and immediately executable limit orders are filled as soon as they reach the crowd so there is nothing to leave with the DMM. In the case of a NH order, once a floor broker is given discretion as to time and price, it may not be given to another party.

A DMM's book may look something like the following example:

Buy	XYZ	Sell
5 Goldman 10 Schwab	20	
	20.05	

Buy	XYZ	Sell
	20.10	1 Prudential 5 Fidelity
	20.15	2 Morgan
5 Merrill Stp	20.20	

The inside market for XYZ based on the DMM's book would be:

	Bid	Ask
15 × 6	**20.00**	**20.10**

Buyers are bidding for 1,500 shares and sellers are offering 600 shares of XYZ.

TAKENOTE!

The buy stop entered over the market by Merrill is not contained in the quote, because the order has not been elected.

CROSSING STOCK

A floor broker from time to time may get an order from both a buyer and a seller in the same security. The floor broker may be allowed to pair off, or cross, the orders and execute both orders simultaneously. In order for the floor broker to cross the stock, the DMM must allow it and the floor broker must announce the orders in an effort to obtain price improvement for the orders. The floor broker must offer the stock for sale at a price above the current best bid and may purchase the stock using the buy order if no price improvement has been offered. This will then complete the cross, and both orders will be filled.

DO NOT REDUCE (DNR)

GTC orders that are placed underneath the market and left with the DMM for execution will be reduced for the distribution of dividends. Orders that will be reduced are:

- Buy limits
- Sell stops

These orders are reduced because when a stock goes ex dividend, its price is adjusted downward. To ensure that customer orders placed below the market are only executed as a result of market activity, the order will be adjusted down by the value of the dividend.

EXAMPLE

A customer has placed an order to buy 500 XYZ at 35 GTC. XYZ closed yesterday at 36.10. XYZ goes ex dividend for 20 cents and opens the next day at 35.90. The customer's order will now be an order to purchase 500 XYZ at 34.80 GTC.

If the customer had entered the order and specified that the order was not to be reduced for the distribution of ordinary dividends, it would have remained an order to purchase 500 shares at 35. The order in this case would have been entered as:

Buy 500 XYZ 35 GTC DNR

Orders placed above the market are not reduced for distributions.

ADJUSTMENTS FOR STOCK SPLITS

GTC orders that are left with the DMM must be adjusted for stock splits. Orders that are placed above and below the market will be adjusted so that the aggregate dollar value of the order remains the same.

EXAMPLE

A customer has placed a GTC order. Let's look at what happens to the order if the company declares a stock split:

Type of Split	Old Order	New Order
2:1	Buy 100 at 50	Buy 200 at 25
2:1	Sell 100 at 100	Sell 200 at 50
3:2	Buy 100 at 100	Buy 150 at 66.67
3:2	Sell 100 at 60	Sell 150 at 40

Notice that in all of the examples the value of the customer's order remained the same. To calculate the adjustment to an open order for a forward stock split, multiply the number of shares by the fraction and the share price by the reciprocal of the fraction, such that:

Buy 100 at 50 after a 2:1 stock split

$100 \times 2/1 = 200$

$50 \times 1/2 = 25$

The value of the order was $5,000 both before and after the order. If the stock undergoes a reverse stock split, all open orders will be canceled.

STOPPING STOCK

A DMM, as a courtesy to a public customer, may guarantee an execution price while trying to find an improved or better price for the public customer. This is known as stopping stock.

EXAMPLE

An order comes to the crowd to purchase 500 ABC at the market when ABC is quoted as follows:

	Bid	Ask
15 × 20	**40**	**40.20**

If the DMM stopped the customer, the DMM would guarantee that the customer would pay no more than 40.20 for the 500 shares. The DMM would then try to obtain a better price for the customer and try to attract a seller by displaying a higher bid for that customer's order. ABC may now be quoted after the DMM stopped the stock as:

	Bid	Ask
5 × 20	**40.10**	**40.20**

In this case, the DMM is trying to buy the stock for the customer 10 cents cheaper than the current best offer. If, however, a buyer comes into the crowd and purchases all of the stock that is offered at 40.20, the DMM must sell the customer 500 shares from his or her own account at no higher than 40.20.

COMMISSION HOUSE BROKER

A commission house broker is an employee of a member organization who executes orders for the member's customers and for the member's own account.

TWO-DOLLAR BROKER

A two-dollar broker is an independent member who executes orders for commission house brokers when they are too busy managing other orders. The name originated from the practice of charging a $2 commission for every 100 shares contained in an executed order.

REGISTERED TRADERS

Registered traders are exchange members who trade for their own accounts and for their own profit and loss. Orders may not originate on the floor of the NYSE; however, registered traders are active on other exchanges, such as the Amex.

TAKENOTE!

The hybrid trading model at the NYSE allows for off-floor market makers to qualify as supplemental liquidity providers (SLPs). SLPs must submit bids and offers that are equal to the best bid or offer at least 10% of the time for at least 100 shares in the securities in which they are registered. Unlike the DMM, an SLP is only required to display a one-sided quote.

SUPER DISPLAY BOOK (SDBK)

Most customer orders will never be handled by a floor broker. Floor brokers usually only handle the large complex institutional orders. Customer orders will be electronically routed directly to the trading post for execution via the Super Display Book (SDBK). The SDBK bypasses the floor broker and sends the order right to the DMM for execution. If the order can be executed immediately, the system will send an electronic confirmation of the execution to the submitting broker dealer. All listed securities are eligible to be traded over the SDBK. All preopening orders that can be matched up are automatically paired off by the system and executed at the opening price. Any preopening orders that cannot be paired off are routed to the trading post for inclusion on the SDBK.

SHORT SALES

An investor who believes that a stock price has appreciated too far and is likely to decline may profit from this belief by selling the stock short. In a short sale, the customer borrows the security in order to complete delivery to the buying party. The investor sells the stock high hoping that it can be bought back and replaced at a cheaper price. It is a perfectly legitimate investment strategy. The investor's first transaction is a sell. The investor exits the position by repurchasing the stock. The short sale of stock has unlimited risk because there is no limit to how high the stock price may go. The investor will lose money if the stock appreciates past the sales price.

AFFIRMATIVE DETERMINATION

All firms and agents are required to make an affirmative determination for all sell orders entered on behalf of the firm or a customer. All sell orders must be marked either long or short. A person is considered long the security if the investor:

- Has possession of the security.
- Has purchased the security but the trade has not settled.
- Has issued conversion or exercise instructions for a right, warrant, option, convertible bond, or preferred stock.

If the investor owns rights, warrants, options, or a convertible security but has not issued exercise or conversion instructions, the investor is not considered long the security.

The firm must make a determination if the customer is long the security or if the customer is selling short. If the customer is selling short, the firm must determine if the security can be borrowed for delivery.

An investor is only considered long the security to the extent of the investor's net long position in the security. If an investor is long 1,000 shares of

ABC and is short 600 shares of ABC in another account, the investor may only mark a sell ticket for 400 shares of ABC long.

REGULATION SHO

The SEC has adopted new rules relating to the short sale of securities. Regulation SHO has been adopted to update prior short sale regulations. This regulation covers:

- Definitions and order marking.
- Suspension of uptick and plus bid requirements.
- Borrowing and delivery requirements for securities.

Under Regulation SHO, the SEC has prohibited any SRO from adopting any price criteria as a requirement of executing a short sale.

RULE 200 DEFINITIONS AND ORDER MARKING

Rule 200 updates the definition of who is determined to be long a security. As new derivatives and trading systems and strategies have been introduced, amendments to the short sale rules under the Securities Exchange Act of 1934 have needed to be updated. Most of the prior rules and definitions remain unchanged. The new updates under Rule 200 are:

- A person is considered long the security if the person holds a security future contract and has been notified that he or she will receive the underlying security.
- A broker dealer must aggregate its net positions in securities unless it qualifies to allow each independent trading unit to aggregate its positions independently.

A broker dealer may qualify to have its various trading departments determine their net long or short positions independently if:

- Traders are only assigned to one independent trading unit at any one time.
- Traders in each independent trading unit employ their own trading strategies and do not coordinate their trading with other independent trading units.

- The firm has documented each aggregation unit and the independent trading objectives of each unit.
- The firm supports the independent nature of each trading unit.
- At the time a sell order is entered, each independent aggregation unit determines its net position for the security.

The order-marking requirements of Rule 200 require the broker dealer to mark all orders long, short, or short exempt. The definitions of long and short include the definitions in the affirmative determination rule and have been expanded to include the following:

- An order may be marked long if the investor or broker dealer has possession of the security and can reasonably be expected to deliver the security by the settlement date.
- An order must be marked short if the investor or broker dealer has possession of the security but cannot reasonably be expected to deliver the security by the settlement date.
- An order does not need to be marked short exempt if the seller is only relying on a price test exemption under the tick test or bid test rule.

RULE 203 SECURITY BORROWING AND DELIVERY REQUIREMENTS

A broker dealer may not accept an order to sell short an equity security for the account of a customer or for its own account without having borrowed the security, having arranged to borrow the security, or without having a reasonable belief that the security can be borrowed. A broker dealer can rely on an easy-to-borrow list of securities so long as the list is less than 24 hours old. If a security does not appear on the easy to borrow list or if it is on the hard to borrow list, the broker-dealer must specifically obtain a borrow to complete delivery. An interesting test point relating to this information, is the fact that a security that does not appear on the hard to borrow list, should not be assumed to be included on the easy to borrow list. For sell orders that were marked long, the broker dealer must deliver the securities by the settlement date and may not borrow the securities to complete delivery. However, a broker dealer may borrow securities to complete delivery under the following exceptions:

- To complete delivery to the buyer when a customer fails to deliver.
- The security is being loaned to another broker dealer.
- A fail to deliver resulting from a good faith mistake and a buy in would create an undue hardship.

A broker dealer is exempt from the locating requirements for short sales under any of the following conditions:

- The broker dealer has accepted an order to sell short an equity security from another broker dealer. The broker dealer entering the order is required to locate the securities unless the broker dealer accepting the order has a contractual obligation to comply.
- Transactions in securities futures.
- Transactions that are executed in accordance with bona fide market making.
- Transactions executed by a DMM, block positioner, or dealer.
- An order where the customer has been determined to be long and will deliver the security when restrictions have been removed or expired. The seller must deliver the securities within 35 calendar days. If the broker dealer does not receive the securities, the broker dealer must buy in the customer or borrow the securities.

SEC Rule 204 was adopted as part of Regulation SHO to ensure that broker-dealers buy in securities on a timely basis to close out any failure to deliver. Unless an exemption applies a broker-dealer must closeout any failure to deliver 1 business day past settlement date or T+3. If the failure to deliver was a result of a long sale or part of bona fide market-making the broker-dealer must purchase the securities no later than 3 business days past settlement or T+5. A broker dealer must close out all customer fails to deliver if the customer does not complete deliver within 35 days of the trade date. The broker dealer must borrow the securities or buy in the securities of a like kind and quantity on the 36th calendar day. A broker dealer must close out all customer fails to deliver within 35 days of the trade date. The broker dealer must borrow the securities or buy in the securities of a like kind and quantity.

THRESHOLD SECURITIES

The self-regulatory organizations (SROs) are responsible for the inclusion of securities on the threshold securities list. The SROs monitor reports from the National Securities Clearing Corporation (NSCC) to determine which securities meet the definition of a threshold security. A threshold security is a NYSE, NASDAQ or OTCBB equity security that meets the following criteria:

- The security is registered under Section 12 of the Securities Exchange Act of 1934.
- There is an aggregate fail-to-deliver position at a clearing firm of 10,000 shares or more for five consecutive settlement days and such position represents 0.5 percent or more of the issuer's outstanding securities.
- The security has been included on the threshold securities list by an SRO and the list has been distributed by the SRO to its members.

Under SEC Rule 204 , a broker dealer who has a fail to deliver in a threshold security at a clearing firm for 13 consecutive settlement days must immediately close out the position by buying securities of a like kind and quantity on the 14th business day. If the fail to deliver for a threshold security was the result of securities being sold under Rule 144, after 35 business days, the broker-dealer must buy in the securities on the 36th business day. A broker dealer with a fail to deliver in a threshold security for 13 consecutive settlement days may not accept an order to sell the security short from another person, and may not sell the security short for its own account without having located the security until the fail to deliver has been closed out. Clearing firms that provide clearing services to other broker dealers may allocate or distribute a fail-to-deliver position in threshold securities to its broker dealer customers who are responsible for the fail to deliver. By allocating the fail-to-deliver position to its broker dealer customer who established the position, the obligation to close out the position is transferred from the clearing firm to the correspondent broker dealer who established the position. The 13-day requirement does not apply to any fail-to-deliver position that was established prior to a security becoming a threshold security. If a market maker cannot borrow a threshold security to execute transactions in connection with bona fide market-making activities, the market maker is entitled to an excused withdrawal from that security. A security will cease to be considered a threshold security if it does not exceed the specific fail-to-deliver criteria for five consecutive settlement days.

Firms must maintain a record of customer and firm short positions. The firm must file a short interest report twice per month for short positions that have settled by the 15th and as of the last trading day of each month, using FINRA's Regulation Filing Application (RFA). All reports are required to be filed with the firm's designated examining authority (FINRA or NYSE) by the end of the second business day following the settlement date.

BLOCK TRADES

A firm that purchases a block of stock from a customer with a value of $500,000 or greater is considered to be a block positioner. Block positioners, who have purchased a block of stock with a value of $500,000 or greater, may not purchase the same stock on a plus tick during the last 20 minutes of the normal trading day. If the firm has adequate information barriers between its block-positioning desk and other trading departments, the other trading departments will not be bound by NYSE Rule 97 and may purchase the stock on a plus tick during the last 20 minutes of trading.

TAKENOTE!

If the block-trading desk has any of the block left, even a single stock, it may not purchase the same stock on a plus tick within 20 minutes of the close. If the stock that was purchased had a value less than $500,000, Rule 97 does not apply.

Prior to crossing a block of stock for 10,000 shares or more, or having a market value of $200,000 or greater, the member firm must check the market for the stock to see if there is independent interest in the block. NYSE Rule 127 requires members to follow certain guidelines prior to crossing stock in the crowd. The firm should always check with the DMM to see if there is outside interest in the block and to request permission to cross the block.

TRADING ALONG

NYSE Rule 92 prohibits member firms from executing an order for their own accounts on the same side of the market, for the same listed security, at a price that would satisfy a customer's order, when they have prior knowledge of the customer's order. Rule 92 strictly prohibits trading along with individual customers who are trading in their own name. A firm with written permission from an institutional customer may trade along with the institution's order. Written permission is required on a case-by-case basis, and the customer must get an allocation report detailing how much the customer bought or sold and how much the firm bought or sold. If an Institutional customer wishes to purchase or sell a large block of stock in a single transaction, the broker-dealer may not enter an order for its own account or for the account of an agent prior to the execution and reporting of the block transaction. This would be a front-running violation. The transaction must be reported to tape or disseminated to the public through another medium. If a firm executed an order for its own on account or for that of an agent after the execution but prior to the reporting of the trade, this would be a violation known as shadowing.

CIRCUIT BREAKERS

The NYSE, Nasdaq, and SEC continue to develop and test circuit breakers that will act as a safety net during times of exorbitant price changes in the market as a whole or in the price of individual securities. SEC Rule 201 prohibits the shorting of covered NMS securities which consist of NYSE, Nasdaq, and Amex listed equities at the bid price if the price of the security has declined 10 percent or more from the previous day's close. During the time the single stock circuit breaker is in effect, a broker-dealer may only enter orders to sell a security short at a price that is greater than the national best bid. Market centers are required to establish procedures to ensure that orders are not executed or displayed in violation of the single stock circuit breaker rule. The short-sale circuit breaker stays in effect once enacted through the end of the following trading day. Should the security continue to fall in price the single-stock circuit breaker may be re-triggered and the prohibition on shorting at the bid price extended. Arbitrage transactions, riskless principal transactions, odd lots, volume weighted average price transactions and underwriters executing an order to cover over-allotments are all exempt from this rule. The NYSE has enacted rules to help restore orderly market conditions during periods of heightened volatility. Rule 80B halts all trading if the S & P 500 falls by 7 percent, 13 percent, or 20 percent in any given day. A level 1 (7 percent) or level 2 (13 percent) decline occurring between 9:30 a.m. and 3:25 p.m. EST will result in a trading halt in all stocks for 15 minutes. In the case of a level 1 or level 2 decline on a day when the market closes early trading will be halted for 15 minutes if the decline occurs between 9:30 a.m. and 12:25 p.m. EST. Once trading resumes after a level one halt, trading will not be halted again unless the S & P 500 decline reaches a level 2 or 13 percent decline. Similarly in the case of a level 2 decline trading would not be halted again once resumed until the S & P 500 reached a level 3 or 20 percent decline. A level 3 (20 percent) decline occurring at any time during the day will halt all trading for the rest of the day.

The base level that regulates Rule 80B is based on the daily closing value of the S & P 500. All orders that are in hand or on the book prior to a market halt will be treated as GTC orders except market on close and limit on close orders, which will be canceled.

LIMIT UP LIMIT DOWN (LULD)

The SEC requires market centers to enforce the use of the Limit Up Limit Down (LULD) rule. This rule is designed to ensure that prices of individual securities reflect fundamental prices based on supply and demand and do not move outside of established parameters based on errors or manipulative actions. Upper and lower trading bands will be established based on the average reference price of the security over the preceding 5-minute period. The reference price is the algorithmic mean of all eligible transactions reported during the 5-minute period and does not include transactions reported at a volume weighted average price (VWAP). If the stock price moves outside of the established bands, trading will be paused for 5 minutes if the stock does not trade at or within the limit price within 15 seconds. During this 15-second period the stock will be subject to a state of limit up or limit down. If no trades take place at or inside the limit price, the 5-minute trading pause will occur. During the trading pause market-makers may continue to quote the security and accept orders. However, no orders may be executed until trading resumes. Once the stock reopens the new reference price will be the opening price. When the displayed quote for an NMS security has one side of the quote inside the limit price and one side of the quote outside of the limit price, a straddle state occurs. During a straddle state only the quote displayed inside the limit price is executable. The primary exchange may at its discretion halt a security in a straddle state. The Limit Up Limit Down rule classifies securities as either Tier 1 or tier 2 based on their historic volatility. Tier 1 and tier 2 securities will have trading bands of 5 and 10 percent respectively from 9:45 a.m.–3:35 p.m. EST. During these times the securities may deviate from the reference price by the stated percentage without being subject to a trading pause. To accommodate additional price discovery during the opening and closing of the market, those bands will be expanded to 10 and 20 percent respectively from 9:30 a.m.–9:45 a.m. and from 3:35 p.m.–4:00 p.m. Any aggressive orders placed outside of the price band will be repriced by the Nasdaq system to the price band limit price.

LISTING REQUIREMENTS FOR THE NYSE

Only corporations that meet the strict listing requirements may have their stock traded on the NYSE. In order to become listed, a company must have all of the following:

- At least 400 shareholders owning at least 100 shares.
- At least 1,100,000 publicly held shares with a market value of at least $40 million or $100 million for IPOs or spin-off companies.
- A bid price of at least $4 per share.

Companies must also meet at least one of the following:

- Total pretax earnings of at least $12 million over the last three years, with at least $5 million in the most recent year.
- Total pretax earnings of $10 million over the last three years with at least $2 million in each of the last two years
- Average global market capitalization of $500 million with revenues of at least $100 million for the latest fiscal year.

If the issuer ever wants to have its stock delisted from the NYSE, the following conditions must be met:

- The board of directors must approve the action.
- The 35 largest shareholders must be notified.
- The board's audit committee must approve the action.

OVER-THE-COUNTER/NASDAQ

Securities that are not listed on a centralized exchange trade over-the-counter or on the Nasdaq. Nasdaq stands for National Association of Securities Dealers Automated Quotation System. It is the interdealer network of computers and phone lines that allows securities to be traded between broker dealers. Nasdaq, while considered to be a stock exchange, is not a traditional centralized exchange. It is a negotiated market where one broker dealer negotiates a price directly with another broker dealer. None of the other interested parties for that particular security have any idea of what terms are being proposed. The broker dealers may communicate over their Nasdaq workstations or can speak directly to one another over the phone. The normal business hours for the Nasdaq market are from 9:30 a.m. to 4:00 p.m. EST.

MARKET MAKERS

Because there are no DMMs for the OTC markets, bids and offers are displayed by broker dealers known as market makers. A market maker is a firm that is required to display a two-sided market. A two-sided market consists of a simultaneous bid and offer for the security quoted through the Nasdaq workstation. The market maker must be willing to buy the security at the bid price, which is displayed, as well as be willing to sell the security at the offering price, which also is displayed. These are known as firm quotes. There is no centralized location for the Nasdaq market; it is simply a network of computers that connects broker dealers throughout the world. Market makers purchase the security at the bid price and sell the security at the offering price. Their profit is the difference between the bid and the offer, which is known as the spread. Rule changes and new trading systems known as electronic communication networks, or ECNs, have narrowed the spreads on stocks significantly in recent years. Firms that act as market makers must continuously display two-sided quotes during normal business hours. Firms may remain open for extended hours trading but are not required to display quotes after the close of the market at 4:00 p.m. EST. During extended hours trading the market has greater volatility, lower liquidity, and fewer market participants than trading during the regular session. As a result, there are wider spreads and the risk of poor executions.

NASDAQ SUBSCRIPTION LEVELS

Broker dealers will subscribe to the Nasdaq workstation services that meet their firm's requirements. The Nasdaq levels of subscription service are:

Level I: Provides information relating to the inside market, the last sale, and the daily volume data and provides quotes for registered representatives.

Level II: Allows the subscriber to see the inside market, the quotes of all market makers, the total daily volume, and the high and low for the day.

Level III: The highest level of service offered over the Nasdaq workstation. Level III contains all of the features of Level II and allows the firm to enter and update its own markets. Level III is only for approved market makers.

TotalView: Nasdaq TotalView quotation service allows professionals and nonprofessionals to view the entire book for securities traded over Nasdaq. TotalView displays the price and size quoted by all market makers, exchanges, and ECNs. TotalView also displays the total size of the market for the five best-priced quotes as well as order imbalance information for all Nasdaq crossing sessions.

REGISTERING AS A MARKET MAKER

All broker dealers that wish to register as a market maker must file an application with FINRA and demonstrate that they are in good standing with FINRA and that the firm meets the capital requirements to become a market maker. The broker dealer's registration will become effective upon notification by FINRA. Once approved, a broker dealer must register in each security it wishes to make a market in, prior to quoting that security. The firm will request to quote a security over the Nasdaq workstation and will receive same day approval to enter quotes. If the security to be quoted has been listed on Nasdaq in the last 5 days, the firm may quote the security immediately. Once approved to quote a security, the firm must enter an initial quote within 5 days. If the firm has not entered a quote within this time, it must reapply to quote the security. Broker dealers may not receive any consideration from the issuer or from promoters for making a market in the security. Once a broker dealer is approved as a market maker, it will be assigned a market participant identifier (MPID). The firm's MPID is the symbol by which its bids and offers are identified in the Nasdaq Market Center Execution System (NMCES). The initial MPID assigned to the firm will be known as the firm's primary MPID. Firms may also be assigned supplemental MPIDs to be displayed in the Nasdaq Market Center. A firm may use a supplemental MPID for use by customers under a sponsored access program, its proprietary trading, index arbitrage or prime brokerage business. Firms may not use supplemental MPIDs to engage in passive market making, stabilization, or to quote a security if the firm fails to meet the requirements to quote a security under its primary MPID. A quote displayed under a supplemental MPID may be one sided and may be withdrawn at any time without penalty.

 TAKENOTE!

All approved Nasdaq market makers must display continuous two-sided quotes under its primary MPID and be open for business during normal business hours 9:30 a.m.–4:00 p.m. EST. Market makers are not required to quote pre or post market.

REGISTERING AS A MARKET MAKER IN AN OTCBB SECURITY

Securities traded on the OTCBB must be reporting companies and file 10-Qs, 10-Ks, and 8-Ks with the SEC. There are no other listing requirements for the OTCBB. Securities traded on the OTCBB may be quoted by broker dealers who are registered as OTC market makers. Market makers must obtain detailed information regarding the issuer as required by SEC Rule 15c2-11. Prior to quoting or resuming a quote in an OTCBB security, the market maker must have at least one of the following:

- Forms 10-K, 10-Q, and 8-K.
- An offering circular effective within 40 days.
- A prospectus effective within 90 days.
- Other detailed financial information.
- Foreign financial filings for foreign firms.

The market maker entering the quote must maintain a file containing the following:

- A copy of any SEC trading suspension or public release relating to any of the issuer's securities within the last 12 months.
- A record of the name of the person or people for whom the quote is published and a record of any information provided to the dealer by that person.
- A copy of other information relating to the issuer that the dealer becomes aware of.

The dealer is required to file Form 211 with FINRA at least three business days prior to entering a quote. The firm is also required to provide FINRA with the information required under SEC Rule 15c2-11. The filing should also include:

- The name of the issuer.
- The dealer's initial or resumed quote.
- The basis for the quote.
- The type of security.
- How the firm will display the quote.
- A demonstration of the dealer's compliance with SEC Rule 15c2-11.
- The previous name of the company if the issuer was party to a merger.

 TAKE**NOTE!**

If the dealer's initial quote is not priced and is subsequently changed to a priced quote, the dealer must update its filing and include the new quote and the basis for the quote.

FINRA will respond to the dealer's application within three business days and notify the dealer if the application has been cleared or denied or if additional information is needed.

 TAKE**NOTE!**

SEC Rule 15c2-11 only relates to non-Nasdaq securities. A dealer may be exempt from the requirements of SEC Rule 15c2-11 if:

- The quote is being entered based on an unsolicited customer order. If the dealer is representing unsolicited customer interest in an inactive security the dealer must remove the quote after the order is filled or file Form 211.
- The security is listed on an exchange or trades on Nasdaq.
- The dealer is piggybacking another dealer's quote.

PIGGYBACKING A QUOTE

If an OTCBB security has been quoted by another dealer for a minimum of 30 days, the dealer may simply enter its own quote by piggybacking the current dealer's quote so long as:

- The security has been quoted for at least 12 of the last 30 days (active).
- There have been no more than four consecutive days without a quote (active).
- There is at least one independent market maker quoting the security.

If a market maker piggybacks a sole market maker's quote and the original market maker stops quoting the security, the market maker who piggybacked the quote is not required to file Form 211 or take any other action.

Securities that have been delisted from Nasdaq may be automatically quoted by a dealer on the OTCBB if:

- The issuer is not in bankruptcy.
- The market maker quoted the security on Nasdaq in the last 30 days.
- The security was quoted for 30 days continuously before being halted.
- The issuer is current with all required SEC filings.

If a security being quoted on the OTCBB is the subject of an SEC trading suspension, the market maker should review the information it has in its possession with regard to the issuer to ensure that it is still accurate and that it is still in compliance with SEC Rule 15c2-11. The market maker must obtain updated information if necessary. FINRA has the authority to halt the quoting and trading in securities on the OTCBB, the PINK OTC market as well as for securities that are not publicly quoted. The halt will become effective at the time FINRA's announcement is released. The halt will continue until FINRA lifts the halt or 10 business days have past, whichever occurs earlier.

A broker dealer acting as a market maker in OTC equity securities must honor their displayed quotes for the minimum size based on the price of the security. The minimum size for each quote displayed based on the price of the security is as follows:

Price (Bid or Offer)	Minimum Quote Size
0.0001–0.0999	10,000
0.10–0.1999	5,000
0.20–0.5099	2,500
0.51–0.9999	1,000
1.00–174.99	100
175.00+	1

Each broker dealer acting as a market maker in an OTC equity security must also adhere to the minimum pricing increment for the security. The minimum price increment for equities priced $1 per share or greater is $0.01. For OTC equity securities priced less than $1, the smallest increment allowed to be displayed is $.0001. A firm may accept an order or indication of interest for a security priced less than $1 down to an increment of .000001. While an order with this price increment may be accepted by the firm, the order may not be displayed.

NASDAQ QUOTES

Most actively traded Nasdaq stocks are quoted by a large number of market makers. As market makers enter their quotes, some will be above or below the best quote, which is known as the inside market. A market maker whose quote is above or below the inside market is said to be away from the market. As the market makers adjust their quotes, the market maker who is publishing the highest bid for the security has its bid displayed at the top of the list, and its bid is published as the best bid to anyone with a Nasdaq Level I subscription service or higher. The market maker publishing the lowest offer will have its offer listed at the top of the list and published as the lowest offer to anyone with a Nasdaq Level I subscription service or higher. As a result, the best bid and offer from any two market makers will make up the inside market.

EXAMPLE

XYAD

	Bid	**Ask**
	15.00	**15.05**
MM 1	14.90	15.10
MM 2	15.00	15.20
MM 3	14.85	15.05
MM 4	14.95	15.15
MM 5	14.98	15.18

Notice how the inside market for XYAD consists of the bid from market maker 2 and the offer from market maker 3. All of the other market makers are away from the market.

Additional terms used to describe the inside market include:

- NBBO (national best bid and offer): A composite of all of the quotes from all market participants.

- Nasdaq inside: The best bid and offer entered by Nasdaq market participants through the NMCES.
- Nasdaq BBO: The best bid and offer entered through the Nasdaq Market Center Execution System, excluding quotes from regional exchanges.

LOCKED AND CROSSED MARKETS

Market makers may not enter quotes that would lock or cross the market. A locked market is one where the bid and offer are equal in price. For example, if another market maker, known as market maker 6, came into the above listed market for XYAD and entered a bid of 15.05 or an offer of 15.00, the bid or offer entered would lock the market. A crossed market is one where a bid is entered that is higher than the offer or one where an offer is entered that is lower than the bid. If market maker 6 entered a bid of 15.10 or an offer of 14.95, the bid or offer would cross the market. A market maker who has an order that would cause it to enter a bid or offer that would lock or cross the market must make an effort to trade with all the market makers whose bid or offer it would lock or cross. The NMCES helps alleviate most locked or crossed markets.

NOMINAL NASDAQ QUOTES

All quotes published over the Nasdaq workstation are firm quotes. A dealer who fails to honor its quotes has committed a violation known as backing away. Dealers who provide quotes over the phone, which are clearly indicated as being subject or nominal, cannot be held to trade at those prices. Nasdaq qualifiers are:

- "It looks like"
- "It's around"
- "Subject"
- "Nominal"
- "Work it out"
- "Last I saw"

A response of "it is" would indicate a firm quote. A firm quote is always good for at least one round lot, or 100 shares.

NASDAQ EXECUTION SYSTEMS

Most Nasdaq trades are executed over a Nasdaq workstation using one of Nasdaq's automated execution systems. These systems allow dealers to execute orders without having to speak with one another on the phone.

NASDAQ MARKET CENTER EXECUTION SYSTEM (NMCES)

The Nasdaq Market Center Execution System (NMCES), accepts market orders and immediately executable limit orders for both customer and firm accounts. Orders may be entered for up to 999,999 shares per order. The orders will immediately be routed to dealers on the inside market for automatic execution. Larger orders may be split up to meet the maximum order volume. However, a broker dealer may not split orders that would otherwise be able to be entered into the Nasdaq system in an effort to increase fees or rebates. This is considered order shredding, and it is a violation of FINRA rules. Orders executed through the NMCES are automatically reported to ACT. Orders executed through the NMCES are executed based on the priority of price and time. Orders will be executed against the market maker that is quoting the best price first. If more than one market maker is quoting the same price, orders will be executed against the market maker that quoted the best price first. Orders may be entered in the NMCES by both market makers and order-entry firms. Firms may modify the way that their orders are routed to market makers by selecting:

- Modified price and time; this option takes into consideration access fees that may be charged by the counterparties.
- Price, size, and time, which takes into consideration the size of the counterparties' quotes.

QUOTES ENTERED THROUGH NMCES

Maker makers who quote securities through the NMCES must display the prices for their quotes as well as the size of their quotes. The NMCES will also allow market makers to maintain additional shares to buy or sell in reserve. This reserve size is not seen by other market participants and must be for at least one round lot, or 100 shares.

ABCD				
Market Maker	Bid	Size	Reserve	Refresh from Reserve
MM 1	15	1,000	5,000	1,000
MM 2	15	1,000	4,000	1,000
MM 3	14.95	1,000	3,000	1,000
MM 4	14.95	1,000	2,000	1,000
MM 5	14.90	1,000	1,000	1,000

EXAMPLE

Market makers 1 and 2 are both bidding 15 for ABCD. Market maker 1 is ahead of market maker 2 in time priority. An order to sell 10,000 shares of ABCD would be executed against the displayed size for market maker 1 and market maker 2, respectively. The order would then be executed against market maker 1's reserve size of 5,000 shares. The remaining 3,000 shares in the order would then be executed against market maker 2's reserve and would leave market maker 2 with 1,000 shares to buy at 15. After the execution, the market would look as follows:

ABCD				
Market Maker	Bid	Size	Reserve	Refresh from Reserve
MM 2	15	1,000		
MM 3	14.95	1,000	3,000	1,000
MM 4	14.95	1,000	2,000	1,000
MM 5	14.90	1,000	1,000	1,000
MM 1				

Market maker 1 now needs to update its quote in the system. The transactions that were executed against market maker 1 only constituted one transaction with that market maker, and the transactions that were executed against market maker 2 only constituted one transaction with that market maker.

UPDATING NASDAQ QUOTES

If a market maker's quote is reduced to below one round lot or to zero, the market maker is required to update its quote. Any order that reduces the size of the market maker's quote is said to decrement the quote. Market makers may manually update their quotes or may select the automatic quote refresh (AQR) feature. Market makers may select the price and size that will be automatically entered through the AQR system. This will allow the market maker to set the system's AQR feature to operate in a way that is consistent with the firm's trading patterns. However, if the firm has entered multiple quotes for the security into the NMCES and one of the other quotes is better than the quote that would automatically be created by the AQR feature, the better-priced quote would be displayed. Quotes may be entered into the system:

- By the market maker
- By the system
- On a summary basis

If the market maker enters the quote, the market maker is responsible for the quoted prices. If the market maker's quote is exhausted, the NMCES will generate a quote for the market maker that is one price level up from the worst quote. Quotes entered on a summary basis will allow the market maker to maintain several different quotes in the system.

ORDER ENTRY PARAMETERS

A system order is entered in the Nasdaq system for display or execution. All orders must indicate a limit price and if the order is to buy, sell, or sell short the security for which the order is entered. System orders may be designated with the following time in force parameters:

- Market Hours Immediate or Cancel (MIOC) 9:30 a.m.–4:00 p.m. EST
- Market Hours Good-til-Cancelled (MGTC) 9:30 a.m.–4:00 p.m. EST
- Market Hours Day (MDAY) 9:30 a.m.–4:00 p.m. EST
- System Hours Expire Time (SHEX) expires at a stated time
- System Hours Immediate or Cancel (SIOC) 7:00 a.m.–8:00 p.m. EST
- System Hours Good-til-Cancelled (SGTC) 7:00 a.m.–8:00 p.m. EST
- Good-till-Market Close (GTMC) 7:00 a.m.–8:00 p.m. EST

THE ORDER ROUTING PROCESS

Orders entered by market participants will be routed by the Nasdaq system from 7:00 a.m. to 8:00 p.m. EST. All orders entered into the Nasdaq system are governed by Regulation NMS. The following order routing types are nonroutable Nasdaq only orders:

Intermarket Sweep Order (ISO)—Orders entered as intermarket sweep orders will be executed at the best price displayed in the Nasdaq system and will not be routed to any other market for execution. Firms entering ISO orders must have checked prices in other market centers to ensure better prices are not available. ISO orders are exempt from the order protection rule.

Price to Comply Order—Orders entered as price to comply orders that lock or cross an external market will automatically be adjusted by the Nasdaq system to comply with the locked and crossed market rules of regulation NMS. Buy orders entered at a price above the lowest offer will be adjusted to the price of the lowest offer. Orders to sell entered at a price below the highest bid will be adjusted to the price of the highest bid. If the market changes to cause the adjusted to again lock or cross the market the order will be cancelled.

Minimum Quantity Orders—Orders entered in the Nasdaq system that specify a minimum number of shares to be executed or cancelled may only be entered as market hours immediate or cancel or as system hours immediate or cancel. Market hours IOC orders may not be entered prior to the opening cross or after the closing cross.

Firms may also enter orders in the Nasdaq system that may be sent to other markets for execution. Orders that may be routed to other markets include:

SCAN Order—This order routing type will first try to execute the order in the Nasdaq system at a price better than the NBBO. If the order is not executed it will then route the order to other markets for execution. If any portion of the order is not filled after being routed to other markets, it will be returned to the Nasdaq system and be posted in the Nasdaq book. Once posted to the Nasdaq book, the order will not be rerouted if the order subsequently locks or crosses an external market.

Reactive Electronic STGY Order—This order acts as a SCAN order; however the order will reroute after it is posted to the Nasdaq book if another market locks or crosses the order.

Aggressive Electronic SPDY Order—Limit orders entered as SPDY orders will reroute like STGY orders. Market orders entered as SPDY orders will track the inside market on the same side of the market for which the order is entered. SPDY market orders to buy will track the highest bid while SPDY market orders to sell will track the inside offer.

PEGGED ORDERS

A pegged order is an order entered through Nasdaq that is designed to track the inside market of the stock for which it is entered for execution. A pegged order may be entered as a primary peg, as a midpoint peg, or as a market peg. A primary peg order to buy will track the best bid, while a primary peg order to sell will track the offer. A midpoint peg order to buy or sell will track the midpoint of the spread between the best bid and offer. A market peg order to buy will track the offer and a market peg order to sell will track the bid. As the market for the stock changes the pegged order will automatically adjust to track the market until the order is filled. All pegged orders must be entered as day orders.

HIGH FREQUENCY AND ALGORITHMIC TRADING

Many sophisticated institutions invest significant amounts of money in the development of proprietary computerized trading models. These trading models are often driven by the use of sophisticated algorithms. An algorithm is a set of mathematical procedures and instructions that are designed to execute orders based on many variables. These computerized trading models are able to take advantage of trading opportunities that last only nanoseconds. The trading algorithms are the basis of the high frequency trading module, which route and display a substantial amount of orders for execution based on market conditions that may only last a nanosecond. If the orders are not executed the orders may be immediately canceled by the trading program. The constant routing and canceling of orders can result in flickering quotes. A firm that executes a customer order at an inferior price due to a flickering quote in another market will not have committed a violation due to the extremely temporary nature of the flickering quote.

THE ALTERNATIVE DISPLAY FACILITY (ADF)

FINRA operates the Alternative Display Facility (ADF) from 8:00 a.m. to 6:30 p.m. EST. The ADF allows unlinked ECN participants to enter and match quotes and to report trades. The quotes entered in the ADF will not appear in the NMCES. However, if the quote entered in the ADF would improve the inside market, the quote will be displayed as part of the inside market. The ADF does not provide execution capabilities. All ADF participants are required to provide direct or indirect electronic access to their quotes. Direct electronic access will allow other market participants to execute an order electronically against the firm's quote. Indirect electronic access will allow another market participant to execute an order against the firm's quote through the firm's broker dealer customer. Both direct and indirect electronic access requires:

- No voice communication.
- Equivalent speed, reliability, and availability as offered to participants' customers.
- Equivalent costs as offered to participants' customers.
- A two-second turnaround for accepting or declining an order.
- A three-second or less turnaround for communication between market participants.

FINRA requires that participants who enter quotes in multiple trading centers must display the same quote in the different centers. A market participant may, however, display different sizes in different centers. Only quotes for Nasdaq and CQS stocks will be displayed in the ADF. OTC BB and PINK OTC securities are not displayed in the ADF.

TRADE REPORTING AND COMPARISON SERVICE (TRACS)

The Trade Reporting and Comparison Service (TRACS) collects trade information for market participants who use the ADF. FINRA established TRACS to assist in the reporting of trades for ADF market participants who are not eligible to use the Nasdaq Market Center Trade Reporting Service or ACT. ADF market participants who are also market makers may choose to report trades executed through the ADF either through ACT or the TRACS systems. The TRACS system works in much the same way as ACT. However, the TRACS system will allow ADF market participants to report a three-party trade to assist in the reporting of riskless principal trades. The TRACS system reports trades to the Depository Trust Clearing Corporation (DTCC) and reports the trade to the appropriate securities information processor for public dissemination. FINRA may terminate the TRACS service upon notice to members who fail to abide by the rules of FINRA or the TRACS service.

ELECTRONIC COMMUNICATION NETWORKS (ECNS)

The electronic communication networks (ECNs) operate independently of FINRA. ECNs display and execute third-party orders and are allowed access to the NMCES. ECNs are widely used by both broker dealers and institutional investors to display and execute orders. ECN quotes are included in the Nasdaq quote system, but the ECN is not required to maintain a two-sided market like a market maker, and ECNs do not take positions in the security. There are two ways that the ECN may participate in the NMCES; the ECN may be a full-participation ECN or it may be an order-delivery ECN. Full-participation ECNs may:

- Display quotes.
- Enter and accept directed and nondirected orders.
- Accept automatic executions.
- Send orders for automatic execution through the NMCES.

Order-entry ECNs may display quotes and enter and accept directed and nondirected orders. The order-entry ECN may fill, decline, price improve, or allow an order it has received to expire. If the order sent to the order-entry ECN expires, the order will be canceled and sent to the next participant at the inside market by the NMCES.

UNLISTED TRADING PRIVILEGES

Certain exchanges are given access to the NMCES through unlisted trading privileges. These exchanges are referred to as UTP exchanges. UTP exchanges may enter quotes and directed and nondirected orders as long as the UTP exchange has agreed to accept automatic executions. UTP exchanges that will not accept automatic executions may not participate in the NMCES.

MARKET CENTERS

As a result of the development of multiple order execution systems and centers, the SEC has enacted order execution disclosure rules. SEC Rule 11Ac1-5 requires market centers to disclose certain order execution information for covered securities. A market center is:

- An OTC market maker.
- A market maker that internalizes orders.
- An alternative trading system.
- A national securities association.
- A national securities exchange.

A covered security is a Nasdaq Global market security or any other security for which last sale data and quotes are disseminated through the automated quotation system. A covered order is any market or limit order received and executed during the normal trading hours (9:30 a.m.–4:00 p.m. EST). SEC Rule 11Ac1-6 requires broker dealers to file quarterly reports regarding the execution of nondirected customer orders. A broker dealer does not have to file a report for market centers that make up less than 5 percent of nondirected order execution. A nondirected order is one where the customer did not specify the market center where the order is to be executed. The following items must be included in the report:

- The identity of the market center where nondirected orders were routed for execution.
- Any relationship the broker dealer has with the market center.
- Any payment received for order flow.
- Any profit sharing relationships with the market center.
- Any internalization of orders.

SEC Rule 11Ac1-6 requires that the reports be made public and posted on an Internet website. Customers must be notified at least annually in writing that a copy of the report will be made available to them free of charge upon request. A customer may also request market center information for a specific order that was executed by the broker dealer within the last six months.

TAKENOTE!

A broker dealer that has routed 500 or fewer customer orders per month during the preceding calendar quarter is exempt from the reporting requirement but not from providing the data to customers who request such information.

SEC REGULATION NMS

SEC Regulation NMS was designed to improve the regulation of the U.S. markets as a result of the development of multiple market centers. Under the order protection rule, SEC Regulation NMS requires market centers to establish and enforce policies and procedures to ensure that trades do not get executed at inferior prices to those protected prices displayed in other market centers. A protected price or quote is one that is displayed in a market center that is immediately and automatically accessible. When a broker-dealer receives an order for a security with a limited market, the broker-dealer must establish policies and procedures to help ensure that the customer receives the best execution. Certain OTC BB and PINK OTC securities may have only one or two market-makers. Other times, a broker-dealer may receive an order for a foreign security with no domestic market. As a result, obtaining the best execution for the customer will be substantially harder than for a listed security. In these situations the broker-dealer should contact several interested parties including other broker-dealers who have traded the securities with the firm in the past. The access rule of Regulation NMS requires fair and nondiscriminatory access to quotations and establishes uniform fees for access to various trading platforms and market centers. Regulation NMS prohibits members from engaging in any activity designed to intentionally lock or cross markets and prohibits members from quoting securities valued at more than $1 in subpenny prices. NMS stocks with a bid price of less than $1 may be quoted in increments of $.0001. OTCBB and PINK OTC may be quoted in any increments.

SEC REGULATION ATS

Technological innovations have allowed an increasing number of market participants to develop alternative trading systems such as ECNs and trade-crossing networks. As market participants developed new trading systems, they often chose only to allow access to these systems to subscribers, and this has created hidden markets. Trading activity in these systems has not been regulated in the way that trading is regulated on a registered exchange. As a result, customer orders entered in the systems were not protected to the same degree as if the orders were entered on a registered exchange. As the number of services available through alternative trading systems increased, alternative trading systems began providing services traditionally only offered by registered exchanges. SEC Regulation ATS was designed to help regulate these alternative trading systems and to bring more uniformity to the national marketplace. Regulation ATS allows operators of alternative trading systems the choice to register with the SEC as an exchange or as a broker dealer. Regulation ATS also updated the definition of an exchange to include any organization, association, or group of persons that brings together the orders of multiple buyers and sellers and uses established, nondiscretionary methods (whether by providing a trading facility or by setting rules) under which such orders interact with each other and the buyers and sellers entering such orders agree to the terms of the trade. The SEC also further refined the definition of an exchange by excluding from the definition of an exchange those systems provided by broker dealers that:

- Solely route orders to other facilities for execution.
- Are systems operated by a single registered market maker to display its own bids and offers and the limit orders of its customers and to execute trades against such orders.
- Are systems that allow persons to enter orders for execution against the bids and offers of a single dealer.

DIRECT MARKET ACCESS

Broker dealers who have direct market access, who provide direct market access to customers through the firm's MPID or supplemental MPID, or who provide sponsored access to customers, must maintain strict financial risk and supervisory control systems for firm employees and customers who have direct or sponsored market access. Direct market access is defined as access to trade securities on an exchange or through an alternative trading system as a result of being a member or subscriber. A broker dealer who provides a non-broker dealer customer with access to an alternative trading system will be deemed to have provided direct market access to that customer. The financial controls required for such access include:

- The risk management controls and supervisory procedures must be reasonably designed to systematically limit the financial exposure of the broker dealer that could arise as a result of market access.
- The risk management controls and supervisory procedures must be reasonably designed to prevent the entry of orders that exceed appropriate pre-set credit or capital thresholds in the aggregate for each customer and the broker or dealer and, where appropriate, more finely-tuned by sector, security, or otherwise by rejecting orders if such orders would exceed the applicable credit or capital thresholds.
- The risk management controls and supervisory procedures must be reasonably designed to prevent the entry of erroneous orders, by rejecting orders that exceed appropriate price or size parameters, on an order-by-order basis or over a short period of time, or that indicate duplicative orders.

The regulatory risk management controls and supervisory procedures in place at the broker dealer must be designed to ensure compliance with all industry rules. The risk management controls and supervisory procedures shall be reasonably designed to ensure compliance with all regulatory requirements, including being reasonably designed to:

- Prevent the entry of orders unless there has been compliance with all regulatory requirements that must be satisfied on a pre-order entry basis.
- Prevent the entry of orders for securities for a broker or dealer, customer, or other person if such person is restricted from trading those securities.
- Restrict access to trading systems and technology that provide market access to persons and accounts pre-approved and authorized by the broker or dealer.
- Ensure that appropriate surveillance personnel receive immediate post-trade execution reports that result from market access.

TAKE**NOTE!**

Under a direct market access program the customer will use the broker dealer's order routing and trading infrastructure. Under a sponsored access program the customer will use its own systems and the trades do not route through the broker dealer's systems.

NASDAQ INTERNATIONAL

The Nasdaq operates an international platform that allows European firms to trade domestic equities and other securities during the European trading session. The Nasdaq international service operates from 3:30 a.m. to 9:00 a.m. EST. European non-FINRA members may only participate during the European session, whereas FINRA members may participate in both the domestic and European sessions by registering as an international market maker. Securities that may be traded during the European session include:

- Nasdaq Global Market securities.
- Exchange-listed U.S. securities.
- Non-Canadian foreign securities that are quoted on Nasdaq but not the Global Market.

If a FINRA member firm pulls its quote during the international session it may continue to quote that same security during regular hours.

NON-NASDAQ OTCBB

The OTC Bulletin Board (OTCBB) provides two-sided electronic quotes for OTC securities that cannot meet the listing standard of an exchange or Nasdaq. Direct participation programs (DPPs) and American depositary receipts (ADRs) will often be quoted on the OTCBB. The OTCBB is operational from 7:30 a.m. to 6:30 p.m. The OTCBB displays:

- Real-time quotes
- Volume
- Last sale price

Quotes that may be entered over the OTCBB by a market maker include:

- Bid wanted
- Offer wanted
- Bid only
- Offer only
- Two-sided quotes
- Quote modifications

Quotes displayed over the OTCBB are firm quotes unless they are quoting DPP programs. Quotes entered on the OTCBB must be for the minimum size for that security. The minimum quote size for the security depends on the price of the security being quoted. Quotes for DPP are subject quotes and may only be updated twice per day, once between 8:30 and 9:30 a.m. and at 12:30 p.m.

PINK OTC MARKET

Securities that do not qualify for listing on the Nasdaq or that have been delisted from Nasdaq or one of the exchanges may be quoted on the Pink OTC market. The PINK OTC Market is an electronic marketplace and is registered as an alternative trading system, not as an ECN with the SEC. All two-sided quotes displayed in the Pink OTC Market are firm quotes. The Pink OTC market also provides a list of phone numbers for market makers who display subject quotes. Stocks quoted on the Pink OTC market trading at under $5 per share are known as penny stocks. A firm that executes a customer's order for a Pink OTC market security is required to make a reasonable effort to obtain the best price for the customer.

The firm is required to obtain quotes from at least three market makers for the security prior to executing the customer's order. If the security has fewer than three market makers, the firm is required to obtain a quote from all market makers.

THIRD MARKET

The third market consists of transactions in exchange-listed securities executed over the counter through the Nasdaq workstation. A broker dealer may wish to simply purchase or sell an exchange-listed security directly with another brokerage firm instead of executing the order on the floor of the exchange. These transactions are known as third-market transactions. All third-market transactions are reported through ACT to the consolidated tape for display. Market makers that enter quotes for exchange-listed securities must enter their quotes through the Consolidated Quotation System (CQS). CQS market makers may not execute an order for an exchange-listed IPO prior to the security's opening for trading on its primary exchange. The CQS operates from 7:00 a.m. to 8:00 p.m. EST.

NASDAQ MARKET CENTER FOR LISTED SECURITIES

The Nasdaq Market Center for Listed Securities allows CQS market makers and order-entry firms to execute orders for securities that are listed on the NYSE or on a regional exchange though the Nasdaq workstation. The Intermarket Trading System (ITS) links the primary and regional exchanges for securities that are listed on more than one exchange. Exchange members may execute an order for an exchange-listed security on other exchanges through the ITS system. Regulation NMS discontinued FINRA member participation with the ITS system, and FINRA members now execute orders on the exchanges through private connectivity providers.

FOURTH MARKET

A fourth-market transaction is a transaction between two large institutions without the use of a broker dealer. The computer network that facilitates these transactions is known as INSTINET. Large blocks of stock, both listed and unlisted, trade between large institutional investors in the fourth market. Although many trades in the fourth market are executed through the INSTINET system, many large portfolio managers execute internal crosses, which go unreported. Proprietary trading systems are not considered part of the fourth market because these systems are either registered as broker dealers or are operated by broker dealers. Trades executed by large institutions via proprietary networks are sometimes referred to as dark pools, because the supply or demand for a security is unseen by market participants.

NASDAQ LISTING STANDARDS

Prior to having its stock trade in either the Nasdaq Global Market or Capital Market, an issuer must meet certain standards. Issuers must apply and be accepted to have its stock trade in either marketplace. Issuers that want to have their stock trade in the Global Market must have a bid price of at least $5, meet stringent financial requirements, and be an issue with national interest. Issuers that cannot meet the financial requirements to trade in the Global Market may elect to have their stock trade in the Capital Market. In addition to having to meet lower financial requirements, the price of the security is only required to be $4. Prior to being accepted to trade in either market, an issuer is required to meet FINRA corporate governance standards and meet the following requirements:

- Maintain an audit committee with mostly independent directors.
- Solicit proxies.
- Provide annual and quarterly reports.
- Maintain at least two independent directors.

An issuer that has been informed by Nasdaq that it is in violation of Nasdaq listing standards will be given 30 days to correct any problems or face suspension. Note that if an issuer is suspended from trading in either market for failing to meet the continued listing standards and wants to resume trading in that market the issuer must reapply and meet the initial listing standards.

MARKET MAKER REGULATIONS AND RESPONSIBILITIES

In addition to the requirements to become a market maker, firms must follow strict guidelines when acting as a market maker. Market makers must adhere to all rules relating to their participation in the OTC market. Entering quotes, executing orders, and operating as a market maker during an offering are just some of the activities that have very specific standards of operation. All Series 24 candidates must have an in-depth understanding of market maker rules and regulations in order to successfully complete the Series 24 exam.

TIMES FOR ENTERING A QUOTE

The Nasdaq opens for trading at 9:30 a.m. EST with an opening cross. Market makers, in anticipation of the opening, may enter bids and offers based on orders that the firm has received from customers or for the firm's account. Nasdaq quotes open at 9:25 a.m. Quotes and limit X orders that do not lock or cross the market become part of the book. If a market maker enters a quote or order that locks or crosses the market, the order or quote is sent to the queue to wait for execution. Quotes and orders that are placed in the queue are executed against the best bid or offer available at that time. Orders that cannot be executed in the queue are sent back to the book.

THE OPENING CROSS

The opening cross begins at 9:28 a.m. At this time, the NMCES automatically executes orders. Orders placed after 9:28 a.m. may not be canceled. Orders placed after 9:28 a.m. may only be changed if the change to the order makes the order more aggressive. A change that increases the size of the order or improves the price would make the order more aggressive. For a buy order, an improved price would be a higher limit price; for a sell order, an improved price would be a lower limit price. All orders that are executed during the opening cross will be reported to ACT with a .T modifier. The official Nasdaq opening print is disseminated by the system at 9:30 a.m.

TAKENOTE!

Orders that are entered prior to the opening for execution during regular hours may not be canceled or modified during the opening cross.

ORDER IMBALANCES

Oftentimes during the opening cross, as a result of news or other events, there are either buy-side or sell-side order imbalances for any given security. During the opening cross, starting at 9:28 a.m. order imbalance messages will appear in the Nasdaq system. Between 9:28 a.m. and 9:30 a.m. indications of the imbalance are sent out every second. Among other information, order imbalance indications include the direction and size of the imbalance, the percent away from the current inside market, and the indicative price. The indicative price is the price at which the opening cross would take place if executed at the time the imbalance indication was disseminated.

THE NASDAQ OFFICIAL OPENING PRICE (NOOP)

Nasdaq opens for regular hours trading at 9:30 a.m. EST. At that time, the orders that are held in the queue that have not been paired off are executed and reported to the tape. The first trade that is reported to the tape creates the Nasdaq Official Opening Price (NOOP). If at 9:30:15 no trades in the queue have been matched and reported to the tape, the first, last sale trade that is reportable to the tape becomes the NOOP. Nasdaq has created new types of orders as a result of the creation of the opening cross. The orders are:

- Early regular hours: Orders entered prior to 9:28 a.m. for the regular trading session.
- Late regular hours: Orders entered after 9:28 a.m. for the regular trading session.
- OO on open: Market and limit orders that are entered to be executed at the opening price only.
- IO (imbalance only): Orders that are only to be executed against imbalances on the open that are away from the bid or offer at 9:30 a.m.
- X: Extended hours orders are entered before or after the market opens and can be day, GTC, or IOC.

THE CLOSING CROSS

Nasdaq has developed the closing cross to determine a uniform closing price for securities at the end of the trading day. Customers and firms may enter or cancel on the close orders at any point starting at 7:00 a.m. up until 3:50 p.m. After 3:50 p.m., on the close orders may not be entered, canceled, or modified; orders entered as a legitimate error may be canceled up until 3:55 p.m. On the close orders that may be entered include both market and limit on close orders. Starting at 7:00 a.m. and up until the close of the market, firms may enter imbalance only orders. Imbalance-only orders must be priced and will not be executed prior to the close nor will they be included in the market maker's displayed quote prior to the close.

TAKENOTE!

The Nasdaq crossing network provides intraday and postclosing executions. All crosses will be executed anonymously and provide greater liquidity. The scheduled crossing times are 10:45 a.m., 12:45 p.m., 2:45 p.m., and 4:30 p.m. Orders may be entered for the next cross only, for regular hours crosses, or for all subsequent crosses. Orders entered for all crosses will not be eligible for the opening or closing cross.

THE NASDAQ HALT CROSS

If a security is halted as a result of news or other corporate developments, the security will reopen with an opening cross. The Nasdaq halt cross is designed to provide greater price discovery and allow all market participants and investors an opportunity to execute orders at the best available price once the news has been disseminated. The Net Order Imbalance Indicator (NOII) will disseminate order imbalance information every second between the time quoting begins and the time trading resumes. Prior to the time quotes are allowed market makers may not quote or trade the security or any derivative of the security in any market. This includes foreign markets and internal crossing. The dealer may only maintain an internal book of interest during this time. Trades may only be executed once trading resumes.

WITHDRAWING QUOTES

A market maker may withdraw quotes for a security in two ways. A market maker may withdraw quotes on either a voluntary basis or on an excused basis. If a market maker withdraws its quotes on a voluntary basis, the market maker simply removes or "pulls" the quote. A Nasdaq or ADF market maker that voluntarily withdraws a quote may not reregister as a market maker in that security for 20 business days. A CQS market maker that is trading listed securities in the third market and voluntarily pulls its quotes may reenter quotes for 1 business day. If a market maker removes a quote for any of the following reasons it would be considered a voluntary withdrawal:

- A sudden influx of orders
- Trading losses
- Lack of interest

A market maker may also withdraw its quotes on an excused basis by applying to Nasdaq for permission to withdraw its quotes. An excused withdrawal will generally be granted for up to 5 business days. A market maker may request an excused withdrawal under the following circumstances:

- The firm has three or fewer Nasdaq Level III workstations and key personnel are going on vacation. The application must be made one business day prior to removing the quotes.
- A firm may be granted an excused withdrawal for up to five business days for circumstances beyond the market maker's control, such as illness or acts of God.
- The market maker is participating in a distribution or is acting as a passive market maker.
- The firm may be granted an excused withdrawal for up to 60 days for legal or regulatory reasons (i.e., the firm has inside information regarding the issuer of the security as a result of an investment banking relationship).
- The firm involuntarily fails to maintain a clearing relationship.
- An excused withdrawal may be granted for religious holidays provided that the application to Nasdaq is made one business day prior to the withdrawal.

 **TAKENOTE!**

A market maker that pulls its European quote for a security may continue to quote that security domestically during the U.S. session.

HANDLING AND DISPLAYING CUSTOMER LIMIT ORDERS

If a market maker accepts customer limit orders, it must handle the order in accordance with the limit order display rule. If a market maker accepts a customer's limit order that would improve its quoted price, the market maker must update its quote to reflect the customer's limit order. A market maker is required to update its quote within 30 seconds of receiving the customer's order. The 30-second time frame only applies to normal market conditions and does not include the opening or reopening of a security after a halt.

EXAMPLE In the market for XYAD listed below the inside market is 15.00 bid and 15.05 offered. The size of the bid is for 500 shares and there are 300 shares offered

XYAD

	Bid	Ask	Size
	15.00	**15.05**	**5 × 3**
MM 1	14.90	15.10	10 × 10
MM 2	15.00	15.20	5 × 5
MM 3	14.85	15.05	2 × 3
MM 4	14.95	15.15	15 × 15
MM 5	14.98	15.18	10 × 10

If market maker 2, which offered the best bid, received a customer's limit order to buy 200 shares at 15.02, the market maker would have to update its quote, and the market would look as follows:

XYAD

	Bid	Ask	Size
	15.02	**15.05**	**2 × 3**
MM 1	14.90	15.10	10 × 10
MM 2	15.02	15.20	5 × 5
MM 3	14.85	15.05	2 × 3
MM 4	14.95	15.15	15 × 15
MM 5	14.98	15.18	10 × 10

If market maker 2, which offered the best bid, instead had received a customer's limit order to buy 1,000 shares at 15.00, the market maker would have to update its quote by adding the customer's size to its current quote, and the market would look as follows:

XYAD

	Bid	Ask	Size
	15.00	**15.05**	**15 × 3**
MM 1	14.90	15.10	10 × 10
MM 2	15.00	15.20	15 × 5
MM 3	14.85	15.05	2 × 3
MM 4	14.95	15.15	15 × 15
MM 5	14.98	15.18	10 × 10

If the customer's limit order is equal in price to the firm's displayed quote but is less than 10 percent of its displayed size, the firm does not have to update the size of its quote to reflect the customer's order. Orders that are not required to be displayed include:

- Odd lot orders.
- AON orders.
- Block orders for at least 10,000 shares or $200,000 in market value.
- Orders sent to a qualifying ECN.
- Orders sent to another market maker that complies with the display rule.
- Orders that the customer request not be displayed.
- Orders that are immediately executable.

In order for an ECN to be considered a qualifying ECN under the ECN Display Alternative Rule, the ECN must communicate its quotes to Nasdaq and must allow access to its quotes to broker dealers who do not subscribe to the ECN's service. The ECN may charge a fee to nonsubscribing broker dealers that execute orders against its quotes. If a broker dealer sends a customer's limit order to a qualifying ECN to be displayed, it does not need to improve its quote in Nasdaq. If the broker dealer sends a customer's order to a nonqualifying ECN, the market maker must update its quote to reflect the customer's order. A qualifying ECN is also known as a linked or eligible ECN. The broker dealer that sends a customer's order to a qualified ECN may not trade ahead of the customer's order displayed by the ECN at a price that would satisfy the customer's limit order.

THE ORDER AUDIT TRAIL SYSTEM (OATS)

In order to ensure that customer orders are transmitted to the marketplace in a timely manner, FINRA developed the Order Audit Trail System (OATS). OATS tracks an order through each stage of its life, from receipt to execution or cancellation. Each firm is required to synchronize clocks used for reporting to within one second of the National Institute of Standardized Time's atomic clock and must display time in hours, minutes, and seconds.

Firms are only requested to collect and submit data in milliseconds if the firm collects the data. Firms are required to submit daily electronic OATS reports to FINRA. The business day for OATS is 4:00:01 p.m. to 4:00 p.m. the following business day. OATS reports must be made by 8 a.m. on the day after the trade date. For trades executed on Friday, OATS reports are due by

8 a.m. Saturday morning. Daily OATS reports must be made for each order and each order must have a unique identifier. Information collected on the OATS report includes:

- Customer.
- Date and time of receipt.
- Order ID.
- Terms of the order (i.e., buy, sell, security, price, shares, account type, and handling instructions).
- If the order was received manually or electronically.
- If the order was routed manually or electronically
- Where the order was routed for execution.
- Any modifications to the order, including the date and time of any modifications.
- Execution information, including partial executions, price, date, time, and capacity in which the firm acted in the trade.

TAKENOTE!

On your exam you may see this information tested as OATS or as CATS. CATS is the Consolidated Audit Trail System and serves the same function as OATS, and includes information on option orders.

THE MANNING RULE

In addition to displaying the customer's limit order, a firm that accepts limit orders must protect that order. A firm may not compete with a customer's limit order by executing an order for its own account at a price that would satisfy the customer's limit. If the firm executes an order for its own account at a price that would satisfy the customer's limit order, the firm must execute the customer's order at the same price and for the same number of shares within 60 seconds. Broker dealers that route orders to ECNs or other firms to be displayed must still protect the customer's limit order and are not relieved of their obligations under the Manning Rule. Orders from institutional customers and orders for 10,000 shares and having value of more than $100,000 are not required to be protected under the Manning Rule. If the firm accepts limit orders that will not be protected under the Manning Rule, the firm must disclose the conditions at the time the order is accepted. If the market-making desk is holding a customer's limit order that is subject to the Manning Rule, no trading desk anywhere within the firm may knowingly execute a proprietary order that would compete with the customer's order. If the firm has sufficient barriers between its trading desks and the other desk does not have knowledge of the customer's order, the other desks are not bound by the Manning Rule. If prior to displaying a customer's limit order that is better than the inside market the firm receives an offsetting market order, the firm must execute the market order at a price that at least equals the price of the limit order it is holding. Only customer orders entered for at least one round lot between 9:30 a.m. and 6:30 p.m. EST are required to be protected under the Manning rule.

AUTOMATED CONFIRMATION SYSTEM (ACT)/ TRADE REPORTING FACILITY (TRF)

The ACT system facilitates the reporting, matching, and clearing of trades executed through Nasdaq and other OTC environments. The price that is reported to ACT is the wholesale or protected price, excluding markups and commissions. ACT transactions include:

- Nasdaq Global Market and Capital Market securities
- Non-Nasdaq OTC securities
- Third-market CQS trades
- Nasdaq convertible bonds
- Internal clearable transactions

All ACT-eligible transactions must be reported to ACT by market makers within 10 seconds of the transaction during normal business hours. For trades that are not automatically reported to ACT by the NMCES, market participants must report the Nasdaq and CQS trades to ACT by imputing the trade details into the Trade Reporting Facility (TRF). Trades executed in OTCBB or Pink OTC securities are reported to ACT via the OTC Reporting Facility (ORF).

ACT TRADE SCAN

For trades that are not automatically reported to ACT through the NMCES, order-entry firms and market makers may enter, review, accept, decline, or cancel transactions by using the ACT Trade Scan function of the Nasdaq workstation. The ACT Trade Scan function will also allow the firm to change the capacity in which it acted in the trade. The firm may enter the following qualifiers for each trade:

- A, for agent
- P, for principal
- R, for riskless principal

The ACT Trade Scan function will also allow the parties to a trade to break a trade, if both sides agree. Order-entry firms must enter the terms of the trade to ACT within 20 minutes of the trade when it is required to report through the order-entry function of Level II, or accept or decline the transaction within 20 minutes of the trade when the trade has been reported by the counterparty using the ACT Trade Scan function.

ACT/TRF is only used to match, report, and clear trades that have already been executed. It does not display quotes, and it is not an order execution system.

NASDAQ TRADE REPORTING FACILITY (TRF)

The FINRA/Nasdaq Trade Reporting Facility (TRF) is a trade comparison service operated on the ACT platform. It has been designed to greatly reduce questionable trades and trades that one party does not know (DKs). The TRF facilitates the reporting and clearing of trades in Nasdaq and the NYSE, Amex, and regionally listed stocks executed off the floor. Firms utilizing the TRF may customize reports so that the data may be easily managed. Additional features of the TRF include:

- Collection of last sale data.
- Online access to real-time trade reporting information.
- 10-second trade reporting for all Nasdaq, NYSE, Amex, and regionally listed securities.
- Dissemination of last sale information to the tape and to the media via Nasdaq's Trade Data Dissemination Service.

- Same-day trade confirmation and reconciliation to market makers and order-entry firms.
- Trades locked in within 20 minutes of execution.
- On screen confirmation of trades negotiated over the telephone.

TAKENOTE!

The Series 24 exam may use either TRF or ACT on the exam to test the concepts of trade reporting and clearing. The TRF can be thought of as the user interface a trader would use to submit the trade details to the ACT system.

WHICH SIDE OF THE TRADE REPORTS TO ACT/TRF?

In order to ensure that trades are not reported twice to the ACT/TRF system, the following rules have been enacted to determine who reports the trade:

- In a transaction between two market makers negotiated over the phone, the sell side of the transaction reports.
- In a transaction between two market makers, the executing market maker reports.
- In a transaction between two nonmarket makers, the executing firm reports.
- In a transaction between a member firm and a customer, the member firm reports.

The executing party in a transaction is the party that received the order for handling or to whom the order was directed and against whose quote the order was executed.

All reports to ACT must include the following:

- Nasdaq symbol.
- Price, excluding commissions, markups, and fees.
- Number of shares listed in round lots only.
- The time of execution if being reported late after 10 seconds.
- If the firm bought, sold, or crossed the stock.
- If the sale was a short sale it must be entered into ACT as sell short or sell short exempt.

The following table details the reporting requirements for a trade executed at a given time.

Time of Execution	ACT/TRF Reporting
Midnight–8 a.m.	Domestic equities report between 8:00–8:15 a.m. with a .T modifier. If reported late, a .U modifier is needed.
8:00–9:30 a.m.	Within 10 seconds of trade with .T modifier. If reported late, a .U modifier is needed.
9:30 a.m.–4:00 p.m.	Within 10 seconds of trade. If reported late, a .Z modifier is needed.
4:00–8:00 p.m.	Within 10 seconds of trade with .T modifier. If reported late, a .U modifier is needed.
8:00 p.m.–Midnight	Between 8:00–8:15 a.m. T + 1 as of with time of execution.

Firms that cannot or do not report trades to ACT under the above listed guidelines are required to file Form T weekly with the Market Regulation Department. If ACT is not available or if the firm is having communication problems, the trade must be reported by phone to the Market Operations Department.

The following Nasdaq transactions are exempt from the ACT reporting requirements:

- Private placements.
- Securities that are part of a primary or secondary distribution.
- Transactions automatically reported by another system.
- Transactions related to the exercise of an option or the conversion of a security.
- Transactions where the price is unrelated to the market, such as a gift.

THE ROLE OF ACT/TRF IN THIRD-MARKET TRANSACTIONS

FINRA members that execute third-market transactions must report the details of the trade to the consolidated tape through the TRF system. In order to ensure that third-market trades are not reported twice to the TRF system, the following rules have been enacted to determine who reports the trade:

- In a transaction between two market makers, the executing market maker reports.
- In a transaction between two nonmarket makers, the executing firm reports.
- In a transaction between a member firm and a customer, the member firm reports.

All third-market reports to ACT/TRF must include:

- Stock symbol.
- Price, excluding commissions, markups, and fees.
- Number of shares listed in round lots only.
- The time of execution if being reported late after 10 seconds.
- If the firm bought, sold, or crossed the stock.

Transactions in listed securities that are exempt from the ACT reporting requirements include:

- Transactions executed on the exchange.
- Transactions automatically reported through the Nasdaq market center for listed securities.
- Odd lots are exempt for last sale reporting but still reported to ACT for clearing and settlement.
- Purchases or sales where the parties agree that the price is not reasonably related to the market.
- Purchases or sales relating to the exercise of options or the conversion of another security.
- Private placements.
- Transactions that are part of a primary or secondary distribution.
- Purchases made off the exchange floor as part of a tender offer.
- Principal purchases by a member in anticipation of making an exchange distribution or exchange offering.

The following table details reporting requirements for a third-market trade executed at a given time.

Time of Execution	ACT/TRF Reporting
Midnight–8 a.m.	Report between 8:00–8:15 a.m. with a .T modifier. If reported late, a .U modifier needed.
8:00–9:30 a.m.	Within 10 seconds of trade with .T modifier. If reported late, a .U modifier needed.
9:30 a.m.–4:00 p.m.	Within 10 seconds of trade. If reported late, a .Z modifier is needed.
4:00–8:00 p.m.	Within 10 seconds of trade with .T modifier. If reported late, a .U modifier is needed.
8:00 p.m.–Midnight	Between 8:00–8:15 a.m. T + 1 as of with time of execution.

STEP OUT TRADES

Broker dealers will often execute orders that are to be assigned, or stepped out, to other broker dealers for comparison, clearance, and settlement through NSCC. This is especially true for prime broker transactions. A step out transaction will act as a position transfer rather than a trade execution when reported to ACT. The executing broker enters the trade into the ACT Trade Scan function as a step out transaction against the receiving broker. The receiving broker is then required to accept the transaction or submit a contra report to confirm the details of the step out.

MARKET MAKING DURING SYNDICATION

The SEC has set strict guidelines regarding the activity of market participants and other interested parties during syndication. Regulation M sets guidelines for:

- Syndicate members
- Issuers
- Passive market makers
- Stabilization of the issue
- Short sales prior to the issue's effective period

REGULATION M, RULE 101

Rule 101 regulates the activities of distribution participants, including syndicate members, selling group members, and other interested broker dealers. The focus of Rule 101 is to keep distribution participants from manipulating the secondary market for an issue during the distribution of a registered secondary or subsequent primary offering of shares. Rule 101 sets a restricted period that prohibits the participants from bidding for or buying the subject security for the period just prior to the effective date. The length of the restricted period depends on the level of trading activity in the security and the value of the public float. The lower the trading volume and value of the public float, the greater the ability of an interested party to manipulate the price of the security. The restricted period will begin as listed below or when the broker dealer becomes a participant, whichever occurs later.

Average Daily Trading Volume	Value of Public Float	Restricted Period
Less than $100,000	Less than $25 million	Five days prior to effective date
$100,000 or greater	At least $25 million	One day prior to effective date
$1,000,000 or greater	At least $150 million	No restricted period

The following are exceptions to Rule 101:

- Government and municipal securities.
- Nonconvertible investment grade bonds and preferred stock.
- Investment company securities.
- Unsolicited customer orders may be executed on an agency or principal basis.
- Odd lot orders.
- Exercising of options, rights, or warrants.

PENALTY BIDS

A syndicate manager may enter a penalty bid that will require the syndicate member, who sells securities back to the syndicate, to return the selling concession it originally received for selling the shares. A penalty bid will have the identifier PBID next to the market maker's Nasdaq symbol.

REGULATION M, RULE 102

Rule 102 regulates the activities of issuers during the restricted period. Issuers and selling shareholders may not bid for or purchase a covered security or encourage others to do so during the restricted period. An issuer during the restricted period also may not:

- Bid for or purchase actively traded securities of the issuer or an affiliate.
- Execute inadvertent orders or small orders known as de minimis orders.
- Participate in basket transactions that include the covered security.

The following are exempt from Rule 102:

- 144a transactions
- Conversion of convertible bonds or preferred shares
- Odd lot orders
- Unsolicited purchases
- Transactions in exempt securities

REGULATION M, RULE 103

Rule 103 regulates the activity of market makers participating in a distribution. Market makers that are participating in a distribution may only act as passive market makers during the restricted period. Passive market makers may not enter a bid or buy the security at a price that exceeds the highest bid entered by an independent party. If the highest independent bid entered by a nonparticipant drops below the bid of the passive market maker, the passive market maker may remain as the highest bid until it purchases an amount equal to its volume restriction. The volume restriction in this case would be the lesser of two times the passive market maker's displayed size or the balance of its daily purchase limit. If there are no independent market makers, passive market making will not be allowed. The syndicate manager must apply for passive market making status on behalf of all syndicate members by filing part of the Underwriting Activity Form no later than one business day prior to the first full trading day of the restricted period. All participants who act as a passive market maker during the offering will have the identifier PSSM next to the market maker's Nasdaq symbol. A passive market maker is still required to display customer limit orders even if the displayed order would cause the firm to increase its bid above the highest independent bid. Passive market making may only take place for firm commitment underwritings.

PASSIVE MARKET MAKERS' DAILY PURCHASE LIMIT

A passive market maker's daily purchase limit is the greater of 30 percent of its ADTV or 200 shares. The number of shares in a passive market maker's displayed bid cannot exceed the size of its daily purchase limit. If a passive market maker exceeds this limit, it must withdraw from the market for the rest of the day. Only a passive market maker's net purchases count toward its daily purchase limit. A sell order, reported within 30 seconds of a purchase, will reduce the passive market maker's net purchase.

TAKENOTE!

A market maker that is approaching its daily purchase limit may execute any single order, even if executing the order would cause the market maker to exceed its daily purchase limit.

REGULATION M, RULE 104

Rule 104 allows for the stabilization of a new issue in the secondary market provided that the issue is not being distributed at the market offering. In order to provide for an orderly distribution, and to ensure that the shares do not fall dramatically in the secondary market as a result of the increased supply, a syndicate may enter a stabilizing bid. A stabilizing bid may be entered at or below the issue's offering price. At no time may a syndicate member enter a stabilizing bid at a price that exceeds the issue's offering price. However, a stabilizing bid may have a lower price limit if the stabilizing bid is entered when the principal market for the security is open, and:

- The security traded in the principal market on the day preceding the initiation of stabilization or on the day stabilization began.
- The security is offered at a price that is greater than or equal to the last independent trade in the principal marketplace.

If the above conditions are met, then the stabilizing bid may be no higher than the last independent trade in the principal market. If the above conditions are not met, then the stabilizing bid may not be higher than the highest independent bid in the principal market. If a syndicate member is going to enter an initial stabilizing bid when the principal market is closed, then the stabilizing bid will be limited to the lower of the following:

- The price at which a stabilizing bid may have been entered in the primary market based on the closing price in the primary market.

  or

- The last independent bid or transaction in the marketplace where the issue will be stabilized.

Syndicates must notify the market in which it intends to stabilize the issue. Stabilization is the only form of security price manipulation allowed by the SEC. There is no time limit as to how long an issue may be stabilized; however, all syndicate accounts must be settled 90 days from the day the issuer delivers the securities to the syndicate. The following conditions apply to stabilizing bids entered on behalf of a syndicate:

- Only one stabilizing bid may be entered.
- The stabilizing bid will be a one-sided quote with no offer.
- The identifier SYND will identify the bid as a stabilizing bid.
- The market maker entering the stabilizing bid must confirm the request to stabilize the issue by filing an Underwriting Activity Report (UAR) no later than the end of the first day it entered the stabilizing bid.
- The UAR must include the identity of the security, the estimated effective date and pricing date, a copy of the cover page of the preliminary or final prospectus, and the date when the SYND identifier should appear next to the market maker's ID.
- Only issues sold through a fixed price offering on a firm commitment basis may be stabilized. Best efforts and at the market offerings may not be stabilized.

SYNDICATE SHORT POSITIONS

In an effort to cover a short position created in the syndicate account as a result of overallotments, the syndicate manager may enter a covering bid. The syndicate manager must record information relating to the syndicate's short position within 30 days of the issue's effective date. If offered, a syndicate may also exercise its greenshoe option, which will allow the syndicate to purchase up to an additional 15 percent of the offering from the issuer. The syndicate will purchase the securities from the issuer at the original price to cover overallotments. The syndicate agreement will detail how any losses that result from covering the syndicate short position will be distributed.

REGULATION M, RULE 105

Rule 105 restricts the purchase of subject securities to cover short positions. Rule 105 states that securities purchased through an offering may not be used to cover short positions established during the restricted period. The restricted period for selling securities short begins five days prior to pricing the issue. If the issue is priced within five days of the filing of the registration, then the restricted period under Rule 105 begins with the filing date. Offerings not done on a firm commitment basis as well as shelf registrations are exempt.

TRADE REPORTING AND COMPLIANCE ENGINE (TRACE)

Most transactions in fixed-income securities take place in the OTC market. FINRA members must use the Trade Reporting and Compliance Engine (TRACE) system to report transactions in eligible fixed-income securities. Eligible fixed-income securities include:

- Domestic and foreign corporate debt registered with the SEC.
- Dollar-denominated debt that is depository eligible.
- Investment grade and noninvestment grade issues.
- Dollar-denominated debt securities sold under Rule 144 or 144A.
- U.S. Treasury securities issued or guaranteed by a government-sponsored entity.
- Certain asset-backed and mortgage-backed securities.

Securities that are exempt from the TRACE reporting requirements include:

- Municipal debt
- Repurchase agreements
- Money market instruments

- Development bank debt
- Foreign sovereign debt

The following table details the reporting requirements for a TRACE-eligible trade executed at a given time.

Time of Execution	TRACE Reporting
8:00 a.m.–6:15:01 p.m. EST	As soon as practical but no later than within 15 minutes of the trade
6:15–11:59:59 p.m. EST	T + 1 within 15 minutes of TRACE opening as of transaction date.
Midnight–7:59:59 a.m. EST	Report within 15 minutes (by 8:15 a.m. T+1) of TRACE opening.
Nonbusiness Day	Next business day as if the trade was executed on the day the trade is reported to TRACE. The trade must be reported to TRACE within 15 minutes of TRACE opening. The execution time must be 12:01:00 a.m., and the report must include the actual date and time in the special price field.

If a transaction is executed in a TRACE-eligible security with fewer than 15 minutes left until the closing of TRACE, that trade may be reported any time prior to the closing of TRACE but must be reported by 8:15 a.m. on T+1. All TRACE reports must include the following:

- Number of bonds
- Price and accrued interest
- Buy, sell, or cross data
- Time of execution
- Agent or principal
- Yield to maturity or yield to call
- Commissions, mark up, or mark down
- Contra party
- Give up for introducing or executing broker dealer
- Trade modifiers
- Date of execution for as of trades
- CUSIP number

TRACE is not a trade-execution system; it is only a trade-reporting system. Both parties must report the trade to the TRACE system. FINRA will disseminate information relating to transactions to the market. The information that is disseminated includes:

- The symbol
- The number of bonds
- The yield and price
- The CUSIP number

TAKE**NOTE!**

FINRA may report transactions involving noninvestment grade issues if there is significant volume and interest in the security.

Noninvestment grade bonds will not have information disseminated if:

- The bonds have been called.
- The bonds have been upgraded to investment grade.
- The bonds have been downgraded below minimum quality.
- The bonds have matured.

BROKER VS. DEALER

The term *broker dealer* actually refers to the two capacities in which a firm may act when executing a transaction. When a firm is acting as a broker, it is acting as the customer's agent and is merely executing the customer's order for a fee known as a commission. The role of the broker is simply to find someone willing to buy the investor's securities if the customer is selling or to find someone willing to sell the investor the securities if the customer is seeking to buy. The firm acts as a dealer when it participates in the transaction by taking the opposite side of the trade. For example, the firm may fill a customer's buy order by selling the securities to the customer from the firm's own account or the dealer may fill the customer's sell order by buying the securities for its own account. A brokerage firm is always acting as a dealer or in a principal capacity when it is making markets over the counter.

Broker	Dealer
Executes customer's orders.	Participates in the trade as a principal.
Charges a commission.	Charges a markup or markdown.
Must disclose the amount of the commission.	Makes a market in the security. Must disclose the fact that it is a market maker, but not the amount of the markup or markdown.

FINRA 5 PERCENT MARKUP POLICY

FINRA has set a guideline to ensure that the prices investors pay and receive for securities are reasonably related to the market for the securities. As a general rule, FINRA considers a charge of 5 percent to be reasonable. The 5 percent policy is a guideline, not a rule. Factors that go toward what is considered reasonable are:

- The price of the security.
- The value of the transaction.
- The type of security.
- The value of the member's services.
- Execution expenses.

When a customer is executing an order for a low priced or low total dollar amount, a firm's minimum commission may be greater than 5 percent of the transaction.

EXAMPLE A customer wants to purchase 1,000 shares of XYZ at $1. If the firm's minimum commission is $100, that would be 10 percent of the trade. But in this case it would be ok.

Stocks generally carry a higher degree of risk than bonds and, as a result, stocks justify a higher commission or profit to the dealer. Full-service firms may be able to justify a larger commission simply based on the value of the services they provide.

MARKUPS/MARKDOWNS WHEN ACTING AS A PRINCIPAL

A firm that executes customer orders on a principal basis is entitled to a profit on those transactions. If the firm is selling the security to the customer, it will charge the customer a markup. In the case of the firm buying the securities from the customer, it will charge the customer a markdown. The amount of the markup or markdown that a firm charges the customer is based on the inside market for the security.

EXAMPLE

Let's assume that the brokerage firm is a market maker in ABCD. In the morning, the firm purchased shares of ABCD for its own account at 9.50. The stock has been trading higher all day and is now quoted as follows:

Bid	Ask
10.00	**10.05**

If a customer wants to purchase 100 shares of ABCD from the dealer in the above example, the customer's markup would be based on the current offering price of 10.05. As a result, the maximum amount the firm could charge the customer for the stock would be 10.552 per share, or $1,055.20 for the entire order, which would include a 5 percent markup. Notice that the markup to the customer did not take into consideration the firm's actual cost. The firm is entitled to the profit because it took on risk by purchasing the shares for its own account with no offsetting customer order. Alternatively, if the firm had purchased the shares of ABCD at $11 instead of $9.50 the markup would still be based on the inside offer of $10.05.

If a customer wanted to sell 100 shares of ABCD using the above quote, the minimum proceeds to the customer would be 9.50 per share, or $950 for the entire order, which would include a 5 percent markdown.

To determine the maximum or minimum prices for a customer, use the following:

- 105 percent of the offer price for customers who are purchasing the security.
- 95 percent of the bid price for customers who are selling the security.

When determining the amount of the markup or markdown the following are excluded:

- The firm's actual cost.
- The firm's quote if it is a market maker in the security.

RISKLESS PRINCIPAL TRANSACTIONS

If a brokerage firm receives a customer order to buy or sell a security and the firm does not have an inventory position in the security, the firm may still elect to execute the order on a principal basis. If the firm elects to execute the order on a principal basis, it is known as a riskless principal transaction. Because the dealer is only taking a position in the security to fill the customer's order, the dealer is not taking on any risk. As a result, the markup or markdown on riskless transactions will be based on the dealer's actual cost, not on the inside market. Let's look at an example:

EXAMPLE

Bid	Ask
10.00	**10.05**

A customer wants to purchase 100 shares of ABCD from the dealer, and the dealer executes the order on a principal basis by purchasing the shares for its own account at $10.02, only to immediately resell the stock to the customer. The markup in this case must be based on the dealer's actual cost of $10.02, and the maximum the dealer could charge the customer would be $10.521 per share, or $1,052.10 for the entire order.

PROCEEDS TRANSACTIONS

In a proceeds transaction, the customer sells a security and uses the proceeds from that sale to purchase another security on the same day. FINRA's 5 percent policy states that a firm may only charge the customer a combined commission or markup and markdown of 5 percent for both transactions, not 5 percent on each.

DOMINATED AND CONTROLLED MARKETS

FINRA's 5% markup policy is a guideline for charging markups and commissions for transactions in securities with active and competitive markets. Some small OTC securities do not have active and competitive markets because of lack of national interest in the company. As a result, the market for these securities can be dominated or controlled by one market maker. Market makers who dominate or control the market for a security must base the markup charged to the customer on their contemporaneous cost, not on the inside market for the security. All markups will be based on the price the market maker paid for the stock when it was purchased for their inventory account.

EXAMPLE

Market Maker 1 is one of two market makers in MNBV, an OTC BB security. Market Maker 1 brought MNBV public and is the only firm with a retail sales force recommending the stock to its customers. Market Maker 1 has been accumulating shares from its customers, who are selling MNBV at 6.00 per share, when the market for MNBV was 6.25 to 6.75. After accumulating a significant number of shares, Market Maker 1 raises its quote to 10.00 to 10.50 knowing that it will not have to purchase shares from other dealers at this level. In this case, if Market Maker 1's sales force recommends MNBV to its customers and the customer purchases the stock at the current market price of 10.50 plus a 50 cent markup, Market Maker 1 would have a profit of $5 per share. Because Market Maker 1 can display any quote it wants for the stock, the inside market displayed may not have any relation to the actual market for the stock. In these cases, the markup must be based on Market Maker 1's actual cost for the security, or 6.00 in this example. Firms and registered representatives who charge or receive excessive markups can be held accountable for their actions. Traders who execute the transaction can also be held accountable for excessive markups, as one of the responsibilities of a trader is to determine the inside market for a security in addition to executing orders.

NET TRANSACTIONS WITH CUSTOMERS

FINRA sets forth specific guidelines for broker dealers who execute orders for customers on a net transaction basis. A broker dealer who, after receiving a customer's order, executes that order on a principal basis with another broker dealer and subsequently fills the order at a net price to the customer, must first obtain the customer's consent. A broker dealer must obtain the customer's written consent and acknowledgment prior to executing a net transaction for any noninstitutional customer. Institutional customers may agree to the terms of net transactions in writing or orally on a trade-by-trade basis or may be sent a negative consent letter detailing the terms under which net transactions may be executed by the broker dealer. The negative consent letter must provide the institutional customer a reasonable opportunity to object to net transactions. If the customer does not object, the broker dealer may assume that the institutional customer has consented to the potential terms of any net transaction. All documentation relating to customer consent must be maintained under FINRA rules.

FIRM QUOTE RULE

SEC Rule 11Ac1-1 states that all market makers that publish quotes over the Nasdaq system must execute an order that is presented to the firm at a price and size that is at least equal to its published quote. A market maker's firm quote obligation begins when an order is presented to the firm for execution against its quote either electronically or over the phone. A market maker is not bound by the firm quote rule under the following circumstances:

- The market maker is publishing a quote for a security not covered by the rule.
- The market maker has just affected a trade and is in the process of updating its quote.
- The market maker has just updated and published a new quote, and the new quote was published prior to, or at the same time as, the receipt of the order.

TAKENOTE!

A market maker that fails to honor its firm quote has committed a violation known as backing away.

Liability orders create firm quote obligations for the market maker. Should a liability order expire or be canceled prior to execution, the market maker is still required to offer the counterparty an execution. If a liability order expires, or times out, and the receiving market maker fails to honor the order or offer the party an execution, the market maker could be found to have committed a backing-away violation.

THE FIRM QUOTE COMPLIANCE SYSTEM (FQCS)

To assist in the enforcement of the firm quote rule and to assist in the resolution of backing away allegations, FINRA has developed the Firm Quote Compliance System (FQCS). A firm that feels that a market maker failed to honor their quote must file a complaint within five minutes of the incident. The Market Regulation Department will enter the complaint into the FQCS. The FQCS allows FINRA to review the market conditions at the time of the allegation and to look for patterns of backing away. If FINRA feels that a firm failed to honor its quote it will usually award the aggrieved party a contemporaneous execution. A contemporaneous execution will result in a transaction at a price that is representative of the market conditions at the time of the allegation. If the aggrieved party fails to file a compliant within five minutes it does not relieve the firm who allegedly backed away of responsibility. However, failing to file a complaint on a timely basis makes the award of a contemporaneous execution less likely.

TRADE COMPLAINTS BETWEEN MEMBERS

A member who feels that a trade was reported in error may have the trade reviewed by Nasdaq Market Operations if the member is unable to resolve the issue with the contra broker dealer. The party bringing the complaint must submit a written request to Nasdaq Market Operations by fax or other acceptable means by 10:30 a.m. EST for trades occurring prior to 10:00 a.m. EST and within 30 minutes for trades occurring after 10:00 a.m. EST. Once a complaint has been filed, the firm bringing the complaint has 30 minutes to provide additional documentation. The broker dealer responding to the complaint will receive telephone notification and will be given 30 minutes to submit documentation. Once both parties have indicated that they have submitted all documentation, they may not submit additional documentation. The matter will then be reviewed by a Nasdaq Market Operations hearing officer. The hearing officer may cancel the trade, modify the trade, or allow the trade to stand. Both parties will receive telephone notification and a written report. If the Nasdaq system causes erroneous reports to take place, Nasdaq Market Operations can automatically correct or break the trade within 30 minutes of detection.

Nasdaq may correct trades caused by system malfunctions up to 6:00 p.m. EST on the day after the trade date.

ROGUE TRADING PREVENTION

The actions of bad actors on a trading desk can have significant financial repercussions to a firm and to the integrity of the market as a whole. A broker dealer is required to ensure that it has established the proper supervisory systems to detect and prevent the actions of potential rogue traders. Several firms have collapsed as a result of traders hiding significant losses from the firm. Part of the checks and balances require that traders and other persons in sensitive positions take mandatory vacations every year. These vacations must be for a minimum of 10 consecutive business days. A trader who says he / she does not want to take a vacation is a red flag that the trader may be hiding losses from his / her firm. The firm should keep information regarding its monitoring systems confidential from those who are being monitored so the systems may not be bypassed. Additionally, only authorized persons should have access to the firm's trading systems and the use of multiple passwords should be required for sensitive systems.

ARBITRAGE

Arbitrage is an investment strategy used to take advantage of market inefficiencies and to profit from the price discrepancies that result from those inefficiencies. There are three types of arbitrage:

- Market arbitrage
- Security arbitrage
- Risk arbitrage

MARKET ARBITRAGE

Securities that trade in more than one market will sometimes be quoted and traded at different prices. Market arbitrage consists of the simultaneous purchase and sale of the same security in two different markets to take advantage of the price discrepancy.

SECURITY ARBITRAGE

Securities that give the holder the right to convert or exercise the security into the underlying stock may be purchased or sold to take advantage of price discrepancies between that security and the underlying common stock. Securities arbitrage consists of the purchase or sale of one security and the simultaneous purchase or sale of the underlying security.

RISK ARBITRAGE

Risk arbitrage tries to take advantage of the price discrepancies that come about as a result of a takeover. A risk arbitrageur will short the stock of the acquiring company and purchase the stock of the company being acquired.

CHAPTER 4

Pretest

TRADING SECURITIES

1. Which of the following are true for an issuer who has been suspended from Nasdaq?
   - I. The issuer may reapply if it meets the Nasdaq minimum maintenance requirements.
   - II. The issuer may not reapply for listing for 180 days.
   - III. The issuer must reapply to the Nasdaq initial listing requirements.
   - IV. The issuer was unable to correct any deficiencies within 30 days.
     - a. III and IV
     - b. I and II
     - c. II, III, and IV
     - d. II and III

2. If a Nasdaq-listed company is informed by Nasdaq that it is in violation of the Nasdaq listing requirements, the issuer will be given how many days to correct the problem?
   - a. 15
   - b. 30
   - c. 45
   - d. 60

3. Which of the following may NOT trade on the floor of the NYSE?
   - a. Two-dollar broker
   - b. Regular member
   - c. Commission house broker
   - d. Allied member

4. Your brokerage firm acts as a market maker for several high-volume stocks that are quoted on Nasdaq. What is the firm's consideration for being a market maker?

   a. Commission
   b. Fees
   c. Spread
   d. 5 percent

5. Which of the following are NOT types of orders?

   I. All or none
   II. Fill or kill
   III. Mini-maxi
   IV. Best efforts

   a. I and II
   b. II and IV
   c. I and IV
   d. III and IV

6. INTC has been hitting a lot of resistance at $30. A technical analyst who wants to buy the stock would most likely place what type of order?

   a. Limit order to buy at $30
   b. Market order
   c. Buy stop at $31
   d. Buy limit at $29

7. The inside market consists of the which of the following?

   I. Highest offer
   II. Lowest offer
   III. Highest bid
   IV. Lowest bid

   a. II and III
   b. I and II
   c. I and IV
   d. I and III

8. Which of the following is true of DMMs on the NYSE?
   a. They work for themselves.
   b. They are appointed by a vote of the company's board.
   c. They work for the exchange.
   d. They work for the company whose stock they trade.

9. Which of the following is NOT a feature of the NMCES?
   a. Automatic refreshing of quotes
   b. Automatic ACT reporting
   c. ADF quotes
   d. UTP executions

10. XYZ is quoted 20.30 × 20.50. Your firm receives a customer limit order to purchase 1,000 shares of XYZ at 20.40. Prior to displaying the customer limit order, your firm receives an order from another customer to sell 1,000 shares of XYZ at the market. Which of the following is true?
    I. Your firm must display the purchase order.
    II. The market order to sell may be executed at the best price displayed in the market.
    III. The firm may not execute the customer's sell order at a price that is less than the limit order it is holding.
    IV. Both orders may be routed to a qualifying ECN.
    a. I and III
    b. II and IV
    c. III only
    d. IV only

11. Which of the following assist in the execution of third-market trades?
    a. ACES
    b. TRACE
    c. Nasdaq Market Center
    d. AutoEX

12. ACT does not:
    a. report.
    b. quote.
    c. match.
    d. clear.

13. A market maker who wants to enter an initial quote for an OTCBB security must file Form 211:
    a. five business days prior to entering the quote.
    b. three business days prior to entering the quote.
    c. two business days prior to entering the quote.
    d. one business day prior to entering the quote.

14. The daily purchase limit for passive market makers is:
    a. the greater of 20 percent of their ADTV or 200 shares.
    b. the lesser of 20 percent of their ADTV or 200 shares.
    c. the greater of 30 percent of their ADTV or 200 shares.
    d. the lesser of 30 percent of their ADTV or 200 shares.

15. Your firm is a market maker and is participating in an offering of securities as a syndicate member. Your firm is acting as a passive market maker and has purchased 12,000 shares, which is 98% of its ADTV. An order comes into the firm's trading desk to sell 3,000 shares at 2:40 p.m. Which of the following is true?
    a. Your firm may not purchase the stock, because it would cause the firm to exceed its purchase limit.
    b. Your firm may purchase the stock.
    c. Your firm may purchase the stock, as long as it finds an offsetting customer order within 30 seconds.
    d. Your firm may purchase the stock, as long as it finds an offsetting customer order within 90 seconds.

16. A firm that is acting as a passive market maker has just executed an order that caused it to exceed its daily purchase limit by 12%. Which of the following is true?
    a. The firm may execute any single order even if that order would cause it to exceed its volume limitations. Once the firm has exceeded the volume limit, it must withdraw for the rest of the day.
    b. Upon executing the order the firm has committed a violation of passive market making regulations, and the firm will be subject to disciplinary action from the Nasdaq Market Operations Department.
    c. Upon executing the order the firm must find an offsetting order within 90 seconds.
    d. Upon executing the order the firm has committed a violation of passive market making regulations, and the firm will be out of the box for 20 days, during which time it may not enter quotes.

17. Which of the following would be considered firm?

 I. A price quoted for a non-Nasdaq security received from a dealer over the phone
 II. A two-sided quote for a non-Nasdaq DPP
 III. A two-sided bond quote
 IV. A two-sided priced quote from a dealer listed in the Pink OTC

 a. I and II
 b. I, III, and IV
 c. II and IV
 d. I, II, III, and IV

18. An investor enters an order to buy 1,000 ABC MOC. Which of the following is FALSE?

 a. The order will be executed as close to the closing price as possible.
 b. The order will be canceled if trading on the exchange is halted.
 c. The order will be canceled if trading in ABC is halted.
 d. The order may be executed at any price within the last 4 minutes of the trading day because it is a market order.

19. The consolidated tape reads 30s/s XYZ Pr C 84.15. What does this mean?

 a. 30,000 shares of XYZ Pr C sold at 84.15.
 b. 30 Shares of XYZ Pr C sold at 84.15.
 c. 3,000 shares of XYZ Pr C sold at 84.15.
 d. 300 shares of XYZ Pr C sold at 84.15.

20. As it relates to a market maker's quotes, which of the following is FALSE?

 a. CQS market makers may pull their quotes on a voluntary basis and reenter the market on the third business day.
 b. The NMCES will prevent a firm from locking markets.
 c. A firm with fewer than five Nasdaq workstations may obtain an excused withdrawal if key personnel are going on vacation.
 d. The NMCES will allow the market maker to keep additional size hidden in its reserve.

21. ABC Technologies, a very volatile stock, closes at $180 per share. Your customer has placed an order to sell 500 ABC at 165 stop limit 160 GTC.

After the close, the company announces bad earnings and the stock opens at 145. What happened to your customer's order?

a. It has been canceled because the stock price is below the limit price.

b. It has been elected and has become a limit order.

c. It has been elected and executed.

d. It has been canceled because the stock price is below the stop price.

CHAPTER 5

Recommendations to Customers

INTRODUCTION

All recommendations to customers must be suitable, based on the customer's investment objectives, financial profile, and attitude toward investing. Representatives usually make recommendations to customers verbally. The representative will review the customer's investment objectives and offer facts to support his or her basis for the recommendation as well as an explanation as to how the recommendation will help the customer meet his or her objectives. Any predictions about the performance of an investment should be stated strictly as an opinion or belief, not as a fact. If the firm uses reports that cite past performance of the firm's pervious recommendations, the report must contain:

- The prices and dates when the recommendations were made.
- General market conditions.
- Recommendations in all similar securities for 12 months.
- A statement disclosing that the firm is a market maker (if applicable).
- A statement regarding whether the firm or its officers or directors own any of the securities being r
- If the firm managed or comanaged an underwriting of any of the issuer's securities in the last three years.
- A statement regarding the availability of supporting documentation for the recommendations.

When making a recommendation, a representative may not:

- Guarantee or promise a profit or no loss.
- Make false, misleading, or fraudulent statements.
- Make unfair comparisons to dissimilar products. ecommended or options or warrants for the same security.

INVESTMENT OBJECTIVES

All investors want to make or preserve money. There are, however, different ways to achieve these objectives. Some of the different investment objectives are:

- Income
- Growth
- Preservation of capital
- Tax benefits
- Liquidity
- Speculation

INCOME

Many investors are looking to have their investments generate additional income to help meet their monthly expenses. Some investments that will help to meet that objective are:

- Corporate bonds
- Municipal bonds
- Government bonds
- Preferred stocks
- Money market funds
- Bond funds

GROWTH

Investors who are seeking capital appreciation over time want their money to grow in value and are not seeking any current income. The only investments that will achieve this goal are:

- Common stock
- Common stock fund

PRESERVATION OF CAPITAL

People who have preservation of capital as an investment objective are very conservative investors and are more concerned with keeping the money they have saved. For these investors, high-quality debt will be an appropriate recommendation. Some choices are:

- Money market funds
- Government bonds

- Municipal bonds
- High-grade corporate bonds

TAX BENEFITS

For investors seeking tax advantages, the only two possible recommendations are:

- Municipal bonds
- Municipal bond funds

LIQUIDITY

Investors who need immediate access to their money need to own liquid investments that will not fluctuate wildly in value, in case they need to use the money. The following is a list from the most liquid to the least liquid:

- Money market fund
- Stocks/bonds/mutual funds
- Annuities
- CMOs
- Direct participation programs
- Real estate

SPECULATION

A customer investing in a speculative manner is willing to take a high degree of risk in order to earn a high rate of return. Some of the more speculative investments are:

- Penny stocks
- Small cap stocks
- Some growth stocks
- Junk bonds

CAPITAL ASSET PRICING MODEL (CAPM)

The capital asset pricing model (CAPM) operates under the assumption that investors are risk averse. Investors who take on risk through the purchase of an investment must be compensated for that risk through a higher expected rate of return known as the risk premium. A security's risk is measured by its beta. Therefore, securities with higher betas must offer investors a higher expected return in order for the investor to be compensated for taking on the additional risk associated with that investment.

RISK VS. REWARD

Risk is the reciprocal of reward. An investor must be offered a higher rate of return for each unit of additional risk the investor is willing to assume. There are many types of risk involved with investing money. They are as follows:

- Capital risk
- Market risk
- Nonsystematic risk
- Legislative risk
- Timing risk
- Credit risk
- Reinvestment risk
- Interest rate risk
- Call risk
- Opportunity risk
- Liquidity risk

CAPITAL RISK

Capital risk is the risk that an investor may lose all or part of the capital they have invested. Investors who purchase securities are not assured of the return of their invested principal.

MARKET RISK

Market risk is also known as a systematic risk and it is the risk that is inherent in any investment in the markets. For example, you could own stock in the greatest company in the world and you could still lose money because the value of your stock is going down, simply because the market as a whole is going down.

NONSYSTEMATIC RISK

Nonsystematic risk is the risk that pertains to one company or industry. For example, the problems that the tobacco industry faced a few years ago would not have affected a computer company.

LEGISLATIVE RISK

Legislative risk is the risk that the government will do something that adversely affects your investment. For example, beer manufacturers probably did not fare too well when the government enacted prohibition.

TIMING RISK

Timing risk is simply the risk that an investor will buy and sell at the wrong time and will lose money as a result.

CREDIT RISK

Credit risk is the risk of default inherent in debt securities. Investors may lose all or part of their money because the issuer has defaulted and cannot pay the interest or principal payments owed to the investors.

REINVESTMENT RISK

When interest rates decline and higher yielding bonds have been called or have matured, investors will not be able receive the same return given the same amount of risk. This is reinvestment risk and the investor is forced to either accept the lower rate or take more risk to obtain the same rate.

INTEREST RATE RISK

Interest rate risk is the risk that the price of bonds will fall as interest rates increase. As interest rates rise, the value of existing bonds falls and may subject the bondholder to a loss if they need to sell the bonds.

CALL RISK

Call risk is the risk that, as interest rates decline, higher yielding bonds and preferred stocks will be called and investors will be forced to reinvest the proceeds at a lower rate of return or at a higher rate of risk to achieve the same return. Call risk only applies to preferred stocks and bonds with a call feature.

OPPORTUNITY RISK

Investors who hold long-term bonds until maturity must forgo the opportunities to invest that money in other potentially higher-yielding investments.

LIQUIDITY RISK

Liquidity risk is the risk that investors will not be able to liquidate their investment when they need to or that they will not be able to liquidate their investment without adversely affecting the price.

ALPHA

A stock's or portfolio's alpha is its projected independent rate of return or the difference between an investment's expected (benchmark) return and its actual return. Portfolio managers whose portfolios have positive alphas are adding value through their asset selection. The outperformance as measured by alpha indicates the portfolio manager is adding additional return for each unit of risk taken on in the portfolio.

BETA

A stock's beta is its projected rate of change relative to the market as a whole. If the market was up 10 percent for the year, a stock with a beta of 1.5 could reasonably be expected to be up 15 percent. A stock with a beta greater than 1 has a higher level of volatility than the market as a whole and is considered to be more risky than the overall market. A stock with a beta of less than 1 is less volatile than prices in the overall market and is considered to be less risky. An example of a low beta stock would be a utility stock. The price of utility stocks does not tend to move dramatically. A security's beta measures its nondiversifiable or systematic risk. For each incremental unit of risk investors take on, they must be compensated with additional expected returns. If the portfolio's actual return exceeds that of its expected return, the portfolio has generated excess returns.

DEVELOPING THE CLIENT PROFILE

Recommendations to a client must be suitable based on the client's investment objective and client profile. The suitability obligation is triggered at the time the recommendation is made. The agent should obtain enough information about the customer to ensure that their recommendations are suitable, based on a review of the client's:

- Investment objectives
- Financial status
- Income
- Investment holdings
- Retirement needs
- College and other major expenses

- Tax bracket
- Attitude toward investing

The more an agent knows about a client's financial position, the more she will be able to help the client meet his or her objectives. Agents should always ask questions like:

- How long have you been making these types of investments?
- Do you have any major expenses coming up?
- How long do you usually hold investments?
- How much risk do you normally take?
- What tax bracket are you in?
- How much money do you have invested in the market?
- Have you done any retirement planning?
- How old are you?
- Are you married?
- Do you have any children?
- How long have you been employed at your current job?

Agents, who help people invest to meet a specific objective, must make sure that their recommendations meet that client's objective. Should a person have a primary and a secondary objective, an agent must make sure that the recommendation meets the investor's primary objective first and the secondary objective second. When developing the client's profile agents should also calculate clients':

- Assets
- Liabilities
- Net worth
- Monthly discretionary cash flow or income

If a client does not provide complete financial and suitability details the broker dealer may still make recommendations to the client if the broker dealer can determine suitability through the information provided. If suitability cannot be determined, recommendations should be withheld until the client provides more information.

SUITABILITY STANDARDS

Products made available through member firms must meet a reasonable basis suitability requirement. The reasonable basis suitability requirement has two parts. The member must understand the risks and performance characteristics of the investment and the agents offering the products for sale must understand the risks and performance characteristics of the investment. The member is required to educate its agents about the risks and rewards of the products it allows agents to recommend to clients. If a member maintains a new product committee to review potential investments offered to clients the committee must believe that the products are suitable for at least some of the firm's clients. FINRA member firms should train representatives about the characteristics relating to specific products including product features, risks, and pricing. Members should also provide representatives with suitability guidance for recommending products and product related risk assessments and reviews. It is the responsibility of the representative to meet the client specific suitability requirement. The representative's principal will review the transaction promptly to ensure client specific suitability

TAKENOTE!

If the firm's product committee understands the risks and allows agents to offer the securities to clients, but the representative does not, neither the firm nor the representative has met their obligations under suitability standards.

PROFESSIONAL CONDUCT WHEN MAKING RECOMMENDATIONS

All industry participants are expected to uphold high professional standards and to adhere to just and equitable practices. All broker dealers, investment advisers, and agents are prohibited from:

- Implying that any securities regulator has approved or endorsed any security, firm, or agent.
- Using excessive hedge clauses.
- Misrepresenting an account status or commissions to be charged.
- Making inaccurate market quotes.
- Misrepresenting a company's earnings.
- Guaranteeing results or promising "no loss."

- Making predictions about a security's future performance without clearly stating that it is an opinion and not a fact.
- Stating that a security will be listed on an exchange without knowledge of such listing.
- Trading or making recommendations based on inside information.
- Manipulating the market for a security.
- Unreasonably delaying a customer's request that a check or certificate be sent to them.
- Splitting or sharing commissions or advisory fees with individuals who are not properly registered.
- Offering free services without the intent to provide them or charging a fee for the free service.

REGULATION BEST INTEREST

Regulation Best Interest (Reg BI) was adopted by the SEC in June of 2019 as an amendment to the Securities Exchange Act of 1934. All broker dealers, investment advisers, and agents are subject to standards of conduct that require the firm and its agents to act in the best interest of retail customers. Regulation BI covers all recommendations to effect securities transactions as well as all recommendations regarding account establishment. That is to say, when recommending that a client open a joint, transfer on death, trust, or fee-based account, the type of account established must be in the client's best interest. In June of 2020, as part of Regulation BI, all broker dealers and investment advisers will be required to provide retail clients with a client relationship summary (CRS) and will be required to post the CRS on their publicly available website. The CRS may be provided in hardcopy or electronically. If the CRS is provided in hardcopy, the CRS may not be more than two pages long and the CRS must be the first page among any documents sent in the same package. The following rules are in place relating to the CRS:

- The CRS must be written in plain English using everyday terms.
- The CRS should be written using "active voice" with a strong, direct, and clear meaning.
- The CRS must follow the standard format and order as detailed by the SEC.
- The CRS should be written as if speaking to the retail investor directly.
- The CRS must be factual and avoid boilerplate, vague, or exaggerated language.
- The CRS may not include disclosures other than those required under Regulation BI.

- Electronic CRSs should use graphs and charts, specifically dual column charts to compare services.
- Electronic CRSs may use videos and popups and must provide access to any referenced information via hyperlink or other means.
- Electronic CRSs may be delivered via email provided that the email contains a direct link to the CRS.

Some of the required disclosures are referred to as "conversation starters." These conversation starters should be in bold or in other text to ensure that they are more noticeable than other disclosures. These conversation starters include questions such as:

1. Who is my primary contact and does he or she represent a broker dealer or an investment adviser?
2. Who can I speak to about how the person is treating me?
3. Given my financial situation, should I choose a brokerage service? Why or why not?
4. Given my financial situation, should I choose an investment advisory service? Why or why not?
5. How will you choose investments to recommend to me?
6. What is your relevant experience, including licenses, education, and qualifications? What do these qualifications mean?
7. What fees will I pay?
8. How will these fees affect my investments? If I give you $10,000, how much will go toward fees and expenses and how much will be invested for me?
9. What are your legal obligations to me when providing recommendations (broker dealer)?
10. What are your legal obligations to me when acting as my investment adviser?
11. How else does your firm make money?
12. How do your financial professionals make money?
13. What conflicts of interest do you have?
14. Does the firm or its financial professionals have legal or disciplinary history?

Both broker dealers and investment advisers are required to adhere to the standards of conduct under Regulation BI. As such, both must disclose that they must put the interests of the client ahead of theirs when making a recommendation and that the way the firm makes money for providing the services causes a conflict of interest. These conflicts include recommending proprietary products, receiving payments from third parties, principal trading, or revenue sharing.

Online broker dealers who only provide access to trading, as well as investment advisers who only offer automated services and who do not offer access to specific registered individuals must disclose this fact in the CRS and must provide a section on their website that answers questions relating to the conversation starters. If a broker dealer or investment adviser provides both online services and access to registered personnel, a registered person must be made available to discuss the conversation starters.

Broker dealers are required to provide the CRS to customers before or upon the earlier of recommending the type of account to establish or an investment strategy or upon opening an account or placing an order. Investment advisers must provide the CRS to clients prior to or at the time the contract is entered into even if the contract is oral. The CRS is now known as ADV part 3. For entities who are registered as both a broker dealer and as an investment adviser, the CRS must be delivered upon the earliest requirement for either registration. Any changes required to be made to the CRS must be completed within 30 days and an updated CRS clearly reflecting the changes must be sent to existing customers within 60 days. All broker dealers and investment advisers are required to file the CRS along with any changes with the SEC. Broker dealers will file through the Central Registration Depository (CRD) system and investment advisers will file through the Investment Adviser Registration Database (IARD). The relationship summary must be provided to a client upon request within 30 days.

RECOMMENDING MUTUAL FUNDS

A representative recommending a mutual fund should ensure that the mutual fund's investment objective meets the customer's investment objective. If the mutual fund company or broker dealer distributes retail communication regarding the mutual fund, the following should be disclosed:

- The highest sales charge charged by the fund.
- The fund's current yield based on dividends only.
- Graph performance of the fund versus a broad-based index.
- The performance of the fund for 10 years or the life of the fund, whichever is less.
- Nothing that implies that a mutual fund is safer than other investments.
- The source of graphs and charts.

If a client wants to diversify an investment among several different mutual fund portfolios with different investment objectives, the agent should find a fund family with a large variety of portfolios to choose from. This will allow the client to invest the funds with one company and to take advantage of breakpoint sales charge reductions. An agent who spreads the money among different portfolios at different companies may have committed a breakpoint sale violation.

PERIODIC PAYMENT PLANS

When recommending or advertising a periodic payment plan, the following must be disclosed:

- A statement that a profit is not guaranteed.
- A statement that investors are not protected from a loss.
- A statement that the plan involves continuous investments, regardless of market conditions.

MUTUAL FUND CURRENT YIELD

When advertising or recommending a mutual fund, any statement or claim regarding its current yield must be based solely on the annual dividends paid by the fund and may not include any capital gains distributions. Additionally, the public offering price (POP) used to calculate the current yield must contain the highest sales charge charged by the fund and may not be based on a breakpoint schedule or sales reduction charge.

FAIR DEALINGS WITH CUSTOMERS

All broker dealers are required to act in good faith in all of their dealings with customers and are required to uphold just and equitable trade practices. FINRA's Rules of Fair Practice, also known as the Rules of Conduct, regulate how business is conducted with members of the general public. The Rules of Conduct prohibit the following:

- Churning.
- Manipulative and deceptive practices.
- Unauthorized trading.
- Fraudulent acts.
- Blanket recommendations.

- Misrepresentations.
- Omission of material facts.
- Making guarantees.
- Selling dividends.
- Recommending speculative securities without knowing if the customer can afford the risk.
- Short-term trading in mutual funds.
- Switching fund families.

CHURNING

Most representatives are compensated when customers make transactions based on their recommendations. Churning is a practice of making transactions that are excessive in size or frequency, with the intention of generating higher commissions for the representative. When determining if an account has been churned, regulators will look at the frequency of the transactions, the size of the transactions, and the amount of commission earned by the representative. Customer profitability is not an issue when determining if an account has been churned.

In addition to churning where the agent or firm executes too many transactions to increase revenue, a practice known as reverse churning is also a violation. Reverse churning is the practice of placing inactive accounts or accounts that do not trade frequently into fee-based programs that charge an annual fee based on the assets in the account. This fee covers all advice and execution charges. Since these inactive accounts do not trade frequently it will cause the total fees charged to the account to increase and makes a fee-based account unsuitable for inactive accounts and for accounts that simply buy and hold securities for long periods of time. These accounts will generally be charged an annual fee in the range of 1–2 percent of the total value of the assets in lieu of commissions when orders are executed.

MANIPULATIVE AND DECEPTIVE PRACTICES

It is a violation for a firm or representative to engage in or employ any artifice or scheme that is designed to gain an unfair advantage over another party. Some examples of manipulative or deceptive practices are:

Capping: A manipulative act designed to keep a stock price from rising or to keep the price down.

Pegging: A manipulative act designed to keep a stock price up or to keep the price from falling.

Front running: The entering of an order for the account of an agent or firm prior to the entering of a large customer order. The firm or agent is using the customer's order to profit on the order it has entered for its own account.

Trading ahead: The entering of an order for a security based on the prior knowledge of a soon to be released research report.

Painting the tape/matched purchases and sales: A manipulative act by two or more parties designed to create false activity in the security without any beneficial change in ownership. The increased activity is used to attract new buyers.

Participating in rings or pools: Investors many not act in concert to manipulate the price of a security or for the purpose of concealing the actual ownership or control of the security.

UNAUTHORIZED TRADING

An unauthorized transaction is one that is made for the benefit of a customer's account at a time when the customer has no knowledge of the trade and the representative does not have discretionary power for the account. Additionally, a representative may not accept an order from any third party who is not listed on the account and who does not have discretionary authority on the account.

EXAMPLE

On April 1, a husband mails in two IRA contributions, one for his account and one for his nonworking wife's account. The next week the husband phones the agent and asks the agent to invest both contributions into the mutual fund that he and his wife have been contributing to for years.

ANALYSIS

The agent would only be allowed to execute the order entered by the husband for his own IRA even though the husband wrote the check for both IRA contributions. Once the money was deposited into the wife's IRA it became her property and the wife would have to call the agent and place the mutual fund order personally. The wife would have to sign a third party trading authorization to allow the husband to be able to place orders for the spouse's IRA.

FRAUDULENT ACTS

Fraud is defined as any act that is employed to obtain an unfair advantage over another party. No member may engage in any fraudulent dealings in the securities industry. Some examples of fraudulent acts are:

- Forgery
- Material omission
- Lying

BLANKET RECOMMENDATIONS

It is inappropriate for a firm or a representative to make blanket recommendations for any security, especially low-priced speculative securities. No matter what type of investment is involved, a blanket recommendation to a large group of people will always be wrong for some investors. Different investors have different objectives, and the same recommendation will not be suitable for everyone.

EXAMPLE

Mr. Jones, an agent with XYZ brokers, has a large customer base that ranges from young investors who are just starting to save to institutions and retirees. Mr. Jones has been doing a significant amount of research on WSIA Industries, a mining and materials company. Mr. Jones strongly believes that WSIA is significantly undervalued based on its assets and earning potential. Mr. Jones recommends WSIA to all his clients. In the next six months the share price of WSIA increases significantly as new production dramatically increases sales, just as Mr. Jones's research suggested. The clients then sell WSIA at Mr. Jones's suggestion and realize a significant profit.

ANALYSIS

Even though the clients who purchased WSIA based on Mr. Jones's recommendation made a significant profit, Mr. Jones has still committed a violation because he recommended WSIA to all of his clients. Mr. Jones's clients have a wide variety of investment objectives, and the risk or income potential associated with an investment in WSIA would not be suitable for every client. Even if an investment is profitable for the client, it does not mean it was suitable for the client. Blanket recommendations are never suitable.

TAKENOTE!

An investment adviser who has discretion over client accounts may in certain circumstances be found to have made unsuitable blanket recommendations if the adviser purchases a significant amount of an illiquid security for a large number of client accounts. This action could also be deemed to be market manipulation.

SELLING DIVIDENDS

Selling dividends is a violation. Registered representatives may not use the pending dividend payment as the sole basis of their recommendation to purchase a stock. Using the pending dividend as a means to create urgency on the part of the investor to purchase the stock is a prime example of this type of violation. If the investor were to purchase the shares just prior to the ex dividend date simply to receive the dividend, the investor, in many cases, would end up worse off. The dividend in this case will actually be a return of the money that the investor used to purchase the stock, and then the investor will have a tax liability when the dividend is received.

MISREPRESENTATIONS

A representative or a firm may not knowingly make any misrepresentations regarding:

- A client's account status
- The representative
- The firm
- An investment
- Fees to be charged

OMITTING MATERIAL FACTS

A representative of a firm may not omit any material fact, either good or bad, when recommending a security. A material fact is one that an investor would need to know in order to make a well-informed investment decision. The representative may omit an immaterial fact.

MAKING GUARANTEES

A representative, a broker dealer, or an investment adviser may not make any guarantees of any kind. A profit may not be guaranteed, and a promise of no loss may not be made.

RECOMMENDATIONS TO AN INSTITUTIONAL CUSTOMER

FINRA recognizes an institutional customer as one that has at least $10,000,000 in assets. The agent's or member's suitability determination can be met if the customer:

- Can independently evaluate the investment risks and merits.
- Can independently make its own investment decisions.

If the customer meets the above criteria, the member or agent may recommend almost any investment to the customer and allow the customer to determine if it is suitable.

TAKE**NOTE!**

If the person who is making decisions on behalf of an institutional account clearly cannot determine the risks and suitability of recommendations, the responsibility to make suitable recommendations will revert back to the representative and the member firm.

SHORT SALES IN CONNECTION WITH RECOMMENDATIONS

If a customer of a broker dealer accepts the firm's recommendation to purchase a security, and the firm sells the security short to fill the customer's order, the firm must purchase the security promptly in order to deliver the security to the customer.

ISSUING RESEARCH REPORTS

Broker dealers that issue research reports must carefully supervise their associated people who issue the research reports. The review and approval of research is exclusively conducted by the research department and supervisory analysts. The member's investment banking department is strictly prohibited from exercising any control over the member's research department. Neither the investment banking nor any other non research department may have any review, approval, or veto power over the issuance of research reports. The investment banking department may only be contacted by the research department to ensure the accuracy of information. All written communications, including emails and instant messaging, between the two departments must be conducted through the legal or compliance department or the department must be copied on the communication. If the contact is oral, the communication must be done through an official of the legal or compliance department or in the presence of a member from the legal or compliance department. All other communication between investment banking and research is strictly prohibited. FINRA has recognized that certain small firms may not be able to absorb the costs associated with ensuring the barriers between research and investment banking. In order to alleviate the undue hardship, in limited circumstances, FINRA will allow personnel to act in a dual capacity. If during the last three years, on average, the member firm has participated in 10 or fewer underwritings as a manager or co-manager and has received $5 million or less in compensation, an investment banker may also function as a research analyst. This exception relieves the member from the obligation for the legal and compliance department to serve as the intermediary between investment banking and research. Further, this exemption also relieves the member firm from the prohibition regarding investment banking having a supervisory role in research. While this exception alleviates many provisions of the firewall or gatekeeper provisions, it does not eliminate the prohibition regarding communication between research and the issuer. Compensation for analysts may not be based on:

- Deal-related bonuses
- Percentage of investment deals
- Specific investment banking deals

If the analyst's compensation is in any way tied to the investment banking department it must be clearly disclosed in the research reports issued by that analyst. All analyst compensation should be reviewed by the firm's compensation committee and supervisory analysts. In order to ensure that analysts who issue research reports do not profit by trading the security just before or after they issue the report, the following rules have been enacted:

- Analysts may not trade against their recommendations.
- An analyst who is working on a research report may not trade the security that is the subject of the report until such time as the intended recipients of the report have had an opportunity to act on the report.
- Analysts may not receive pre-IPO shares from a company in a sector the analyst covers.

The personal trading rules apply to accounts owned by the analyst or under the control of the analyst or any member of the analyst's household. Exceptions would be made for hardship or emergency sales by analysts. Each exemption would have to be approved by the firm's legal or compliance department. It's important to note that a hardship exemption would not allow the analyst to trade against their own recommendation to cover expenses they knew were coming up, such as college tuition. Analysts may invest in mutual funds without restriction so long as the analyst does not own 1 percent or more of the fund and the fund does not invest more than 20 percent of its assets in a sector covered by the analyst. A broker dealer may prohibit analysts from owning securities issued by the companies or in the sector covered by the analyst. Should a broker dealer hire an analyst or assign a company to an analyst who already owns the stock in the company or sector they are now going to cover, the broker dealer must handle the sale of the securities in line with its policy of not allowing an analyst to own such securities. Research analysts who are primarily engaged in the preparation of research reports and those who report directly or indirectly to such persons must register with FINRA and are subject to both firm element and regulatory CE requirements. Individuals who only occasionally produce or prepare research do not meet the definition of a research analyst. In addition to the trading rules for analysts, the firm itself is precluded from establishing or adjusting it's inventory position in a security based on the prior knowledge of a research report. This is another variation of the prohibited practice known as trading ahead. Excluded from this rule are inventory adjustments solely based on the receipt of unsolicited customer orders, orders received from other broker-dealers, and adjustments made based on internal research reports that will not be made available to the public. Firms must maintain adequate supervisory systems to ensure all research related rules are followed but are not required to attest annually or otherwise relating to the adequacy of its research supervisory system.

REQUIRED DISCLOSURES FOR RESEARCH REPORTS

The issuance of research reports requires the member to make certain disclosures about the firm's ownership and relationship with the subject company. The firm must disclose:

- If the firm makes a market in the security.
- If the firm owns 1 percent or more of the subject security.
- If the analyst or a member of the analyst's household owns the security, has an interest in the issuer, or is an officer, director, or adviser to the issuer.
- If the member has received investment banking fees from the subject company within the last 12 months.
- If the member is seeking investment banking business from the subject company within the next three months.

- Any material conflict of interest known by the firm.

The disclosures required by the firm must appear on the first page of the research report in type of equal size. If the report contains research reports on six or more companies, the report may direct the reader to a location as to where the information may be found in print or electronic form. The firm must also disclose certain information relating to the firm's research and the market conditions. The research must disclose:

- A clear explanation of its rating system and an explanation of what each rating means.
- The percentage of subject securities that are rated buy, sell, or hold.
- Rationale to support the recommendation.
- The percentage of subject companies in each category with whom the firm has an investment banking relationship.
- Risk factors that may keep the security from reaching the firm's price target.
- The market price of the security at the time the recommendation was made.
- A three-year price chart for the subject security and information relating the firm's target prices and any changes to the target price for securities covered for at least one year.

If an analyst makes a public appearance on a television or radio program, the analyst is required to make similar disclosures if predictions are made. The disclosures that are required during the interview are:

- If the firm owns 1 percent or more of the subject security.
- If the analyst or a member of the analyst's household owns the security, has an interest in the issuer, or is an officer, director, or adviser to the issuer.
- If the issuer of the subject security is an investment banking client.
- Any material conflict of interest known by the firm.

A public appearance by an analyst is defined as any appearance where there are 15 or more attendees in person in a seminar, on a conference call, or through a webinar. A public appearance would also be defined as any event or call attended by one or more members of the media. Firms must maintain guidelines for disclosing all of the potential conflicts of interest by an analyst as part of the written supervisory procedures. Firms issuing research reports may not submit research reports to subject companies, and subject companies may not be informed of a ratings change until the end of the trading day one day prior to the public announcement. The only exception is for factual clarification. If the analyst requires a clarification from the subject company, only the part dealing with the facts in question may be sent to the subject company, with the approval of the legal or compliance department. Managers, co-managers and syndicate members participating in the underwritings of IPO's may not issue research reports relating to the IPO until 10 days have passed from the offering's effective date. The quiet period for mangers and co-managers is reduced for secondary and follow on offerings to 3 days from the effective date. Syndicate members have no quiet period for follow on offerings. It is important to note that these rules are not in effect for the underwriting of debt securities. In addition to preparing its own research, broker dealers may also use third-party and independent third-party research prepared by others. Third-party research is prepared by an affiliated party, and the broker dealer has control over the content of the report. The broker dealer is required to approve the research prior to its distribution. Independent third-party research is prepared by an unaffiliated party, and the broker dealer has no control over the content of the report. As a result, the broker dealer is not required to approve the content of the report. Regulation AC requires an analyst to certify each and every report issued by the analyst. This certification states that the opinion expressed in the research report is based on the analyst's own personal beliefs. Additionally, within 30 days of the end of every quarter, the analyst must recertify that each research report issued during the quarter reflects the analyst's personal beliefs. If the analyst fails to recertify all reports at the end of the quarter, each research report for the next 120 days issued by the analyst must be marked as uncertified.

REGULATION FD

Regulation FD was adopted by the SEC in order to prevent the selective disclosure of nonpublic material information to securities industry professionals. Issuers may not disclose nonpublic material information in the content of a conference call with analysts and research professionals without making that information known to the general public. If the issuer intentionally discloses such information in a conference call, the issuer must simultaneously disclose it through a public filing or announcement. A filing such as an 8K or an announcement through a press release on the issuer's website or the use of social media such as Twitter are all sufficient. If the information is unintentionally released, the issuer has 24 hours to announce it publicly or until the next opening of the NYSE, whichever is later. Regulation FD applies to the senior management of the issuer as they communicate to financial professionals and large investors who may reasonably be expected to trade on the information. Regulation FD does not regulate communications between the issuer and its accountants or lawyers.

RECOMMENDATIONS THROUGH SOCIAL MEDIA

The use of social media such as LinkedIn, Facebook, and Twitter needs to be closely supervised by the member firm, specifically in cases where the communication posted by the firm or its agents could be deemed to be a recommendation. Being able to determine when communication reaches the level of a recommendation is a key element on the exam and for supervisors in general. When communication is deemed to be a recommendation it becomes subject to the suitability requirements of FINRA Rule 2111. Certain types of communications that are deemed to be recommendations are as follows:

- Targeted email distributions and tweets that advise the reader to buy or sell a security or securities within a sector.
- Targeted pop-up, redirect, and mouse-over messages displayed to website visitors that advise the visitor to buy or sell a security or securities within a sector.

If the firm maintains a website that allows access to a library of research containing previous buy and sell recommendations, the ability to access the library will not constitute a recommendation.

Due to the complex compliance issues social media present, member firms are within their rights to limit or restrict employees' use of social media. Should a member firm allow its representatives to communicate over social media the level of supervision required will depend on the type of social media used and the content of the communication. Member firms must properly train its employees on the use of social media and maintain written policies and procedures regarding its use and supervision. Static content that may be accessed by any visitor at any time requires prior approval from a principal before the static post is made and is considered part of retail communication. Static content includes Facebook walls, LinkedIn profiles, blogs, and Twitter posts as well as interactive content that is copied and pasted to any static media. Aggressively tweeting positive or negative messages about an investment is a cause for concern and may result in sanctions being imposed on both the agent and the firm. Only agents who have the approval of their firms to tweet about investments should do so. Interactive blogs and chatroom conversations are deemed to be public appearances. These public appearances do not require prior principal approval but are subject to FINRA rules. Statements made must be factual and not exaggerated and no statements should be made about a security during a quiet period. It is important to note that most blogs are static and require prior approval for posts; merely updating a blog on a regular basis does not constitute an interactive blog. While registered representatives may use interactive social media, member firms may not post to interactive media that automatically deletes. FINRA members must carefully supervise the use of social media by its agents and must have systems in place designed to detect potential violations. These systems should be designed to detect red flag words and phrases such as "guarantee" and "can't lose." Member firms are required to supervise and maintain records of the use of all social media for business purposes for 3 years regardless of the device the rep uses to post to a social media account. This is true even if the representative uses a personal cell phone or other personal electronic device to post, text or instant message. All text messages, chat logs and posts for business purposes are subject to the retention requirement. Representatives need to be particularly careful when liking or sharing social media posts. These social media activities are subject to FINRA's communication rules and in some instances liking and sharing can raise to the level of a testimonial. If the activity is deemed to be a testimonial, a link to the important testimonial information must be clearly displayed. Agents who have a history of questionable sales practices or who have been sanctioned should be prohibited from using social media for business purposes. A post on social media from a client of the firm or from an unrelated third party will not be deemed to have been made by the firm and is not subject to supervision unless the firm assisted in preparing the post or approved the content. If the firm assisted in the preparation of the post, the broker-dealer has become subject to entanglement. If the firm explicitly or otherwise endorsed or approved the content posted by a third party, the broker-dealer is considered to have adopted the content. If a firm adopts or becomes entangled with posts or links to third party websites it becomes responsible for the content. By posting a link on its website or sharing a link through email, a broker-dealer will be considered to have adopted the full content of the site or article. However, the broker-dealer will not be considered to have adopted the content accessible through an external link from the adopted content. Further, firms and representatives may not link to third party sites that they believe or have reason to believe contain misleading information. An interesting situation can arise when a registered representative sends personalized communications to a client and links to information made available by the firm but does not promote the business of the firm. In this case, the communication would not be deemed communications with the public. Such is the case when the firm sponsors a golf outing, tennis match, or charity event.

TAKENOTE!

One way for a firm to closely supervise representatives who make recommendations using social media is to have a preapproved catalog of research available for the representatives to use.

CHAPTER 5

Pretest

RECOMMENDATIONS TO CUSTOMERS

1. A customer seeking to balance her portfolio's growth and income is asking for a recommendation to invest $32,000 of her savings. She has a large portfolio of common stock. Her agent responds that the NGK Corporation is about to announce a new product and that the stock should appreciate significantly. Which of the following is true?
   - **a.** The representative is helping the customer make an informed investment decision by pointing out alternatives.
   - **b.** The customer would be better off investing in the company because she would make more money.
   - **c.** The representative should point out other facts relating to NGK as well.
   - **d.** The representative has made an unsuitable recommendation.

2. An investor has a large amount of money to invest in different portfolios. Her representative invests the money with several different fund families. Which of the following is true regarding the representative's recommendations?
   - **a.** The representative has made appropriate recommendations by diversifying a large portfolio.
   - **b.** The investor will realize a reduced sales charge on her investments.
   - **c.** The representative may have engaged in breakpoint sales.
   - **d.** The investor will have diversified out of systematic risk.

3. Which of the following is NOT required to be disclosed in a research report?
   a. If the firm has received investment banking fees in the last 18 months.
   b. If the firm owns 1 percent or more of the issuer
   c. An explanation of the rating system used by the firm
   d. A three-year price chart showing the performance of the security if the security has been covered for longer than one year

4. A conservative investor is seeking to diversify a large amount of money. She is seeking current income and safety of principal. Which of the following would you recommend?
   a. Intermediate-term Treasury bonds, fixed annuities, and money market funds
   b. Long-term Treasury bonds, money market funds, and balanced funds
   c. Short-term corporate bonds, variable annuities, and money market funds
   d. GNMAs, high-yield bonds, and fixed annuities

5. An agent's requirement to determine suitability of a recommendation may be satisfied if:
   a. the customer can judge the investment and he is an accredited investor.
   b. the customer can judge the investment and he is a qualified purchaser.
   c. the customer can judge the investment and is an institution with at least $5,000,000.
   d. the customer can judge the investment and is an institution with at least $10,000,000.

6. Which of the following are true relating to recommendations made by a firm to an investor?
   - **I.** The firm may not sell the recommended security short to fill the customer's order under any circumstances.
   - **II.** A mutual fund's current yield may be based on all distributions.
   - **III.** A research report containing reports on more than five companies may direct the reader electronically to the required disclosures.
   - **IV.** A firm's investment banking department may participate in the creation of reports only to the extent of fact verification.
     - **a.** I and II
     - **b.** III and IV
     - **c.** II and III
     - **d.** I and IV

7. Your firm's research department is issuing a report on a newly covered company. As it relates to the analyst, which of the following is true?
   - **a.** The analyst may call the investment banking department directly.
   - **b.** The analyst must wait 30 days after the issuance of the report to trade in the security.
   - **c.** The subject company may not receive any excerpts from the report from the analyst.
   - **d.** The analyst is required to make disclosures during interviews.

8. The analyst may not trade the security he or she covers in a research report:
   - **a.** until the transaction is approved by the principal.
   - **b.** until the recipients have had a chance to act on the report.
   - **c.** not until 10 trading days have elapsed.
   - **d.** only after the opening of the business day following the day the report was released.

9. In which of the following situations may an analyst invest in mutual funds without restriction?

   I. The analyst does not own 1 percent or more of the fund.
   II. The analyst does not own 3 percent or more of the fund.
   III. The fund does not invest more than 20 percent of its assets in a sector covered by the analyst.
   IV. The fund does not invest more than 10 percent of its assets in a sector covered by the analyst.

   a. I and III
   b. I and IV
   c. II and III
   d. I and IV

10. If an analyst makes a public appearance on a television or radio program, the analyst is required to disclose all of the following, EXCEPT:

   a. risk factors that may keep the security from reaching the firm's price target.
   b. if the firm owns 1 percent or more of the subject security.
   c. if the analyst or the analyst's household owns the security, has an interest in the issuer, or is an officer, director, or adviser to the issuer.
   d. if the issuer of the subject security is an investment banking client.

11. Analysts may:

   a. short a stock they rate a sell.
   b. sell a stock they rate a buy.
   c. trade 15 days prior to the issuance of a report.
   d. trade three days after the issuance of a report.

12. Which of the following are misleading?

   I. Multiple hedge clauses
   II. An implied regulatory endorsement
   III. Promises of free services
   IV. Use of outside research

   a. I and II
   b. II and IV
   c. I and III
   d. I, II, III, and IV

CHAPTER 6

General Supervision

INTRODUCTION

The foundation of a firm's supervisory system is its written supervisory manual, also known as the firm's policy and procedures manual. All members are required to have a policy and procedures manual that outlines the supervisory structure of the firm and that designates a principal to be responsible for each business area of supervision. The policy and procedures manual must include the title, location, and registration status of all supervisors and a copy of the manual must be kept in each office of the firm where supervised activities are conducted. The purpose of the written policy and procedures manual is to ensure compliance with the firm's rules, as well as the rules of the industry. The manual must be updated to reflect the adoption of new policies, a change in personnel, or new industry regulations. The manual must also clearly outline the way the periodic compliance examinations are conducted and documented. Both the SEC and FINRA can take action against a firm or principal for failing to supervise its operations and agents.

THE ROLE OF THE PRINCIPAL

Prior to any firm being admitted as a member of FINRA, it must have at least two principals to supervise the firm's activities. At a minimum, one must be a principal to supervise employees, and the other must be a financial operations principal, or FINOP, to supervise the financial and operational activities of the firm. It is the principal's responsibility to ensure that all rules in the policy and procedures manual are followed by the firm's employees. It is also the responsibility of the principal to review and approve all of the following:

- New accounts
- Retail communication (advertising and sales literature)
- Transactions

The principal reviews and approves the above listed items in writing by signing or initialing the item. In the case of transactions, a principal may initial each ticket or initial a daily trade run. This supervisor's initials will indicate the fact that the trades have been reviewed and approved. As most firms now execute orders using electronic "tickets," the principal may review the trade runs electronically and check a box for approval. There is no requirement that a principal approve a trade prior to its execution, but the trade must be reviewed and approved promptly. A firm may also employ a risk based review system designed to identify trades that pose the greatest financial or regulatory risks to the firm or its customers. Monitoring trades executed in certain products, or by producing managers or representatives with disciplinary history may all be considerations for the risk based system. Each registered representative must be assigned to a specific supervisor. A principal of a member firm who fails to supervise the actions of the agents under his or her control may be subject to action by both FINRA and the SEC. A principal will not be subject to action if there are written procedures in place that are designed to detect and prevent violations. These procedures must have been enacted and the supervisor must not have reason to believe the system is not operating properly. Additionally, the principal will not be found to have failed to supervise if an agent has employed extreme measures to conceal his or her actions. Each member firm must designate at least one principal to establish and review the firm's supervisory control systems. This person is responsible for recommending changes in the system to the firm's senior management and reporting the effectiveness of the firm's compliance system at least once per year. This report must include the areas where the system is working well, where it can be improved and a description of the compliance issues experienced by the firm in the previous year. This person must be identified to FINRA as the principal in charge of reviewing the firm's compliance control systems. This report must include the areas where the system is working well, where it can be improved and a description of the compliance issues experienced by the firm in the previous year. In addition to identifying the person responsible for testing the firm supervisory systems, broker-dealers must appoint and identify to FINRA, an executive representative and a chief compliance officer. The executive representative will be the person FINRA contacts to discuss matters relating to the firm's business. For example, if FINRA had a question regarding an ad that the member ran in a newspaper, FINRA would call the executive representative, not the principal who approved the ad. The appointment of the executive representative should be reviewed quarterly within 17 business days of the end of the quarter. A firm's Chief Compliance Officer is the ultimate decision maker for the broker-dealer regarding compliance matters. The appointment of the chief compliance officer/ CCO must be certified annually by the Chief Executive Officer no later than April 1st of each year.

SUPERVISOR QUALIFICATIONS AND PREREQUISITES

People who supervise or train agents generally must register as a principal with FINRA and qualify by training or experience. Prior to taking a principal exam, the individual must have successfully completed the appropriate registered representative examination. A principal of a FINRA member firm will usually take the General Securities Principal Exam, which is known as the Series 24. Series 24 general securities principals may manage or supervise the firm's corporate securities business, including investment banking, direct participation programs, investment company products, and variable contracts. A Series 24 does not qualify an individual as a(n):

- Registered options principal.
- General securities sales supervisor for options or municipal securities.
- Municipal securities principal.
- Financial and operations principal.
- Introducing broker/dealer financial and operations principal.

All portions of FINRA administered exams are proprietary and to be held in the strictest of confidence. FINRA considers it a violation of its rules for any individual to:

- Disclose exam questions or content to anyone.
- Reproduce exam questions.
- Receive exam questions or content from anyone.
- Compromise the content of any exam.
- Remove any portion of an exam from the exam location.

CONTINUING EDUCATION

Most registered agents and principals are required to participate in industry-mandated continuing education (CE) programs. The CE program consists of a firm element, which is administered by the broker dealer, and a regulatory element, which is administered by the regulators.

FIRM ELEMENT CONTINUING EDUCATION

Every FINRA member firm must identify the training needs of its covered employees at least annually and develop a written training plan based on its employees' needs. A covered employee is a registered person who engages in sales of securities to customers, trading, and investment banking, as well as that employee's immediate supervisors. The firm, at a minimum, should institute a plan that increases the covered employees' securities knowledge and should focus on the products offered by the firm. The plan should also highlight the risks and suitability requirements associated with the firm's investment products and strategies. The firm is not required to file the continuing education plan with FINRA unless it is specifically requested to do so. However, firms that fail to adequately document their CE program, including their covered agents' compliance with the program, may be subject to disciplinary action.

REGULATORY ELEMENT

All registered agents who were not registered on or before July 1, 1988, must participate in the regulatory element of the CE requirement. Agents subject to the requirement must complete the computer-based training at an approved facility or through FINRA's continuing education portal on the second anniversary of their initial registration and every three years thereafter. The content of the exam is developed by the Securities Industry Regulatory Council on Continuing Education and is not the responsibility of the broker dealer. FINRA will notify the agent 30 days prior to his or her anniversary date. This notification provides the agent with a 120-day window to complete the regulatory continuing education requirement. The registration of an agent who fails to complete the requirement within that period will become inactive. Agents whose registrations have become inactive may not engage in any securities business that requires a license and may not receive commissions until their registration is reactivated. Series 7 registered representatives are subject to Series 101 of the regulatory element, whereas registered principals are subject to Series 201 of the requirement. Agents who were exempt from the regulatory element as a result of having been registered for 10 years or more with a clean disciplinary history on July 1, 1998, who become the subject of a significant disciplinary action, will now be required to participate in the regulatory element of the CE requirement. Additionally, if an agent who was exempt from the regulatory element subsequently becomes registered as a principal, the agent will become subject to the Series 201 requirement. The one-time exemption is only for the regulatory element; there is no exemption from the firm element of the CE program. If an agent leaves the industry for less than 24 months, the date of their regulatory requirement will be based on the date of their initial industry registration, not upon the date of association. An agent who leaves the industry for more than 24 months will have to requalify by exam and will have a regulatory education requirement based on the date of reassociation (the date they passed the exam for the second time). An agent who becomes subject to sanctions or disciplinary action by FINRA may be required to retake the regulatory CE requirement as part of the penalty. This will change the base date for the person's regulatory requirement to the date of the sanction.

TAPE RECORDING EMPLOYEES

Certain firms may be subject to special supervision requirements if a significant amount of its registered agents came from a firm or firms that have been disciplined by regulators. A firm that is subject to the taping rule must implement special written procedures and begin taping the conversations of its registered personnel and customers within 60 days of being notified by FINRA that the firm has become subject to the taping rule. The firm also must implement written procedures to retain, review, and classify the recordings. Firms that fall into the following categories must tape their employees:

- Has more than five but fewer than 10 registered representatives and 40 percent or more have come from disciplinary firms within the last three years.
- Has at least 10 but fewer than 20 registered representatives and four or more have come from disciplinary firms within the last three years.
- Has 20 or more employees and at least 20 percent have come from disciplinary firms within the last three years.

A broker dealer that has been notified by FINRA that it is subject to the taping rule has a one-time option to reduce its number of registered representatives. If the firm elects to reduce a portion of the subject agents to eliminate the taping requirement, the firm may not rehire the subject agents who were eliminated for 180 days. Also, the firm may not hire additional agents to dilute the percentage of agents with disciplinary histories to avoid the taping requirement.

HEIGHTENED SUPERVISORY REQUIREMENTS

In addition to having to record agents under certain conditions, FINRA has enacted rules to ensure that heightened supervision is in place for:

- Representatives who have been sanctioned by FINRA.
- Managers who turn a blind eye to violations.
- Complex structured or proprietary products.

- Producing managers who generate 20 percent or more of the production where they supervise, based on the trailing 12 months, commissions at the location.

Individuals who supervise producing managers must be financially independent of the managers they supervise. These supervisors should be located at an office that is independent from the office of the producing manger they supervise and they must have the authority to correct the actions of the manager including terminating the manager. Firms must maintain written policies and procedures to detect red flags and to implement heightened supervision where required. A key red flag for producing branch office managers would be an unusual number of cancel and rebill transactions, where trades are cancelled out of one account and placed in another after execution.

INFORMATION OBTAINED FROM AN ISSUER

If a broker dealer obtains information during the performance of duties to an issuer of securities it may not use that information to solicit business. A broker dealer may obtain information from an issuer while acting as:

- An underwriter
- A transfer agent
- A paying agent
- An investment banker

CUSTOMER COMPLAINTS

All written complaints received from a customer or from an individual acting on behalf of the customer must be reported promptly to the principal of the firm. The firm is required to:

- Maintain a copy of the complaint at a supervising office of supervisory jurisdiction.
- Electronically report all complaints to FINRA within 15 days of the end of each calendar quarter. If no complaints were received, no report is due.
- Report complaints within 10 days to FINRA, if the complaint alleges misappropriation of funds or securities or forgery.

The firm must maintain a separate customer complaint folder, even if it has not received any written customer complaints. If the firm's file contains complaints, the file must state what action was taken by the firm, if any, and it must disclose the location of the file containing any correspondence relating to the complaint. All records relating to customer complaints must be maintained by the firm for 4 years.

TAKE**NOTE!**

A principal is required to review all written customer complaints but there is no required time frame to respond or take action.

INVESTOR INFORMATION

All broker dealers that carry customer accounts must send their customers information detailing FINRA's BrokerCheck public disclosure program at least once per calendar year. The BrokerCheck program, accessible via the FINRA website, provides detailed registration and disciplinary history for firms and agents and is maintained at the central registration depository (CRD). The information must contain the program's 800 number, FINRA's website address, and a statement that an investor brochure includes the same information and is available.

MEMBER OFFICES

As a member's business grows, it will often wish to open new offices. The classification of the additional offices depends on the type of activity that is conducted. There are three types of offices that a member may open. They are:

- An office of supervisory jurisdiction
- A branch office
- A satellite office

OFFICE OF SUPERVISORY JURISDICTION

A member firm must inform FINRA which offices it has identified as being offices of supervisory jurisdiction, or OSJs. An OSJ is any office that conducts one or more of the following activities at that location:

- Has custody of customer funds or securities.
- Has final approval for retail communications (advertising or sales literature).

- Has final approval of customer accounts.
- Reviews and approves customer orders.
- Executes orders or makes markets in securities.
- Forms or structures offerings.
- Supervises employees at other branch offices.

At least one resident principal must manage the OSJ. The resident principal must enforce the policies and procedures of the firm, review all customer activity, and inspect the branch offices within his or her jurisdiction. Each OSJ should have one resident onsite principal who is assigned to the office and who maintains a consistent physical presence at the office. FINRA's guidelines assume that each principal will have supervisory responsibility for only one OSJ. However, if a member's business requires it to assign the supervisory responsibilities for more than one OSJ to a principal, the member must document the supervisory arrangement in its written supervisory procedures manual. FINRA would not be required to approve the arrangement but the member should give special consideration to the experience level of the principal, the geographic location of the offices, the number of representatives and if the principal is a producing agent. An office that solely has final approval over the issuance of research reports need not be classified as an OSJ so long as it does not engage in the activities of an OSJ detailed above.

TAKENOTE!

A copy of the firm's policy and procedures manual as well as a copy of the FINRA manual must be kept at each OSJ. The FINRA manual must be made available to a customer upon request. The manual may be provided to the customer in hard or electronic copy.

BRANCH OFFICES

A branch office is any location that is identified to the public as being a place where the member conducts business but does not engage in any of the activities that would require it to be considered an OSJ. Branch offices are inspected by an OSJ. A branch office may operate without a resident principal. A registered representative may act as the branch manager. The supervisory responsibility is with the OSJ. An office of convenience, such as temporary office space provided by an office sharing company for a daily rate, a temporary office maintained as part of the firm's business continuity plan, an insurance sales office where less than 25 securities transactions take place per year, and an office where only back office functions are conducted would not be considered to be branch offices and are classified as non-branch locations. A branch office with the responsibility to supervise the activities of non-branch locations would be classified as a supervising branch office. Should the member firm move or relocate a branch office, whether it is a traditional office, house boat, or yacht, FINRA must be notified within 30 days.

SATELLITE OFFICES

A satellite office is usually a smaller office that does not meet the definition of a branch. A satellite office may not have any signs or advertising. The home office of a registered representative that works out of his or her house would be considered a satellite office. Any business cards, letterhead, or email signatures must have the address and phone number of the branch office or OSJ responsible for that agent. An agent who works out of a home office may not meet with clients or handle customer checks or securities at the home. Any orders entered by the agent from the home office must be entered over a system that can be monitored by the branch office to which the agent is assigned. An agent who has a second home or vacation home may work out of that home for up to 30 days. If the agent works out of the vacation home for more than 30 days the agent must be assigned to a branch office for supervision.

ANNUAL COMPLIANCE REVIEW

At least once per year the member must conduct a compliance review of each OSJ, supervising branch office, and each registered representative. The individuals who conduct the review are generally prohibited from being assigned to the office being inspected. The person inspecting the office should not directly or indirectly report to or be supervised by anyone at the office being inspected. Persons assigned exclusively to the firm's compliance department and supervised by the compliance department are generally excluded from this rule. Non supervising branch offices should be directly reviewed every three years. When the member reviews the OSJ, the member is automatically inspecting the activities of the branch offices under the jurisdiction of the OSJ. Each member must designate a principal to test the firm's supervisory and compliance controls. This principal must file a report with senior management detailing the results of these tests. Controls must be in place to provide daily supervision of any producing managers.

BUSINESS CONTINUITY PLAN

One of the regulations developed as a result of the attack on 9/11 is the requirement for FINRA member firms to develop and maintain plans and backup facilities to ensure that the firm can meet its obligations to its customers and counterparties, in the event that its main facilities are damaged, destroyed, or inaccessible. The plan must provide for alternative means of communication between the firm, its employees, customers, and regulators as well as a data backup. The plan must provide for data back up in both hard copy and electronic format. All mission-critical functions, including financial and operational systems and regulatory reporting, must be addressed in the plan. The plan must be approved and reviewed annually by a senior member of the firm's management team and provide plans to ensure that customers have access to their funds. The plan must be provided to FINRA upon request. Should the firm's business materially change, the business continuity plan should be updated promptly to reflect the change in the member's business. The plan must identify two members of senior management as emergency contacts, one of whom must be a registered principal with the firm. Should one of the contact people change, FINRA must be notified within 30 days. Customers of the firm must be advised of the business continuity plan at the time the account is open and in writing upon request. The plan must also be posted on the firm's website. Small firms with one office should provide a contact number to the clearing firm. Each member firm is required to evaluate its potential vulnerabilities as well as any areas of weakness that may arise from its relationships with other firms and service providers. The firm's business continuity plan must adequately address each of these issues. A significant business disruption event may require the firm to go out of business temporarily or permanently and customers must be informed of this fact. The firm must inform customers how they will have access to their assets in such an event.

CURRENCY TRANSACTIONS

The Bank Secrecy Act requires that all member firms must guard against money laundering. Every member must report any currency receipt of $10,000 or more from any one customer on a single day. The firm must fill out and submit a currency transaction report (CTR), also known as Form 4789, to the Internal Revenue Service (IRS) within 15 days of the receipt of the currency. Multiple deposits that total $10,000 or more will also require the firm to file a CTR. Additionally, the firm is required to maintain a record of all international wire transfers of $3,000 or greater.

THE PATRIOT ACT

The Patriot Act, as part of the Bank Secrecy Act, requires broker dealers to have written policies and procedures designed to detect suspicious activity. The firm is required to file a Suspicious Activity Report (SAR) for any transaction of more than $5,000 that appears questionable. The firm must file the report within 30 days of identifying any suspicious activity. Anti-money-laundering rules require that all firms implement a customer identification program to ensure that the firm knows the true identity of its customers. All customers who open an account with the firm, as well as individuals with trading authority, are subject to this rule. The firm must ensure that its customers do not appear on any list of known or suspected terrorists. A firm's anti-money-laundering program must be approved by senior management. Should the approving member of management leave the firm, the plan should be reapproved by the new member of senior management. All records relating to the SAR filing, including a copy of the SAR report, must be maintained by the firm for 5 years. FINRA Rule 3310 requires member firms to identify to FINRA the name of the person in charge of the firm's AML program, as well as the name and full contact details of the person(s) who are to oversee the day to day operation of the AML program. A member firm may outsource its chief AML officer duties to an outside party who has sufficient knowledge of the Bank Secrecy Act. Any changes to AML persons identified to FINRA must be updated within 30 days. Members must also conduct an annual independent test of the program. The person conducting the test may not perform the daily AML duties at the firm or report to anyone in charge of the program. The person should have substantial knowledge of the Bank Secrecy Act and its related rules and regulations.

The money-laundering process begins with the placement of the funds. This is when the money is deposited in an account with the broker dealer. The second step of the laundering process is known as layering. The layering process consists of multiple deposits in amounts less than $10,000. The funds will often be drawn from different financial institutions, which is known as structuring. The launderers will then purchase and sell securities in the account. The integration of the proceeds back into the banking system completes the process. At this point, the launderers may use the money, which now appears to have come from legitimate sources, to purchase goods and services. Firms must also identify the customers who open the account and must make sure that they are not conducting business with anyone on the OFAC list. This list is maintained by the Treasury Department Office of Foreign Assets Control. It consists of known and suspected terrorists, criminals, and members of pariah nations. Individuals and entities who appear on this list are known as Specially Designated Nationals and Blocked Persons. Conducting business with anyone on this list is strictly prohibited. Registered representatives who aid in the laundering of money are subject to prosecution and face up to 20 years in prison and a $500,000 fine per transaction. The representative does not even have to be involved in the scheme or even know about it to be prosecuted.

FinCEN is a bureau of the U.S. Department of the Treasury. FinCEN's mission is to safeguard the financial system, guard against money laundering, and promote national security. FinCEN collects, receives, and maintains financial transactions data; analyzes and disseminates that data for law enforcement purposes; and builds global cooperation with counterpart organizations in other countries and with international bodies. FinCEN will email a list of individuals and entities to a designated principal every few weeks. The principal is required to check the list against the firm's customer list. If a match is found the firm must notify FinCEN within 14 calendar days.

U.S. ACCOUNTS

Every member must obtain the following from U.S. customers:

- Social Security number/documentation number
- Date of birth
- Address
- Place of business

FOREIGN ACCOUNTS

All non-U.S. customers must provide at least one of the following:

- A passport number and country of issuance
- An alien ID number
- A U.S. tax ID number
- A number from another form of government-issued ID and the name of the issuing country

IDENTITY THEFT

The fraudulent practice of identity theft may be used by criminals in an attempt to obtain access to the assets or credit of another person. The Federal Trade Commission (FTC) requires banks and broker dealers to establish and maintain written identity theft prevention programs. A broker dealer's written supervisory procedures manual must reference its identity theft program. The program must be designed to detect red flags relating to the known suspicious activity employed during an attempt at identity theft. The identity theft prevention program should be designed to allow the firm to respond quickly to any attempted identity theft to mitigate any potential damage.

FINRA RULES ON FINANCIAL EXPLOITATION OF SENIORS

While many people are living active and productive lives well into their eighties and beyond, FINRA has enacted rules designed to protect the financial interests of seniors who are 65 or older. FINRA is particularly concerned about clients being taken advantage of by unscrupulous or otherwise self-serving people. Registered representatives should have a clear understanding of the financial needs, resources, and behavior of their clients. This is specifically important when dealing with older clients who may require the assets to meet their current financial needs and who can fall victim to bad actors. Registered representatives should be particularly concerned with any requests to withdraw money from an account that is outside the normal actions of the client.

EXAMPLE

Sally is a retired school administrator who is 83 years old and is living on her assets. Sally and her late husband had planned well for their retirement. She has the proceeds from her husband's life insurance policy and a significant savings and retirement account, as well as her social security. Sally has been a client of your firm for 10 years and generally moves $1,800 to $2,000 per month from her brokerage account to her checking account. Twice per year she travels and moves $5,000 to her checking account to pay her travel expenses. One day Sally calls up and says she needs $35,000 wired to an out-of-state bank account. When the agent inquires what this is for, Sally says her friend has told her of an investment opportunity in real estate that she would like to take advantage of. When the agent inquiries about the opportunity, the details Sally provides do not sound right to the agent.

ANALYSIS

This is a serious red flag, and in this situation the agent has a significant conflict. On the one hand, the agent is required to do as the client requests. On the other, the agent feels a duty to protect the client and senses that their client may be the victim of senior exploitation. Even discussing the matter with a principal of the firm is not enough to determine if the client is being taken advantage of.

FINRA's rules allow broker dealers to withhold distributions to senior and other specified clients who may have mental impairments for 15 business days in cases of suspected financial exploitation. During this time the broker dealer should investigate the client's request and obtain as much information regarding the receiving party as they can. To further protect seniors, broker dealers should obtain the name and contact information of a "trusted contact" for senior clients. The firm in very limited circumstances may contact the trusted contact to inquire about requests to withdraw money when financial exploitation is suspected. The firm may also contact the person to inquire as to the welfare of the client and to inquire as to the identity of any individual who may hold power of attorney or who may be named as executor of the client's will. The firm should notify the trusted contact as well as any individuals who are authorized to transact business in the account within two business days of placing the hold on the transfer. If at the end of 15 business days the firm has gathered information relating to the request that indicates that this is a case of financial exploitation, it may withhold the funds for another 10 business days. The firm should share their findings with the National Center for Elder Abuse as well as with law enforcement.

CHAPTER 6

Pretest

GENERAL SUPERVISION

1. A branch office may do which of the following?
   - I. Advertise in the phone book
   - II. Approve new accounts
   - III. Execute customer orders on a wire basis
   - IV. Conduct the member's business with the public
     - a. I and IV
     - b. II and III
     - c. I, II, and IV
     - d. I, II, III, and IV

2. A member would be required to record which of the following as part of its anti-money-laundering efforts?
   - a. A customer's large transaction executed on a cash basis
   - b. A customer's purchase of $70,000 of stock for next-day settlement
   - c. A wire transfer from a Canadian client for $4,800
   - d. The firm transferring $7,000 to its trading account

3. An office of supervisory jurisdiction (OSJ) may conduct which of the following activities?

I. Final approval of retail communication

II. Execution of customer orders

III. Structuring of investment banking

IV. Review of branch offices

a. I and III

b. II and IV

c. I, II, and IV

d. I, II, III, and IV

4. A firm's business continuity plan must provide for which of the following?

I. Cash reserve account for customers needing access to funds

II. Secondary communication facilities

III. The designation of a FINOP who can calculate the firm's net capital in case of an emergency

IV. Contact information for two emergency contacts

a. I and III

b. II and IV

c. III and IV

d. I, II, III, and IV

5. A satellite office may do which of the following?

a. Advertise its location

b. Transact business with the public

c. Conduct compliance reviews of its agents

d. Approve new accounts

6. Which of the following is true?

I. An OSJ must have at least two resident principals.

II. An OSJ is responsible for the activities of the branch offices in its area.

III. A registered representative may act as the manager of a branch office.

IV. An OSJ must have a resident FINOP.

a. I and III
b. II and III
c. I and IV
d. II and IV

7. As it relates to a member firm's annual compliance review, which of the following is FALSE?
   a. All branch offices must be directly inspected by the member.
   b. All registered representatives are subject to the review.
   c. All OSJs must be directly inspected by the member.
   d. All branch offices do not need to be directly inspected by the member.

8. A general securities firm carrying customer accounts must perform which of the following?
   I. Advise customers of FINRA's public disclosure program.
   II. Give investors the 800 number for the public disclosure program.
   III. Provide customers with the address for FINRA's website.
   IV. Provide all of the items listed in writing twice per year.
      a. I and III
      b. II and IV
      c. I, II, and III
      d. I, II, III, and IV

9. A Suspicious Activity Report must be filed for questionable actions exceeding:
   a. $3,000.
   b. $5,000.
   c. $10,000.
   d. $15,000.

10. A firm's anti-money-laundering program must be approved by:
    a. the resident principal at the OSJ.
    b. the branch manager.
    c. a compliance officer.
    d. the senior compliance official only.

CHAPTER 7

Customer Accounts

INTRODUCTION

Prior to opening an account for any new customer a registered representative must complete and sign a new account form. The five main types of account ownership are:

- Individual
- Joint
- Corporate
- Trusts
- Partnership

The registered representative should try to obtain as much information about the customer as possible. The representative should obtain the customer's:

- Full name and address.
- Home and work phone numbers.
- Social Security or tax ID number.
- Employer, occupation, and employer's address.
- Net worth.
- Investment objectives.
- Estimated annual income.
- Bank/brokerage firm reference.
- Whether the customer is employed by a bank or broker dealer.
- Any third-party trading authority.

- Citizenship.
- Legal age.
- How account was obtained.
- Whether the client is an officer, director, or 10 percent stockholder of a publicly traded company.
- Name of trusted contact.

At the time a registered representative opens a new account for a retail customer, the rep should attempt to obtain the name and contact information for a trusted contact for the client. The trusted contact must be at least 18 years old and the firm may contact this individual if they have been unable to reach the customer after multiple attempts, the account may have been subject to fraud or exploitation or if the customer appears to be suffering from diminished mental capacity. If a new retail customer does not wish to provide a trusted contact, the representative should make note of that fact and the account may still be open by the firm.

All new accounts must be accepted and signed by a principal of the firm. The principal must accept the account in writing for the firm either before or promptly after the first trade is executed. The principal accepts the account by signing the new account card. While the vast majority of new accounts are opened electronically and approved electronically, the test may still use the older language. The representative who introduced the account to the firm as well as the agent who will be handling the account should be noted. The customer never has to sign anything to open a new cash account. Some firms have the customer sign a customer agreement when opening a new account, but this is not required. The customer agreement will state the firm's policies and will usually contain a predispute arbitration clause. The predispute clause requires that any potential dispute arising out of the relationship be settled in binding arbitration. The predispute arbitration clause must be presented in a certain format and include:

- A disclosure that arbitration is final and binding.
- A disclosure that the findings of the arbitrators are not based on legal reasoning.
- A statement that the discovery process is generally more limited than the discovery process in a legal proceeding.
- A statement that the parties are waiving their right to a jury trial.
- A statement that the customer must be provided with a copy of the predispute clause and must verify its receipt with a signature.

- A disclosure that a minority of the arbitration panel will be affiliated with the securities industry.
- If the predispute clause is contained in the customer agreement, there must be a highlighted disclosure just above the signature line.

A firm may also have the customer sign a signature card. A signature card will allow the firm to verify the customer's written instructions that are sent in to the firm or the fund sponsor. A copy of the information collected on the customer's account must be sent to the customer within 30 days of account opening or with the next statement. Firms must also reconfirm the customer's information no later than 36 months from the time the information was last sent to the customer. The information must contain the customer information that was collected at the time the account was opened, as well as the definitions of the terms used to describe the investment objectives. Any changes in the customer's investment objectives, name, or address must be confirmed within 30 days or when the next statement is sent. Customers who do not wish to disclose financial information may still open an account if there is reason to believe that the customer can afford to maintain the account. All registered representatives should update the customer's information regularly and note any changes in the following:

- Address
- Phone number
- Employer
- Investment objectives
- Marital status

Registered representatives are also required to maintain an accurate and up-to-date listing of all of their customer's transactions and investment holdings.

HOLDING SECURITIES

Upon opening an account, investors must decide where they want their securities to be held. The following methods are available:

- Transfer and ship
- Transfer and hold in safekeeping
- Hold in street name

TRANSFER AND SHIP

Securities that are to be transferred and shipped will be registered in the customer's name and the certificates will be sent to the customer's address of record.

TRANSFER AND HOLD IN SAFEKEEPING

Securities that are to be transferred and held in safekeeping will be registered in the customer's name and will be held by the brokerage firm. The broker dealer may charge a fee for the safekeeping of the securities. Customers may now elect to hold securities registered in their names electronically in book-entry form through the Direct Registration System (DRS). The DRS system offered through the Depository Trust Company allows investors to hold their securities on the books of the issuer or the transfer agent. Investors who hold securities with the DRS will receive a statement from the issuer or transfer agent.

HOLD IN STREET NAME

Securities that are held in street name are registered in the name of the brokerage firm as the nominal owner of the securities and the customer is the beneficial owner. Most securities are held in this manner to make transfer of ownership easier. When opening an account, the customer will also decide what to do with the distributions from the account. Investors may have the distributions sent directly to them or they may have them reinvested or swept into a money market account.

THE DEPOSITORY TRUST COMPANY (DTC)

The Depository Trust Company (DTC) is a centralized securities depository that acts as a national clearinghouse for the settlement of trades in DTC-eligible securities. DTC transfers securities on a book- or journal-entry basis. DTC eligible securities include:

- Corporate equity and debt securities
- U.S. Treasury and agency issues
- Municipal bonds
- Money market instruments
- Mortgage-backed bonds

MAILING INSTRUCTIONS

All confirmations and statements will be sent to the customer's address of record. Statements and confirmations may be sent to an individual with power of attorney if the duplicates are requested in writing. A customer's mail may be held by a brokerage firm for up to two months if the customer is traveling within the United States and for up to three months if the customer is traveling outside the United States. If a customer provides a valid reason and submits a written request, the broker-dealer may hold the customer's mail for up to six months. A customer who is in the military who will be deployed for an extended period of time should open a military PO Box to receive statements and confirmations.

INDIVIDUAL ACCOUNT

An individual account is an account that is owned by one person. That person makes the determination as to what securities are purchased and sold. In addition, that person receives all of the distributions from the account.

JOINT ACCOUNT

A joint account is an account that is owned by two or more adults. Each party to the account may enter orders and request distributions. The registered representative does not need to confirm instructions with both parties. Joint accounts require the owners to sign a joint account agreement prior to the opening of the account. All parties must endorse all securities, and all parties must be alive. Checks drawn from the account must be made out in the names of all of the parties.

JOINT TENANTS WITH RIGHTS OF SURVIVORSHIP (JTWROS)

In a joint account with rights of survivorship (JTWROS), all the assets are transferred into the name of the surviving party in the event of one tenant's death. The surviving party becomes the sole owner of the assets in the account. Both parties on the account have an equal and undivided interest in the assets in the account.

JOINT TENANTS IN COMMON (JTIC)

In a joint account that is established as tenants in common, the assets of the tenant who has died become the property of the decedent's estate. They do not become the property of the surviving tenant. An account registered as JTIC allows the assets in the account to be divided unequally; one party on the account could own 60% of the account's assets.

 TAKENOTE!

Any securities registered in the names of two or more parties must be signed by all parties and all parties must be alive to be considered good delivery.

TRANSFER ON DEATH (TOD)

An account that has been registered as a transfer on death (TOD) account allows the account owner to stipulate to whom the account is to go to in the event of the account owner's death. The party who will become the owner of the account in the event of the account holder's death is known as the beneficiary. The beneficiary may only enter orders for the account if he or she has power of attorney for the account. Unlike an account that is registered as JTWROS, the assets in the account will not be at risk should the beneficiary become the subject of a lawsuit, such as in a divorce proceeding.

DEATH OF A CUSTOMER

If an agent is notified of the death of a customer, the agent must immediately cancel all open orders and mark the account "deceased." The representative must await instructions from the executor or administrator of the estate. In order to sell or transfer the assets, the agent must receive:

- Letters testamentary
- Affidavit of domicile
- Inheritance tax waivers
- Certified copy of the death certificate

The death of a customer with a discretionary account automatically terminates the discretionary authority.

TAKE**NOTE!**

In the event an account owner cannot be located after a significant effort by the dealer, the account will be considered to be abandoned and the state will claim the account through the escheatment process. The state will hold the account as a bookkeeping entry, against which the former account owner may make a claim.

CORPORATE ACCOUNTS

Corporations, like individuals, will purchase and sell securities. In order to open a corporate account, the registered representative must obtain a corporate resolution that states which individuals have the power to enter orders for the corporation. If a corporation wants to purchase securities on margin, the registered representative must obtain a corporate charter that states that the corporation may purchase securities on margin.

TRUST ACCOUNTS

Trusts may be revocable or irrevocable. With a revocable trust, the individual who established the trust and contributes assets to the trust, known as the grantor or settlor, may, as the name suggests, revoke the trust and take the assets back. The income generated by a revocable trust is generally taxed as income to the grantor. If the trust is irrevocable, the grantor may not revoke the trust and take the assets back. With an irrevocable trust, the trust usually pays the taxes as its own entity or the beneficiaries of the trust are taxed on the income they receive. If the trust is established as a simple trust, all income generated by the trust must be distributed to the beneficiaries in the year the income is earned. If the trust is established as a complex trust, the trust may retain some or all of the income earned and the trust will pay taxes on the income that is not distributed to the beneficiaries. The grantor of an irrevocable trust is generally not taxed on the income generated by the trust unless the assets in the trust are held for the benefit of the grantor, the grantor's spouse, or if the grantor has an interest in the income of the trust of greater than 5 percent. A trust may also be established to hold or to distribute assets after a person's death under the terms of their Will. Trusts that are established under the terms of a Will are known as Testamentary trusts. All assets placed into a Testamentary trust are subject to both estate taxes and probate.

PARTNERSHIP ACCOUNTS

When a professional organization, such as a law partnership, opens an account, the registered representative must obtain a copy of the partnership agreement. The partnership agreement will state who may enter orders for the account. If the partnership wishes to purchase securities on margin, it must not be prohibited by the partnership agreement. A family limited partnership is often used for estate planning. Parents may place significant assets into a family limited partnership as a way to transfer their ownership. Usually the parents will act as the general partners and will transfer limited partnership interests to their children. As the interests are transferred to the children, the parents may become subject to gift taxes. However, the gift taxes will usually be lower than they would have suffered without the partnership.

TRADING AUTHORIZATION

From time to time, someone other than the beneficial owner of the account may be authorized to enter orders for the account. All discretionary authority must be evidenced in writing for the following accounts:

- Discretionary account
- Custodial account
- Fiduciary account

If a customer dies, any trading authorization is automatically canceled.

OPERATING A DISCRETIONARY ACCOUNT

A discretionary account allows the registered representative to determine the following, without consulting the client first:

- The asset to be purchased or sold.
- The amount of the securities to be purchased or sold.
- The action to be taken in the account, whether to buy or sell.

The principal of the firm must accept the account and review it more frequently to ensure against abuses. The customer is required to sign a limited power of attorney that awards discretion to the registered representative. The limited power of attorney is good for up to three years. The customer is bound by the decisions of the representative, but may still enter his or her own orders. Once discretion is given to the representative, the representative may not give discretion to another party. If the representative leaves the firm or stops managing the customer's account, the discretionary authority is automatically terminated. A full power of attorney allows an individual to deposit and withdraw cash and securities from the account. A full power of attorney is usually not given to a registered representative. A full power of attorney is more appropriate for fiduciaries, such as a trustee, custodian, or a guardian.

A standard power of attorney will terminate upon the death or incapacitation of the grantor. A durable power of attorney will remain in full force during the incapacitation of the grantor and will only terminate upon the grantor's death. Discretion may not be exercised by the representative until the power of attorney has been received and approved.

MANAGING DISCRETIONARY ACCOUNTS

All discretionary accounts must have the proper paperwork kept in the account file and must have:

- Every order entered marked discretionary, if discretion was exercised by the representative.
- Every order must be approved promptly by a principal.
- A designated principal to review the account.
- A record of all transactions.

THIRD-PARTY AND FIDUCIARY ACCOUNTS

A fiduciary account is one that is managed by a third party for the benefit of the account holder. The party managing the account has responsibility for making all of the investment decisions and other decisions relating to the account. The individual with this responsibility must act as a prudent person would and may not speculate. This is known as the prudent man rule. Many states have an approved list of securities known as the legal list that may be purchased by fiduciaries. The authority to transact business for the account must be evidenced in writing by a power of attorney. The fiduciary may have full power of attorney, also known as full discretion, under which the fiduciary may purchase and sell securities as well as withdraw cash and securities from the account. Under a limited power of attorney, or limited discretion, the fiduciary may only buy and sell securities and may not withdraw assets. The fiduciary has been legally appointed to represent the account holder and may not use the assets in the account for his or her own benefit. The fiduciary may, however, be reimbursed for expenses incurred in connection with the management of the account.

Examples of fiduciaries include:

- Administrators
- Custodians
- Receivers
- Trustees
- Conservators
- Executors
- Guardians
- Sheriffs/marshals

When opening a third-party or fiduciary account, the registered representative is required to obtain documentation of the individual's appointment and authority to act on behalf of the account holder. Trust accounts require that the representative obtain a copy of the trust agreement. The trust agreement will state who has been appointed as the trustee and any limitations on the trust's operation. Most trusts may only open cash accounts and may not purchase securities on margin unless specifically authorized to do so in the agreement. When opening an account for a guardian, the representative must obtain a copy of the court order appointing the guardian. The court order must be dated within 60 days of the opening of the account. If the court order is more than 60 days old, the representative may not open the account until a new court order is obtained. Guardians are usually appointed in cases of mentally incompetent adults and orphaned children.

TAKE**NOTE!**

In the case of a person who is deemed mentally incompetent, the registered representative will need a certificate of incumbency dated within 60 days of the account opening.

UNIFORM GIFTS TO MINORS ACT (UGMA)

Minors are not allowed to own securities in their own name because they are not of age to enter into legally binding contracts. The decision to purchase or sell a security creates a legally binding contract between two parties. The Uniform Gifts to Minors Act (UGMA) regulates how accounts are operated for the benefit of minors. All UGMA accounts must have:

- One custodian.
- One minor.
- UGMA and the state in the account title.
- Assets registered to the child's name after he or she reaches the age of majority.

All securities in a UGMA account will be registered in the custodian's name as the nominal owner for the benefit of the minor, who is the beneficial owner of the account. For example, the account should be titled: Mr. Jones as custodian for Billy Jones under New Jersey Uniform Gifts to Minors Act.

Only one custodian and one minor are allowed on each account. A husband and wife could not be joint custodians for their minor child. If there is more than one child, a separate account must be opened for each. The same person may serve as custodian on several accounts for several minors, and the minor may have more than one account established by different custodians. The donor of the security does not have to be the custodian for the account, and if neither of the parents are the custodian of the account, they have no authority over the account.

RESPONSIBILITIES OF THE CUSTODIAN

The custodian has a fiduciary duty to manage the account prudently for the benefit of the minor child within certain guidelines, such as:

- No margin accounts.
- No high-risk securities, such as penny stocks.
- Custodian may not borrow from the account.
- No commodities.
- No speculative option strategies.
- Custodian may not give discretion to a third party.
- All distributions must be reinvested within a reasonable time.
- The custodian may not let rights or warrants expire. They must be exercised or sold.
- The custodian must provide support for all withdrawals from the account.
- Withdrawals may only be made to reimburse the custodian for expenses incurred in connection with the operation of the account or for the benefit of the minor.

CONTRIBUTIONS TO A UGMA ACCOUNT

Gifts of cash and securities or other property may be given to the minor. There is no dollar limit as to the size of the gift that may be given. The limit on the size of the tax-free gift is $15,000 per year. An individual may give gifts valued at up to $15,000 to any number of people each year without incurring a tax liability. Once a gift has been given, it is irrevocable. Gifts to a UGMA account carry an indefeasible title and may not be taken back for any reason. The custodian may, however, use the assets for the minor's welfare and educational needs.

UGMA TAXATION

The minor is responsible for the taxes on the account. However, any unearned income that exceeds $2,200 per year will be taxed at the parents' marginal tax rate if the child is younger than 14 years. For gifts that exceed $15,000 per year, the tax liability is on the donor of the gift, not on the minor.

DEATH OF A MINOR OR CUSTODIAN

If the minor dies, the account becomes part of the minor's estate. It does not automatically go to the parents. If the custodian dies, a court or the donor may appoint a new custodian.

UNIFORM TRANSFER TO MINORS ACT

Some states have adopted the Uniform Transfer to Minors Act (UTMA) rather than the UGMA. The main difference is that with a UTMA account the custodian may determine when the assets become the property of the child. The maximum age is 25 years old.

No evidence of custodial rights is required to open a UGMA or UTMA account.

ABLE ACCOUNTS

An ABLE account, sometimes referred to as a 529 ABLE account, may be established as a tax-advantaged savings account to provide for the care of individuals with disabilities. The Achieving a Better Life Experience (ABLE) account regulations were passed in order to recognize the unique financial burdens inherent in caring for a disabled person. Individuals with disabilities may have only one ABLE account at a time and the individual with the disability is deemed to be both the account owner and the designated beneficiary. ABLE accounts may be transferred or rolled over into new ABLE accounts for the same beneficiary. Contributions to the account are made with after-tax dollars and are allowed to grow tax deferred. The contributions and the growth may be used tax free by the beneficiary for qualified care and quality-of-life expenses. Tax-free withdrawals may be made by the beneficiary to cover qualified expenses incurred or in anticipation of paying expenses to be incurred. Qualified expenses would include things such as:

- Medical care
- Wellness care
- Transportation
- Housing expenses (including mortgage, tax, rent, insurance, and utility payments)
- Assistive technology
- Education
- Job training

Withdrawals from an ABLE account for expenses that do not meet the definition of qualified expenses will be seen as part of the beneficiary's resources if retained past the month the distribution occurred. In order to qualify for an ABLE account, the individual must have been disabled by the time he or she reached their 26th birthday. The maximum annual contribution to an ABLE account is equal to the annual tax-free gift limit of $15,000 and is subject to change each year. Anyone may make contributions to an ABLE account and the account may be rolled over to another family member if that person meets the eligibility guidelines. The assets in the ABLE account will not impact the disabled person's eligibility for many assistance programs. When calculating eligibility for assistance, the first $100,000 in assets in the ABLE account are excluded when estimating the amount of resources available. However, ABLE account balances that exceed $100,000 can cause the beneficiary of the account to be placed in a suspended status for receiving supplemental security income (SSI) until all resources in the ABLE and other accounts owned by the individual fall to $100,000 or lower. Upon the death of the beneficiary of an ABLE account, the remaining assets will be used to repay Medicaid for any payments made to the beneficiary.

ACCOUNTS FOR EMPLOYEES OF OTHER BROKER DEALERS

If an account is opened for the employee of another FINRA member firm or for the spouse or minor child of the employee, the opening firm will:

- Notify the employer in writing.
- Send duplicate copies of confirmations and statements upon written request.

FINRA Rule 3210 regulates the opening of brokerage accounts by employees of broker dealers. This rule requires an employee of a broker dealer who wishes to open an account at another broker dealer to obtain the employer's written permission prior to opening the account. The employee must present written notification to the broker dealer opening the account that he/she is employed by a FINRA member firm at the time the account is opened. This rule is in effect for the employee or any of the employee's immediate family members. This rule will also require the employee to obtain the employer's written permission for accounts that were opened within 30 days of the start of employment. Excluded from this rule are accounts opened by the employee where no transactions may take place in individual securities such as accounts opened to purchase open-end mutual funds, variable annuities, UITs and back accounts.

NUMBERED ACCOUNTS

A broker dealer, at the request of the customer, may open an account that is simply identified by a number or a symbol, as long as there is a statement signed by the customer attesting to the ownership of the account.

PRIME BROKERAGE ACCOUNTS

A prime brokerage account allows customers to utilize several broker dealers to execute their orders while designating a central or main firm to maintain custody of their assets. The firm that carries and receives the customer's cash and securities is known as the prime broker. Prime brokerage accounts are usually established by institutional investors and larger retail investors. In order to open a prime brokerage account, the client must have at least $500,000 in equity. If the account is managed by a registered investment adviser, the minimum account equity is $100,000. A prime brokerage account will allow the client to receive execution and research reports from a variety of broker dealers known as executing brokers. The executing broker will buy and sell securities for the customer, and the customer will report the trade to the prime broker. The trade will then be entered into the customer's account at the prime broker. The executing broker will confirm the trade through the DTC institutional ID system, and the prime broker will affirm the trade.

ACCOUNT TRANSFER

Clients from time to time will wish to have their accounts transferred from one brokerage firm to another. This is usually accomplished through the Automated Client Account Transfer Service (ACATS). ACATS provides transfer and delivery instructions to the firm, which will be required to deliver the account to the client's new firm. Once transfer instructions are received and validated, the account will be frozen, no new orders may be accepted, and all open orders must be canceled, except for open orders for options that expire within seven days. The firm that receives the transfer instructions, known as the carrying member, is required to validate the instructions or take exception to them within one business day. Upon validation, the transfer instructions must be sent back to the receiving firm with a list of the positions to be transferred. Once the instructions have been validated, the firm has another three business days to complete the account transfer. A firm may only take exception to the instructions for the following reasons:

- The customer's signature is missing or invalid (both live and electronic signatures are valid).
- The account title does not match the carrying firm's account title.
- The Social Security number does not match.
- The account number is wrong.
- In extreme cases a broker-dealer may protest the transfer of a client's account if the client has any unsatisfied judgments, tax liens or is subject to a court order.
- A receiving firm may reject delivery if the account to be received is operating outside its credit or risk policies.

A difference in securities positions and free credit balances is not a reason to take exception to the transfer instructions. From time to time, certain investment positions will not be able to be transferred from the old firm to the new firm. The customer must be informed of this fact in writing, and the customer is required to give specific instructions as to what should be done with that investment. The customer may elect to:

- Leave the investment at the old firm.
- Have it liquidated.
- Have it shipped.

If the position is liquidated, the proceeds must be forwarded to the customer within five business days. If the customer is transferring an account that has a checking account, debit card, or credit card connected to the account, the customer must return or destroy the checks and/or card. If a registered representative leaves a broker-dealer during the term of a non-compete clause prohibiting the representative from soliciting existing clients, the firm may not dispute the transfer of a customer's account once valid transfer instructions have been received. A firm may seek a temporary restraining order against the former rep in order to stop the solicitation of clients. However, even with the existence of the temporary restraining order, the firm may not delay or dispute the transfer of the customers' accounts. Broker dealers that engage in partial account transfers from one broker dealer to another use the DTC to settle the transfers. If the old firm fails to deliver a position to the new firm, the old firm has a fail to deliver and the new firm has a fail to receive. Any disputes between the two firms must be resolved within 5 business days. A registered rep who changes firms may utilize a bulk account transfer process for his clients' account so long as the clients have provided affirmative consent. FINRA does not allow customer accounts to be transferred or the broker of record to be changed through a negative consent letter.

Variable contracts and redeemable mutual fund shares held at the issuer (fund company or annuity company) may not use a negative consent letter to change the broker of record. Customers must provide affirmative consent to change the broker of record.

A firm may in limited circumstances use a negative consent letter to bulk transfer customer accounts. A negative consent letter may be used in cases where an introducing broker dealer is changing clearing firms so long as the letter is sent giving the customer 30 days' notice. The letter must explain the reason for the change and if any charges may be incurred by the customer. The customer must also be notified of the option to move his or her account to another firm. The firm sending the negative consent letter may not share any customer personal confidential information with the receiving firm unless the sharing of the information is in line with Regulation S-P. If a broker dealer is going out of business or is at risk of going out of business, closing a line of business, or is merging or acquired by another firm, a negative consent letter may be used to accomplish a bulk account transfer. A firm seeking to use a negative consent letter must file an application with FINRA regarding the proposed transfer and must have received the approval of the proposed transfer, prior to sending the negative consent letter.

MARGIN ACCOUNTS

A margin account allows the investor to purchase securities without paying for the securities in full. The investor is required to deposit a portion of the securities' purchase price and may borrow the rest from the broker dealer. The portion of the securities' purchase price that an investor must deposit is called the margin. The amount of the required deposit or margin is controlled by the Federal Reserve Board (FRB) under Regulation T of the Securities Exchange Act of 1934. Regulation T gave the FRB the authority to regulate the extension of credit for securities purchases.

The FRB controls:

- Which securities may be purchased on margin.
- The amount of the initial required deposit.
- Payment dates.

Customers who purchase Securities on margin must receive a separate margin disclosure statement at the time the account is opened and annually thereafter detailing the risks of purchasing securities on margin. If the broker-dealer allows customers to open accounts online, the margin disclosure statement must be clearly displayed on the firm's website.

Unlike when a customer opens a cash account, when opening a margin account the customer will be required to sign certain account documents. The customer will be asked to sign the following:

- Credit agreement
- Hypothecation agreement
- Loan consent

THE CREDIT AGREEMENT

The credit agreement states the terms and conditions under which credit will be extended to the customer. It will include information about how interest is charged as well as information about the rates that will be charged. A margin loan does not amortize, meaning that the principal is not paid down on a regular schedule. The brokerage firm simply charges interest to the account.

THE HYPOTHECATION AGREEMENT

The hypothecation agreement pledges the customer's securities that were purchased on margin as collateral for the loan. It also allows the brokerage firm to take the same securities and repledge or rehypothecate them as collateral for a loan at a bank to obtain a loan for the customer.

LOAN CONSENT

By signing a loan consent agreement, the customer allows the brokerage firm to lend out the securities to customers who wish to sell the securities short. This is the only part of the margin agreement that the customer is not required to sign. The credit and hypothecation agreement must be signed prior to the account being approved to purchase securities on margin.

All securities purchased in a margin account will be held in street name, that is, the name of the brokerage firm, so that the broker dealer may sell the securities to protect itself if the value of the securities falls significantly.

GUARANTEEING A CUSTOMER'S ACCOUNT

A customer may guarantee the account of another customer, as long as the guarantee is received by the member in writing. The most likely case for using a customer's account to guarantee the account of another customer is to provide the proper equity for a margin account. Both accounts will be closely monitored to ensure the proper equity is maintained in both accounts.

DAY TRADING ACCOUNTS

Day trading is an investment strategy defined by the entering of round-trip orders, consisting of both a buy and sell order, on the same day for the same security. Firms that promote the use of day trading strategies to individual investors must adhere to special account opening requirements. A broker dealer will be considered to be promoting day trading strategies if it holds seminars, advertises, or uses another company to promote its services. If the firm promotes day trading, it must provide the customer with a risk disclosure document and approve the account for day trading. If the customer is not approved for day trading, the customer may still open an account so long as the firm obtains a written statement from the customer stating that he or she will not be engaging in day trading strategies.

TAKENOTE!

A firm will be considered to be promoting day trading if the registered representatives promote day trading strategies with the knowledge of the firm's principal.

COMMINGLING CUSTOMER'S PLEDGED SECURITIES

A broker dealer may not commingle a customer's pledged securities with that of another customer's pledged securities as joint collateral to obtain a loan from a bank without the written authorization of both customers. This authorization is required by SEC Rule 15c2-1 and is part of most margin agreements. A customer's securities may never be commingled with the firm's securities.

WRAP ACCOUNTS

A wrap account is an account that charges the customer a set annual fee for both advice and execution costs. The fee is based on the assets in the account. Wrap account holders must be given a Schedule H, which details the fees and charges, prior to opening the account. Broker dealers offering wrap accounts must also be registered as investment advisers. Wrap accounts and other asset-based fee accounts are usually not appropriate for clients who trade infrequently and use a buy and hold strategy.

REGULATION S-P

Regulation S-P requires that the firm maintain adequate procedures to protect the financial information of its customers. Firms must guard against unauthorized access to customer financial information and must employ policies to ensure its safety. Special concerns arise over the ability of a person to "hack" into a firm's customer database by gaining unauthorized access. Firms must develop and maintain specific safeguards for their computer systems and WiFi access.

Regulation S-P was derived from the privacy rules of the Gramm-Leach-Bliley Act. A firm must deliver:

- An initial privacy notice to customers when the account is opened.
- An annual privacy notice to all customers.

The annual privacy notice may be delivered electronically via the firm's website, as long as the customer has agreed to receive it electronically in writing and it is clearly displayed. The privacy notice must describe the type of information that is collected and the type of nonaffiliated parties with whom it may be shared. Regulation S-P also states that a firm may not disclose non-public personal information to nonaffiliated companies for clients who have opted out of the list. The method by which a client may opt out may not be unreasonable. It is considered unreasonable to require a customer to write a letter to opt out. Reasonable methods are emails or a toll-free number. The rule also differentiates between who is a customer and who is a consumer. A customer is anyone who has an ongoing relationship with the firm (i.e., has an account). A consumer is someone who is providing information to the firm and is considering becoming a customer or who has purchased a product from the firms and has no other contact with the firm. The firm must give the privacy notice to consumers prior to sharing any nonpublic information with a nonaffiliated company.

TAKE**NOTE!**

A client of a brokerage firm may not opt out of the sharing of information with an affiliated company.

Regulation S-AM prohibits broker dealers from soliciting business based upon information received from affiliated third parties unless the potential marketing had been clearly disclosed to the potential customer, and the potential customer was provided an opportunity to opt out and did not opt out.

CHAPTER 7

Pretest

CUSTOMER ACCOUNTS

1. The nominal owner in a Uniform Gifts to Minors Account (UGMA) is the:
   a. custodian.
   b. minor.
   c. donor.
   d. parent or guardian.

2. A customer and his spouse have an account registered as joint tenants in common. If the customer dies, what would happen to the account?
   a. The spouse would get the assets in the account.
   b. The decedent's assets will be distributed according to his will.
   c. All of the assets in the account will be distributed according to the trustee.
   d. The executor of the estate will determine how all of the assets are to be distributed.

3. All of the following are required in the account title for a custodial account, EXCEPT:
   a. the minor's Social Security number.
   b. the state.
   c. UGMA.
   d. the name of the custodian.

4. An investor has given her representative the authority to purchase and sell securities in her account without first consulting her. Which of the following is FALSE?
   a. The authority must be evidenced in writing.
   b. The account must be reviewed more frequently.
   c. All transactions must be approved by a principal prior to execution.
   d. The investor is bound by the transactions made by the representative.

5. An UTMA allows the assets in the account to:
   a. remain there until the custodian decides to transfer them to the beneficial owner.
   b. be invested more aggressively than in a UGMA.
   c. remain in the account until the beneficial owner reaches the age of 25.
   d. remain in the account until the beneficial owner reaches the age of 21.

6. Joint accounts are allowed in all of the following situations, EXCEPT:
   a. a registered representative and a customer.
   b. a registered representative and a spouse.
   c. a registered representative and a friend.
   d. a registered representative and his 16-year-old child.

7. All of the following are true of the ACAT process, EXCEPT:
   a. the customer must be informed in writing that certain positions may not be able to be transferred.
   b. the instructions must be validated in one business day.
   c. the account must be transferred within three days of validation.
   d. the receiving firm need not send a position report to the new firm.

8. Which of the following is true with regard to the management of a discretionary account?
   a. The client may reject the agent's selections after reviewing the transaction.
   b. The agent may give discretion to another agent while on vacation.
   c. The discretionary authority given to the agent is a special power of attorney that survives the death of a client so the agent may liquidate the account for the estate.
   d. All tickets must clearly state whether discretion was exercised.

9. An agent has just been informed of the death of a client. The agent must do all of the following, EXCEPT:

a. cancel all open orders.

b. mark the account deceased.

c. inform the IRS and request inheritance tax waivers.

d. await instructions from the executor.

10. A broker dealer carrying customer accounts and providing credit to customers for margin purposes may jointly pledge customers' securities as joint collateral:

a. under no circumstances.

b. only if it benefits the customers by offering them a lower interest rate.

c. only if the margin loans are amortized.

d. if all parties agree in writing.

CHAPTER 8

Margin Accounts

INTRODUCTION

Investors may borrow a portion of a security's purchase price directly from the broker dealer to establish a position. Investors who borrow money to purchase securities are said to be buying on margin. The term *margin* refers to the portion of the securities' purchase price that must be deposited by the customer to establish the position.

REGULATION OF CREDIT

One of the main reasons the stock market crashed in 1929 was the aggressive lending of money to investors who wanted to purchase securities on margin. In an effort to ward off future excessive lending practices, authority was given to the Federal Reserve Board to regulate the extension of credit for securities purchases. Regulation T of the Securities Exchange Act of 1934 allowed the Federal Reserve Board to regulate the extension of credit by broker dealers.

REGULATION T

Once a customer has established a margin account, Regulation T sets the minimum initial requirement that must be met by the customer to purchase securities on margin. Regulation T currently requires that the customer deposit 50 percent of the securities' purchase price. However, the NYSE and FINRA require that a customer meet a minimum initial equity requirement of $2,000 before a firm may lend money to an investor. In order to establish a position in a new margin account, the investor must deposit the greater of $2,000 or 50 percent of the securities' purchase price. The broker dealer may pledge or rehypothecate the customer's securities to obtain a loan at a bank for the customer. The broker dealer may pledge the customer's securities with a value of 140 percent of the customer's debit balance to obtain the loan for the customer. All excess margin securities must be segregated.

EXAMPLE

Purchased	Minimum Equity	Reg. T at 50%	Required Deposit
1,000 ABC at 10	$2,000	$5,000	$5,000
1,000 XYZ at 5	$2,000	$2,500	$2,500
1,000 RTY at 3	$2,000	$1,500	$2,000
100 KLM at 15	$2,000	$750	$1,500

TAKENOTE!

A customer may never be required to deposit more than the purchase price of the securities.

Investors who purchase securities on margin are charged interest monthly on the amount of the loan. An investor, in theory, may hold the securities on margin indefinitely and will be required to repay the principal amount of the loan upon the sale of the securities. Investors purchasing securities on margin must hypothecate or pledge the securities they purchased as collateral for the loan. All securities purchased on margin will be held in the name of the broker dealer, or street name. Holding the securities in the name of the broker dealer will allow the firm to liquidate the securities to protect the loan if the securities fall too far in value. Regulation T also establishes which securities may be purchased on margin. Marginable securities include:

- All exchange-listed stocks and bonds.
- All Nasdaq Global Market stocks.
- All securities on the Federal Reserve Board's approved list.

Investors who purchase securities on margin must deposit the required amount within four business days. If the investor is unable to make the deposit by the fourth business day, the broker dealer can apply for an extension on behalf of the customer. The broker dealer must request the extension by writing a letter to either the NYSE or FINRA by the expiration of the fourth business day. An investor may meet the margin requirement by:

- Depositing cash equal to the requirement,

  or

- Depositing marginable securities with a loan value equal to the amount of the requirement.

 TAKE**NOTE!**

Broker dealers may waive a call for $1,000 or less.

A marginable security's loan value is equal to the complement of Reg. T. When Reg. T is 50 percent, the security's loan value is 50 percent.

EXAMPLE

An investor purchasing $20,000 worth of securities in a margin account may meet the Reg. T requirement by:

- Depositing $10,000.

  or

- Depositing $20,000 worth of fully paid for marginable securities.

Nonmarginable securities include:

- Non-Nasdaq OTC securities
- Options
- IPOs and new issues for 30 days
- When issued, nonexempt securities

Certain securities are exempt from the margin requirements of Reg. T. Although an investor may still borrow money from the broker dealer to purchase these securities, the investor is not required to deposit 50 percent of the purchase price. The following securities are exempt from Reg. T:

- U.S. government securities
- U.S. government agencies
- Municipal securities
- Nonconvertible corporate debt

The initial margin requirement for exempt securities is set by the NYSE or FINRA. The initial margin requirement for U.S. government securities is 1–7 percent of the par value. For municipal securities, it is the greater of 7 percent of par or 15 percent of the market value.

HOUSE RULES

A broker dealer may elect to increase the minimum amount of margin that must be deposited by the investor or it may elect not to extend credit to customers at all. A broker dealer may never lower the amount of the required deposit below Reg. T or below the requirements of the NYSE or FINRA.

ESTABLISHING A LONG POSITION IN A MARGIN ACCOUNT

A customer's long margin account will consist of the customer's equity and loan amount or debit balance. The customer's equity represents the portion of the securities that the customer has paid for in full. The customer's debit balance represents the portion of the securities' purchase price that was loaned to the customer by the broker dealer. To determine the equity in the account, use the following formula:

equity = long market value − debit

EXAMPLE A customer in a new margin account purchases 1,000 shares of XYZ at $40 per share and makes the required deposit when Reg. T is 50 percent. The investor's margin account will now look like this:

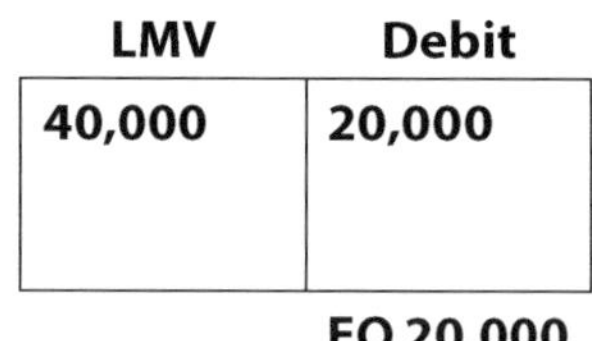

The long market value (LMV) of the stock is $40,000. The customer has a debit balance or has borrowed $20,000 and has equity of $20,000.

In order to gain an understanding of the debit balance and equity components, one could compare a long margin account to home ownership. The homeowner's equity represents the portion of the home's market value that is fully paid for. The mortgage balance is the amount of money owed on the home. As the home's market value changes, so does the homeowner's equity. The mortgage balance, however, does not change as a result of a change in the market value of the home. A long margin account operates in much the same way. As the LMV of the account increases, so does the account holder's equity. Alternatively, if the LMV of the account falls, the account holder's equity falls with it. The customer's debit balance or the amount that the customer has borrowed does not change as a result of a change in the market value of the securities. A broker dealer will closely monitor the relationship between the purchase price of the securities and the current market value of the securities through a process known as marking to the market.

AN INCREASE IN THE LONG MARKET VALUE

As the LMV in a margin account increases, the customer's equity will also increase. Let's look at our original example and see what happens to our customer's account if XYZ increases in value to $50 per share.

Original Position

LMV	Debit
40,000	20,000

EQ 20,000

XYZ at $50

LMV	Debit
50,000	20,000

EQ 30,000

As the LMV increased by $10,000, the customer's equity also increased by $10,000. Notice that the debit balance, or the amount of the customer's loan, was not affected. As the LMV increases, the rise in value creates excess equity for the customer. Excess equity is the amount of the customer's equity that exceeds the initial Reg. T. requirement at the current market value. Using our current example, the customer's excess equity (EE) is calculated as follows:

LMV	Debit
50,000	20,000

EQ 30,000
Reg. T 25,000
EE 5,000

The customer may do all of the following with the excess equity:

- Withdraw an amount equal to the excess equity.
- Use the excess equity to purchase two times the amount of marginable securities.
- Use the excess to purchase an equal amount of nonmarginable securities.

A customer may request that the brokerage firm send a check in an amount equal to the excess equity. Withdrawing the excess equity will increase the customer's debit balance. If the customer in our example withdraws the excess equity, the customer's account will look as follows:

LMV	Debit
50,000	25,000

EQ 25,000
Reg. T 25,000
EE 0

The customer's debit balance increased by the amount of the excess equity that was withdrawn. The customer may also use the excess equity to purchase marginable stock. To determine the customer's buying power, use the following formula:

buying power = excess equity/the complement of Reg. T

or, when Reg. T is 50%,

buying power = excess equity × 2

If the customer uses the excess equity to purchase $10,000 worth of marginable stock, the account would appear as follows:

LMV	Debit
60,000	30,000

EQ 30,000
Reg. T 30,000
EE 0

The LMV and the debit have increased by the amount of the purchase.

SPECIAL MEMORANDUM ACCOUNT (SMA) LONG MARGIN ACCOUNT

When a customer's equity increases to over 50 percent of the LMV, it is credited to the special memorandum account, or SMA. A customer's SMA is like a line of credit. Once SMA has been created, it will remain in place until it is used by the customer. A customer may use SMA to:

- Purchase additional securities.
- Have funds sent out by check.

A decline in the LMV in the account will not affect the customer's SMA. Customers may always use their SMAs unless doing so would cause the account to fall below the minimum equity requirement. SMA will be created by any of the following:

- An increase in the LMV.
- A nonrequired cash deposit.
- Receipt of dividends or interest.
- A nonrequired deposit of fully paid for marginable securities.
- 50 percent of the proceeds from a sale of securities will be credited to the SMA.

TAKENOTE!

A customer's SMA is the greater of the excess equity or the amount of SMA already established by the account.

EXAMPLE A customer's margin account is as follows:

LMV	Debit
60,000	40,000

EQ 20,000
Reg. T 30,000
EE 0
SMA 5,000

TAKENOTE!

The customer's margin account is restricted because the equity is below the Reg. T requirement. If the customer in this case uses the SMA of $5,000 to purchase $10,000 worth of stock, their account will look as follows:

LMV	Debit
70,000	50,000

EQ	20,000
Reg. T	35,000
EE	0
SMA	0

The customer was able to use the SMA to purchase the stock because doing so did not cause the account to fall below the minimum equity requirement of 25 percent. An investor may never use SMA to meet a margin call.

A DECREASE IN THE LONG MARKET VALUE

A decrease in the LMV of the securities in a margin account will cause the customer's equity to fall. Should the equity in the customer's account fall below 50 percent of the current market value, the account becomes restricted. A customer whose account is restricted may still:

- Buy additional marginable securities and deposit 50 percent.
- Sell securities and withdraw 50 percent of the proceeds.
- Withdraw securities by depositing 50 percent of their value in cash or by depositing securities with a loan value of 50 percent.

TAKENOTE!

If a customer wants to withdraw cash from a restricted margin account, they must deposit marginable securities with a loan value equal to the amount of the cash withdrawn from the account.

THE MINIMUM EQUITY REQUIREMENT FOR LONG MARGIN ACCOUNTS

Once the Reg. T deposit has been made by the investor, the NYSE or FINRA set the minimum account equity that must be maintained by the investor. An investor is required to maintain a minimum equity equal to 25 percent of the LMV of the account. If the investor's equity falls below the minimum, the investor will receive a margin or maintenance call. A maintenance call can be met by:

- Depositing cash.
- Depositing marginable securities with a loan value equal to the call.
- Selling securities.

All margin calls must be met promptly. If the investor fails to meet the call, the firm will liquidate enough of the customer's securities to satisfy the call.

To determine the minimum equity at a given LMV, use the following formula:

minimum equity = LMV × 25%

EXAMPLE

A customer has a margin account with a LMV of $50,000. The customer's minimum equity would be found as follows:

$50,000 × .25 = $12,500

To determine how far a customer's account value can fall in order to be at the minimum equity requirement, use the following formula:

minimum equity = debit balance/.75

If a customer purchased $40,000 worth of securities and made the required deposit, the customer's account would look as follows:

LMV	Debit
40,000	20,000

EQ 20,000

Using the above formula to determine how low the market value could fall for the account to be at the minimum equity, we get:

$20,000/.75 = $26,667

At the $26,667 level, the account is at the minimum equity of 25 percent. If the value falls any lower, the investor will receive a margin call.

ESTABLISHING A SHORT POSITION IN A MARGIN ACCOUNT

All short sales must be done in a margin account. Prior to establishing the short position, the customer must first borrow the stock that he or she wishes to sell short. The customer is required to deposit 50 percent of the market value of the borrowed shares to ensure that the customer has the resources to repurchase the shares if the stock price rises. The customer's deposit establishes the customer's equity in the account. The customer may meet the Reg. T requirement by depositing cash or fully paid for marginable securities with a loan value equal to the Reg. T requirement. In order to establish a short position in a new margin account, the investor must deposit the greater of $2,000 or 50 percent of the borrowed securities' market value. Special rules are in place for customers who want to sell low-priced stocks short. If the stock sold short is less than $5 per share the required deposit is the greater of 100% of the market value or $2.50 per share.

EXAMPLE

Sold Short	Minimum Equity	Reg. T at 50%	Required Deposit
1,000 ABC at 50	$2,000	$25,000	$25,000
1,000 XYZ at 20	$2,000	$10,000	$10,000
100 RTY at 30	$2,000	$1,500	$2,000
100 KLM at 15	$2,000	$750	$2,000
1,000 FGTK @ 3	$2,000	$1,500	$3,000

The credit balance in a short margin account remains constant while the short market value (SMV) changes. To determine the equity in a short margin account, use the following formula:

equity = credit balance – short market value

Let's look at the account of a customer who sells 1,000 XYZ short at $40 per share. The customer's account will look as follows:

Credit	SMV
60,000	40,000

EQ 20,000

The credit of $60,000 was created from the proceeds from the short sale of 1,000 XYZ at 40 and the investor's Reg. T deposit of $20,000.

A DECREASE IN THE SHORT MARKET VALUE

A customer who has sold stock short hopes that the value of the stock will fall and that he will be able to buy it back cheaper and replace it. As a result, as the SMV of the account falls, the investor's equity will increase. The credit balance in a short margin account remains constant while the SMV changes.

Let's look at what happens to the same account if XYZ falls to $30 per share:

Original Position

Credit	SMV
60,000	40,000
	EQ 20,000

XYZ at $30

Credit	SMV
60,000	30,000
	EQ 30,000

Notice that as the SMV of the account fell from $40,000 to $30,000 the investor's equity increased from $20,000 to $30,000.

SPECIAL MEMORANDUM ACCOUNT (SMA) SHORT MARGIN ACCOUNT

When a customer's equity increases to over 50 percent of the SMV, it is credited to the special memorandum account, or SMA. A customer may use SMA in a short margin account to:

- Sell short additional securities.
- Have it sent out by check.

To determine if the customer has excess equity in a short margin account, use the following formula:

excess equity = customer's equity – Reg. T requirement of SMV

Let's look at the account again after XYZ has fallen to $30 per share.

Credit	SMV
60,000	30,000

EQ 30,000
Reg. T at 30 15,000
EE 15,000
SMA 15,000

As the SMV of the account has fallen, the investor's equity has increased. The customer's excess equity is credited to SMA, just as in a long margin account. In this case, the customer may sell short an additional $30,000 worth of securities based on the SMA.

Let's look at the account if the investor sells short additional securities valued at $30,000.

Credit	SMV
90,000	60,000

EQ 30,000
Reg. T 30,000
EE 0
SMA 0

The customer's account has exactly 50 percent equity, as required by Reg. T.

Let's look at the account if the customer withdraws the excess equity instead of selling additional securities short.

Credit	SMV
45,000	30,000

EQ 15,000
Reg. T at 30 15,000
EE 0
SMA 0

AN INCREASE IN THE SHORT MARKET VALUE

An increase in the SMV in a short margin account will cause the investor's equity to fall. Should the equity in the customer's account fall below

50 percent of the current SMV, the account becomes restricted. A customer whose account is restricted may still:

- Sell short additional securities and deposit 50 percent.
- Cover the short securities and withdraw 50 percent.

An increase in the SMV of the account will not affect the customer's SMA. The customer's SMA will be the greater of:

- The excess equity,

  or

- The SMA already established.

THE MINIMUM EQUITY REQUIREMENT FOR SHORT MARGIN ACCOUNTS

Once the Reg. T deposit has been made by the investor, the NYSE or FINRA set the minimum account equity that must be maintained by an investor who sells securities short. Because selling stock short involves unlimited risk, a higher level of minimum equity is required to be maintained. An investor is required to maintain a minimum equity equal to 30 percent of the short market value of the account. If the investor's equity falls below the minimum, the investor will receive a margin or maintenance call. A maintenance call can be met by:

- Depositing cash.
- Depositing marginable securities with a loan value equal to the call.
- Repurchasing securities.

All margin calls must be met promptly. If the investor fails to meet the call, the firm will repurchase enough of the customer's securities to satisfy the call.

To determine the minimum equity at a given SMV, use the following formula:

minimum equity = SMV × 30%

EXAMPLE

A customer has a margin account with a short market value of $50,000. The customer's minimum equity would be found as follows:

$50,000 × .30 = $15,000

To determine how high the short market value can rise in order to be at the minimum equity requirement, use the following formula:

minimum equity = total credit balance/1.30

If a customer sold short $50,000 worth of securities and made the required deposit, the customer's account would look as follows:

Credit	SMV
75,000	50,000
	EQ 25,000

Using the above formula to determine how high the market value could rise for the account to be at the minimum equity we get:

$75,000/1.3 = $57,693

At the $57,693 level, the account is at the minimum equity of 30 percent. If the value rises any higher, the investor will receive a margin call. If the investor has sold short low-priced securities the minimum is as follows:

- 100 percent of the market value or $2.50 per share, whichever is greater for stock under $5.
- 30 percent of the market value or $5 per share, whichever is greater for stock over $5.

MARGIN REQUIREMENTS FOR DAY TRADING

Special margin requirements are in place for pattern day traders. A pattern day trader is one who day trades four or more times in a five-day period. A day trade is defined as a purchase and sale entered for the same security on the same day for the same number of shares; this is also called a round trip. The customer is flat at the end of the day. Also included in determining a day trade are positions held overnight and closed out the next day, prior to establishing another position. The minimum initial equity requirement for a pattern day trader increases from $2,000 to $25,000. A pattern day trader's buying power is four times the investor's maintenance margin excess. If the trader exceeds this limit during the course of a day, the trader will receive a day trading margin call. The trader must meet the call within five business days. During the time the call is outstanding, the trader's buying power is limited to twice the maintenance excess. If the call is not met within four business days, the account will become restricted for 90 days, and the buying power will be limited to the available cash in the account. All deposits used to meet a day trading margin call must remain in the account for at least two business days. Pattern day traders may not use cross guarantees. This means that the resources of the day trading account must meet the requirements for that account independently. Day traders may not use the accounts of others or use other accounts owned by the day trader to meet the obligations of the day trading account.

TAKE**NOTE!**

If a customer meets the requirements of a pattern day trader but the number of day trades in a five-day period is 6 percent or less of all the trades in the account during the five-day period, the individual will not be considered a pattern day trader.

COMBINED MARGIN ACCOUNTS

Investors may wish to purchase securities that they feel will rise and sell short securities that they feel will fall. An investor establishing both long and short positions in a margin account is said to have a combined account. The investor will have to determine:

- The Reg. T requirement on the long side.
- The Reg. T requirement on the short side.
- The minimum equity on the long side.
- The minimum equity on the short side.

Let's look at a combined account that has the following:

LMV = $60,000

Debit = $25,000

SMV = $40,000

Credit = $62,000

To determine the customer's equity in a combined account, use the following formula:

(LMV – debit) + (credit – SMV) = equity

Using the above example, we get:

(60,000 – 25,000) + (62,000 – 40,000) = $57,000

If you are asked to determine the minimum equity for a combined account, you must determine the minimum equity on the long side and the minimum equity on the short side and then add them together.

PORTFOLIO MARGIN ACCOUNTS

Broker dealers may offer sophisticated investors who properly hedge their positions portfolio-based margin. In contrast to strategy-based margin, which calculates the margin requirement for all positions in the account separately, portfolio-based margin calculates the potential losses in the account based on all of the positions and offsetting hedges to determine the investor's margin requirement. An institutional investor who is long a basket of S&P 500 stocks and short S&P 500 futures has dramatically lower risk than an investor who is outright long with no hedges. Broker dealers will use an SEC-approved risk modeling system to determine both the risk to the portfolio and the amount of margin required to hold the positions. Portfolio-based margin calculations generally result in lower overall margin requirements and increased leverage. As a result, portfolio margin is only offered to the largest and most sophisticated investors, such as hedge funds, broker dealers, members of a futures exchange, and accounts with $5,000,000 or more in equity who have been approved for uncovered option writing. If an account approved for portfolio margin receives a margin call, it must be met in three business days.

SECURITIES BACKED LINES OF CREDIT

Some broker dealers allow customers to have a line of credit attached to their account, which allows the investor to borrow funds based on the value of the fully paid for assets in the account. This is not a margin loan used to purchase securities. In some ways it functions like a home equity line of credit that allows the investor to borrow from the broker dealer to meet their cash needs or to pay for a large purchase such as a home renovation. Firms must have proper procedures in place to make sure the customers and the representatives understand the loan restrictions and features. Customers must understand how a fall in the market value of the securities in the account can impact their ability to borrow. Additionally, a significant fall in the value may also require additional collateral or a portion of the loan to be repaid.

MINIMUM MARGIN FOR LEVERAGED ETFs

To determine the minimum equity requirement for an exchange-traded fund that employs leverage to return a multiple of the performance or inverse performance of an index, you must multiply the minimum equity requirement by the leverage factor. Therefore, buying an ETF that uses a leverage factor of 2:1 or 200% would have a minimum equity requirement of 50%. (25% × 2). Buying an ETF that uses a leverage factor of 3:1 would have a minimum equity requirement of 75% (25% × 3). Investors who sell a leveraged ETF short would be subject to the 30% minimum requirement times the leveraged factor. Therefore selling an ETF short with a leverage factor of 3:1 or 300% would have a minimum equity requirement of 90% (30% × 3).

CHAPTER 8

Pretest

MARGIN ACCOUNTS

1. The minimum maintenance for a new margin account is set by:
   a. the Federal Reserve Board.
   b. Regulation T.
   c. NYSE/FINRA.
   d. the brokerage firm.

2. The initial minimum for a new margin account is:
   a. 50 percent of the purchase price.
   b. the greater of $2,000 or 50 percent of the purchase price.
   c. set by the Federal Reserve Board.
   d. set by the MSRB.

3. A margin customer must sign which of the following to pledge securities as collateral for the loan?
   a. Loan consent
   b. Rehypothecation agreement
   c. Hypothecation agreement
   d. Collateral agreement

4. An investor has an open margin account with $48,000 in LMV and a debit balance of $10,000. What is the investor's minimum equity at this level?

a. $24,000

b. $12,000

c. $13,333

d. $10,000

5. The initial margin requirement for municipal bonds is set by:

a. the NYSE.

b. Regulation T.

c. the MSRB.

d. the Federal Reserve Board.

6. A margin account has the following positions:

Long 500 ABC at 27
Long 1,500 XYZ at 42
Long 250 MCX at 80

The debit balance is $28,200. What is the minimum maintenance?

a. $24,125

b. $48,250

c. $22,500

d. $37,600

7. A customer buys $100,000 principal amount of New York Bridge and Tunnel revenue bonds at 54 in a margin account. How much must the customer deposit?

a. $7,000

b. $27,000

c. $54,000

d. $8,100

8. An investor in a new margin account purchases 200 XYZ at 20 and deposits $2,000. XYZ falls to $18, and the investor's equity falls to $1,600. Which of the following is true?
   a. The investor will receive a margin call for $200.
   b. No action by the investor is required at this time.
   c. The investor must deposit $400 to maintain the $2,000 minimum equity requirement.
   d. The position could be liquidated if the investor doesn't meet the current margin call.

9. You have an open margin account with an LMV of $125,000 and a debit balance of $54,000. How low can the value of the securities drop before you get a margin call?
   a. $72,000
   b. $100,000
   c. $67,500
   d. $93,750

10. Which of the following is true if a client uses SMA to withdraw $2,500 from a margin account?
    a. The SMA is reduced and the debit balance is reduced.
    b. The SMA is increased and the debit balance is increased.
    c. The SMA is reduced and the debit balance is increased.
    d. The SMA is reduced and the debit balance is not affected.

CHAPTER 9

Investment Companies and Other Products

INTRODUCTION

In this chapter, we will look at how an investment company pools investors' funds in order to purchase a diversified portfolio of securities. Series 24 principals will be supervising firms that transact business in investment company products, so it is imperative that candidates have a complete understanding of this material. Some of the test focus points will be on:

- Types of investment companies.
- Investment company structure.
- Investment company registration.
- Investment company taxation.
- Investment strategies and recommendations.
- Investor benefits.

INVESTMENT COMPANY PHILOSOPHY

An investment company is organized as either a corporation or as a trust. Individual investors' money is then pooled together in a single account and used to purchase securities that will have the greatest chance of helping the investment company reach its objectives. All investors jointly own the portfolio that is created through these pooled funds, and each investor has an undivided interest in the securities. No single shareholder has any right or claim that exceeds the rights or claims of any other shareholder, regardless of the size of the investment. Investment companies offer individual investors the opportunity to have their money managed by professionals who may otherwise only offer their services to large institutions. Through diversification, the investor may participate in the future growth or income generated from the large number of different securities contained in the portfolio. Both diversification and professional management should contribute significantly to the attainment of the objectives set forth by the investment company. There are many other features and benefits that may be offered to investors that will be examined later in this chapter.

TYPES OF INVESTMENT COMPANIES

All investment company offerings are subject to the Securities Act of 1933, which requires the investment company to register with the Securities and Exchange Commission (SEC) and to give all purchasers a prospectus. Investment companies are also subject to the Investment Company Act of 1940, which sets forth guidelines on how investment companies must operate. The Investment Company Act of 1940 breaks down investment companies into three different types:

- Face-amount certificate company
- Unit investment trust (UIT)
- Management investment company (mutual fund)

FACE-AMOUNT CERTIFICATE COMPANY

An investor may enter into a contract with an issuer of a face-amount certificate to contract to receive a stated or fixed amount of money (the face amount) at a stated date in the future. In exchange for this future sum, the investor must deposit an agreed lump sum or make scheduled installment payments over time. Face-amount certificates are rarely issued these days because most of the tax advantages that the investment once offered have been lost through changes in the tax laws.

UNIT INVESTMENT TRUST (UIT)

A unit investment trust (UIT) will invest either in a fixed portfolio of securities or a nonfixed portfolio of securities. A fixed UIT will traditionally invest in a large block of government or municipal debt. The bonds will be held until maturity, and the proceeds will be distributed to investors in the UIT. Once the proceeds have been distributed to the investors, the UIT will have achieved its objective and will cease to exist. A nonfixed UIT will purchase mutual fund shares in order to reach a stated objective. A nonfixed UIT is also known as a contractual plan. Both types of UITs are organized as a trust and operate as a holding company for the portfolio. UITs are not actively managed, and they do not have a board of directors or investment advisers. Both types of UITs issue units or shares of beneficial interest to investors, which represent an undivided interest in the underlying portfolio of securities. UITs must maintain a secondary market in the units or shares to offer some liquidity to investors.

MANAGEMENT INVESTMENT COMPANY (MUTUAL FUND)

A management investment company employs an investment adviser to manage a diversified portfolio of securities designed to obtain its stated investment objective. The management company may be organized as either an open-end company or as a closed-end company. The main difference between an open-end company and a closed-end company is how the shares are purchased and sold. An open-end company offers new shares to any investor who wants to invest. This is known as a continuous primary offering. Because the offering of new shares is continuous, the capitalization of the open-end fund is unlimited. Stated another way, an open-end fund may raise as much money as investors are willing to put in. An open-end fund must repurchase its own shares from investors who want to redeem them. There is no secondary market for open-end mutual fund shares. The shares must be purchased from the fund company and redeemed to the fund company. A closed-end fund offers common shares to investors through an initial public offering (IPO), just like a stock. Its capitalization is limited to the number of authorized shares that have been approved for sale. Shares of the closed-end fund will trade in the secondary market in investor-to-investor transactions on an exchange or in the over-the-counter market (OTC), just like common shares.

OPEN-END VS. CLOSED-END FUNDS

Although both open-end and closed-end funds are designed to achieve their stated investment objectives, the manner in which they operate is different. The following is a side-by-side comparison of the important features of both open-end and closed-end funds and shows how those features differ between the fund types:

Feature	Open End	Closed End
Capitalization	Unlimited continuous primary offering	Single fixed offering through IPO
Investor may purchase	Full and fractional shares	Full shares only
Securities offered	Common shares only	Common and preferred shares and debt securities
Shares are purchased and sold	Shares are purchased from the fund company and redeemed to the fund company	Shares may be purchased only from the fund company during IPO; secondary market transactions are between investors
Share pricing	Shares are priced by formula: NAV + SC = POP	Shares are priced by supply and demand
Shareholder rights	Dividends and voting	Dividends, voting, and preemptive

EXCHANGE-TRADED FUNDS (ETFS)

An exchange-traded fund, or ETF, is an equity security that represents an ownership interest in a basket or portfolio of underlying securities. Many ETFs are designed to track the performance of an underlying index, such as the S&P 500 or the Dow Jones Industrial Average. Both large and small investors use ETFs as a way to gain exposure to the performance of an index or an industry sector, such as technology or energy. ETFs, like traditional closed-end funds, allow investors to buy and sell the securities in the open market at any time during the trading day. Most ETFs are passively managed and maintain a fixed portfolio of securities. As a result, the expense ratios charged by these ETFs will be lower than the fees charged by the actively managed portfolios of traditional mutual funds or actively managed ETFs. ETFs provide investors with tax efficiency, reduced transaction costs, and diversification within an industry, sector, or geographic region. Not all ETFs will be suitable for all investors. The ETF's portfolio and objectives must meet the individual's investment objectives and risk tolerance.

EXCHANGE-TRADED NOTES (ETNs)

Exchange-traded notes (ETNs), sometimes known as equity linked notes or index linked notes, are debt securities that base a maturity payment on the performance of an underlying security or group of securities such as an index. ETNs do not make coupon or interest payments to investors during the time the investor owns the ETN. ETNs may be purchased and sold at any time during the trading day and may be purchased on margin and sold short. One very important risk factor to consider when evaluating an ETN is the fact that ETNs are unsecured and carry the credit risk of the issuing bank or broker dealer. Similarly, principal protected notes (PPNs), which are structured products that guarantee the return of the investor's principal if the note is held until maturity, carry a principal guarantee that is only as good as the issuer's credit rating and therefore are never 100 percent guaranteed.

ETFs THAT TRACK ALTERNATIVELY WEIGHTED INDICES

Investing in ETFs that track indexes has become a popular investment strategy. As a result, new products have come to market that track the performance of alternative indexes. Equal weight, alternatively weighted, fundamentally weighted, and volatility weighted ETFs offer exposure to other investment styles and may provide enhanced performance. These ETFs present additional risk factors that both registered representatives and investors need to understand. These funds are sometimes marketed as having better performance than other indices, which could be a cause for a concern as the ETFs that track these indices may be complex, thinly traded, and hard to understand for both representatives and retail investors. The lack of liquidity can lead to wider spreads, causing the product to be expensive to buy and sell for investors. The portfolios often have high turnover, which can lead to increased transaction costs for an ETF.

DIVERSIFIED VS. NONDIVERSIFIED

Investors in a mutual fund will achieve diversification through their investments in the fund. However, in order to determine if the fund itself is a diversified fund, the fund must meet certain requirements. The Investment Company Act of 1940 has laid out an asset allocation model that must be followed in order for the fund to call itself a diversified mutual fund. It is known as the 75-5-10 test, and the requirements are as follows:

75%: Seventy-five percent of the fund's assets must be invested in securities of other issuers. Cash and cash equivalents are counted as part of the 75 percent. A cash equivalent may be a Treasury bill or a money market instrument.

5%: The investment company may not invest more than 5 percent of its assets in any one company.

10%: The investment company may not own more than 10 percent of any company's outstanding voting stock.

EXAMPLE

XYZ fund markets itself as a diversified mutual fund. It has $10,000,000,000 in net assets. The fund's investment adviser thinks that the ABC Company would be a great company to acquire for $300,000,000. Because XYZ markets itself as a diversified mutual fund, it would not be allowed to purchase the company, even though the price of $300,000,000 would be less than 5 percent of the fund's assets. The investment company must meet both the diversification requirements of 5 percent of assets *and* 10 percent of ownership in order to continue to market itself as a diversified mutual fund.

INVESTMENT COMPANY REGISTRATION

Investment companies are regulated by both the Securities Act of 1933 and by the Investment Company Act of 1940. An investment company must register with the SEC if the company operates to own, invest, reinvest, or trade in securities. A company must also register with the SEC as an investment company if the company has 40 percent or more of its assets invested in securities other than those issued by the U.S. government or one of the company's subsidiaries.

REGISTRATION REQUIREMENTS

Before an investment company may register with the SEC, it must meet certain minimum requirements. An investment company may not register with the SEC unless it meets the following criteria:

- Minimum net worth of $100,000.
- At least 100 shareholders.
- Clearly defined investment objectives.

An investment company may be allowed to register without having 100 shareholders and without a net worth of $100,000 if it can meet these requirements within 90 days.

Investment companies must file a full registration with the SEC before the offering becomes effective. The investment company is considered to have registered when the SEC receives its notice of registration. The investment company's registration statement must contain:

- The type of investment company (open end, closed end, and so forth).
- Biographical information on the officers and directors of the company.
- Name and address of each affiliated person.
- Plans to concentrate investments in any one area (such as a sector fund).
- Plans to invest in real estate or commodities.
- Plans to borrow.
- Conditions under which investment objectives may be changed through a vote by shareholders.

Once registered the investment company may:

- Raise money through the sale of shares.
- Lend money to earn interest.
- Borrow money on a limited basis.

An investment company obtains its investment capital from shareholders through the sale of shares. Once it is operating, it may lend money to earn interest, such as by purchasing bonds or notes. An investment company may not, however, lend money to employees. An investment company may borrow money for such business purposes as to redeem shares. If the investment company borrows money, it must have $3 in equity for every dollar that it wants to borrow. Another way of saying this is that the investment company must maintain an asset-to-debt ratio of at least 3:1, or at least 300 percent.

An investment company is prohibited from:

- Taking over or controlling other companies.
- Acting as a bank or a savings and loan.
- Receiving commission for executing orders or for acting as a broker.
- Continuing to operate with less than 100 shareholders or less than $100,000 net worth.

Unless the investment company meets strict capital and disclosure requirements it may not engage in any of the following:

- Selling securities short.
- Buying securities on margin.
- Maintaining joint accounts.
- Distributing its own shares.

Regardless of the makeup of its investment holdings, all of the following are exempt from the registration requirements of an investment company:

- Broker dealers
- Underwriters
- Banks and savings and loans
- Mortgage companies
- Real estate investment trusts (REITs)
- Security holder protection committees

INVESTMENT COMPANY COMPONENTS

Investment companies have several different groups that serve specialized functions. Each of these groups plays a key role in the investment company's operation. They are:

- The board of directors
- The investment adviser
- The custodian bank
- The transfer agent

BOARD OF DIRECTORS

Management companies have an organizational structure that is similar to that of other companies. The board of directors oversees the company's president and other officers who run the day-to-day operations of the company. The board and the corporate officers concern themselves with the business and administrative functions of the company. They do not manage the investment portfolio. The board of directors:

- Defines the investment objectives.
- Hires the investment adviser, custodian bank, and transfer agent.
- Determines what type of funds to offer, such as growth or income.

The board of directors is elected by a vote of the shareholders. The Investment Company Act of 1940 governs the makeup of the board. All directors must serve for a minimum of 1 year and may not serve for more than 5 years without being reelected. The Investment Company Act of 1940 requires that at least a majority of the board be noninterested persons. A noninterested person is a person whose only affiliation with the fund is as a member of the board. Therefore, a maximum of 49 percent or less than 50 percent of the board may hold another position within the fund company or may otherwise be interested in the fund. A noninterested person is not deemed to be an interested person simply due to the fact that he or she is a member of the board or advisory committee. An affiliated person is anyone who could exercise control over the company, such as:

- Officers, directors, and employees of the investment company.
- The investment adviser.
- A company in which the investment company owns at least 5 percent of the voting stock.
- Any entity owning 5 percent or more of the investment company's voting stock.
- The person who deposits the assets of a UIT into the custodian bank.

An interested person includes:

- All broker dealers.
- Anyone who has been an attorney, investment adviser, affiliated person, or the principal underwriter for the investment company within the last two years.
- The principal underwriter.
- Employees of the investment adviser.
- Most affiliated persons.
- Immediate family of an affiliated person.
- Anyone else the SEC designates.

Both affiliated and interested parties are prohibited from selling securities or property to the investment company or any of its subsidiaries. Anyone who has been convicted of any felony or securities-related misdemeanor or who has been barred from the securities business may not serve on the board of directors.

BONDING OF KEY INVESTMENT COMPANY EMPLOYEES

The investment company is required to obtain a bond to cover itself and each officer, director, and employee with access to the investment company's assets. The company may obtain a bond for each employee or it may obtain a blanket bond for all employees that are required to be bonded. In the case of a blanket bond, the company must list the names of the employees to be covered. The bond only covers the employees for negligence. Any criminal acts or acts of bad faith are not covered.

INVESTMENT ADVISER

The investment company's board of directors hires the investment adviser to manage the fund's portfolio. The investment adviser is a company, not a person. The investment adviser must determine the tax consequences of distributions to shareholders and ensure that the fund's investment strategies are in line with its stated investment objectives. The investment adviser's compensation is a percentage of the net assets of the fund, not a percentage of the profits, although performance bonuses are allowed. The investment adviser's fee is typically the largest expense of the fund, and the more aggressive the objective, the higher the fee. The investment adviser may not borrow from the fund and may not have any securities-related convictions. The investment adviser's contract requires initial and annual reapproval by a majority vote of the board of directors and the outstanding shares.

CUSTODIAN BANK

The custodian bank, or the exchange member broker dealer that has been hired by the investment company, physically holds all of the fund's cash and securities. The custodian holds all of the fund's assets for safekeeping and provides other bookkeeping and clerical functions for the investment company, such as maintaining books and records for accumulation plans for investors. All fund assets must be kept segregated from other assets. The custodian must ensure that only approved persons have access to the account and that all distributions are done in line with SEC guidelines.

TRANSFER AGENT

The transfer agent for the investment company handles the issuance, cancellation, and redemption of fund shares. The transfer agent also handles name changes and may be part of the fund's custodian bank or a separate company. The transfer agent receives an agreed upon fee for its services.

MUTUAL FUND DISTRIBUTION

Most mutual funds do not sell their own shares directly to investors. The distribution of the shares is the responsibility of the underwriter. The underwriter for a mutual fund is also known as the sponsor or distributor. The underwriter is selected by the fund's board of directors and receives a fee in the form of a sales charge (SC) for the shares it distributes. As the underwriter receives orders for the mutual fund shares, it purchases the shares directly from the fund at the net asset value (NAV). The sales charge is then added to the NAV as the underwriter's compensation. This process of adding the sales charge to the NAV is responsible for the mutual fund pricing formula, which is NAV + SC = public offering price (POP). The underwriter may purchase shares from the mutual fund only to fill customer orders. It may not hold mutual fund shares in inventory in anticipation of receiving future customer orders.

TAKENOTE!

Mutual fund wholesalers will often visit member firms to update the firm and its employees on the features of the funds offered. On many occasions, the wholesalers will cater a lunch for the firm. All employees, both registered and unregistered, may have a meal provided by the fund company.

SELLING GROUP MEMBER

Most brokerage firms maintain selling agreements with mutual fund distributors, which allows them to purchase mutual fund shares at a discount from the POP. Selling group members may then sell the mutual fund shares to investors at the POP and earn part of the sales charge. In order to purchase mutual fund shares at a discount from the POP, the selling group member must be a member of FINRA. All non-FINRA members and suspended members must be treated as members of the general public and pay the POP.

DISTRIBUTION OF NO-LOAD MUTUAL FUND SHARES

No-load mutual funds do not charge a sales charge to its investors. Because there is no sales charge, the mutual fund may sell the shares directly to investors at the NAV.

DISTRIBUTION OF MUTUAL FUND SHARES

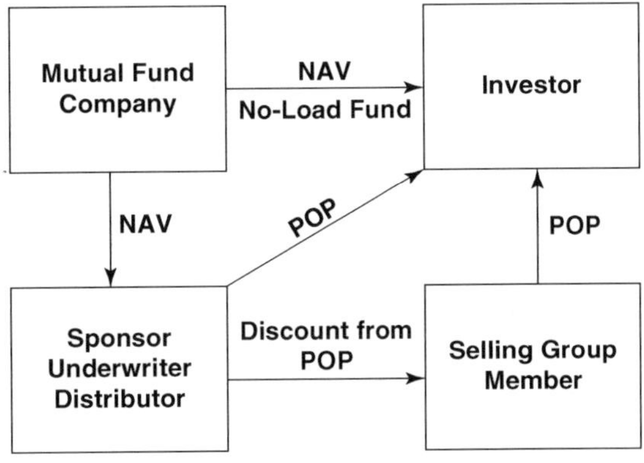

MUTUAL FUND PROSPECTUS

The prospectus is the official offering document for open-end mutual fund shares. The prospectus, or information on where to obtain a prospectus, must be presented to all purchasers of the fund either before or during the sales presentation. The prospectus is the fund's full-disclosure document and provides details regarding:

- The fund's investment objectives.
- Sales charges.
- Management expenses.
- Fund services.
- Performance data for the past one, five, and 10 years or for the life of the fund.

The prospectus that is given to most investors is the summary prospectus. If the investor wants additional information regarding the mutual fund, the investor may request a statement of additional information. The statement of additional information will include details regarding the following as of the date it was published:

- The fund's securities holdings.
- A balance sheet.
- An income statement.
- Portfolio turnover data.
- Compensation paid to the board of directors and investment advisory board.

A summary prospectus that contains past performance data is known as an advertising prospectus. A mutual fund prospectus:

- Should be updated by the fund every 12 months.
- Must be updated by the fund every 13 months.
- May be used by a representative for up to 16 months.
- Should be discarded after 16 months from publication.

TAKENOTE!

The date of the financial information is the date that is used to calculate when a mutual fund prospectus must be updated and how long it may be used. This is not always the same date that is on the cover of the prospectus.

Mutual funds are also required to disclose either in the prospectus or in its annual report to shareholders:

- A performance comparison graph showing the fund's performance.
- Names of the officers and directors who are responsible for the portfolio's day-to-day management.
- Disclosure of any factors that materially affected performance over the latest fiscal year.

All mutual fund investors must receive an annual audit report and a semiannual update. The annual report must include:

- A balance sheet.
- An income statement.
- The valuation of all securities held in the investment company's portfolio.
- A complete statement regarding compensation to the board of directors, officers, and investment adviser.
- A statement detailing the total value of all securities purchased and sold.

Mutual funds are required to include summary information at the front of its statutory prospectus. The purpose of this summary information is to clearly convey all of the most pertinent information an investor would require to make an informed decision about the fund. The terms to be detailed in the summary information include the fund's investment objectives, past performance, costs, and the biographical information for the management of the fund. Also covered in the summary information will be the principal investment strategies, compensation, purchase and redemptions, and tax implications. Mutual funds may use this information to create a "mutual fund profile" for investors. Investors may use the profile to purchase the mutual fund shares but the investor must be given information on where to obtain a statutory prospectus and the statement of additional information for the fund.

ADDITIONAL DISCLOSURES BY A MUTUAL FUND

An open-end mutual fund must disclose in its statement of additional information how it votes the proxies it receives for securities held by the fund. A closed-end fund will disclose this on Form N-CSR. All management companies must file their complete proxy voting record annually by August 31 for the 12 months ending June 30. They will file the information on Form N-PX. Shareholders that request this information must be sent a copy within three business days.

ANTI-RECIPROCAL RULE

A mutual fund may not select a broker dealer to execute the orders for its portfolios based on the dollar amount of the mutual fund that the broker dealer sells. The fund's selection of broker dealers to execute orders and to provide other services must be based solely on the merits of the broker dealer performing the service. Alternatively, a brokerage firm may not recommend a mutual fund to a client based on the amount of commission the firm receives from executing the mutual fund's securities transactions. A broker dealer also may not:

- Allow a registered representative to share in the commission revenue generated by the execution of the fund's order to induce the representative to sell more mutual fund shares.
- Use the amount of sales of the fund as a way to leverage a higher rate on the fund's execution business.
- Create a list of preferred funds based on the amount of commission business that the funds give the clients.

MONEY MARKET FUNDS

Money market funds invest in short-term money market instruments, such as bankers' acceptances, commercial paper, and other debt securities with less than one year remaining to maturity. Money market funds are no-load funds that offer the investor the highest degree of safety of principal as well as current income. The NAV for money market funds is always equal to $1; however, this is not guaranteed. Investors use money market funds as a place to hold idle funds and to earn current income. Interest is earned by investors daily and is credited to their accounts monthly. Most money market funds offer check-writing privileges, and investors must receive a prospectus prior to investing or opening an account.

MONEY MARKET GUIDELINES

Money market funds must adhere to certain guidelines in order to qualify as a money market fund, such as:

- The prospectus must clearly state on its cover that the fund is not insured or guaranteed by the U.S. government and that the fund's net asset value may fall below $1.
- Securities in the portfolio may have a maximum maturity of 13 months.
- The average maturity for securities in the portfolio may not exceed 90 days.

- No more than 5 percent of the fund's assets may be invested in any one issuer's debt securities.
- Investments are limited to the top two ratings awarded by a nationally recognized ratings agency such as Standard & Poor's or Moody's.
- 95 percent of the portfolio must be in the top ratings category with no more than 5 percent being invested in the second tier.

VALUING MUTUAL FUND SHARES

Mutual funds must determine the NAV of the fund's shares at least once per business day. Most mutual funds will price their shares at the close of business of the NYSE (4 p.m. EST). The mutual fund prospectus will provide the best answer as to when the fund calculates the price of its shares. The calculation is required to determine both the redemption price (NAV) and the purchase price (POP) of the fund's shares. The price that is received by an investor who is redeeming shares and the price that is paid by an investor who is purchasing shares will be based on the price that is next calculated after the fund has received the investor's order. This is known as forward pricing. To calculate the fund's NAV, use the following formula:

assets – liabilities = net asset value (NAV)

To determine the NAV per share, simply divide the total net asset value by the total number of outstanding shares.

$$\frac{\textbf{total NAV}}{\textbf{total \# of shares}}$$

If XYZ mutual fund has $10,000,000 in assets and $500,000 in liabilities, what is the fund's NAV?

assets – liabilities = NAV

$10,000,000 – $500,000 = $9,500,000

If XYZ has 1,000,000 shares outstanding, its NAV per share would be:

$$\frac{\textbf{total NAV}}{\textbf{total \# of shares}} \qquad \frac{\textbf{\$9,500,000}}{\textbf{1,000,000}}$$

NAV per share = $9.50

CHANGES IN THE NAV

The net asset value of a mutual fund is constantly changing as security prices fluctuate and as the mutual fund conducts its business. The following illustrates how the NAV per share will be affected given certain events.

INCREASES IN THE NAV

The net asset value of the mutual fund will increase if:

- The value of the securities in the portfolio increases.
- The portfolio receives investment income, such as interest payments from bonds.

DECREASES IN THE NAV

The net asset value will decrease if:

- The value of the securities in the portfolio falls.
- The fund distributes dividends or capital gains.

NO EFFECT ON THE NAV

The following will have no effect on the net asset value of the mutual fund share:

- Investor purchases and redemptions
- Portfolio purchases and sales of securities
- Sales charges

SALES CHARGES FOR OPEN-END FUNDS

The maximum allowable sales charge that an open-end fund may charge is 8.5 percent of the POP. The sales charge that may be assessed by a particular fund will be detailed in the fund's prospectus. It is important to note that the sales charge is not an expense of the fund; it is a cost of distribution, which is borne by the investor. The sales charges pay for all of the following:

- Underwriters' commission.
- Commission to brokerage firms and registered representatives.

SALES CHARGES FOR CLOSED-END FUNDS

Closed-end funds do not charge a sales charge to invest. An investor who wants to purchase a closed-end fund will pay the current market price, plus whatever the brokerage firm charges to execute the order.

FRONT-END LOADS

A front-end load is a sales charge that the investor pays when purchasing shares. The sales charge is added to the NAV of the fund, and the investor purchases the shares at the POP. The sales charge, in essence, is deducted from the gross amount invested, and the remaining amount is invested in the portfolio at the NAV. Shares that charge a front-end load are known as A shares.

EXAMPLE XYZ mutual fund has a NAV of $9.50, a POP of $10, and a sales charge of 5 percent. How much in sales charges would an investor pay when investing $10,000 in the fund?

$10,000
× 5%
$500 = sales charge

$10,000
– $500
$9,500 invested in the portfolio at NAV

BACK-END LOADS

A back-end load is also known as a contingent deferred sales charge (CDSC). An investor in a fund that charges a back-end load will pay the sales charge at the time of redemption of the fund shares. The sales charge will be assessed on the value of the shares that have been redeemed, and the amount of the sales charge will decline as the holding period for the investor increases. The following is a hypothetical back-end load schedule:

Years Money Left in Portfolio	Sales Charge
1	8.5%
2	7%
3	5%
4	3%
5	1.5%
5 years or more	0%

The mutual fund prospectus will detail the particular schedule for back-end load sales charges. Mutual fund shares that charge a back-end load are also known as B shares.

OTHER TYPES OF SALES CHARGES

A mutual fund can assess sales charges in a variety of other ways. Shares that charge a level load based on the NAV are known as level-load funds, or C shares. Shares that charge an asset-based fee and a back-end load are known as D shares.

RECOMMENDING MUTUAL FUNDS

Mutual funds are designed to be longer term investments and are generally not used to time the market. When determining suitability for investors the registered representative must first make sure that the investment objective of the mutual fund matches the investor's objective. Once several funds have been selected that meet the client's objective, the representative must then compare costs, fees, and expenses among the funds. Priority should be given to any fund company with whom the investor maintains an investment. If the client's objective has changed, the fund most likely offers conversion privileges, which will allow the investor to move into another portfolio without paying any sales charge. If the investor is committing new capital the fund company most likely offers combination privileges and rights of accumulation, which will help the investor reach a sale charge reduction. Switching fund companies and/or spreading out investment dollars among different fund companies are red flags for breakpoint sale violations and abusive sales practices. The amount of time the investor is seeking to hold the investment will be a determining factor as to which share class is the most appropriate. Investors who have longer holding periods may be better off in B shares that assess a sales charge upon redemption based on their holding period. Investors who have shorter time horizons will be better off choosing A shares over B shares as the expenses associated with B shares tend to be higher. Important to note is that making a large investment in class B shares is a red flag for a breakpoint sale violation as the large dollar amount would have most likely resulted in a reduced sales charge for the investor. Investors with relatively short holding periods or who want to actively move money between funds to try to time the market would be best off with C shares, which charge a level load each year.

TAKENOTE!

Based on the fees and CDSC, a mutual fund with a front-end load may be more suitable for an investor with a shorter holding period if all other suitability requirements have been met by both funds.

12B-1 FEES

Most mutual funds charge an asset-based distribution fee to cover expenses related to the promotion and distribution of the fund's shares. The amount of the fee will be determined annually as a percentage of the NAV or as a flat fee. The 12B-1 fee will be charged to the shares quarterly, reducing the investor's overall return on the fund. Because a 12B-1 fee reduces the return, it is a type of sales load. 12B-1 fees cover such things as the printing of prospectuses and certain sales commissions to agents. To start and continue a 12B-1 fee, three votes must initially approve the fee and annually reapprove it. The three votes that are required are:

- A majority vote of the board of directors.
- A majority vote of the noninterested board of directors.
- A majority vote of the outstanding shares.

To terminate a 12B-1 fee, only two votes are required. They are:

- A majority vote of the noninterested board of directors.
- A majority vote of the outstanding shares.

LIMITS OF A 12B-1 FEE

A mutual fund that distributes its own shares and markets itself as a no-load fund may charge a 12B-1 fee that is no more than .25 percent. If the fund charges a 12B-1 fee that is greater than .25 percent, it may not be called a no-load fund. Other funds that do not call themselves a no-load fund are limited to .75 percent of assets, and the amount of the 12B-1 fee must be reasonably related to the anticipated level of expenses incurred for promotion and distribution. All 12B-1 fees are reviewed quarterly.

CALCULATING A MUTUAL FUND'S SALES CHARGE PERCENTAGE

Oftentimes an investor may know only the NAV and the POP for a given mutual fund and not the sales charge percentage that is charged by the fund.

To determine the sales charge percentage given the NAV and the POP, use the following formula:

$$SC\% = \frac{(POP - NAV)}{POP}$$

$$SC\% = \frac{(POP - NAV)}{POP} = \frac{(10 - 9.50)}{10} = \frac{.50}{\$10} = 5\%$$

FINDING THE PUBLIC OFFERING PRICE

There will also be times when an investor knows the NAV of a fund and the sales charge percentage but does not know the POP that must be paid to invest in the fund. To calculate the POP given the sales charge percentage and the NAV, use the following formula:

$$POP = \frac{NAV}{(100\% - SC\%)}$$

TESTFOCUS!

Again using fund XYZ, which has a NAV of $9.50 and a sales charge percentage of 5%, determine the POP by plugging the numbers into the formula as follows:

$$POP = \frac{9.50}{(100\% - SC\%)} = \frac{9.50}{(100\% - 5\%)} = \frac{9.50}{.95} = \$10.00$$

SALES CHARGE REDUCTIONS

The maximum allowable sales charge that may be assessed by an open-end mutual fund is 8.5 percent of the public offering price. If a mutual fund charges 8.5 percent, it must offer the following three privileges to investors:

- Breakpoint sales charge reductions that reduce the amount of the sales charge based on the dollar amount invested.
- Rights of accumulation that will reduce the sales charge on subsequent investments based on the value of the investor's account.

- Automatic reinvestment of dividends and capital gains at the NAV.

If a mutual fund does not offer all three of these benefits to investors, the maximum allowable sales charge that may be charged drops to 6.5 percent. Although a mutual fund that charges 8.5 percent must offer these features, most mutual funds that charge less than 8.5 percent also offer them. If the mutual fund pays a service fee to broker dealers for providing ongoing services to shareholders, the maximum sales charge that may be charged by the fund is 7.25 percent. FINRA members are prohibited from selling mutual funds that charge a service fee in excess of .25 percent.

BREAKPOINT SCHEDULE

As an incentive for investors to invest larger sums of money into a mutual fund, the mutual fund will reduce the sales charge based on the dollar amount of the purchase. Breakpoint sales charge reductions are available to any "person," including corporations, trusts, couples, and accounts for minors. Breakpoint sales charge reductions are not available to investment clubs or to parents and their adult children investing in separate accounts. The following is an example of a breakpoint schedule that a family of funds might use:

Dollar Amount Invested	Sales Charge
$1–24,999	8.5%
$25,000–74,999	7%
$75,000–149,999	5%
$150,000–499,999	3%
$500,000 or greater	1.5%

A breakpoint schedule benefits all parties—the fund company, the investor, and the representative. It is important to note that the fund's distributor will keep track of the investor's contributions to determine if the investor qualifies for a breakpoint. If the same investor holds the fund at different broker dealers the value of both accounts will be combined to determine breakpoint eligibility.

LETTER OF INTENT

An investor who might not be able to reach a breakpoint with a single purchase may qualify for a breakpoint sales charge reduction by signing a letter of intent. A letter of intent will give the investor up to 13 months to reach the dollar amount to which he or she subscribed. The letter of intent is binding only on the fund company, not on the investor. The additional shares that will be purchased as a result of the lower sales charge will be held by the fund company in an escrow account. If the investor fulfills the letter of intent, the shares are released. Should the investor fail to reach the breakpoint, the investor will be charged an adjustment to the sales charge. The investor may choose to pay the adjusted sales charge by either sending a check or by allowing some of the escrowed shares to be liquidated.

BACKDATING A LETTER OF INTENT

An investor may backdate a letter of intent up to 90 days to include a prior purchase, and the 13-month window starts from the back date. For example, if an investor backdates a letter of intent by the maximum 90 days allowed, then the investor has only 10 months to complete the letter of intent.

BREAKPOINT SALES

A breakpoint sale is a violation committed by a registered representative who is trying to earn larger commissions by recommending the purchase of mutual fund shares in a dollar amount that is just below the breakpoint, which would allow the investor to qualify for a reduced sales charge. A breakpoint violation may also be considered to have been committed if a representative spreads out a large sum of money over different families of funds. A registered representative must always notify an investor of the availability of a sales charge reduction, especially when the investor is depositing a sum of money that is close to the breakpoint.

RIGHTS OF ACCUMULATION

Rights of accumulation allow the investor to qualify for reduced sales charges on subsequent investments by taking into consideration the value of the investor's account, including the growth. Unlike a letter of intent, there is no time limit and, as the investor's account grows over time, the investor can qualify for lower sales charges on future investments. The sales charge reduction is not retroactive and does not reduce the sales charges on prior purchases. To qualify for the breakpoint, the dollar amount of the current purchase is calculated into the total value of the investor's account.

EXAMPLE

Using the breakpoint schedule from the previous page, let's look at an investor's account over the last three years:

	Deposit	Sales Charge
Year 1	$5,000	8.5%
Year 2	$5,000	8.5%
Year 3	$5,000	8.5%

Let's assume that the investor's account has increased in value by $6,000, making the total current value of the account $21,000. The investor has another $5,000 to invest this year, and because there is a sales charge reduction available at the $25,000 level, the investor will pay a sales charge of 7 percent on the new $5,000.

AUTOMATIC REINVESTMENT OF DISTRIBUTIONS

Investors may elect to have their distributions automatically reinvested in the fund and use the distributions to purchase more shares. Most mutual funds will allow the investor to purchase the shares at the NAV when they reinvest distributions. This feature has to be offered by mutual funds charging a sales charge of 8.5 percent. However, it is offered by most other mutual funds as well.

COMBINATION PRIVILEGES

Most mutual fund companies offer a variety of portfolios to meet different investment objectives. The different portfolios become known as a "family" of funds. Combination privileges allow an investor to combine the simultaneous purchases of two different portfolios to reach a breakpoint sales charge reduction.

EXAMPLE

An investor purchases $15,000 worth of an income fund and at the same time invests $40,000 in a growth portfolio offered by the same fund company. If the fund company offers a breakpoint sales charge reduction at $50,000, the investor would qualify for the lower sales charge under combination privileges.

CONVERSION OR EXCHANGE PRIVILEGES

Most mutual fund families will offer its investors conversion or exchange privileges that allow an investor to move money from one portfolio to another offered by the same fund company without paying another sales charge. Another way of looking at this is that the fund company allows the investor to redeem the shares of one portfolio at the NAV and use the proceeds to purchase shares of another portfolio at the NAV. The IRS sees this as a purchase and a sale, and the investor will have to pay taxes on any gain on the sale of portfolio shares. Investors who move money between portfolios charging a CDSC will have the amount of the CDSC based on the date of the purchase of the original portfolio.

Other exchange conditions are as follows:

- The dollar value of the purchase may not exceed the sales proceeds.
- The purchase of the new portfolio must occur within 30 days.
- The sale may not include a sales charge refund.
- No commission may be paid to a registered representative or broker dealer.

EXAMPLE

An aggressive investor has $20,000 invested in ABC high growth fund, which has a NAV of $12 and a POP of $12.60. The investor wants to move the money into the ABC biotech fund, which has a NAV of $17.20 and a POP of $17.90. ABC offers conversion privileges, so the investor will redeem the shares of the growth portfolio at $12 and will purchase 1,162.79 shares of the biotech portfolio at $17.20.

30-DAY EMERGENCY WITHDRAWAL

Many mutual funds will provide investors with access to their money in a time of unexpected financial need. If the investor needs to liquidate mutual fund shares for emergency purposes, the investor will be able to reinvest an equal sum of money at the portfolio's NAV if they reinvest the money within 30 days. This is usually a one-time privilege, and the NAV used to purchase the shares is the NAV on the day of the reinvestment.

TAKENOTE!

If a client redeems mutual fund shares within seven business days of purchase, the sales charge earned by the broker dealer and the representative is returned to the fund company.

VOTING RIGHTS

Mutual fund investors have the right to vote on major issues regarding the fund. All votes are won be a simple majority; that is, 51 percent of the outstanding shares will win the vote. It is important to distinguish that shares vote, not shareholders. An investor with 5,000 shares has five times as many votes as an investor with 1,000 shares, even though they are both shareholders. Among the major issues to be voted on are:

- Changing capitalization (going from an open-end to a closed-end fund).
- Changing the sales load (going from a loaded fund to a no-load fund).
- Changing or terminating business.
- Changing the investment objectives.
- Lending money.
- Entering into real estate transactions.
- Issuing or underwriting other securities.
- Changing borrowing policies.
- Electing the board of directors.
- Electing the investment adviser.
- Changing 12B-1 fees.

YIELDS

A mutual fund's current yield is found by dividing its annual dividends by its current market price, or POP. The higher the yield, the more income the fund produces for every dollar invested. A mutual fund's current yield may be based on dividends only, not on capital gains distributions.

annual income/POP = current yield

PORTFOLIO TURNOVER

Portfolio turnover rates will tell you how long the fund holds its securities. The higher the rate, the shorter the fund's holding period. Higher portfolio turnover causes the fund to incur additional expenses in the form of execution charges. A turnover rate of 100 percent means that the fund replaces its portfolio annually.

VOLUNTARY ACCUMULATION PLANS

Mutual fund investors may set up a schedule to invest regularly into a specific mutual fund. The investor may simply send the money to the fund or may allow the fund to debit a checking account. Some funds require a minimum initial investment. An investor should check the fund prospectus for particulars. If the investor skips a scheduled investment, there is no penalty.

DOLLAR-COST AVERAGING

One of the more popular methods to accumulate mutual fund shares is through a process known as dollar-cost averaging. An investor purchases mutual fund shares through regularly scheduled investments of a fixed dollar amount. An investor may elect to invest $100 a month into a mutual fund by having the fund company debit a checking account. As the share price of the mutual fund fluctuates, the investor's $100 investment will purchase fewer shares when the market price of the mutual fund share is high and will purchase more shares when the market price is low. As the market price of the mutual fund share continues to fluctuate over time, the investor's average cost per share should always be lower than their average price per share, allowing the investor to liquidate the shares at a profit. Dollar-cost averaging does not, however, guarantee a profit, because a mutual fund share could continue to decline until the share price hits zero. All Series 6 candidates should be able to determine an investor's average cost and average price per share.

 TESTFOCUS!

Let's look at the dollar-cost averaging results for an investor who is depositing $100 a month into a mutual fund whose share price has been fluctuating widely over that time.

Investment	Share Price	Number of Shares Purchased
$100	$20	5
$100	$12.5	8
$100	$10	10
$100	$25	4
$400	$67.5	27 total shares

In order to calculate the investor's average cost per share, use the following formula:

$$\text{average cost} = \frac{\text{total dollars invested}}{\text{total \# of shares invested}}$$

Using the numbers from the example, we get:

$$\text{average cost} = \frac{\$400}{27} = \$14.81$$

In order to determine the average price that the investor paid per share, use the following formula:

$$\text{average price} = \frac{\text{total of purchase prices}}{\text{number of purchases}}$$

Using the numbers from the example we get:

$$\text{average price} = \frac{67.5}{4} = \$16.875$$

The example illustrates the effects of dollar-cost averaging in a mutual fund with a fluctuating market price. The result is an average cost per share that is significantly lower than the investor's average price per share. The change in the mutual fund share price is more dramatic than will usually be experienced in real life, and the investor would normally have to invest in the fund for a longer period of time before achieving similar results.

HEDGE FUNDS

A hedge fund is a private investment fund that pools the assets of sophisticated investors. Hedge funds are not regulated in the same way that traditional mutual funds are. However, the fund is still subject to the anti-fraud provisions of the Securities Acts and the Investment Advisers Act of 1940. Hedge funds will employ sophisticated and aggressive investment strategies utilizing enhanced leverage and derivative instruments. Hedge funds often take both long and short positions in the market depending on their investment objectives and outlook on the markets. Hedge funds are only suitable for the most sophisticated investors who are willing to speculate with their investment capital. Hedge fund participants at a minimum should be accredited investors. Many funds have high minimum investments of $5 million or more and often have lock-up periods during which withdrawals are not allowed. The legal structure of most hedge funds is as a limited liability company or a partnership. Some of the more speculative hedge funds are special purpose acquisition companies (SPAC), also known as blind pools or blank check companies. These types of companies raise money without identifying the specific assets to be acquired. Many of these funds will simply detail the industry in which they would like to make an acquisition but the specific target company is not identified. A blank check company often does not even state the industry it is looking to invest in.

Alternative funds, also known as alt funds or liquid alts, invest in non-traditional assets or illiquid assets and may employ alternative investment strategies. There is no standard definition for what constitutes an alt fund, but alt funds are often marketed as a way for retail investors to gain access to hedge funds and actively managed programs that will perform well in a variety of market conditions. These funds claim to reduce volatility, increase diversification, and produce higher returns when compared to long only equity funds and income funds, while providing liquidity. Recommendations for alt funds must be based on the specific strategies employed by the fund, not merely as one overall investment. Retail communication must accurately and fairly detail each fund's operations and objectives in line with the information in the prospectuses. FINRA is concerned that registered representatives and retail investors will not understand how funds will react in certain market conditions or how the fund managers will approach those market conditions. These funds must be reviewed during the new product review process even if the firm has a selling agreement with the fund.

FLOATING RATE BANK LOAN FUNDS

These funds invest in bank loans that are traditionally designed for institutional investors. More and more funds and ETFs available to retail investors are investing in these products. The loans are designed to hedge interest rate risk. However, the floating rate loans contain increased liquidity, credit, and call risks to the funds who invest in these products. Floating rate bank loans are also difficult to value and have long settlement times. Funds that invest in these products may have liquidity issues if faced with large redemptions.

STRUCTURED RETAIL PRODUCTS/SRPs

Members firms have been creating their own proprietary products for distribution and sale to retail investors. These SRPs include complex products such as structured notes with complicated payout structures. These SRPs may use proprietary indexes as reference assets that are hard to track, making the products difficult to understand for retail investors. The payout structure may also be based on longer terms and other conditions, adding to the complexity of the products. Firms must ensure that its representatives understand the performance characteristics and operational risks prior to recommending these products to investors. All members who create retail communications relating to SRPs must file the communications with FINRA within 10 business days of first use. FINRA is concerned that member firms, in an effort to increase revenue, will offer complex SRPs through distributors who do not have the knowledge or expertise to properly understand or recommend the products. If the member engages a wholesaler to sell its SRPs the member must have written supervisory procedures in place to "know your distributor," to ensure that the distribution channels have controls in place regarding the proper training of representatives who sell the products to customers. Additional concerns are created when there are potential conflicts of interest between the creator of the SRP and the wholesale distributor, such as when the two companies are affiliated.

REAL ESTATE INVESTMENT TRUSTS (REITs)

A real estate investment trust, or REIT, is a special type of equity security. REITs are organized for the specific purpose of buying, developing, or managing a portfolio of real estate. REITs may also be organized to provide mortgage financing and are known as mortgage REITs. Some hybrid REITs hold both a portfolio of real estate and mortgages. REITs are organized as a corporation or as a trust, and publicly traded REITs will trade on the exchanges or in the over-the-counter market just like other stocks. A REIT is organized as a conduit for the investment income generated by the portfolio of real estate. REITs are entitled to special tax treatment under Internal Revenue Code subchapter M. A REIT will not pay taxes at the corporate level so long as:

- It receives 75% of its income from real estate.
- It distributes at least 90% of its taxable income to shareholders.
- At least 95% of its income is derived from real estate activities

So long as the REIT meet the above requirements, the income will be allowed to flow through to the shareholders and will be taxed at their rate. Dividends received by REIT shareholders will continue to be taxed as ordinary income. It is important to note that REITs do not pass through gains and losses only income to investors.

NON-TRADED REITs

Non-traded real estate investment trusts or REITs lack liquidity, have high fees, and can be difficult to value. The fees for investing in a non-traded REIT may be as much as 15% of the per shares price. These fees include commissions and expenses which cannot exceed 10% of the offering price. Investors are often attracted to the high yields offered by these investments. Firms who conduct business in these products must conduct ongoing suitability determination on the REITs they recommend. Firms must react to red flags in the financial statements and from the REIT's management and adjust the recommendation process accordingly or stop recommending if material changes take place that would make the REIT unsuitable. Holding periods can be eight years or more and the opportunities to liquidate the investments may be very limited. Furthermore, the distributions from the REITs themselves may be based on the use of borrowed funds and may include a return of principal which may be adversely impacted and cause the distributions to be vulnerable to being significantly reduced or stopped altogether. Distributions may exceed cash flow and the amount of the distributions, if any, are at the discretion of the Board of Directors. Non-traded REITs like exchange-traded REITs must distribute 90% of the income to shareholders and must file annual reports (10-Ks) and quarterly reporrs (10-Qs) with the SEC. Broker dealers who sell non-traded REITs must provide investors with a valuation of the REIT within 18 months of the closing of the offering of shares. The issuer of the REIT must agree to provide valuation data within 150 days of the second anniversary of the offering's effective date (breaking of escrow) and annually thereafter.

NAV REAL ESTATE INVESTMENT TRUST

In an effort to attract investors who may otherwise not invest in non-traded REITs, many private offerings of REITs are now known as NAV REITs. These NAV REITs are designed to provide liquidity to investors while still paying the high distributions normally associated with non-traded REITs. The NAV REIT allows the investor to redeem their shares at the net asset value that is calculated by the sponsor on a daily, weekly, or monthly basis. In addition to the added liquidity, NAV REITs provide additional transparency regarding the value of each share or unit. Many of the same suitability requirements must be met prior to an investor purchasing shares in an NAV REIT; however, the ability to lock up their capital for an extended period of time is a much lower consideration when considering an NAV REIT.

COLLATERALIZED MORTGAGE OBLIGATION (CMO)

A collateralized mortgage obligation (CMO) is a mortgage-backed security issued by Government-sponsored entities (such as Fannie Mae and Freddie Mac), broker-dealers and private finance companies . The securities are structured much like a pass-through certificate and the terms are set into different maturity schedules, known as tranches. Pools of mortgages on one- to four-family homes collateralize CMOs. Investors in most CMOs receive monthly interest and principal payments based on the mortgage payments made by the homeowners. CMOs issued by Fannie Mae and Freddie Mac have largely had their credit risk offset through government guarantees. However, private label CMOS issued by broker-dealers carry the credit risk of the issuing entity even if all of the mortgages in the pool have been insured by government entities. Changing interest rates will impact the price of the CMO and the cash flow received by the investor. As interest rates change, homeowners tend to refinance homes based on the prevailing market rates. If interest rates rise, refinancing activity slows and in times of falling rates, refinancing activity accelerates. As a result the expected life and the ultimate yield for the CMO is subject to change. All retail communications relating to collateralized mortgage obligations must clearly disclose this fact to investors. Specifically, the communications must contain statements advising the client that the information regarding the yield and life of the CMO is based on certain prepayment assumptions and that those assumptions may or may not be met. To ensure that these required disclosures are included in print advertisements FINRA has created a standard CMO advertising template for use by member firms. Broker-dealers are free to use this template or to create their own provided that all of the required disclosures detailed in FINRA'S template are included. Television and radio advertisements are required to contain the same disclosures that appear in the template. Further, broker-dealers are required to provide retail investors with educational material covering the performance and risk characteristics of CMOs. This material must detail the impact changing interest rates have on CMOS, an explanation of the various tranches and a glossary detailing the relevant terms used. Because of the unique characteristics of CMOS, CMOS may not be compared to other interest-bearing investments such as bonds or other debt securities. Additionally, there are specific disclosures which must be made on a customer's confirmation. The nominal face value, nominal yield, anticipated average life and yield, final maturity date, the specific tranche and underlying securities must be disclosed on a customer's confirmation.

CHAPTER 9

Pretest

INVESTMENT COMPANIES AND OTHER PRODUCTS

1. An investor with $20,000 invested in the XYZ growth fund is:
   a. a stockholder in XYZ.
   b. an owner of XYZ.
   c. an owner of an undivided interest in the XYZ growth portfolio.
   d. both an owner of XYZ and an owner of an undivided interest in the XYZ growth portfolio.

2. All of the following benefit an investor, EXCEPT:
   a. combination privileges.
   b. emergency withdrawal privileges.
   c. breakpoint sales.
   d. Form 1099.

3. A mutual fund investor has 500 shares of XYZ growth fund, which has a NAV of 22.30 and a POP of 23.05. The investor wants to invest the money in the biotech fund offered by XYZ, which has a NAV of 17.10 and a POP of 18. If XYZ offers conversion privileges, how many shares will the investor be able to purchase of the biotech fund?
   a. 652
   b. 619
   c. 640
   d. 605

4. A mutual fund's custodian bank does which of the following?
   a. Holds customer's securities
   b. Cancels certificates
   c. Maintains records for accumulation plans
   d. Issues certificates

5. A no-load mutual fund may charge a 12B-1 fee that is:
   a. up to .25 of 1 percent of the NAV.
   b. less than .25 of 1 percent of the NAV.
   c. up to .25 of 1 percent of the POP.
   d. less than .25 of 1 percent of the POP.

6. The ex dividend date on a closed-end mutual fund is set by the:
   a. fund's board of directors.
   b. SEC.
   c. Board of Governors.
   d. FINRA/NYSE.

7. A mutual fund has been seeking to attract new customers to invest in its growth fund. It has been running an advertising campaign that markets the fund as a diversified mutual fund. How much of any one company may the fund own?
   a. 15 percent
   b. 5 percent
   c. 10 percent
   d. 9 percent

8. An investor wires $10,000 into his mutual fund on Tuesday, March 11, and the money is credited to his account at 3 p.m. He will be the owner of record on:
   a. Friday, March 14.
   b. Wednesday, March 12.
   c. Tuesday, March 11.
   d. Tuesday, March 18.

9. As it relates to the bonding of mutual fund employees, which of the following is true?
   a. All fund employees are required to be listed on the bond coverage.
   b. Only key employees are required to be listed on the bond coverage.
   c. All employees must have an individual bond posted for them.
   d. All employees with access to assets must be listed on the bond coverage.

10. A long-term growth fund has a portfolio turnover ratio of 25 percent. How often does the fund replace its total holdings?
    a. Every four years
    b. Once a year
    c. Every four months
    d. Every six months

CHAPTER 10

Variable Annuities and Retirement Plans

INTRODUCTION

This chapter will cover a variety of important topics relating to annuity products and retirement plans. Many investors choose to purchase annuities to help plan for retirement. Over the years, a wide range of annuity products have been developed to meet different investment objectives and risk profiles. This section will also cover various types of retirement plans and their participation and funding options. Series 24 candidates will need to understand how an annuity functions in order to successfully complete the exam.

ANNUITIES

An annuity is a contract between an individual and an insurance company. Once the contract is entered into, the individual becomes known as the annuitant. The three basic types of annuities are designed to meet different objectives. The three types of annuities are:

- Fixed annuity
- Variable annuity
- Combination annuity

Although all three types allow the investor's money to grow tax-deferred, the type of investments made and how the money is invested varies according to the type of annuity.

FIXED ANNUITY

A fixed annuity offers investors a guaranteed rate of return regardless of whether the investment portfolio can produce the guaranteed rate. If the performance of the portfolio falls below the rate that was guaranteed, the insurance company owes investors the difference. Because the purchaser of a fixed annuity does not have any investment risk, a fixed annuity is considered an insurance product, not a security. Representatives who sell fixed-annuity contracts must have an insurance license. Because fixed annuities offer investors a guaranteed return, the money invested by the insurance company will be used to purchase conservative investments such as mortgages and real estate, investments whose historical performance is predictable enough so that a guaranteed rate can be offered to investors. All of the money invested into fixed-annuity contracts is held in the insurance company's general account. Because the rate that the insurance guarantees is not very high, the annuitant may suffer a loss of purchasing power due to inflation risk.

VARIABLE ANNUITY

An investor seeking to achieve a higher rate of return may elect to purchase a variable annuity. Variable annuities seek to obtain a higher rate of return by investing in stocks, bonds, or mutual fund shares. These securities traditionally offer higher rates of return than more conservative investments. A variable annuity does not offer the investor a guaranteed rate of return, and the investor may lose all or part of the principal. Because the annuitant bears the investment risk associated with a variable annuity, the contract is considered both a security and an insurance product. Representatives who sell variable annuities must have both their securities license and their insurance license. The money and securities contained in a variable annuity contract are held in the insurance company's separate account. The separate account is named as such because the variable annuity's portfolio must be kept separate from the insurance company's general funds. The insurance company must have a net worth of $1,000,000 or the separate account must have a net worth of $1,000,000 in order for the separate account to begin operating. Once the separate account begins operations, it may invest in one of two ways:

- Directly
- Indirectly

DIRECT INVESTMENT

If the money in the separate account is invested directly into individual stocks and bonds, the separate account must have an investment adviser to actively manage the portfolio. If the money in the separate account is actively managed and invested directly, then the separate account is considered an open-end investment company under the Investment Company Act of 1940 and must register as such.

INDIRECT INVESTMENT

If the separate account uses the money in the portfolio to purchase mutual fund shares, it is investing in the equity and debt markets indirectly, and no investment adviser is required to actively manage the portfolio. If the separate account purchases mutual fund shares directly, then the separate account is considered a unit investment trust (UIT) under the Investment Company Act of 1940 and must register as such.

COMBINATION ANNUITY

For investors who feel that a fixed annuity is too conservative and that a variable annuity is too risky, a combination annuity offers the annuitant features of both a fixed and variable contract. A combination annuity has a fixed portion that offers a guaranteed rate and a variable portion that tries to achieve a higher rate of return. Most combination annuities will allow the investor to move money between the fixed and variable portions of the contract. The money invested in the fixed portion of the contract is invested in the insurance company's general account and used to purchase conservative investments such as mortgages and real estate. The money invested in the variable side of the contract is invested in the insurance company's separate account and used to purchase stocks, bonds, or mutual fund shares. Representatives who sell combination annuities must have both their securities license and their insurance license.

BONUS ANNUITY

An insurance company that issues annuity contracts may offer incentives to investors who purchase their variable annuities. Such incentives are often referred to as bonuses. One type of bonus is known as premium enhancement. Under a premium enhancement option, the insurance company will make an additional contribution to the annuitant's account based on the premium paid by the annuitant. For example, if the annuitant is contributing $1,000 per month, the insurance company may offer to contribute an additional 5 percent, or $50, per month to the account. Another type of bonus offered to annuitants is the ability to withdraw the greater of the account's earnings or up to 15 percent of the total premiums paid without a penalty. Although the annuitant will not have to pay a penalty to the insurance company, there may be income taxes and a 10 percent penalty tax owed to the IRS. Bonus annuities often have higher expenses and longer surrender periods than other annuities, and these additional costs and surrender periods need to be clearly disclosed to prospective purchasers. Fixed annuity contracts may not offer bonuses to purchasers.

EQUITY-INDEXED ANNUITY

Equity-indexed annuities offer investors a return that varies according to the performance of a set index, such as the S&P 500. Equity-indexed annuities will credit additional interest to the investor's account based on the contract's participation rate. If a contract sets the participation rate at 70 percent of the return for the S&P 500 index, and the index returns 5 percent, then the investor's account will be credited for 70 percent of the return, or 3.5 percent. The participation rate may also be shown as a spread rate. If the contract had a spread rate of 3 percent and the index returned 10 percent the investor's contract would be credited 7 percent. Equity-index annuities may also set a floor rate and a cap rate for the contract. The floor rate is the minimum interest rate that will be credited to the investor's account. The floor rate may be zero or it may be a positive number, depending on the specific contract. The contract's cap rate is the maximum rate that will be credited to the contract. If the return of the index exceeds the cap rate, the investor's account will only be credited up to the cap rate. If the S&P 500 index returns 11 percent and the cap rate set in the contract is 9 percent, the investor's account will only be credited 9 percent. Most equity-indexed annuities combine the guarantee features of a fixed annuity with the potential for additional returns like that of a variable annuity. Equity-indexed annuities may also be referred to as equity indexed contracts or EICs. The following table compares the features of fixed and variable annuities:

Feature	Fixed Annuity	Variable Annuity
Payment received	Guaranteed/fixed	May vary in amount
Return	Guaranteed minimum	No guarantee/return may vary in amount
Investment risk	Assumed by insurance company	Assumed by investor
Portfolio	Real estate, mortgages, and fixed-income securities	Stocks, bonds, or mutual fund shares
Portfolio held in	General account	Separate account
Inflation	Subject to inflation risk	Resistant to inflation
Representative registration	Insurance license	Insurance and securities license

RECOMMENDING VARIABLE ANNUITIES

There are a number of factors that will determine if a variable annuity is a suitable recommendation for an investor. Variable annuities are meant to be used as supplements to other retirement accounts such as IRAs and corporate retirement plans. Variable annuities should not be recommended to investors who are trying to save for a large purchase or expense such as college tuition or a second home. Variable annuity products are more appropriate for an investor who is looking to create an income stream. A deferred annuity contract would be appropriate for someone seeking retirement income at some point in the future. An immediate annuity contract would be more appropriate for someone seeking to generate current income and who is perhaps already retired. Many annuity contracts have complex features and cost structures which may be difficult for both the representative and investor to understand. The benefits of the contract should outweigh the additional costs of the contract to ensure the contract is suitable for the investor. Illustrations regarding performance of the contract may use a maximum growth rate of 12 percent and all annuity applications must be approved or denied by a principal based on suitability within 7 business days of receipt. A series 24 or series 26 principal may approve or deny a variable annuity application presented by either a series 6 or series 7 registered representative. 1035 exchanges allow investors to move from one annuity contract to another without incurring tax consequences. 1035 exchanges can be a red flag and a cause for concern over abusive sales practices. Because most annuity contracts have surrender charges that may be substantial, 1035 exchanges may result in the investor being worse off and may constitute churning. FINRA is concerned about firms who employ compensation structures for representatives, which may incentivize the sale of annuities over other investment products with lower costs and which may be more appropriate for investors. Firms should guard against incentivizing agents to sell annuity products over other investments. Members should ensure proper product training for registered representatives and principals for annuities and must have adequate supervision to monitor sales practices and to test their product knowledge. The focus should be to detect problematic and abusive sales practices. L share annuity contracts are designed with shorter surrender periods but have higher costs to investors. The sales of L share annuity contracts can be a red flag for compliance personnel and may constitute abusive sales practices. All retail communications regarding variable annuities must be filed within 10 days of first use. Contracts which are redeemed by investors within 7 business days will result in the return of all sale commissions.

TAKENOTE!

The suitability obligation for variable annuities covers the initial purchase and subaccount allocation as well as the exchange of one annuity contact for any other contract. Exempt from suitability determination are any changes made to the allocation of assets among the available subaccounts.

ANNUITY PURCHASE OPTIONS

An investor may purchase an annuity contract in one of three ways:

- Single-payment deferred annuity
- Single-payment immediate annuity
- Periodic-payment deferred annuity

SINGLE-PAYMENT DEFERRED ANNUITY

With a single-payment deferred annuity, the investor funds the contract completely with one payment and defers receiving payments from the contract until some point in the future, usually after retirement. Money being invested in a single-payment deferred annuity is used to purchase accumulation units. The number and value of the accumulation units varies as the distributions are reinvested and the value of the separate account's portfolio changes.

SINGLE-PAYMENT IMMEDIATE ANNUITY

With a single-payment immediate annuity, the investor funds the contract completely with one payment and begins receiving payments from the contract immediately, normally within 60 days. The money that is invested in a single-payment immediate annuity is used to purchase annuity units. The number of annuity units remains fixed, and the value changes as the value of the securities in the separate account's portfolio fluctuates.

PERIODIC-PAYMENT DEFERRED ANNUITY

With a periodic-payment deferred annuity, the investor purchases the annuity by making regularly scheduled payments into the contract. This is known as the accumulation stage. During the accumulation stage, the terms are flexible and, if the investor misses a payment, there is no penalty. The money invested in a periodic-payment deferred annuity is used to purchase accumulation units. The number and value of the accumulation units fluctuate with the securities in the separate portfolio.

ACCUMULATION UNITS

An accumulation unit represents the investor's proportionate ownership in the separate account's portfolio during the accumulation or deferred stage of the contract. The value of the accumulation unit will fluctuate as the value of the securities in the separate account's portfolio changes. As the investor makes contributions to the account or as distributions are reinvested, the number of accumulation units will vary. An investor will only own accumulation units during the accumulation stage, when money is being paid into the contract or when receipt of payments is being deferred by the investor, such as with a single-payment deferred annuity.

TAKENOTE!

Most annuities allow the investor to designate a beneficiary, who will receive the greater of the value of the account or the total premiums paid if the investor dies during the accumulation stage.

ANNUITY UNITS

When an investor changes from the pay-in or deferred stage of the contract to the payout phase, the investor is said to have annuitized the contract. At this point, the investor trades in the accumulation units for annuity units. The number of annuity units is fixed and represents the investor's proportional ownership of the separate accounts portfolio during the payout phase. The number of annuity units that the investor receives upon annuitizing a contract is based on the payout option selected, the annuitant's age and sex, the value of the account, and the assumed interest rate.

ANNUITY PAYOUT OPTIONS

An investor in an annuity has the choice of taking a lump sum distribution or receiving scheduled payments from the contract. If the investor decides to annuitize the contract and receive scheduled payments, once the payout option is selected it may not be changed. The following is a list of typical payout options in order from the largest monthly payment to the smallest:

- Life only/straight life
- Life with period certain
- Joint with last survivor

LIFE ONLY/STRAIGHT LIFE

This payout option will give the annuitant the largest periodic payment from the contract, and the investor will receive payments from the contract for his or her entire life. When the investor dies, however, no additional benefits are paid to the estate. If an investor has accumulated a large sum of money in the contract and dies unexpectedly shortly after the contract is annuitized, the insurance company keeps the money in the investor's account.

LIFE WITH PERIOD CERTAIN

A life with period certain payout option will pay out from the contract to the investor or to the investor's estate for the life of the annuitant or for the period certain, whichever is longer. If an investor selects a 10-year period certain when the contract is annuitized and the investor lives for 20 years more, payments will cease upon the annuitant's death. However, if the same investor died only two years after annuitizing the contract, payments would go to the investor's estate for another eight years.

JOINT WITH LAST SURVIVOR

When an investor selects a joint with last survivor option, the annuity is jointly owned by more than one party and payments will continue until the last owner of the contract dies. For example, if a husband and wife are receiving payments from an annuity under a joint with last survivor option and the husband dies, payments will continue to the wife for the rest of her life. The payments received by the wife could be at the same rate as when the husband was alive or at a reduced rate, depending on the contract. The monthly payments will initially be based on the life expectancy of the youngest annuitant.

FACTORS AFFECTING THE SIZE OF THE ANNUITY PAYMENT

All of the following determine the size of the annuity payments:

- Account value.
- Payout option selected.
- Age.
- Sex.
- Account performance vs. the assumed interest rate (AIR).

THE ASSUMED INTEREST RATE (AIR)

When an investor annuitizes a contract, the accumulation units are traded for annuity units. Once the contract has been annuitized, the insurance company sets a benchmark for the separate account's performance, known as the assumed interest rate (AIR). The AIR is not a guaranteed rate of return; it is only used to adjust the value of the annuity units up or down based on the actual performance of the separate account. The AIR is an earnings target that the insurance company sets for the separate account. The separate account must meet this earnings target in order to keep the annuitant's payments at the same level. As the value of the annuity unit changes, so does the amount of the payment that is received by the investor. If the separate account outperforms the AIR, an investor would expect the payment to increase. If the separate account's performance falls below the AIR, the investor can expect the payment to decrease. The separate account's performance is always measured against the AIR, never against the previous month's performance. An investor's annuity payment is based on the number of annuity units owned by the investor multiplied by the value of the annuity unit. When the performance of the separate account equals the AIR, the value of the annuity unit will remain unchanged, and so will the investor's payment. Selecting an AIR that is realistic is important. If the AIR is too high and the separate account's return cannot equal the assumed rate, the value of the annuity unit will continue to fall, and so will the investor's payment. The opposite is true if the AIR is set too low. As the separate account outperforms the AIR, the value of the annuity unit will continue to rise, and so will the investor's payment. The AIR is only relevant during the payout phase of the contract, when the investor is receiving payments and owns annuity units. The AIR does not concern itself with accumulation units during the accumulation stage or when benefits are being deferred.

TAXATION

Contributions made to an annuity are made with after-tax dollars. The money the investor deposits becomes the cost basis and is allowed to grow tax-deferred. When the investor withdraws money from the contract, only the growth is taxed. Their cost base is returned tax-free. All money in excess of the investor's cost base is taxed as ordinary income.

SALES CHARGES

There is no maximum sales charge for an annuity contract. The sales charge that is assessed must be reasonable in relation to the total payments over the life of the contract. Most annuity contracts have back-end sales charges or surrender charges similar to a contingent deferred sales charge.

VARIABLE ANNUITY VS. MUTUAL FUND

Feature	Variable Annuity	Mutual Fund
Maximum sales charge	No max	8.5%
Investment adviser	Yes	Yes
Custodian bank	Yes	Yes
Transfer agent	Yes	Yes
Voting	Yes	Yes
Management	Board of managers	Board of directors
Taxation of growth and reinvestments	Tax-deferred	Currently taxed

RETIREMENT PLANS

For most people, saving for retirement has become an important investment objective for at least part of their portfolio. Investors may participate in retirement plans that have been established by their employers, as well as those they have established for themselves. Both corporate and individual plans may be qualified or nonqualified, and it is important for an investor to understand the difference before deciding to participate. The following is a comparison of the key features of both types of plans:

Feature	Qualified	Nonqualified
Contributions	Pre-tax	After-tax
Growth	Tax-deferred	Tax-deferred
Participation must be allowed	For everyone	The corporation may choose who gets to participate
IRS approval	Required	Not required
Withdrawals	100% taxed as ordinary income	Growth in excess of cost base is taxed as ordinary income

INDIVIDUAL PLANS

Individuals may set up a retirement plan that is qualified and allows contributions to the plan to be made with pre-tax dollars. Individuals may also purchase investment products, such as annuities, that allow their money to grow tax-deferred. The money used to purchase an annuity has already been taxed, making an annuity a nonqualified product.

INDIVIDUAL RETIREMENT ACCOUNTS (IRAs)

All individuals with earned income may establish an Individual Retirement Account (IRA). Contributions to traditional IRAs may or may not be tax deductible depending on the individual's level of adjusted gross income and whether the individual is eligible to participate in an employer-sponsored plan. Individuals who do not qualify to participate in an employer-sponsored plan may deduct their IRA contributions regardless of their income level. The level of adjusted gross income that allows an investor to deduct their IRA contributions has been increasing since 1998. These tax law changes occur too frequently to make them a practical test question. Our review of IRAs will focus on the four main types:

- Traditional
- Roth
- SEP
- Educational

TRADITIONAL IRA

A traditional IRA allows an individual to contribute a maximum of 100 percent of earned income, or $6,000 per year or up to $12,000 per couple. If only one spouse works, the working spouse may contribute $6,000 to an IRA for him- or herself and $6,000 to a separate IRA for the nonworking spouse. Investors over 50 may contribute up to $7,000 of earned income to their IRA. Regardless of whether the IRA contribution was made with pre- or after-tax dollars, the money is allowed to grow tax-deferred. All withdrawals from an IRA are taxed as ordinary income regardless of how the growth was generated in the account. Withdrawals from an IRA prior to age 59 1/2 are subject to a 10 percent penalty tax as well as ordinary income taxes. The 10 percent penalty will be waived for first-time homebuyers; for educational expenses for the taxpayer's child, grandchildren, or spouse; if the account holder becomes disabled; or if the payments are part of a series of substantially equal payments. Withdrawals from an IRA must begin by April 1st of the year following the year in which the taxpayer reaches 70 1/2. (It's important to note that the Secure Act of 2020 increased the age of required minimum distributions to 72.) If an individual fails to make withdrawals that are sufficient in size and frequency, the individual will be subject to a 50 percent penalty on the insufficient amount. An individual who makes a contribution to an IRA that exceeds 100 percent of earned income, or $6,000, whichever is less, will be subject to a penalty of 6 percent per year on the excess amount for as long as the excess contribution remains in the account.

ROTH IRA

A Roth IRA is a nonqualified account. All deposits that are made to a Roth IRA are made with after-tax dollars. The same contribution limits apply for Roth IRAs. An individual may contribute the lesser of 100% of earned income, to a maximum of $6,000 per person, or $12,000 per couple. Any contribution made to a Roth IRA reduces the amount that may be deposited in a traditional IRA and vice versa. All contributions deposited in a Roth IRA are allowed to grow tax-deferred, and all of the growth may be taken out of the account tax-free provided that the individual has reached age 59 1/2 and that the assets have been in the account for at least five years. A 10 percent penalty tax will be charged on any withdrawal of earnings prior to age 59 1/2, unless the owner is purchasing a home, has become disabled, or has died. There are no requirements for an individual to take distributions from a Roth IRA by a certain age.

SIMPLIFIED EMPLOYEE PENSION (SEP) IRA

A simplified employee pension (SEP) IRA is used by small corporations and self-employed individuals to plan for retirement. A SEP IRA is attractive to small employers because it allows them to set up a retirement plan for their employees rather quickly and inexpensively. The contribution limit for a SEP IRA far exceeds that of traditional IRAs. The contribution limit is the lesser of 25% of the employee's compensation or $57,000 per year. Should employees wish to make their annual IRA contribution to their SEP IRA, they may do so, or they may make their standard contribution to a traditional or Roth IRA.

PARTICIPATION

All eligible employees must open an IRA to receive the employer's contribution to the SEP. If the employee does not open an IRA account, the employer must open one for the employee. The employee must be at least 21 years old, have worked during three of the last five years for the employer, and have earned at least $400. All eligible employees must participate, as well as the employer.

EMPLOYER CONTRIBUTIONS

The employer may contribute between 0 and 25 percent of the employee's total compensation to a maximum of $57,000. Contributions to all SEP IRAs, including the employer's SEP IRA, must be made at the same rate. An employee who is over 70 1/2 must also participate and receive a contribution. All eligible employees are immediately vested in the employer's contributions to the plan.

SEP IRA TAXATION

Employer's contributions to a SEP IRA are immediately tax-deductible by the employer. Contributions are not taxed at the employee's rate until the employee withdraws the funds. Employees may begin to withdraw money from the plan at age 59 1/2. All withdrawals are taxed as ordinary income, and withdrawals prior to age 59 1/2 are subject to a 10 percent penalty tax. The employer may contribute up to 25 percent of the employee's income, up to $57,000.

EDUCATIONAL IRA

An educational IRA allows individuals to contribute up to $2,000 in after-tax dollars to an educational IRA for each student who is under 18 years of age. The money is allowed to grow tax-deferred, and the growth may be withdrawn tax-free as long as the money is used for educational purposes. If all of the funds have not been used for educational purposes by the time the student reaches 30 years of age, the account must be rolled over to another family member who is under 30 years of age or distributed to the original student and subject to a 10 percent penalty tax as well as ordinary income taxes.

Qualified tuition plans more frequently referred to as 529 plans may be set up either as a prepaid tuition plan or as a college savings plan. With the prepaid tuition plan, the plan locks in a current tuition rate at a specific school. The prepaid tuition plan can be set up as an installment plan or one where the contributor funds the plan with a lump sum deposit. Many states will guarantee the plans but may require that either the contributor or the beneficiary to be a state resident. The plan covers only tuition and mandatory fees. A room and board option is available for some plans. A college cost-savings account may be opened by any adult and the donor does not have to be related to the child. The assets in the college savings plan can be used to cover all costs of qualified higher education including tuition, room and board, books, computers, and mandatory fees. These plans generally have no age limit when assets must be used. College savings accounts are not guaranteed by the state and the value of the account may decline based on the investment results of the account. College savings accounts are not state specific and do not lock in a tuition rate. Contributions to a 529 plan are made with after-tax dollars and are allowed to grow tax deferred. The assets in the account remain under the control of the donor, even after the student reaches the age of majority. The funds may be used to meet the student's educational needs and the growth may be withdrawn federally tax-free. Most states also allow the assets to be withdrawn tax free. Any funds used for non-qualified education expenses will be subject to income tax and a 10% penalty tax. If funds remain or if the student does not attend or complete qualified higher education the funds may be rolled over to another family member within 60 days without incurring taxes and penalties. There are no income limits for the donors and contribution limits vary from state to state. 529 plans have an impact on a student's ability to obtain need based financial aid. However, because the 529 plans are treated as parental assets and not as assets of the student, the plans are assessed at the expected family contribution (EFC) rate of 5.64%. This will have a significantly lower impact than plans and assets that are considered to be assets of the student. Student assets will be assessed at a 20% contribution rate. For your exam, it is important to note that assets in a 529 savings plan may also be used to meet tuition payments for private K–12 schools.

IRA CONTRIBUTIONS

Contributions to IRAs must be made by April 15 of the following calendar year, regardless of whether an extension has been filed by the taxpayer. Contributions may be made between January 1 and April 15 for the previous year, the current year, or both. All IRA contributions must be made in cash.

IRA ACCOUNTS

All IRA accounts are held in the name of the custodian for the benefit of the account holder. Traditional custodians include banks, broker dealers, and mutual fund companies.

IRA INVESTMENTS

Individuals who establish IRAs have a wide variety of investments to choose from when deciding how to invest the funds. Investors should always choose investments that fit their investment objectives. The following is a comparison of allowable and non\allowable investments:

Allowable	Non-Allowable
Stocks	Margin accounts
Bonds	Short sales
Mutual funds, exchange-traded funds, and notes	Tangibles/collectibles/art
Annuities	Speculative option trading
UITs	Term life insurance
Limited partnerships	Rare coins
U.S. minted coins	Real estate

IT IS UNWISE TO PUT A MUNICIPAL BOND IN AN IRA

Municipal bonds or municipal bond funds should never be placed in an IRA because the advantage of those investments is that the interest income is free from federal taxes. Because their interest is free from federal taxes, the interest rate that is offered will be less than the rates offered by other alternatives. The advantage of an IRA is that money is allowed to grow tax-deferred; therefore, an individual would be better off with a higher yielding taxable bond of the same quality.

ROLLOVER VS. TRANSFER

An individual may want or need to move an IRA from one custodian to another. This can be accomplished by rolling over the IRA or transferring the IRA.

ROLLOVER

With an IRA rollover, the individual may take possession of the funds for a maximum of 60 calendar days prior to depositing the funds into another qualified account. An investor may only rollover an IRA once every 12 months. Investors have 60 days from the date of the distribution to deposit 100 percent of the funds into another qualified account or they must pay ordinary income taxes on the distribution and a 10 percent penalty tax if under 59 1/2.

TRANSFER

An investor may transfer an IRA directly from one custodian to another by simply signing an account transfer form. The investor never takes possession of the assets in the account. Investors may directly transfer their IRAs as often as they like.

DEATH OF AN IRA OWNER

Should the owner of an IRA die, the account will become the property of the beneficiary named on the account by the owner. If the beneficiary is the spouse of the owner, special rules apply. The spouse may elect to roll over the IRA into his or her own IRA or retirement plan, such as a 401(k). If this is elected there will be no tax presently due on the money. However, the spouse is still subject to the required minimum distribution rule at age 70 1/2. The surviving spouse may also elect to cash in the IRA. The distributions will be subject to income tax but will not be subject to the 10 percent penalty tax. If the beneficiary is not the spouse, the money may not be rolled into another IRA or retirement account. If the account owner died prior to age 70 1/2, when the required distributions need to be made, the money must all be distributed prior to the end of the fifth year or the money may be distributed in equal installments based upon the beneficiary's life expectancy. If the account owner has died after the start of the required minimum distributions, the payment schedule of distributions will now be based on the life expectancy of the beneficiary.

KEOGH PLANS (HR-10)

A Keogh plan is a qualified retirement plan set up by self-employed individuals, sole proprietors, and unincorporated businesses. If the business is set up as a corporation, a Keogh may not be used.

CONTRIBUTIONS

Keoghs may only be funded with earned income during a period when the business shows a gross profit. If the business realizes a loss, no Keogh contributions are allowed. A self-employed person may contribute the lesser of 25 percent of postcontribution income or $57,000. If the business has eligible employees, the employer must make a contribution for the employees at the same rate as his or her own contribution. Employee contributions are based on the employee's gross income and are limited to $57,000 per year. All money placed in a Keogh plan is allowed to grow tax-deferred and is taxed as ordinary income when distributions are made to retiring employees and plan participants. From time to time, a self-employed person may make a nonqualified contribution to a Keogh plan; however, the total of the qualified and nonqualified contributions may not exceed the maximum contribution limit. Any excess contribution may be subject to a 10 percent penalty tax.

An eligible employee is defined as one that:

- Works full time (at least 1,000 hours per year).
- Is at least 21 years old.
- Has worked at least one year for the employer.

Employees who participate in a Keogh plan must be vested after five years. Withdrawals from a Keogh may begin when the participant reaches 59 1/2. Any premature withdrawals are subject to a 10 percent penalty tax. A Keogh, like an IRA, may be rolled over every 12 months. In the event of a participant's death, the assets will go to the individual's beneficiaries.

TAX-SHELTERED ANNUITIES (TSAs) AND TAX-DEFERRED ACCOUNTS (TDAs)

Tax-sheltered annuities (TSAs) and tax-deferred accounts (TDAs) are established as retirement plans for employees of nonprofit and public organizations such as:

- Public educational institutions
- Nonprofit organizations
- Religious organizations
- Nonprofit hospitals

TSAs/TDAs are qualified plans, and contributions are made with pretax dollars. The money in the plan is allowed to grow tax-deferred until it is withdrawn. TSAs/TDAs offer a variety of investment vehicles for participants to choose from, such as:

- Stocks
- Bonds
- Mutual funds
- CDs

PUBLIC EDUCATIONAL INSTITUTIONS [403(B)]

In order for a school to be considered a public school and qualify to establish a TSA/TDA for its employees, the school must be supported by the state, the local government, or a state agency. State-supported schools are:

- Elementary schools
- High schools
- State colleges and universities
- Medical schools

Any individual who works for a public school, regardless of the position held, may participate in the school's TSA/TDA.

NONPROFIT ORGANIZATIONS/TAX-EXEMPT ORGANIZATIONS [501(C)(3)]

Organizations that qualify under the Internal Revenue Code 501(c)(3) as a nonprofit or tax-exempt entity may set up a TSA or TDA for their employees. Examples of nonprofit organizations are:

- Private hospitals
- Charitable organizations
- Trade schools
- Private colleges
- Parochial schools
- Museums
- Scientific foundations
- Zoos

All employees of organizations that qualify under the IRC 501(c)(3) or 403(b) are eligible to participate as long as they are at least 21 years old and have worked full time for at least one year.

CONTRIBUTIONS

In order to participate in a TSA or TDA, employees must enter into a contract with their employer agreeing to make elective deferrals into the plan. The salary reduction agreement will state the amount and frequency of the elective deferral to be contributed to the TSA. The agreement is binding on both parties and covers only one year of contributions. Each year a new salary reduction agreement must be signed to set forth the contributions for the new year. The employee's elective deferral is limited to a maximum of $19,500 per year. Employer contributions are limited to the lesser of 25 percent of the employee's earnings or $57,000.

TAX TREATMENT OF DISTRIBUTIONS

All distributions for TSAs/TDAs are taxed as ordinary income in the year in which the distribution is made. Distributions from a TSA/TDA prior to age 59 1/2 are subject to a 10 percent penalty tax as well as ordinary income taxes. Distributions from a TSA/TDA must begin by age 70 1/2 or be subject to an excess accumulation tax.

CORPORATE PLANS

Corporations may establish a variety of retirement plans for its employees. The type of plan that is established will be based on the type of entity and the employment of the participant. A corporate retirement plan can be qualified or nonqualified. We will first review the nonqualified plans.

NONQUALIFIED CORPORATE RETIREMENT PLANS

Nonqualified corporate plans are funded with after-tax dollars and the money is allowed to grow tax-deferred. If the corporation makes a contribution to the plan, it may not deduct the contribution from its corporate earnings until the plan participant receives the money. Distributions from a nonqualified plan that exceed the investor's cost base are taxed as ordinary income. All nonqualified plans must be in writing, and the employer may discriminate as to who may participate.

PAYROLL DEDUCTIONS

The employee may set up a payroll deduction plan by having the employer make systematic deductions from the employee's paycheck. The money that is deducted from the employee's check may be invested in a variety of ways. Mutual funds, annuities, and savings bonds are all usually available for the employee to choose from. Contributions to a payroll deduction plan are made with after-tax dollars.

DEFERRED COMPENSATION PLANS

A deferred compensation plan is a contract between an employee and an employer. Under the contract, the employee agrees to defer the receipt of money owed to the employee from the employer until after the employee retires. After retirement, the employee will traditionally be in a lower tax bracket and will be able to keep a larger percentage of the money. Deferred compensation plans are traditionally unfunded and, if the corporation goes out of business, the employee becomes a creditor of the corporation and may lose all of the money due under the contract. The employees may only claim the assets if they retire or become disabled, or, in the case of death, their beneficiaries may claim the money owed. Money due under a deferred compensation plan is paid out of the corporation's working funds when the employee or the employee's estate claims the assets. Should the employee leave the corporation and go to work for a competing company, the employee may lose the money owed under a noncompete clause. Money owed to the employee under a deferred compensation agreement is traditionally not invested for the benefit of the employee and, as a result, does not increase in value over time. The only product that traditionally is placed in a deferred compensation plan is a term life policy. In the case of the employee's death, the term life policy will pay the employee's estate the money owed under the contract.

QUALIFIED PLANS

All qualified corporate plans must be in writing and established as a trust. A trustee or plan administrator will be appointed for the benefit of all plan holders.

TYPES OF PLANS

The two main types of qualified corporate plans are defined benefit plans and defined contribution plans.

DEFINED BENEFIT PLAN

A defined benefit plan is designed to offer the participant a retirement benefit that is known, or defined. Most defined benefit plans are set up to provide employees with a fixed percentage of their salaries during their retirement, such as 74 percent of their average earnings during their five highest-paid years. Other defined benefit plans are structured to pay participants a fixed sum of money for life. Defined benefit plans require the services of an actuary to determine the employer's contribution to the plan based on the participant's life expectancy and benefits promised.

DEFINED CONTRIBUTION PLAN

With a defined contribution plan, only the amount of money that is deposited into the account is known, such as 6 percent of the employee's salary. Both the employee and the employer may contribute a percentage of the employee's earnings into the plan. The money is allowed to grow tax-deferred until the participant withdraws it at retirement. The ultimate benefit under a defined contribution plan is the result of the contributions into the plan as well as the investment results of the plan. The employee's maximum contribution to a defined contribution plan is $19,500 per year. Some types of defined contribution plans are:

- 401(k)s
- Money purchase plans
- Profit-sharing plans
- Thrift plans
- Stock bonus plans

All withdrawals from pension plans are taxed as ordinary income in the year in which the distribution is made.

EMPLOYEE STOCK OWNERSHIP PLANS (ESOPs)

ESOP plans are established by employers to provide a way for the employees to benefit from ownership of the company's stock. The plan allows the employer to take a tax deduction based on the market value of the stock.

PROFIT-SHARING PLANS

Profit-sharing plans let the employer reward the employees by letting them share in a percentage of the corporation's profits. Profit-sharing plans are based on a preset formula, and the money may be paid directly to the employee or placed in a retirement account. In order for a profit-sharing plan to be qualified, the corporation must have substantial and recurring profits. The maximum contribution to a profit-sharing plan is the lesser of 25 percent of the employee's compensation or $57,000.

401(k)s AND THRIFT PLANS

401(k)s and thrift plans allow employees to contribute a fixed percentage of their salaries to their retirement accounts and have the employers match some or all of their contributions. The employer's contributions provide a current tax deduction to the employer, and the employee is not taxed on the contributions until they are withdrawn.

ROLLING OVER A PENSION PLAN

An employee who leaves an employer may move a pension plan to another company's plan or to another qualified account. This may be accomplished by a direct transfer or by rolling over the plan. With a direct transfer, the assets in the plan go directly to another plan administrator, and the employee never has physical possession of the assets. When the employee rolls over a pension plan, the employee takes physical possession of the assets. The plan administrator is required to withhold 20 percent of the total amount to be distributed, and the employee has 60 calendar days to deposit 100 percent of the assets into another qualified plan. The employee must file with the federal government at tax time to receive a return of the 20 percent of the assets that were withheld by the plan administrator.

EMPLOYEE RETIREMENT INCOME SECURITY ACT OF 1974 (ERISA)

The Employee Retirement Income Security Act of 1974 (ERISA) is a federal law that establishes legal and operational guidelines for private pension and employee benefit plans. Not all decisions directly involving a plan, even when made by a fiduciary, are subject to ERISA's fiduciary rules. These decisions are business judgment–type decisions and are commonly called settlor functions. This caveat is sometimes referred to as the business decision exception to ERISA's fiduciary rules. Under this concept, even though the employer is the plan sponsor and administrator, it will not be considered as acting in a fiduciary capacity when creating, amending, or terminating a plan. The following decisions would be considered settlor functions:

- Choosing the type of plan or options in the plan.
- Amending a plan, including changing or eliminating plan options.
- Requiring employee contributions or changing the level of employee contributions.
- Terminating a plan, or part of a plan, including terminating or amending a plan as part of a bankruptcy process.

ERISA also regulates all of the following:

- Pension plan participation
- Funding
- Vesting
- Communication
- Beneficiaries

PLAN PARTICIPATION

All plans governed by ERISA may not discriminate among who may participate in the plan. All employees must be allowed to participate if:

- They are at least 21 years old.
- They have worked at least one year full time (1,000 hours).

FUNDING

Plan funding requirements set forth guidelines on how the money is deposited into the plan and how the employer and employee may contribute to the plan.

VESTING

Vesting refers to the process of how the employer's contribution becomes the property of the employee. An employer may be as generous as it likes, but it may not be more restrictive than either one of the following vesting schedules:

- Three- to six-year gradual vesting schedule.
- Three-year cliff, whereby the employee is not vested at all until three years, at which point the employee becomes 100 percent vested.

COMMUNICATION

All corporate plans must be in writing at inception, and the employee must be given annual updates.

BENEFICIARIES

All plan participants must be allowed to select a beneficiary who may claim the assets in case of the plan participant's death.

THE DEPARTMENT OF LABOR FIDUCIARY RULES

The Department of Labor has enacted significant new legislation for financial professionals who service and maintain retirement accounts for clients. These new rules subject financial professionals to higher fiduciary standards. These standards require financial professionals to place the interest of the client ahead of the interest of the broker dealer or investment advisory firm. Professionals who service retirement accounts are still permitted to earn commissions and/or a fee based on the assets in the account and may still offer proprietary products to investors. However the rule requires that the client receive significant disclosures relating to the fees and costs associated with the servicing of the account. Simply charging the lowest fee will not ensure compliance with the fiduciary standard. Both the firm and the individual servicing the account must put the interests of the client ahead of their own. Broker dealers and advisory firms must establish written supervisory procedures and training programs designed to supervise and educate their personnel on the new requirements for retirement accounts. Many representatives will now be required to obtain the Series 65 or Series 66 license to comply with the new Department of Labor rules.

CHAPTER 10

Pretest

VARIABLE ANNUITIES AND RETIREMENT PLANS

1. A doctor makes the maximum contribution to his Keogh plan while earning $300,000 per year. How much can he contribute to an IRA?
   a. $57,000
   b. $6,000
   c. $8,000
   d. $6,000

2. An individual owns a variable annuity with an assumed interest rate of 5%. If the separate account earns 4%, the individual would expect:
   I. The monthly payment to go up
   II. The monthly payment to go down
   III. The value of the annuity unit to go up
   IV. The value of the annuity unit to go down

   a. II and IV
   b. I and III
   c. I and II
   d. II and III

3. A school principal has deposited $15,000 in a tax-deferred annuity through a payroll deduction plan. The account has grown in value to $22,000. The principal plans to retire and take a lump sum distribution. On what amount does he pay taxes?
   a. $22,000
   b. $15,000
   c. $7,000
   d. $0

4. The maximum amount that a couple may contribute to their IRAs at any one time is:
   a. $2,000.
   b. $6,000.
   c. $12,000.
   d. 400 percent of the annual individual limit.

5. An investor has deposited $100,000 into a qualified retirement account over a 10-year period. The value of the account has grown to $175,000, and the investor plans to retire and take a lump sum withdrawal. The investor will pay:
   a. capital gains tax on $75,000 only.
   b. ordinary income taxes on the $75,000 only.
   c. ordinary income taxes on the whole $175,000.
   d. ordinary income taxes on the $100,000 and capital gains on the $75,000.

6. A 42-year-old investor wants to put $20,000 into a plan to help meet the educational expenses of his 12-year-old son. He wants to make a lump sum deposit. Which would you recommend?
   a. A 529 plan
   b. A Coverdell IRA
   c. A Roth IRA
   d. A growth mutual fund

7. A client who is 65 years old has invested $10,000 in a Roth IRA. It has now grown to $14,000. He plans to retire and take a lump sum distribution. He will pay taxes on:
   a. $0.
   b. $14,000.
   c. $4,000.
   d. $10,000.

8. A fixed annuity guarantees all of the following, EXCEPT:
   a. income for life.
   b. protection from inflation.
   c. a rate of return.
   d. protection from investment risk.

9. A self-employed individual opens a SEP IRA to plan for his retirement. The maximum contribution to the plan is:
   a. $3,000.
   b. $10,000.
   c. $20,000.
   d. the lesser of 25 percent of his postcontribution income, up to $57,000.

CHAPTER 11

Securities Industry Rules and Regulations

INTRODUCTION

Federal and state securities laws, as well as industry regulations, have been enacted to ensure that all industry participants adhere to a high standard of just and equitable trade practices. In this chapter, we will review the rules and regulations, as well as the registration requirements, for firms, agents, and securities.

THE SECURITIES EXCHANGE ACT OF 1934

The Securities Exchange Act of 1934 was the second major piece of legislation that resulted from the market crash of 1929. The Securities Exchange Act regulates the secondary market that consists of investor-to-investor transactions. All transactions between two investors that are executed on any of the exchanges or in the over-the-counter (OTC) market are secondary market transactions. In a secondary market transaction, the selling security holder receives the money, not the issuing corporation. The Securities Exchange Act of 1934 also regulates all individuals and firms that conduct business in the securities industry. The Securities Exchange Act of 1934:

- Created the Securities and Exchange Commission (SEC).
- Requires the registration of broker dealers and agents.
- Regulates the exchanges and FINRA.
- Requires net capital for broker dealers.

- Regulates short sales.
- Regulates insider transactions.
- Requires public companies to solicit proxies.
- Requires segregation of customer and firm assets.
- Authorized the Federal Reserve Board to regulate the extension of credit for securities purchases under Regulation T.
- Regulates the handling of client accounts.
- Regulates interstate securities transactions.

THE SECURITIES AND EXCHANGE COMMISSION (SEC)

One of the biggest components of the Securities Exchange Act of 1934 was the creation of the SEC. The SEC is the ultimate securities industry authority and is a direct government body. Five commissioners are appointed to five-year terms by the president, and each must be approved by the Senate. No more than three members may be from any one political party. During their term as a commissioner, individuals may only act as a commissioner and may not engage in any outside employment. The SEC is not a self-regulatory organization (SRO) or a designated examining authority (DEA). An SRO is an organization that regulates its own members, such as the NYSE or FINRA. A DEA is an entity that inspects a broker dealer's books and records, and it can also be the NYSE or FINRA. All broker dealers, exchanges, agents, and securities must register with the SEC. All exchanges are required to file a registration statement with the SEC that includes the exchange's articles of incorporation, bylaws, and constitution. All new rules and regulations adopted by an exchange must be disclosed to the SEC as soon as they are enacted. Issuers of securities with more than 500 shareholders and with assets exceeding $10,000,000 or issuers whose securities are traded on an exchange or Nasdaq must register with the SEC, file quarterly (10-Q) and annual (10-K) reports, and follow certain rules relating to the solicitation of proxies from stockholders. The issuer must file the proxy with the SEC, and the proxy must be in the required form and must be accompanied by certain information. A broker dealer that conducts business with the public must register with the SEC and maintain a certain level of financial solvency known as net capital. All broker dealers are required to forward a financial statement to all customers of the firm. Additionally, all employees of the broker dealer who are involved in securities sales, have access to cash and securities, or who supervise employees must be fingerprinted.

EXTENSION OF CREDIT

The Securities Act of 1934 gave the authority to the Federal Reserve Board to regulate the extension of credit by broker dealers for the purchase of securities by their customers. The following is a list of the regulations of the different lenders and the regulations that gave the Federal Reserve Board the authority to govern their activities:

- Regulation T: Broker dealers
- Regulation U: Banks
- Regulation G: All other financial institutions

TAKENOTE!

Exempt securities issued by the U.S. government and municipal governments are exempt from most of the conditions of the Securities Exchange Act of 1934, including Regulation T, antimanipulation rules, proxy requirements, and insider reporting.

TRADING SUSPENSIONS

The SEC may impose trading suspensions in nonexempt securities or on an exchange or Nasdaq if certain emergency conditions exist. In the case of significant and excessive price fluctuations, or the prospect of significant and excessive price fluctuations that would disrupt the orderly operation of the security or market, the SEC may suspend trading in the security or in the market as a whole. The SEC may suspend the trading in a security for up to 10 business days, including any extension of the order. The SEC may suspend the trading on an exchange or in a market as a whole for up to 90 days. In the case of a market-wide suspension, the SEC must notify the president of the United States, and he or she must not disapprove the suspension.

ISSUERS REPURCHASING THEIR OWN SECURITIES

Issuers may repurchase their own shares in order to fund stock purchase plans or stock option plans or to retain control of the company. These are just a few of the legitimate reasons a company may repurchase its own shares. Certain restrictions are placed upon issuers who repurchase their own shares in order to ensure that they are not trying to manipulate their share prices. SEC Rule 10b-18 sets guidelines for how an issuer or an affiliate may repurchase its own shares. SEC Rule 10b-18 states:

- For Nasdaq Global Market and listed securities (reported securities), the issuer may not buy on the opening print or within 30 minutes of the close of the market.
- For actively traded issues with ADTV of greater than $1,000,000 and a public float of at least $150,000,000, the safe harbor will begin 10 minutes prior to the close.
- For Nasdaq Capital Market securities, purchases may not be made unless there is at least one independent bid.
- The issuer may only enter orders through one broker dealer or market maker on a given trading day.
- For reported or Capital Market issues, the issuer may purchase the greater of 25 percent of the ADTV for the preceding four calendar weeks or one round lot.
- For non-Nasdaq securities, the issuer is limited to the greater of one round lot or an amount that does not exceed 1/20 of 1 percent of the outstanding shares for the preceding five days, exclusive of securities owned by affiliates.
- For reported securities, the issuer may not enter a bid that is higher than the best independent bid or make a purchase at a price that is higher than the last independent sale, whichever is higher.
- For Capital Market securities, the purchase price or bid price may not be higher than the lowest independent offer.
- For non-Nasdaq OTC equities, the price may not be higher than the lowest independent offer obtained after a reasonable inquiry has been made.

Within these safe harbor guidelines, the repurchasing of securities by issuers or affiliates will not be deemed manipulative. If the repurchase of securities by an issuer would cause the number of shareholders to fall below 300 or cause the securities to be delisted from an exchange or from the Nasdaq, the issuer must file Form 13e-3 with the SEC. This is typically the result of a going private transaction. In addition to form 13 e-3 issuers who go private must file financial reports and the opinions of any financial advisors with the SEC. The issuer will forward a term sheet detailing the transaction and proxies to investors. Should the issuer engage in subsequent transactions that would materially affect the filing, the issuer must notify the SEC within 10 days after the transactions are executed.

TAKENOTE!

Once per week, an issuer will be able to make block purchases that do not count toward its purchase limit of 25 percent of its ADTV so long as the issuer does not make any other purchases on that day.

TENDER OFFERS

A tender offer is made by a person or firm who is seeking to purchase all or part of the outstanding securities of an issuer at a specific price. The SEC has issued strict guidelines that must be followed by both the person making the tender and investors who tender their securities.

If the issuer, another company or person makes a tender offer for securities the offeror must file form TO with the SEC as soon as practical but no later than the commencement date of the tender. Should any entity other than the issuer itself purchase more than 5% of an issuer's outstanding securities, that entity must file form 13D with the SEC in addition to form TO. Form TO will provide investors with the details of the offer being made and will generally be the basis for the information in the proxy statement. In addition to the terms of the offering, schedule TO will include:

- Background information on the parties making the offer
- The purpose of the transaction
- Information on the subject (target) company

The guidelines to be followed by parties making a tender offer include:

- The offer must be open for 20 business days from the day it is announced.
- If any of the terms of the tender are changed, the tender must remain open for at least 10 business days from the day the change in the terms was announced.
- A party making a tender offer for stock may not buy the stock or the convertible securities of the issuer during the term of the tender. However, the party may purchase nonconvertible bonds.

- If the duration of the offer is extended, the announcement extending the offer must be released no later than the opening of the exchange on the business day following the original expiration date for exchange-listed securities. The announcement must include the amount of securities tendered to date.
- If a tender offer is extended for securities that are not listed on an exchange, the announcement must be made no later than 9:00 a.m. EST the business day following the original expiration and must also include the amount of securities tendered to date.
- Shareholders must be notified of the tender offer no later than 10 business days after the tender is announced.
- Management of the company subject to the tender offer must advise shareholders as to management's opinion on the offer (i.e., accept, decline, or neutral).
- A party making a tender offer must pay the price offered for the securities to the extent the offer was made.

Investors may only tender securities that they actually own. An investor may not sell short into a tender, which is known as short tendering. Investors are considered long the security if they have possession of the security or have issued exercise or conversion instructions for an option, warrant, or convertible security. Additionally, investors may only tender their securities to the extent of their net long position. If an investor is short against the box or has written calls with a strike price lower than the tender price, then the investor's net long position will be reduced.

EXAMPLE

If an investor owns 1,000 XYZ and has written 5 XYZ June 40 calls when a tender offer is announced at $42 for XYZ, the investor could only tender 500 shares.

During a partial tender the exact amount of securities to be accepted from all tendering parities is not known. As a result, an investor who has a convertible security may tender an amount equal to the amount to be received upon conversion. If the investor is informed that its tender has been accepted, it must convert the securities and deliver the subject securities.

Another type of tender offer you may see on your exam is known as a Dutch auction. During a Dutch auction the issuer will announce a range of prices at which it is willing to repurchase its own securities. For example, TRY Inc. announces that it is willing to repurchase 10 million of its class A common shares between $45 and $50 per share. Investors who are interested in selling their shares will tender their shares at a stated price. Based on the prices received during the Dutch auction, the issuer will set a final price for the tender. All shares tendered at or below the final price will be purchased by the issuer up to the maximum number of shares stated in the tender. Investors who tendered shares at a price above the final price will have their shares returned to them.

SEC REPORTING

The Securities Exchange Act requires that individuals or entities who acquire 5 percent or more of an issuer's equity securities must file Form 13D with the SEC within 10 days of reaching the 5 percent stake. Rule 13D requires that the SEC, the exchange where the securities are listed, and the issuer be informed of the size of the investor's holdings and the purpose for the investment. Rule 13D does not require that the stockholders be informed directly by the investor. An entity may acquire more than 5 percent of the issuer's securities for investment purposes, for control, or for acquisition.

Other entities must also disclose their large holdings in an issuer's securities. Investment companies who acquire 5 percent or more of an issuer will file a notice of their ownership on Form 13G. Investment advisers who have discretion over $100 million or more in assets must disclose all of their holdings without regard to amount within 45 days of the end of each calendar quarter on Form 13F.

Certain market participants who directly or indirectly exercise investment discretion over one or more accounts are required to register as large traders with the SEC. These large traders will be assigned a large trader ID (LTID). The large trader is required to provide its LTID to each broker dealer that executes orders for the large trader. The executing broker dealer is required to record all transactions executed for the large trader and the LTID and time must be noted on each order. The large trader must file form 13H with the SEC within 45 days of the end of each calendar year. A large trader is defined as an entity that:

- Executes a trade or trades in an NMS security of 2 million shares or greater, or with a value of $20 million or greater on a single day; or
- Executes a trade or trades in an NMS security of 20 million shares or greater or with a value of $200 million or greater in a calendar quarter; or

- Executes a trade or trades in options that meet the daily or quarterly limits above based on the value or number of the underlying shares covered by the option contracts

Officers and directors who own shares of the company he / she work for must file form 3 at the time the shares are initially purchased or received from the company. If the officer or director buys or sells shares he / she is required to file form 4 within 2 days of the transaction.

THE NATIONAL ASSOCIATION OF SECURITIES DEALERS (NASD)

The Maloney Act of 1938 was an amendment to the Securities Exchange Act of 1934 that allowed the creation of the NASD, which is now part of FINRA. The NASD became the SRO for the OTC market, and its purpose was to regulate the broker dealers who conduct business in the OTC market. The NASD was organized into four major bylaws:

- The Rules of Fair Practice
- The Uniform Practice Code
- The Code of Procedure
- The Code of Arbitration

THE RULES OF FAIR PRACTICE (RULES OF CONDUCT)

The Rules of Fair Practice are designed to ensure just and equitable trade practices among members in their dealings with the public. In short, they require members to deal fairly with the public. The Rules of Fair Practice may also be called the Conduct Rules or the Rules of Conduct. They govern, among other things:

- Commissions and markups
- Retail and institutional communications
- Customer recommendations
- Claims made by representatives

THE UNIFORM PRACTICE CODE

The Uniform Practice Code sets forth guidelines for how FINRA members transact business with other members. It sets standards of business practices among its members and regulates:

- Settlement dates
- Ex dividend dates
- Rules of good delivery
- Confirmations
- Don't know (DK) procedures

THE CODE OF PROCEDURE

The Code of Procedure regulates how the FINRA investigates complaints and violations. It regulates the discovery phase of alleged violations of the Rules of Fair Practice. The Code of Procedure is not concerned with money; it is only concerned with rule violations.

THE CODE OF ARBITRATION

The Code of Arbitration provides a forum to resolve disputes. Arbitration provides a final and binding resolution to disputes involving a member and:

- Another member
- A registered agent
- A bank
- A customer

FINRA is divided into districts based on geography. Each district elects a committee to administer the association's rules. The committee is composed of up to 12 members who serve up to a three-year term. The committee appoints the Department of Enforcement to handle all trade practice complaints within the district and has the power to assess penalties against members who have violated one or more of the association's rules. The FINRA Executive Committee, which consists of the Board of Governors, oversees the national business of FINRA.

BECOMING A MEMBER OF FINRA

FINRA sets forth strict qualification standards that all prospective members must meet prior to being granted membership with FINRA. FINRA (or the new firm's SRO) is required to inspect each newly formed broker dealer within 6 months of the firm's registration with the SEC to ensure the firm is in compliance with the SEC's financial requirements. FINRA (or the new firm's SRO) is required to conduct second inspections within 12 months of the firm's registration to ensure compliance with all other rules. Each firm will appoint an executive representative who is authorized to deal with the association with regard to the member's business. Any firm that engages in interstate securities transactions with public customers is required to become a member of FINRA. Additionally, any broker dealer that wishes to participate as a selling group member in the distribution of mutual fund shares must also be a member of FINRA.

In order to become a member of FINRA, a firm must:

- Meet net capital requirements (solvency).
- Have at least two principals to supervise the firm.
- Have an acceptable business plan detailing its proposed business activities.
- Attend a premembership interview.

Members must also agree to:

- Abide by all of the associations rules.
- Abide by all federal and state laws.
- Pay dues, fees, and membership assessments as required by the association.

The FINRA member must pay the following fees:

- Basic membership fee.
- Fee for each representative and principal.
- Fee based on the firm's gross income.
- Fee for all branch offices.

A member failing to pays fees may be suspended or have its membership canceled upon 15 days written notice from FINRA.

The following are not eligible for membership with FINRA:

- Firms that have been expelled, barred, or suspended by a national securities association or exchange.
- Firms that are subject to a court injunction barring them from engaging in the securities business.
- Firms deemed nonqualified or unsuitable by the Board of Governors.
- Firms that have been barred from association with members of a national securities association or exchange.

All members must deal with nonmembers as members of the general public and may not offer nonmembers selling concessions. All suspended or expelled members must also be treated as members of the general public. Exempt from this rule are:

- Transactions in government securities.
- Transactions in municipal securities.
- Transactions executed on an exchange.
- Foreign broker dealers ineligible for registration with FINRA that have a correspondent relationship with a member or that have agreed to treat nonmembers in the United States as members of the general public.

FOREIGN BROKER DEALERS

As the financial markets continue to become more global in scope, more and more broker dealers are conducting international securities transactions. Foreign broker dealers that maintain offices within the United States must register as broker dealers in the United States. If the foreign broker dealer does not maintain an office in the United States but does solicit and execute orders from U.S. investors, the firm must register in the United States. If the firm only executes unsolicited orders or issues research reports that are distributed by a U.S. broker dealer, the firm need not register. The U.S. broker dealer distributing the foreign broker dealer's research must accept responsibility for the content of the report, and all orders must be directed to the U.S. broker dealer. Foreign broker dealers that do not maintain offices in the United States but who transact business with institutional clients do not have to register. If an employee of a foreign broker dealer comes to the United States to speak with clients or potential clients, that employee should be chaperoned by a registered representative if that person is not registered in the United States.

COMPENSATION PAID TO UNREGISTERED PERSONS

No member shall pay directly or indirectly any commissions, concessions, discounts, or fees to any person or entity without the person or entity being duly registered. A member may pay a foreign national person or entity a finder's fee for business introduced to the member, provided the member has made a diligent effort to be assured that the compensation received by the finder will not subject the finder to registration and such finder would not be subject to statutory disqualification. Additionally, the customers introduced by the finder must be foreign nationals or entities domiciled abroad. The customers must be given a written disclosure of the compensation arrangement and all confirmations must note the compensation arrangement with the finder. The finder's agreement must be made available for inspection by FINRA and maintained on the member's books.

REGISTRATION OF AGENTS/ASSOCIATED PERSONS

All individuals who engage in securities transactions with the public are required to be registered as associated persons. Failing to register people who engage in securities transactions can result in disciplinary charges being brought against the member. Prior to becoming registered as an associated person, all individuals must be sponsored by a member firm. All sponsoring firms are required to ascertain the applicant's:

- Business character
- Educational background
- Professional background

Once a member has certified the above information regarding the applicant, it may formally submit the individual's application for becoming an associated person, known as a U4. The applicant must fill out the form completely and submit the form with a set of fingerprints. A principal of the member firm must sign the application and certify that he or she has reviewed the applicant's background. All employees of the broker dealer who engage in any of the following activities must be fingerprinted:

- Sale of securities.
- Has access to or contact with cash or securities.

- Has access to or prepares records of original entry.
- Supervision of individuals engaged in any of the activities listed.

RETIRING REPRESENTATIVES/CONTINUING COMMISSIONS

Retiring representatives may continue to receive commissions on the business that they have built over their careers provided that a contract is in place prior to the representative's retirement. A retiring representative may continue to receive commissions on old business only and may not receive commissions on any new business and may not receive finder's fees. If the retired representative dies, the representative's beneficiary may continue to receive the commissions that were due the representative.

STATE REGISTRATION

In addition to registering with FINRA, all broker dealers and agents must register in their home states as well as in any state in which they transact business with the general public.

RETAIL COMMUNICATIONS/ COMMUNICATIONS WITH THE PUBLIC

Member firms will seek to increase their business and exposure through the use of both retail and institutional communications. Strict regulations are in place in order to ensure that all communications with the public adhere to industry guidelines. Some communications with the public are available to a general audience and include:

- Television/radio
- Publicly accessible websites
- Motion pictures
- Newspapers/magazines
- Telephone directory listings
- Signs/billboards
- Computer/Internet postings
- Videotape displays

- Other public media
- Recorded telemarketing messages

Other types of communications are offered to a targeted audience. These communications include:

- Market reports
- Password-protected websites
- Telemarketing scripts
- Form letters or e-mails (sent to more than 25 people)
- Circulars
- Research reports
- Printed materials for seminars
- Option worksheets
- Performance reports
- Prepared scripts for TV or radio
- Reprints of ads or retail communication

FINRA RULE 2210 COMMUNICATIONS WITH THE PUBLIC

FINRA Rule 2210 replaces the advertising and sales literature rules previously used to regulate member communications with the public. FINRA Rule 2210 streamlines member communication rules and reduces the number of communication categories from six to three. The three categories of member communication are:

- Retail communication
- Institutional communication
- Correspondence

RETAIL COMMUNICATION

Retail communication is defined as any written communication distributed or made available to more than 25 retail investors in a 30-day period. The communication may be distributed in hard copy or in electronic formats. The definition of a *retail investor* is any investor who does not meet the definition of an institutional investor. Retail communication contains all components of advertising and sales literature. All retail communications must be approved by a registered principal prior to first use. All retail communications must be maintained for three years from the date of the last use. A copy should be readily accessible for the first two years and the file should contain the name of the principal who approved communication as well as the date it was first and last used. If the member firm is a new member firm that has been in existence for less than 12 months based on the firm's approval date in the Central Registration Depository (CRD), the member must file all retail communications with FINRA 10 days prior to its first use unless the communication has been previously filed and contains no material changes or has been filed by another member, such as an investment company or ETF sponsor. Member firms that have been established for more than 12 months may file retail communications with FINRA 10 days after the communication is first used. Should FINRA determine that a member firm is making false or misleading statements in its retail communications with the public, FINRA may require the member to file all of its retail communication with the public with the association 10 days prior to its first use.

Knowing what communications are filed with FINRA and when they are filed with FINRA can present challenges for many test takers. The information that is contained in the communication and its intended recipients dictate when or if the communication is filed with FINRA. Exempt from FINRA's filing requirements are:

- Recruiting and generic advertisements
- Retail Communications created from a template previously filed with FINRA
- Retail Communications that do not promote a product or service
- Retail Communications that merely contain a list of products the member offers
- Retail Communications that do not contain investment advice
- Mutual fund profiles
- Reprints and excerpts of articles published by non-affiliated third parties
- Press releases issued only to media outlets
- Institutional communications
- Correspondence
- Internal communications

- Tombstone ads, preliminary and statutory / final prospectus filed with the SEC

It is important to note that while preliminary and statutory prospectus that are filed with the SEC are exempt from being filed with FINRA, free writing prospectus prepared by the broker-dealer are required to be filed with FINRA as part of retail communication.

The following types of retail communication must be filed with FINRA within 10 days of first being used:

- Storyboards for television or video Communications
- mutual fund communications that do not include raking information
- Communications containing information relating to publicly traded direct participation programs and sec-registered collateralized mortgage obligations
- SEC registered securities whose value is based on an index, a basket of securities, commodities, debt securities, or currencies. This includes ETFs, ETNs and other publicly offered structured products
- Free writing prospectus is prepared by the broker-dealer
- Report templates created from an investment analysis tool

Investment analysis tools allow individuals to input a set of criteria and have a computer software program model portfolios, potential outcomes or hypothetical returns using statistical analysis. If a member firm allows retail investors to access investment analysis tools,the firm must provide access to that tool to FINRA's advertising department within 10 days of its first use.

FINRA members are required to pre file the following retail communications 10 days prior to use:

- Communications containing single stock and other security futures
- Communications containing mutual fund ranking or comparisons created by the investment company
- Communications containing volatility ranking information concerning bond funds
- Communications prepared by member firms less than 1 year old
- Communications prepared by sanctioned firms or firms directed to pre-file my FINRA

For most retail communications, the term first use means when it is first published, broadcast, distributed or made available by the member.

All retail communication is required to be approved by a principal of the firm prior to its first use. A securities principal (Series 24) may approve most retail communication. Any retail communication relating to options must be approved by a registered options principal. Research reports must be approved by a supervisory analyst.

TAKE**NOTE!**

Research reports concerning only securities listed on a national securities exchange are excluded from Rule 2210's filing requirements.

INSTITUTIONAL COMMUNICATIONS

Institutional communication is defined as any written communication distributed or made available exclusively to institutional investors and should have a mark stating "for institutional use only." The communication may be distributed in hard copy or in electronic formats. Institutional communications do not have to be approved by a principal prior to first use so long as the member has established policies and procedures regarding the use of institutional communications and has trained its employees on the proper use of institutional communication. Institutional communication is also exempt from FINRA's filing requirement, but like retail communications it must be maintained by a member for three years and readily accessible for the first two years. If the member believes that the institutional communication or any part thereof may be seen by even a single retail investor, the communication must be handled as all other retail communication and is subject to the approval and filing requirements as if it was retail communication. This would be the case if an institutional client distributed the communication to its own individual clients. An institutional investor is a person or firm that trades securities for his or her own account or for the accounts of others. Institutional investors are generally limited to large financial companies. Because of their size and sophistication, fewer protective laws cover institutional investors. It is important to note that there is no minimum size for an institutional account. Institutional investors include:

- Broker dealers.
- Investment advisers.
- Investment companies.

- Insurance companies.
- Banks.
- Trusts.
- Savings and loans.
- Government agencies.
- Employment benefit plans with more than 100 participants.
- Any individuals or entities with more than $50,000,000 in assets.

CORRESPONDENCE

Correspondence consists of electronic and written communications between the member and up to 25 retail investors in a 30-day period. With the increase in acceptance of email as business communication, it would be impractical for a member to review all correspondence between the member and a customer. The member instead may set up procedures to review a sample of all correspondence, both electronic and hard copy. These procedures may include the use of automated lexicon screening tools. A firm using automated screening tools must know the limits of the tools and where required must supplement the automated review with human screening. If the member reviews only a sample of the correspondence, the member must train its associated people on the firm's procedures relating to correspondence and must document the training and ensure that the procedures are followed. Even though the member is not required to review all correspondence, the member must still retain all correspondence. The member should, where practical, review all incoming hard copy correspondence. Letters received by the firm could contain cash, checks, securities, or complaints. A principal of the firm may delegate the review of correspondence to a unregistered employee but the principal still retains all supervisory responsibility.

BROKER DEALER WEBSITES

A broker dealer will not be deemed to have a place of business in a state where it does not maintain an office simply by virtue of the fact that the publicly available website established by the firm or one of its agents is accessible from that state, so long as the following conditions are met:

- The website clearly states that the firm may only conduct business in states where it is properly registered to do so.
- The website only provides general information about the firm and does not provide specific investment advice.
- The firm or its agent may not respond to Internet inquiries with the intent to solicit business without first meeting the registration requirements in the state of the prospective customer.

The content of any website must be reviewed and approved by a principal prior to its first use and must be filed with FINRA within 10 days of use. If the firm or its agent updates the website and the update materially changes the information contained on the website, the updates must be reapproved by a principal and refiled with FINRA. It is important to note that a representaitve may never post to the firm's website without prior principal approval. All versions of the website are subject to a 3 year retention requirement. The website may (but is not required to) use the FINRA logo so long as the use is only to demonstrate that the firm is a FINRA member and a hyperlink to the FINRA website is included in close proximity to the logo.

BLIND RECRUITING ADS

A blind recruiting ad is an ad placed by the member firm for the specific purpose of finding job applicants. Blind recruiting ads are the only form of advertising that does not require the member's name to appear in the ad. The ads may not distort the opportunities or salaries of the advertised positions. All other ads are required to disclose the name of the member firm, as well as the relationship of the member to any other entities that appear in the ad.

GENERIC ADVERTISING

Generic advertising is designed to promote firm awareness and to advertise the products and services generally offered through the firm. Generic ads will generally include:

- Securities products offered (i.e., stocks, bonds, mutual funds).
- Contact name, number, and address.
- Types of accounts offered [i.e., individual, IRA, 401(k)].

TOMBSTONE ADS

A tombstone ad is an announcement of a new security offering coming to market. Tombstone ads are the only type of advertising that may be run while the securities are still in registration with the SEC. During the cooling-off period, only a preliminary prospectus may be sent to gather interest. A tombstone ad may only include:

- A description of the securities.
- A description of the business.
- A description of the transaction.
- Required disclaimers.
- Time and place of any stockholders' meetings regarding the sale of the securities.

Tombstone ads must include:

- A statement that the securities registration has not yet become effective.
- A statement that responding to the ad does not obligate the prospect.
- A statement as to where a prospectus may be obtained.
- A statement that the ad does not constitute an offer to sell the securities and that an offer may only be made by the prospectus.

TESTIMONIALS

From time to time, broker dealers will use testimonials made by people of national or local recognition in an effort to generate new business for the firm. If the individual giving the testimonial is quoting past performance relating to the firm's recommendations, it must be accompanied by a disclaimer that past performance is not indicative of future performance. If the individual giving the testimony received compensation in excess of $100, the fact that the person received compensation must also be disclosed. Should the individual's testimony imply that the person making the testimony is an expert, a statement regarding that person's qualifications as an expert must also be contained in the ad or sales literature. Research prepared by outside parties must disclose the name of the preparer.

FREE SERVICES

If a member firm advertises free services to customers or to people who respond to an ad, the services must actually be free to everyone and with no strings attached.

MISLEADING COMMUNICATIONS

The following are some examples of misleading statements that are not allowed to appear in advertising or sales literature:

- Excessive hedge clauses.
- Implying an endorsement by FINRA, the NYSE, or the SEC.
- Printing the FINRA logo in type that is larger than the type of the member's name.
- Implying that the member has larger research facilities than it actually has.
- Implying that an individual has higher qualifications than he or she actually has.

SECURITIES INVESTOR PROTECTION CORPORATION ACT OF 1970

The Securities Investor Protection Corporation (SIPC) is a government-sponsored corporation that provides protection to customers in the event of a broker dealer's failure. All broker dealers that are registered with the SEC are required to be SIPC members. All broker dealers are required to pay annual dues to SIPC's insurance fund to cover losses due to broker dealer failure. If a broker dealer fails to pay its SIPC assessment, it may not transact business until it is paid. Should a firm fall below its net capital requirement, it is deemed to be insolvent, and SIPC will petition in court to have a trustee appointed to liquidate the firm and protect the customers. The trustee must be a disinterested party, and, once the trustee is appointed, the firm may not conduct business or try to conceal any assets.

CUSTOMER COVERAGE

SIPC protects customers of a brokerage firm in much the same way that the FDIC protects customers of banks. SIPC covers customer losses that result from broker dealer failure, not for market losses. SIPC covers customers for up to $500,000 per separate customer. Of the $500,000, up to $250,000 may be in cash. Most broker dealers carry additional private insurance to cover larger accounts, but SIPC is the industry-funded insurance and is required by all broker dealers. The following are examples of separate customers:

Customer	Securities Market Value	Cash	SIPC Coverage
Mr. Jones	$320,000	$75,000	All
Mr. & Mrs. Jones	$290,000	$90,000	All
Mrs. Jones	$397,000	$82,000	All

All of the accounts shown would be considered separate customers, and SIPC would cover the entire value of all of the accounts. If an account has in excess of $250,000 in cash, the individual would not be covered for any amount exceeding $250,000 in cash and would become a general creditor for the rest. SIPC does not consider a margin account and cash account as separate customers, and the customer would be covered for the maximum of $500,000. SIPC does not offer coverage for commodities contracts, and all member firms must display the SIPC sign in the lobby of the firm. Customers must be notified at the time of account opening that the firm is an SIPC member. The firm must notify the customer in writing at the time of account opening and annually thereafter where the customer may obtain an SIPC brochure by contacting SIPC. The firm is required to provide SIPC's phone number and website address to the customer. If a broker dealer introduces customer accounts to a clearing broker dealer only one of the firms would be required to notify the customer of the availability of SIPC information. Many firms purchase excess insurance for customers that go above and beyond SIPC coverage. If the firm reduces or eliminates this excess coverage it must inform customers 30 days prior to the effective date of the change. Only bona fide customers are offered SIPC coverage. Officers and directors of the broker dealer and other personnel who are in control of a broker dealer would not have their accounts covered by SIPC. Coverage would be provided to the accounts of registered representatives and others at the firm who are not in a position to control the broker dealer.

Additionally, subordinated lenders and the firm's trading account would not be covered under SIPC.

TAKENOTE!

A customer's margin account is covered by SIPC only to the extent of the equity in the customer's account up to the $500,000 limit

THE SECURITIES ACTS AMENDMENTS OF 1975

The Securities Acts Amendments of 1975 gave the authority to the Municipal Securities Rulemaking Board (MSRB) to regulate the issuance and trading of municipal bonds. The MSRB has no enforcement division. Its rules are enforced by other regulators.

THE INSIDER TRADING AND SECURITIES FRAUD ENFORCEMENT ACT OF 1988

The Insider Trading and Securities Fraud Enforcement Act of 1988 set forth guidelines and controls for the use and dissemination of nonpublic material information. Nonpublic information is information that is not known by people outside of the company. Material information is information regarding a situation or development that will materially affect the company in the present or in the future. It is not only just for insiders to have this type of information, but it is required in order for them to do their jobs effectively. It is, however, unlawful for an insider to use this information to profit from a forthcoming move in the stock price. An insider is defined as any officer, director, 10 percent stockholder, or anyone who is in possession of nonpublic material information, as well as the spouse of any such person. Additionally, it is unlawful for the insider to divulge any of this information to any outside party. Trading on inside information has always been a violation of the Securities Exchange Act of 1934, and the Insider Trading Act prescribed penalties for violators, which include:

- A fine of the greater of 300 percent of the amount of the gain or 300 percent of the amount of the loss avoided or $1,000,000 for the person who acts on the information.
- A fine of up to $1,000,000 for the person who divulges the information.
- Insider traders may be sued by the affected parties.

- Criminal prosecutions.

Information becomes public information once it has been disseminated over public media. The SEC will pay a reward of up to 10 percent to informants who turn in individuals who trade on inside information. In addition to the insiders already listed, the following are also considered insiders:

- Accountants
- Attorneys
- Investment bankers

FIREWALL

Broker dealers that act as underwriters and investment bankers for corporate clients must have access to information regarding the company in order to advise the company properly. The broker dealer must ensure that no inside information is passed between its investment banking department and its retail trading departments. The broker dealer is required to physically separate these divisions by a firewall. The broker dealer must maintain written supervisory procedures to adequately guard against the wrongful use or dissemination of inside information.

THE TRUST INDENTURE ACT OF 1939

The Trust Indenture Act of 1939 requires that corporate bond issues in excess of $5,000,000 dollars that are to be repaid during a term in excess of one year, sold interstate, issue a trust indenture for the issue. The trust indenture is a contract between the issuer and the trustee. The trustee acts on behalf of all of the bondholders and ensures that the issuer is in compliance with all of the promises and covenants made to the bondholders. The trustee is appointed by the corporation and is usually a bank or a trust company. If the issuer defaults the trustee will take possession of the collateral pledged if any and liquidate it in an effort to repay bondholders. The Trust Indenture Act of 1939 only applies to corporate issuers. Both federal and municipal issuers are exempt.

TELEMARKETING RULES

FINRA Rule 3230 regulates how telemarketing calls are made by businesses. On your exam you may see the telemarketing rule tested under the telephone

Consumer Protection Act of 1991, FINRA Rule 3230, or as telemarketing rules. Telemarketing calls that are designed to have consumers invest in or purchase goods, services, or property must adhere to the strict guidelines. All firms must:

- Call only between the hours of 8 a.m. and 9 p.m. in the potential customer's time zone.
- Maintain a do-not-call list. Individuals placed on the do-not-call list may not be contacted by anyone at the firm for five years.
- Ensure that the solicitor gives the prospect the firm's name, address, and phone number. Caller ID must display the firm name and phone number, and caller ID blocking may not be used.
- Maintain adequate policies and procedures to maintain a firm-specific do-not-call list.
- Maintain adequate policies and procedures to ensure that numbers called do not appear on the National Do Not Call Registry.
- Train representatives on calling policies and use of the do-not-call list.
- Ensure that any fax solicitations have the firm's name, address, and phone number, and prohibit the use of unsolicited faxes.

TAKENOTE!

An interesting situation can arise when a customer of the firm who maintains an account with the firm is on the firm-specific do-not-call list. In these cases, a representative may not contact the customer unless it is to verify account information such as the mailing address. The customer may not be contacted to discuss holdings in the account or to make a recommendation.

DO-NOT-CALL LIST EXEMPTIONS

The following are exempt from the prohibited calls listed previously:

- Calls to existing customers who have executed a transaction or who have had an account containing cash or securities on deposit within the last 18 months or to a person who has contacted the member within the last 3 months.
- Calls when the caller has a personal relationship with the recipient.

- Calls to a person who has given written permission to be contacted by the firm and the number where the person may be contacted.
- Inadvertent calls to a number that now appears on the National Do Not Call Registry but was not included on the do-not-call list used by the member, so long as that list was not more than 31 days old.

THE PENNY STOCK COLD CALL RULE

SEC Rules 15g-2–15g-9, collectively known as the penny stock cold calling rule, were enacted in order to ensure that investors do not purchase penny stocks without knowing the risks. A penny stock is an unlisted security that trades below $5 per share and whose issuer does not meet the minimum financial listing requirements for an exchange or Nasdaq. Prior to purchasing a penny stock:

- The agent must make sure that the purchase is suitable.
- The customer must sign a suitability statement.
- The firm must supply a current quote.
- The firm must disclose the amount of commission earned by the firm and the agent.

TAKENOTE!

Established customers are exempt from the penny stock cold call rule. An established customer is one who has made three transactions in three different penny stocks on three different days. An established customer is also one who has had cash or securities on deposit with the firm during the previous 12 months. Also exempt from the rule are:

- Transactions executed by broker dealers whose commissions or markups from penny stock transactions do not exceed 5 percent of their total commissions or markups.
- Transactions with institutional investors.
- Private placements.
- Unsolicited transactions.
- Transactions with officers, directors, or 5 percent stockholders.

If a customer has an account containing a penny stock, the broker dealer carrying the customer's account must send the customer an account statement detailing the name and amount of each penny stock held in the customer's account and the value of the securities to the extent that the value can be determined.

VIOLATIONS AND COMPLAINTS

FINRA's Code of Procedure sets forth guidelines for the investigation of alleged violations and complaints against a member firm or a registered representative. FINRA staff originates many complaints against member firms and associated persons during their routine examinations of member firms. Complaints and allegations of wrongdoing may also originate from a customer of the member firm or from another member. If a FINRA staff member has received a complaint that alleges a violation of securities regulations, it is up to FINRA to determine if the complaint is meritorious. FINRA will begin an investigation of the complaint by notifying the member and/or the associated person that a complaint has been received and will request that the member or an associated person respond in writing. All requests for information must be met within 25 days from the day that the request was made. If the member fails to provide the requested information within the 25-day time frame, FINRA will send out a second request for the information. The second request will give the firm or the representative an additional 14 days to provide the information requested. If the information is not provided by the end of the 14 days, FINRA may choose to take action against the firm or the representative for failing to respond.

RESOLUTION OF ALLEGATIONS

Should FINRA find that the allegations are baseless, the association may dismiss it without action. However, if FINRA finds that the allegation has merit, it may be resolved through minor rule violation procedures or through a formal hearing process. If the allegations are uncontested, the firm or representative may sign an acceptance waiver and consent (AWAC) to resolve the issue. By signing the AWAC, the firm or representative does not contest the allegations, accepts whatever penalty is being prescribed, and waives the right to appeal. Additionally, by signing the AWAC, the firm or the representative does not admit to any wrongdoing, but simply does not contest it.

MINOR RULE VIOLATION

A minor rule violation (MRV) letter is traditionally used in cases that involve only small violations. FINRA has outlined a number of rule violations that qualify to be resolved using a MRV procedure. It is offered to respondents in an effort to avoid a costly hearing. Under MRV procedure, the maximum penalty is a censure and a $2,500 fine. If the MRV procedure is offered, the member or associated person has 10 business days to accept it. By signing the MRV letter, the respondent does not admit or deny the allegations and gives up the right to appeal the decision. Should the offer of MRV procedure not be accepted, the Department of Enforcement will proceed with a formal hearing to determine if a violation has occurred. Possible penalties, after a firm or representative has been found to have violated one or more of the association's rules, include:

- Censure
- Suspension for up to one year
- Expulsion for up to 10 years
- Barred for life
- Fined any amount
- Any other penalty deemed appropriate such as restitution

Decisions of the Department of Enforcement may be appealed within 15 days to the National Adjudicatory Council (NAC). If no action is taken, the decision of the Department of Enforcement becomes final in 45 days. Should the NAC determine that the appeal is meritorious, it must start a review within a 45-day period. The decision of the NAC may be appealed to the SEC and finally to the court system. Upon final determination, all fines, penalties, and costs must be paid promptly.

ELECTRONIC BLUE SHEETS

The Intermarket Surveillance Group (ISG) is an organization made up of securities exchanges, market centers, and SROs. The purpose of the ISG is to detect fraudulent and manipulative market activity. Members of the ISG work together to develop programs and procedures designed to identify potential fraudulent activity and to share their findings with the other members. If a member of the ISG, such as FINRA or the SEC, requests information from a broker dealer during the course of an investigation, the broker dealer will submit the requested trade data for the period in question by using the

Electronic Blue Sheet (EBS). The EBS will detail all trade data for the member firm's proprietary accounts as well as trade data for customer accounts.

MEDIATION

Mediation is an informal attempt by two parties to try to resolve a dispute prior to entering into the formal arbitration process. During the mediation process the two parties meet to discuss the contested issue, and the dialog is monitored by a mediator. The mediator is a neutral person with industry knowledge suggested by FINRA who tries to help the parties reach an agreement. If the mediator is not acceptable, the parties may select another mediator from a list of approved mediators or their own independent mediator. Prior to entering into the mediation process, both parties must agree to try to resolve the issue in mediation and must split the mediator's fee. The mediation process begins with an initial joint meeting where both parties lay out their claims for the mediator and the other party. During the second phase of the process, each side meets with the mediator individually in meetings known as caucuses. The mediator is a neutral party and will not disclose information provided during the caucus sessions to the opposing side. The mediation process will continue until an agreement is reached, the mediator declares an impasse with no possible resolution, or one of the parties or the mediator withdraws from the process in writing. The mediation process may provide a resolution for all or some of the contested issues. Issues that are not resolved in mediation may be resolved through formal arbitration. A person who served as a mediator in a dispute that ultimately ends up in arbitration may not serve on the arbitration panel.

CODE OF ARBITRATION

FINRA's Code of Arbitration Procedure provides parties with a forum to resolve disputes. Most claims submitted to arbitration are financial in nature, although other claims may be submitted. Sexual harassment and discrimination claims are not required to be resolved in arbitration unless both parties specifically agree to arbitrate. Class action claims are also not resolved in arbitration. Class action status is awarded by the court system. Arbitration provides a cost-effective alternative to dispute resolution, and many disputes will be resolved much sooner than they otherwise may have been in court. All industry members are required to settle all disputes through arbitration. A public customer, however, must agree in writing to settle any dispute through arbitration. When a customer opens an account with a broker dealer, the broker dealer will often have the customer sign a customer agreement, although this is not required by industry standards. The customer agreement usually contains a predispute arbitration clause whereby the customer agrees to settle any dispute that may arise in arbitration rather than in court. Should the customer request a copy of the predispute arbitration clause the member has 10 business days to provide it to the customer.

THE ARBITRATION PROCESS

Arbitration begins when an aggrieved party, known as the claimant, files a statement of claim, along with a submission agreement, and payment for the arbitration fee with FINRA. The party alleged to have caused the claimant harm must respond to the statement of claim within 45 calendar days and is known as the respondent. The response is sent to both the arbitration director and the claimant, and the claimant then has 10 calendar days to reply to both the arbitration director and respondent. Dispute resolution through arbitration is available for matters involving:

- Member vs. member
- Bank vs. member
- Member vs. bank
- Member vs. registered representative
- Registered representative vs. member
- Customer vs. member
- Member vs. customer

SIMPLIFIED ARBITRATION

Simplified arbitration is available for disputes involving amounts of $50,000 or less. Traditionally, simplified arbitration provides no opportunity for a hearing. Parties submit their case in writing only. One arbitrator reviews the case and renders a decision. If a public customer is involved in arbitration in a matter of $50,000 or less, excluding interest and expenses, the customer can request a hearing in front of a single arbitrator. For amounts that exceed $50,000, a hearing must be held.

LARGER DISPUTES

Larger disputes will be submitted to a panel of up to three arbitrators to render a decision on the matter. A hearing will take place and evidence and testimony will be presented to the panel. The number of arbitrators must always be odd, so the panel will be made up of one or three arbitrators from both the public and the industry. An arbitrator will be deemed to be a non public or industry arbitrator if the person is or was in the securities industry at any point in the last 5 years. Included in this definition are persons associated with hedge funds and accountants and attorneys whose practices dedicated at least 20 percent of their time to industry clients within the last two years. An accountant or attorney will be deemed to be a public arbitrator if 10 percent or less of the business of said professional was dedicated to industry clients in the last two years and the revenue received was less than $50,000.

AWARDS UNDER ARBITRATION

Awards under arbitration are final and binding; there is no appeal. If a monetary payment has been awarded, the party required to pay has 30 days to comply with the decision. A member or a registered representative who fails to pay an award under arbitration is subject to suspension. All pending arbitrations settled prior to final judgement, and arbitrations settled in favor of the customer will be disclosed on BrokerCheck. If an arbitration is settled in favor of the firm or representative it will be removed from BrokerCheck. Any sanction by a regulator that carries a penalty of $15,000 or more will also be disclosed on BrokerCheck.

POLITICAL CONTRIBUTIONS

FINRA enforces the rules enacted by the MSRB for its members that engage in municipal securities business. MSRB Rule G-38 puts strict limits on the amount of political contributions that may be made by a municipal finance professional (MFP). An MFP is an agent who is primarily engaged in any of the following:

- Soliciting municipal underwriting.
- Acting as a financial adviser or consultant.
- Trading or selling municipal securities.
- Providing investment advice or issuing research reports relating to municipal securities to the public.
- Directing supervisors of any agent acting in the above capacity.
- Acting as an executive who oversees municipal dealers or departments.

MFPs may only make political contributions to candidates in an election in which they are eligible to vote. The maximum amount of their contribution is limited to $250 per candidate per election. If an MFP donates more than $250 or makes a contribution to a candidate in an election in which he or she is not able to vote, a violation has occurred, and the employing firm will be banned from engaging in municipal securities business with the issuer for two years. The two-year ban will follow the MFP should the MFP change firms. Both the new firm and the previous employer will be subject to the amount of time that remains on the two-year ban. Should an MFP make a political contribution to an incumbent that would subject the employing firm to a ban, that ban will expire if the incumbent loses the election. This political contribution does not apply to federal elections such as for senators.

EXAMPLE

If an MFP donated $200 to a mayoral candidate in a district where the MFP does not live and, as a result, could not vote in the election, the employing firm could not underwrite that municipality's debt for two years.

If an MFP contributes more than $250 or contributes to a candidate that he or she is not entitled to vote for, the employing firm must notify the issuer by filing forms G37 and G38 by the last day of the month following the end of each calendar quarter. These forms will tell the issuer:

- The amount of the contribution and the contributor category.
- The name and title of the political official and his or her political party.
- A list of the municipal issuers the firm engages in business with.

If the contribution is in line with MSRB Rule 37, the employing firm is not required to file forms G37 and G38. If an executive officer gives more than $250, the donation must be reported, but the firm would not be banned from engaging in municipal securities business with the issuer. Additionally, if the firm employs consultants to help the firm obtain municipal securities business from issuers, the firm must send forms G37 and G38 to the MSRB at the end of each calendar quarter listing:

- The name of the consultant or company.
- The role in which the consultant is acting and the amount of compensation.
- A list of municipal securities business obtained by using the consultant.
- A copy of all consulting agreements.
- Termination dates for consulting agreements.

The dealer also must disclose information relating to the use of consultants to the issuers. The dealer may disclose the information on an issue-specific basis or on an issuer-specific basis. If the dealer notifies issuers on an issuer basis, the dealer must send issuers updated information annually even if there have been no changes.

INVESTMENT ADVISER REGISTRATION

It is unlawful for an investment adviser to conduct securities business without being duly registered or exempt from registration. State registration exemptions are provided for investment advisers who:

- Are federally registered.
- Manage portfolios for investment companies.
- Manage portfolios in excess of $110,000,000.
- Have no office in the state and conduct business exclusively with financial institutions.
- Have no office in the state and offer advice to fewer than five clients in any 12-month period. This is known as the de minimis exemption.

INVESTMENT ADVISER REPRESENTATIVE

All investment adviser representatives who maintain offices within the state must register within the state. An investment adviser representative is an individual who:

- Gives advice on the value of the securities.
- Gives advice on the advisability of buying or selling securities.
- Solicits new advisory clients.
- Is an officer, director, or partner of the investment adviser.

An investment adviser may not employ any representative who is not duly registered. Clerical and administrative employees are not considered representatives and do not need to register.

THE NATIONAL SECURITIES MARKETS IMPROVEMENT ACT OF 1996

The National Securities Markets Improvement Act of 1996 (the Coordination Act) eliminated regulatory duplication of effort and established registration requirements for investment advisers. A federally covered investment adviser must register with the SEC and is any investment adviser that:

- Manages at least $110,000,000.
- Manages investment company portfolios.
- Is not registered under state laws.

All federally registered investment advisers must pay state filing fees and notify the administrator in the states in which they conduct business. The state securities administrator may not audit a federally covered investment adviser unless that adviser's principal office is located in that administrator's state. An investment adviser is required to register with the state if it manages less than $100,000,000. Once the investment adviser reaches $100,000,000 in assets under management (AUM), the adviser becomes eligible for federal registration. An investment adviser that manages between $100,000,000 and $110,000,000 may choose to register either with the state or with the SEC. If the investment adviser thinks that its asset base will exceed $110,000,000, it should register with the SEC. An investment adviser that manages $110,000,000 or more must register with the SEC. If a federally covered investment adviser's AUM falls below $90,000,000, the adviser must withdraw its federal registration by filling form ADV-W and is required to register with the appropriate states within 180 days. Like most regulations, there are rare exceptions to the rule of when an investment adviser may register with the SEC. The Dodd-Frank Wall Street Reform Act of 2010 increased the AUM for federal registration to its current levels and defined three categories of investment advisers:

- Small adviser: Advisers with less than $25,000,000 AUM.
- Midsize advisers: Advisers with $25,000,000–$100,000,000 AUM.
- Large advisers: Advisers with more than $100,000,000 AUM.

Pension consultants must have at least $200,000,000 AUM to be eligible to become federally registered.

INVESTMENT ADVISER REGISTRATION

An investment adviser must file the following with the state securities administrator before becoming registered:

- Application Form ADV.
- Filing fees.
- An audited balance sheet within 90 days of year end.

INVESTMENT ADVISER CAPITAL REQUIREMENTS

An investment adviser must maintain a minimum level of financial solvency. For advisers with custody of customer's cash and securities, the investment adviser must maintain minimum net capital of $35,000. If the adviser is unable to meet this requirement, it may post a surety bond. Deposits of cash and securities will alleviate the surety bond requirement. An adviser is considered to have custody if customers' cash and securities are held at the firm or if the adviser has full discretion over customers' accounts. Full discretion allows the adviser to withdraw cash and securities from the customer's account without consulting the customer. Advisers that have only limited discretionary authority over customers' accounts need to maintain a minimum of $10,000 in net capital. An adviser with limited discretionary authority may only buy and sell securities for the customer's benefit without consulting the customer. It may not withdraw or deposit cash or securities without the customer's consent. Investment adviser representatives are not required to maintain a minimum level of liquidity.

EXAMS FOR INVESTMENT ADVISERS

The state securities administrator may require investment adviser representatives as well as the officers and directors of the firm to take an exam, which may be oral, written, or both. The registration becomes effective at noon 30 days after the application has been filed. The administrator may require that an announcement of the investment adviser's intended registration be published in the newspaper.

INVESTMENT ADVISER ADVERTISING AND SALES LITERATURE

All advertising and sales literature for an investment adviser must be filed with the state securities administrator. The administrator may require prior approval of form letters, prospectuses, and pamphlets.

The following records must be kept for a minimum of five years for investment advisers:

- Advertising and sales literature
- Account statements
- Order tickets/order memorandum

TAKENOTE!

Investment advisers are prohibited from using testimonials or statements regarding a client's experience with the adviser as part of any advertisement or sales literature.

All investment advisers must keep accurate records relating to:

- Cash receipts and disbursements.
- Income and expense ledgers.
- Order tickets, including the customer's name.
- The adviser's name, including the executing broker and discretionary information.
- Ledgers and confirmations for all customers for whom the adviser has custody.
- Financial statements and trial balance.
- All written recommendations to customers.
- Copies of advertisements, circulars, and articles sent to more than 10 people.
- Copies of calculations sent to more than 10 people.

All books and records must be kept for five years readily accessible and for two years at the adviser's office. Records may be kept on a computer or microfiche as long as the data may be viewed and printed.

INVESTMENT ADVISER BROCHURE DELIVERY

An investment adviser is required to provide all prospective clients with a brochure or with Form ADV Part 2 at least 48 hours prior to the signing of the contract or at least at the time of the signing of the contract if the client is given a five-day grace period to withdraw without penalty. The brochure or Form ADV Part 2 will state:

- How and when fees are charged.
- The types of securities the adviser does business in.
- How recommendations are made.
- The type of clients the adviser has.
- The qualifications of officers and directors.

SOFT DOLLARS

Brokerage firms will often provide investment advisers with services that go beyond execution and research to assist the investment adviser in its business. These services are provided in exchange for commission business and are known as soft dollars. The services received should normally be research related. However, in some instances the services received are used for other purposes and benefit the adviser. In order for the soft dollar arrangement to be included in the safe harbor provisions, investment advisers must ensure that the services received are for the benefit of the client and pay careful attention to the disclosure requirements relating to all soft dollar arrangements. If an adviser receives soft dollar compensation from a broker dealer to whom the adviser directs customer transactions (known as directed transactions) the adviser must disclose any arrangement to clients. The fees charged to execute the transactions should be fair and reasonable, in line with what is available in the marketplace and in line with the value of the services offered to the adviser and its clients. The execution fees are not required to be the lowest and simply using a broker dealer whose services are more expensive will not constitute a breach of the adviser's fiduciary duty. If the adviser directs transactions to a broker dealer in exchange services that benefit the adviser, the adviser must disclosure all facts relating to the arrangement and receive the client's written consent to enter into the arrangement, even if such arrangement does not increase the costs to the client. If the adviser selects broker dealers to execute client orders based on the research or other services provided, it must be disclosed on form ADV.

The SEC has divided soft dollar considerations into the following categories:

- Goods/services
- Accounting fees
- Association membership fees
- Cable television
- Commission rebates
- Computer hardware
- Computer software
- Conferences/seminars
- Consulting services
- Courier/postage/express mail
- Custodial fees
- Electronic databases
- Employee salary/benefits
- Execution assistance
- Industry publications
- Legal fees
- Management fees
- Miscellaneous expenses
- Office equipment/supplies
- Online quotation and news services
- Portfolio management software
- Rent
- Research/analysis reports
- Telephone expenses
- Travel expenses
- Tuition/training costs
- Utilities expenses

TAKENOTE!

Only the items that can truly be deemed to be for the benefit of the client are within the safe harbor. Valuation software and other research related items are within the safe harbor, while paying for a laptop or rent for the adviser would not be within the safe harbor.

BROKER DEALERS ON THE PREMISES OF OTHER FINANCIAL INSTITUTIONS

As the financial services business continues to bring together investment services with other more traditional banking services, it is more common to see brokerage services offered at retail bank locations. Broker dealers that offer investment services at bank branches must follow certain guidelines. The setting in which the broker dealer conducts its business should be separate from where the retail banking business is being conducted, if practical. Broker dealers must disclose to the customer, at or before the time that the customer opens the account, that the deposits are not guaranteed by the FDIC or the financial institution and are subject to the loss of principal. These same disclosures must also appear in all advertising and sales literature issued by the broker dealer operating on the location of other financial institutions. The host financial institution must sign an agreement stating that FINRA and SEC are allowed to have access to any location where the member conducts its business. The member is required to promptly notify the financial institution if it terminates an associated person for cause.

THE UNIFORM SECURITIES ACT

In the early half of the twentieth century, each state securities regulator developed its state's rules and regulations for transacting securities business within the state. The result was regulations that varied widely from state to state. The Uniform Securities Act (USA) laid out model legislation for all states in an effort to make each state's rules and regulations more uniform and easier to address. The USA, also known as "The Act," sets minimum qualification standards for each state securities administrator. The state securities administrator is the top securities regulator within the state. The state securities administrator may be the attorney general of that state or an individual appointed specifically to that post. The USA also:

- Prohibits the state securities administrator from using the post for personal benefit or from disclosing information.
- Gives the state securities administrator authority to enforce the rules of the USA within that state.
- Gives the administrator the ability to set certain registration requirements for broker dealers, agents, and investment advisers.
- Allows administrators to set fee and testing requirements.

- Allows administrators to suspend or revoke the state registration of a broker dealer, agent, investment adviser, a security or a security's exemption from registration.
- Sets civil and criminal penalties for violators.

The state-based laws set forth by the USA are also known as blue-sky laws.

SARBANES-OXLEY ACT

The Sarbanes-Oxley Act, also known as the Public Company Accounting Reform and Investor Protection Act of 2002, was enacted to help restore confidence in the financial reports and accounting standards of publicly traded companies. The act created the Public Company Accounting Oversight Board to oversee, regulate, and discipline accounting firms' activities when performing auditing functions for publicly traded companies. Section 302 of the Sarbanes-Oxley Act requires the management of publicly traded companies to affirm the accuracy of the company's financial reports and to accept responsibility for the content of the reports by signing all annual and quarterly reports filed under the Securities Exchange Act of 1934. The principal executive officer as well as the principal financial officer must:

- Sign an acknowledgment that they have read the report.
- Certify to their knowledge that the financial reports do not contain any untrue or misleading statements.
- Certify that to their knowledge the reports do not omit any material fact and accurately represent the company's financial condition for the period covered by the report.
- Establish internal controls to ensure the accurate reporting of all of the issuer's subsidiaries.
- Evaluate the effectiveness of the internal controls within 90 days prior to the filing of the report and file a report relating to the effectiveness of the internal controls.
- Disclose to the audit committee and the board of directors any deficiencies with internal controls, any act of fraud involving management, or any employee significantly involved in the company's internal controls.
- Disclose any material changes to the internal controls or any weaknesses or corrective actions taken.

Section 401 of the Sarbanes-Oxley Act requires financial reports to contain detailed information regarding any off balance-sheet transactions, obligations, and liabilities the company may have engaged in or have outstanding. The statement may not contain any false or misleading information.

Section 402 of the Sarbanes-Oxley Act enhanced conflict of interest rules regarding loans made by the company to any officer. Section 402 of the act made it unlawful for any company to extend or maintain personal loans either directly or indirectly through a subsidiary to or for any officer of the company.

Section 403 of the Sarbanes-Oxley Act requires that the company's management as well as any owner of 10 percent or more of the company's securities file reports regarding holdings and transactions in the company's securities. These reports must be filed within 10 days of the person becoming an officer or a 10 percent holder. If any person subject to the reporting requirements of Section 403 purchases or sells the company's securities or enters into a security-based swap agreement a report of the transaction must be filed within two business days. Such reports may be filed electronically.

Section 404 of the Sarbanes-Oxley Act requires that management file with the annual report a report detailing the company's internal controls over financial reporting. The company's independent auditor is required to certify management's report regarding its internal controls.

SEC REGULATION S-K

SEC Regulation S-K sets forth reporting requirements regarding transactions with an issuer's related persons, promoters, and certain control people, as well as with their immediate family members. Regulation S-K defines an immediate family member as any of the following individuals:

- Spouse
- Parents
- Mother-in-law/father-in-law
- Brother/sister
- Brother-in-law/sister-in-law
- Children/stepchildren/children-in-law

Any transaction entered into with the above identified parties with a value exceeding $120,000 during the issuer's fiscal year must be reported. The issuer is also required to maintain policies for the review, approval, and ratification of related party transactions and is required to disclose such polices even if the issuer has no related parties transactions to report.

TAKENOTE!

The review and disclosure requirements only relate to relationships that are current at the time the transaction occurs. Should a relationship terminate due to divorce prior to the transaction, the transaction is not subject to the disclosure requirements of Regulation S-K.

Regulation S-K also regulates the use of forward-looking settlements as defined in Chapter 3. Issuers must use a reasonable basis and time frame for its forward looking statements and must identify the statements with key words.

SEC REGULATION M-A

SEC Regulation M-A is a subsection of Regulation S-K and was designed to simplify the reporting, communication, and filling requirements and procedures relating to mergers and acquisitions. Regulation M-A requires that a "plain English" term sheet be filed relating to any merger, acquisition, or going-private transaction. This plain English term sheet is designed to clearly communicate with existing shareholders so they may easily understand the terms of the proposed transaction, such as:

- Who is offering to buy my securities?
- What are the types and amounts of securities subject to the offer?
- How much is being offered and what is the form of payment?
- Does the bidder have the ability to make payment?
- How long do I have to tender in the offer?
- Can the offer be changed or extended, and under what circumstances?
- How will I be notified if the offer is changed or extended?

- What are the conditions to the offer?
- How do I tender into the offer?
- How long do I have to withdraw previously tendered shares?
- What steps do I need to take to withdraw previously tendered shares?
- If the transaction is negotiated, is the board of directors for or against the offer?
- Is this the first step in a going-private transaction?
- Will the tender offer be followed by a merger if all the company's shares are not tendered in the offer?
- What will happen if I decide not to tender my shares?
- What is the market value (if traded) or the net asset or liquidation value (if not traded) of my shares as of a recent date?
- Who can I speak to if I have questions about the tender offer?

Regulation M-A also allows additional types of communication with shareholders regarding proposed transactions and allows certain communications to be made or filed electronically.

Regulation M-A permits:

- The dissemination of more information on a timely basis, so long as the written communications are filed on the date of first use.
- More communications before the filing of a registration statement in connection with either a stock tender offer or a stock merger transaction.
- More communications before the filing of a proxy statement (whether or not a business combination transaction is involved).
- More communications regarding a proposed tender offer without commencing the offer and requiring the filing and dissemination of specified information.
- Harmonizing the various communications principles applicable to business combinations under the Securities Act, tender offer rules, and proxy rules.
- Elimination of the confidential treatment currently available for merger proxy statements, except when communications made outside the proxy statement are limited to those specified in Rule 135.
- Combining the existing schedules for issuer and third-party tender offers into one schedule available for all tender offers, entitled Schedule TO.

THE HART-SCOTT-RODINO ACT

The Hart-Scott-Rodino Act requires both parties in certain mergers and acquisitions to file notification of the transaction with the Federal Trade Commission (FTC) and with the Department of Justice (DOJ). Parties required to file premerger notifications may file electronically with the appropriate departments and must wait until a 30-day waiting period expires prior to closing the transaction (15 days for all cash offers). The waiting period begins on the date the notification is first filed and allows the FTC and DOJ to review any anticompetitive or antitrust impact the transaction may have on the economy. Any party required to file may request that the waiting period be terminated before the statutory period expires. A request for early termination may be granted only after compliance with the rules and if both the FTC and DOJ Antitrust Division have completed their review and determined not to take any enforcement action during the waiting period. If after a request for additional information has been issued the agency determines that no further action is necessary, the waiting period may be terminated before full compliance with the second request is made.

Exempt from the filing requirements of the act are things such as:

- Acquisition of real estate.
- Purchase of interests in oil reserves less than $500,000,000.
- Purchase of durable goods.

FINRA RULE 5150 (FAIRNESS OPINION)

Any member who issues a fairness opinion to shareholders in connection with a proposed transaction must establish and maintain procedures under which fairness opinions may be issued. Members must establish a fairness committee and outline the qualifications required for committee members. The processes and methods for evaluating the fairness of any proposed transaction must also be detailed in the procedures. Member issuing fairness options must also disclose any potential conflicts of interest the member may have in connection with the opinion. Members that issue fairness opinions must disclose:

- If the member acted as a financial adviser to either party.
- If the opinion is contingent upon the successful completion of the transaction.

- If the member has received or will receive compensation from either party.
- Any material relationship with either party in the last two years.
- The categories of information used to evaluate the fairness of the transaction.
- Procedures used to establish the opinion.
- If the opinion was approved by the fairness committee.

SEC REGULATION S-X

SEC Regulation S-X sets forth guidelines for how issuers that file reports under the Securities Act of 1933 or the Securities Exchange Act of 1934 account for certain assets that appear on their balance sheets. Issuers that normally would account for the value of assets under an equity method may account for the value of the asset under a fair value method. The value of the asset will be reported on the balance sheet at its fair value, with changes in the asset's value between reporting periods being reported on the issuer's income statement. Under the fair value method the issuer will no longer report its share of income or loss from the investment on its income statement. Issuers of securities whose investment in a subsidiary or entity is equal to 50 percent or less of the subsidiary or entity, and when the income of the subsidiary or entity is 20 percent or more of the issuer's income, are required to file separate financial statements for that subsidiary or entity in connection with the issuer's financial statements, when the value of the investment is accounted for under the equity method. If the income generated by the subsidiary or entity is 10 percent or less than the issuer's income, the issuer may consolidate the income from the investment on its balance sheet and income statements.

A credit default swap (CDS) is a derivative security that is used to transfer the risk of default from the holder of a credit instrument to the seller of the CDS. The buyer of the CDS makes payments to the seller of the contract, much like the premium on an insurance policy. The CDS is based on a notational or stated amount of value of a particular reference issue or issues not on an actual bond. The seller of the CDS will be required to make a payment to the buyer if certain stipulated credit events take place, such as a default or a credit rating downgrade by an NSCO.

A CDS can also be used by speculators to bet on the creditworthiness of the reference issues. Credit default swaps have margin requirements that are based on the contract's term and the interest rate or basis point spread above the London Interbank Offered Rate or LIBOR and based on whether the account holder is long or short the CDS. The contract requirement for an account short a CDS is anywhere from 1 to 50 percent of the notional amount, while the margin requirement for buyers of CDS are usually half that of the seller's margin requirement.

CHAPTER 11

Pretest

SECURITIES INDUSTRY RULES AND REGULATIONS

1. You are looking to increase your book of business and are planning to step up your marketing efforts. Which of the following would NOT be considered retail communication?
   a. A research report
   b. A prospecting script
   c. An invitation to a seminar
   d. A letter to a customer requesting a meeting to discuss her portfolio

2. You have an account with a brokerage firm that has filed for bankruptcy. There is $370,000 in market value in the account and $75,000 in cash. Your spouse also has an account with $300,000 in market value and $90,000 in cash. What will SIPC cover?
   a. A total of $500,000 for both accounts.
   b. Everything is covered.
   c. Only the cash is covered.
   d. Only the securities are covered.

3. Which of the following acts concerns itself with the registration of broker dealers and their required net capital?
   a. SIPC Act of 1970
   b. Securities Exchange Act of 1934
   c. Broker Dealer Fiscal Responsibility Act of 1937
   d. Securities Act of 1933

4. Under the Insider Trading and Securities Fraud Enforcement Act of 1988, the maximum fine for violators is:
   a. three times the amount of money made.
   b. three times the amount of money the investor avoided losing.
   c. unlimited.
   d. treble damages.

5. A brokerage firm wants to appeal the decision of the Department of Enforcement. The appeal will first go to:
   a. the SEC.
   b. the court of appeals.
   c. the national appeal board.
   d. the National Adjudicatory Council (NAC).

6. An MFP donates $2,500 to a candidate in an election where the MFP is not able to vote. The candidate running for municipal office is an old college friend of the MFP. Which of the following is true?
   a. The employing firm has no restrictions due to the relationship between the MFP and the candidate.
   b. If the employing firm wants to bid on an offering in that municipality, it must get prior permission from FINRA.
   c. The firm is restricted from bidding on offerings in that municipality for two years.
   d. The firm is restricted for 270 days.

7. Sanctions imposed by FINRA are effective within how many days of a written decision?
   a. 15 days
   b. 30 days
   c. 45 days
   d. 60 days

8. A registered broker dealer must do which of the following?
   I. Pay SIPC dues.
   II. Display the SIPC sign.
   III. Post a fidelity bond.
   IV. Obtain fingerprint records for associated persons.
      a. I and II
      b. I and III
      c. I, II, and III
      d. I, II, III, and IV

9. A registered broker dealer who is a syndicate member may perform which of the following during the cooling-off period?

   I. Run a tombstone ad.

   II. Gather interest.

   III. Send out the final prospectus.

   IV. Send out retail communications.

   a. I and III
   b. II and IV
   c. I and II
   d. II and III

10. A registered representative who does not contest the accusations of FINRA may sign which of the following to resolve the issue?

   a. An AWAC
   b. A no-contest letter
   c. An offer of settlement
   d. A submission agreement

11. Which of the following are considered retail communications ?

   I. Email to a representative's client list

   II. The firm's website

   III. Invitations to a seminar

   IV. Flyers handed out during a presentation

   a. III and IV
   b. I and II
   c. I, III, and IV
   d. I, II, III, and IV

12. All of the following are exempt from the Do Not Call policies, EXCEPT:

   a. a call from a religious organization.
   b. a call from a nonprofit organization seeking to raise money.
   c. a call to an existing client.
   d. a call to another state.

13. An investor had filed a complaint with FINRA alleging that his firm violated the industry rules. Which of the following bylaws governs the resolution of such matters?

a. Rules of Fair Practice

b. Uniform Practice Code

c. Code of Procedure

d. Code of Arbitration

14. A new member firm that has not filed with FINRA is required to:

a. file its retail communication 10 days after first use.

b. file its retail communication 10 days prior to first use.

c. receive FINRA approval to begin retail communication.

d. file its retail communication five days prior to first use.

15. A syndicate has published a tombstone ad prior to the issue becoming effective. Which of the following must appear in the tombstone ad?

I. A statement that the registration has not yet become effective.

II. A statement that the tombstone ad is not an offer to sell the securities.

III. Contact information.

IV. A no commitment statement.

a. I and III

b. II and IV

c. III and IV

d. I, II, III, and IV

Answer Keys

CHAPTER 1: BROKERAGE OFFICE PROCEDURES

1. (B) A principal is not required to obtain a copy of the employee's U5 directly from the employee. The principal may obtain it from FINRA as well.
2. (C) All gifts given to an employee of another member firm must be given to the member for distribution to the employee and a record must be kept of the gift.
3. (D) The sales assistant who accepts orders would have to register.
4. (C) Shareholders who attend the meeting will not be able to vote by the proxy they received; they will vote at the meeting. The shareholders must return their proxies 10 days prior to the annual meeting.
5. (A) Firms that do not self-clear are required to do all of the choices listed except clear on an omnibus basis.
6. (B) A customer who purchases a security and then decides that it is unsuitable is not a reason to reject delivery.
7. (D) The seller will not keep the dividend.
8. (D) A customer must receive a statement whenever there is activity in the account. The investor purchased the shares two months ago and must have received a statement that month. Because the shares were purchased on margin, interest is being charged on the loan. The debiting of interest to the customer's account is considered activity, and the customer must receive a statement for those months as well.
9. (D) A firm may charge a fee for all of the services listed.
10. (A) A firm may ignore a call for cash for up to $1,000.

CHAPTER 2: RECORD KEEPING, FINANCIAL REQUIREMENTS, AND REPORTING

1. (C) Broker dealers must post trades to the blotter by the end of the following business day, or T + 1.
2. (B) General ledgers must be maintained for six years.
3. (D) Trial balances must be prepared no later than by the 10th business day following the month's end.
4. (C) A new broker dealer may not have an aggregate indebtedness in excess of 8:1 in its first year.
5. (C) Under SEC Rule 15c3-1, if a clearing broker fails to maintain its minimum net capital of $250,000 or if its aggregate indebtedness is greater than 15 times its net capital, it must perform all of the things listed except list the steps being taken to correct the problem.
6. (A) The haircut for an aged fail to deliver is 15 percent for listed, 40 percent otherwise, for contracts more than five business days old.
7. (B) A broker dealer that executes mutual fund orders on a wire basis must have net capital of $25,000.
8. (B) FOCUS Part I reports are filed electronically and are required to be filed by carrying firms within 10 days of the month's end.
9. (C) All of the answers are true except that a subordinated loan is for a minimum of one year.
10. (B) The firm's minimum net capital is $50,000 because it is receiving customers' cash and securities.
11. (D) A broker dealer will subtract its haircuts from its tentative net capital.
12. (C) The OTC security with only two independent market makers will take a larger haircut, but it still may be used when computing net capital.
13. (A) A broker dealer must deposit 105 percent of customer credit balances in a special reserve account.
14. (B) A broker dealer subject to a net capital requirement of less than $100,000 may execute 10 orders for its own investment account without becoming subject to the $100,000 net capital requirement.
15. (D) Broker dealer bank records only need to be kept for three years.
16. (A) A broker dealer may have aggregate indebtedness of 15 times its net capital as long as it has been in business for more than one year. 15 × $800,000 = $12,000,000

17. (C) A broker dealer subject to a $25,000 net capital requirement may execute a customer's order to sell securities if the proceeds are to be reinvested in a mutual fund.
18. (A) The firm must file an early warning report (EWR) within 24 hours.
19. (C) The minutes from board of director's meetings must be kept for the life of the firm and for two years readily accessible.
20. (C) The member must notify both the SEC and FINRA within 24 hours and must detail its corrective measures within 48 hours.

CHAPTER 3: ISSUING CORPORATE SECURITIES

1. (D) All of the items listed must appear in the tombstone ad.
2. (D) All of the parties listed may be held liable to the purchasers of the new issue.
3. (B) A syndicate may only enter a stabilizing bid at or below the offering price.
4. (A) A corporation must issue common stock before it issues any preferred stock.
5. (D) Under Rule 147, 100 percent of the purchasers must be in the state.
6. (C) A greenshoe provision allows the syndicate to purchase up to an additional 15 percent of the offering from the issuer.
7. (A) All of the choices listed are types of offerings except for Rule 149.
8. (B) A business must first hire an underwriter to advise the issuer about the types of securities to issue.
9. (C) The number of nonaccredited investors is limited to 35 in any 12-month period.
10. (D) A company doing a rights offering will use a standby underwriting agreement whereby the underwriter will "standby" ready to purchase any shares not purchased by shareholders.
11. (C) A Regulation A offering covers an offering of $50,000,000 or less in a 12-month period.
12. (B) Rule 145 covers mergers involving a stock swap or offer of another company's securities in exchange for its current stock.
13. (C) Anytime the SEC wants more information, it would most likely issue a deficiency letter.
14. (A) Primary commitment is not a type of underwriting commitment.

15. (B) Purchasers of stock that has just gone public must get a prospectus for 25 days if the stock is Nasdaq listed.
16. (A) All of the answers listed will appear in the preliminary prospectus, except the offering price and the proceeds to the company.
17. (C) An insider may sell securities under Rule 144 for 90 days.

CHAPTER 4: TRADING SECURITIES

1. (A) If an issuer has been suspended from Nasdaq trading, the issuer must reapply to the Nasdaq initial listing requirement. Issuers will be given 30 days to correct any listing deficiencies before being suspended.
2. (B) An issuer will be given 30 days to correct any problems or face suspension.
3. (D) An allied member may not trade on the floor. Allied members are only allowed to call themselves members and have electronic access to the exchange.
4. (C) Firms that act as market makers in Nasdaq securities are trying to make the spread, which is the difference between the bid and the ask.
5. (D) Mini-maxi and best efforts are types of underwriting commitments, not types of orders.
6. (C) A technical analyst would want to buy the stock when it breaks through resistance.
7. (A) The inside market is the highest bid and the lowest offer.
8. (A) Specialists on the NYSE work for themselves or for a specialist firm.
9. (C) All of the answers that are listed are features of the NMCES except it does not display quotes from the alternative display facility.
10. (C) All of the choices listed are false except for III. The firm may not execute the customer's market order to sell at a price that is less than the limit order it is holding.
11. (C) The Nasdaq Market Center for listed securities assists in the execution of third-market trades.
12. (B) The ACT system does not provide quotes. All of the other choices listed are functions of the ACT.
13. (B) A market maker that wants to enter an initial quote for an OTCBB security must file Form 211 three business days prior to entering the quote.
14. (C) The daily purchase limit for a passive market maker is the greater of 30 percent of their ADTV or 200 shares.

15. (B) The firm may execute any single order, even if that order would cause it to exceed its volume limit. Once the firm has exceeded the volume limit, it must withdraw for the rest of the day.
16. (A) The firm may execute any single order even if that order would cause it to exceed its volume limit. Once the firm has exceeded the volume limit, it must withdraw for the rest of the day.
17. (B) Quotes for direct participation programs (DPPs) are not firm.
18. (D) All of the answers are correct with regard to a MOC order except that it must be executed on the closing price or as close to the closing trade as possible. In this case, 4 minutes is too far away from the close to be reasonable.
19. (D) 300 shares traded at 84.15; the s/s means that a round lot for the stock is 10 shares.
20. (C) A firm may only obtain an excused withdrawal due to personnel vacations if the number of workstations is three or fewer.
21. (B) The order has been elected because the stock has traded though the stop price. The order has now become a limit order to sell the stock at 160.

CHAPTER 5: RECOMMENDATIONS TO CUSTOMERS

1. (D) This is an example of an unsuitable recommendation because the client is trying to diversify between growth and income and already owns a large portfolio of common stock. The recommendation does not meet the investor's objective of balancing growth and income.
2. (C) A representative spreading a large amount of money out over a number of different fund families may have engaged in breakpoint sales. Most funds offer combination privileges and a number of different portfolios to meet different objectives.
3. (A) A member must disclose all of the answers listed but is only required to disclose if the firm received investment banking business from the company within the last 12 months.
4. (A) The best choice for an investor seeking current income and safety of principal is a portfolio made up of Treasury bonds, fixed annuities, and money market funds.
5. (D) When making a recommendation to a customer, the representative's suitability determination may be satisfied if the customer is an institution with at least $10,000,000 in assets and can judge the investment for itself.

6. (B) A research report that contains coverage on six or more companies may direct the reader to where the required disclosures may be obtained in electronic format. An investment banking department may only verify facts in connection with the research report.
7. (D) The only answer that is true is that the analyst must make relevant disclosures during interviews.
8. (B) The analyst may not trade a security he or she covers in a research report until the intended recipients have had a chance to act on the report.
9. (A) Analysts may invest in mutual funds without restriction so long as the analyst does not own 1 percent or more of the fund and the fund does not invest more than 20 percent of its assets in a sector covered by the analyst.
10. (A) All of the choices have to be disclosed except risks factors that may keep the security from reaching the firm's price target. This has to be disclosed in research reports, not in interviews.
11. (A) Analysts may only short a stock they rate a sell. All of the other choices are not allowed.
12. (A) Multiple hedge clauses and implied regulatory endorsement are violations and are misleading. Free services must be free to everyone with no payment required.

CHAPTER 6: GENERAL SUPERVISION

1. (A) A branch office may advertise and may conduct the member's business at the branch office. It may not do the other actions listed.
2. (C) The firm is required to record all international transfers in excess of $3,000.
3. (D) An OSJ may do all of the activities listed.
4. (B) A firm's business continuity plan must provide for backup communication facilities and contact information for two emergency contacts, one of whom must be a registered principal.
5. (B) A satellite office may conduct business with the public.
6. (B) All branch offices are required to be supervised by an OSJ, and a registered representative may act as the manager of the branch.
7. (A) All branch offices are not required to be directly inspected by the firm. By inspecting the OSJ, the firm is inspecting the branch as well.

8. (C) A member carrying customer accounts must do choices I, II, and III, but must only inform customers of the information once per year.
9. (B) A Suspicious Activity Report (SAR) must be filed for questionable transactions of more than $5,000 or more.
10. (D) A firm's anti-money-laundering program must be approved by senior management.

CHAPTER 7: CUSTOMER ACCOUNTS

1. (A) The nominal owner of the securities in a UGMA account is the custodian. The securities are registered in the name of the custodian for the benefit of the minor, who is the beneficial owner.
2. (B) The assets of the decedent will be distributed according to the will.
3. (A) Although the minor's Social Security number is listed on the account, it does not appear in the account title.
4. (C) Transactions in discretionary accounts do not need to be approved prior to execution. The transactions need to be approved promptly.
5. (C) A UTMA account allows the assets to remain in the account until the beneficial owner reaches the age of 25.
6. (D) An adult may never have a joint account with a minor.
7. (D) A firm receiving ACAT instructions must send a report of the positions to be transferred to the new firm upon validation.
8. (D) All orders must be marked as to whether discretion was used.
9. (C) It is not the agent's responsibility to inform the IRS.
10. (D) A firm may only jointly pledge customers' securities as joint collateral if all parties agree in writing.

CHAPTER 8: MARGIN ACCOUNTS

1. (C) The NYSE/FINRA set the minimum maintenance for a new margin account.
2. (B) The initial minimum for a new margin account is the greater of $2,000 or 50 percent of the purchase price.
3. (C) The customer must sign the hypothecation agreement.
4. (B) To find the minimum equity given a long market value, simply multiply the market value by .25.

5. (A) Municipal bonds are exempt from Regulation T; the margin requirement is set by the SROs.
6. (A) To find the minimum maintenance, multiply the long market value by .25. In this case, 96,500 × .25 = $24,125.
7. (D) When buying a municipal bond in a margin account, investors must deposit the greater of 7 percent of par value or 15 percent of the market value. In this case, 15% × $54,000 = $8,100.
8. (B) The $2,000 minimum equity requirement is only for the initial deposit.
9. (A) The market value could fall to $72,000. This is found by dividing the debit balance by .75: 54,000/.75 = 72,000.
10. (C) If an investor uses an SMA to withdraw cash, the SMA is reduced and the investor's debit balance is increased by an equal amount.

CHAPTER 9: INVESTMENT COMPANIES AND OTHER PRODUCTS

1. (C) An investor in a mutual fund portfolio has an undivided interest in that portfolio and is not an investor or stockholder in the fund company itself.
2. (C) A breakpoint sale is a violation committed by a representative who is trying to earn a larger commission by not informing the investor that a breakpoint sales charge reduction is available at a slightly higher dollar level.
3. (A) The investor will redeem the shares of the growth portfolio at the NAV and will purchase the shares of the biotech portfolio at the NAV because XYZ offers conversion privileges.
4. (C) A mutual fund's custodian maintains books and records for accumulation plans.
5. (A) A 12b-1 fee may be up to .25 of 1 percent of the NAV.
6. (D) The ex date is set by the NYSE/FINRA for a closed-end fund just like for a stock.
7. (C) A mutual fund calling itself a diversified fund is limited to owning no more than 10 percent of any one company.
8. (C) New shares will be created for the investor as soon as the mutual fund company receives the money. The investor becomes an owner of record on that day.
9. (D) Employees with access to cash and securities must be bonded.

10. (A) A fund with a portfolio turnover ratio of 25 percent replaces its portfolio every four years.

CHAPTER 10: VARIABLE ANNUITIES AND RETIREMENT PLANS

1. (D) Investors may always contribute to their IRAs as long as they have earned income.
2. (A) If the separate account earns less than the assumed interest rate, the monthly payment as well as the value of the annuity unit will go down. As the performance of the separate account is positive, the cash goes up.
3. (C) This is a nonqualified plan, meaning that the money is deposited after taxes. The retiree will only pay taxes on the growth.
4. (D) The maximum amount that a couple may contribute to their IRAs at any one time is $24,000. Between January 1 and April 15, a contribution may be made for the prior year, the current year, or both: $6,000 × 2 × 2 = $24,000.
5. (C) The retirement account is qualified, which means the investor has deposited the money pre-tax. Therefore, all of the money is taxed when it is withdrawn.
6. (A) A 529 plan would allow the investor to make a lump sum deposit.
7. (A) The money has been deposited in a Roth IRA after taxes. It is allowed to grow tax-deferred. If you are over 59 1/2 and the money has been in the IRA for at least five years, then it may all be withdrawn without paying taxes on the growth.
8. (B) A fixed annuity does not provide protection from inflation. If inflation rises, the holder of a fixed annuity may end up worse off due to the loss of value of the dollar.
9. (D) The maximum contribution for a SEP IRA is the lesser of 25 percent of income or $57,000.

CHAPTER 11: SECURITIES INDUSTRY RULES AND REGULATIONS

1. (D) The letter to a particular customer would not be considered retail communication. A letter to a single customer would be correspondence.

2. (B) SIPC covers $500,000 per separate customer, of which up to $250,000 may be cash, so both accounts are fully covered.
3. (B) The Securities Exchange Act of 1934 regulates the activities of broker dealers and their required capital.
4. (C) The maximum fine for someone found to have acted on inside information is unlimited.
5. (D) All appeals will first be heard by the National Adjudicatory Council (NAC).
6. (C) If an MFP donates to the campaign of a candidate in an election in which the MFP may not vote, the firm and the MFP may not bid on municipal underwritings in that municipality for two years.
7. (B) FINRA's decision is effective in 30 days.
8. (D) A registered broker dealer is required to perform all of the items listed.
9. (C) A syndicate member may only run a tombstone ad announcing the issue and gather indications of interest during the cooling-off period.
10. (A) The registered representative may sign an Acceptance Waiver and Consent (AWAC) to resolve the issue.
11. (D) All of the choices listed are considered retail communication if any part of the items listed could be seen by even a single retail investor.
12. (D) A call to another state is not exempt from the Do Not Call requirements.
13. (C) The Code of Procedure handles the resolution of complaints.
14. (B) A new member firm is required to file its retail communication 10 days prior to first use.
15. (D) All of the choices listed must appear in the tombstone ad.

Appendix

The following "Cheat Sheets" are included as an additional study tool to help you review key testable points. These Cheat Sheets have been designed to organize many related topics into one area to aid in your comprehension of the material.

1. Nasdaq Systems
2. Actions and Times
3. Forms and Times
4. Rules and Regulations

The following forms are included for your review to help you better understand how reports are made to the appropriate regulators. Please note that most of the forms are now filed electronically.

Form 1: Page 1 of Form U4

Form 2: Page 1 of Form U5

Form 3: Selected pages from Form BD

Form 4: Selected pages from FOCUS report

Form 5: Currency transaction report

Form 6: Suspicious activity report

Figure A.1 shows the Nasdaq Trade Reporting Facility (TRF), where details of a trade not automatically reported to ACT for clearing and reporting are input manually by a trader. The fields that must be completed include the details of the trade such as:

If the firm acted as a market maker or as an order entry firm

If the firm acted as a principal or as an agent

If the stock was bought or sold by the firm

The number of shares

The security symbol

The price

The contra party's market participant ID (who the trade was done with)

The trade time

Settlement instructions

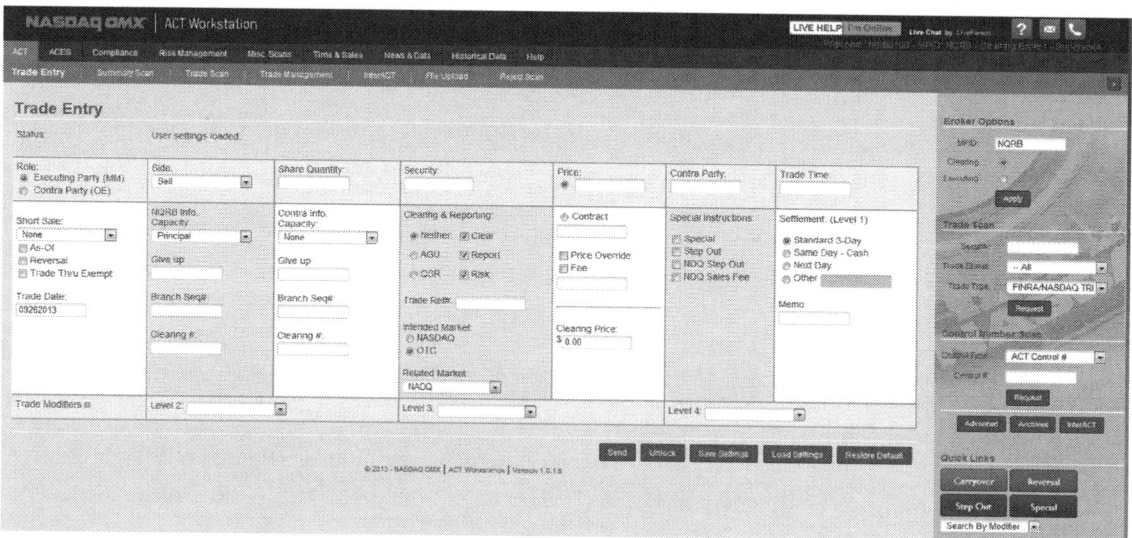

FIGURE A.1 Nasdaq Trade Reporting Facility (TRF)

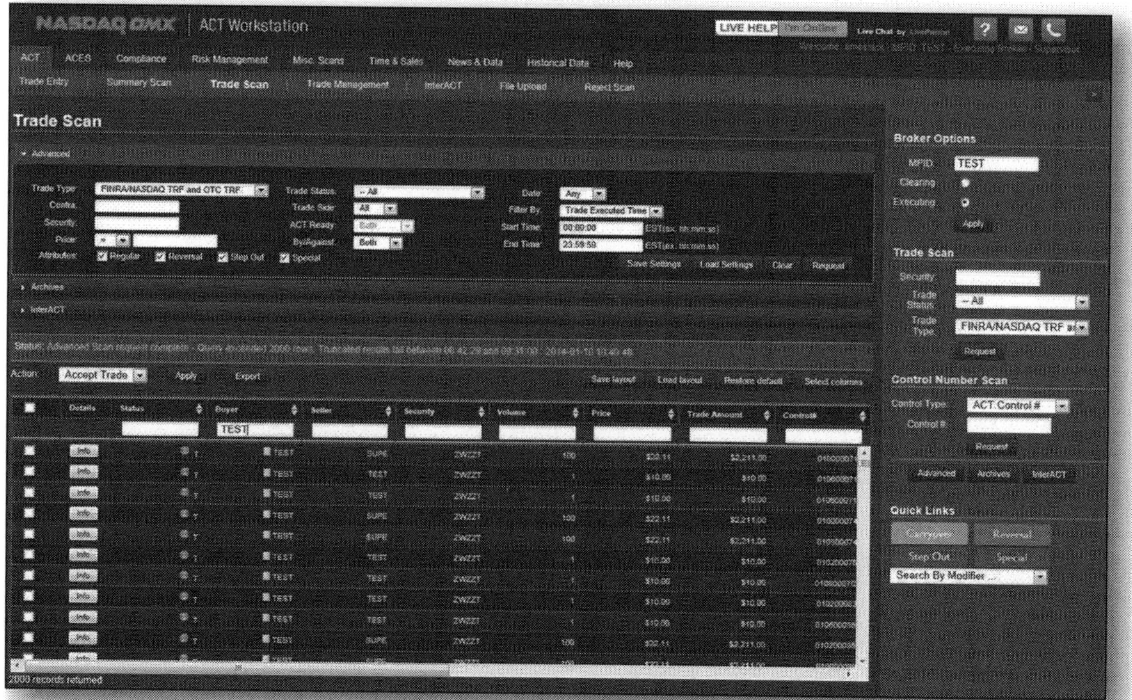

FIGURE A.2 The ACT Trade Scan

INDIVIDUAL NAME:	INDIVIDUAL CRD #:
FIRM NAME:	FIRM CRD #:

1. GENERAL INFORMATION

FIRST NAME:	MIDDLE NAME:	LAST NAME:	SUFFIX:
FIRM CRD #:	*FIRM* NAME:		EMPLOYMENT DATE(MM/DD/YYYY):
FIRM Billing Code:	*INDIVIDUAL CRD* #:		INDIVIDUAL SSN:

Do you have an independent contractor relationship with the above named *firm*?: O Yes O No

Office of Employment Address:

O Registered O Non-Registered	CRD BRANCH #:	NYSE BRANCH CODE#:	*FIRM* BILLING CODE:	O Located At O Supervised From	START DATE:	END DATE:
OFFICE OF EMPLOYMENT ADDRESS STREET 1:	CITY:				STATE:	
OFFICE OF EMPLOYMENT ADDRESS STREET 2:	COUNTRY:				POSTAL CODE:	

Private Residence Check Box: If the Office of Employment address is a private residence, check this box. ☐

O Registered O Non-Registered	CRD BRANCH #:	NYSE BRANCH CODE#:	*FIRM* BILLING CODE:	O Located At O Supervised From	START DATE:	END DATE:
OFFICE OF EMPLOYMENT ADDRESS STREET 1:	CITY:				STATE:	
OFFICE OF EMPLOYMENT ADDRESS STREET 2:	COUNTRY:				POSTAL CODE:	

Private Residence Check Box: If the Office of Employment address is a private residence, check this box. ☐

O Registered O Non-Registered	CRD BRANCH #:	NYSE BRANCH CODE#:	*FIRM* BILLING CODE:	O Located At O Supervised From	START DATE:	END DATE:
OFFICE OF EMPLOYMENT ADDRESS STREET 1:	CITY:				STATE:	
OFFICE OF EMPLOYMENT ADDRESS STREET 2:	COUNTRY:				POSTAL CODE:	

Private Residence Check Box: If the Office of Employment address is a private residence, check this box. ☐

2. FINGERPRINT INFORMATION

Electronic Filing Representation

O By selecting this option, I represent that I am submitting, have submitted, or promptly will submit to the appropriate *SRO* a fingerprint card as required under applicable *SRO* rules; or

Fingerprint card barcode ______________________________

O By selecting this option, I represent that I have been employed continuously by the *filing firm* since the last submission of a fingerprint card to CRD and am not required to resubmit a fingerprint card at this time; or,

O By selecting this option, I represent that I have been employed continuously by the *filing firm* and my fingerprints have been processed by an *SRO* other than FINRA. I am submitting, have submitted, or promptly will submit the processed results for posting to CRD.

Exceptions to the Fingerprint Requirement

O By selecting one or more of the following two options, I affirm that I am exempt from the federal fingerprint requirement because I/*filing firm* currently satisfy(ies) the requirements of at least one of the permissive exemptions indicated below pursuant to Rule 17f-2 under the Securities Exchange Act of 1934, including any notice or application requirements specified therein:

☐ Rule 17f-2(a)(1)(i)

☐ Rule 17f-2(a)(1)(iii)

Investment Adviser Representative Only Applicants

O I affirm that I am applying only as an investment adviser representative and that I am not also applying or have not also applied with this *firm* to become a broker-dealer representative. If this radio button/box is selected, continue below.

O I am applying for registration only in *jurisdictions* that do not have fingerprint card filing requirements, or

O I am applying for registration in *jurisdictions* that have fingerprint card filing requirements and I am submitting, have submitted, or promptly will submit the appropriate fingerprint card directly to the *jurisdictions* for processing pursuant to applicable *jurisdiction* rules.

UNIFORM TERMINATION NOTICE FOR SECURITIES INDUSTRY REGISTRATION

INDIVIDUAL NAME:	INDIVIDUAL CRD #:
FIRM NAME:	FIRM CRD #:

NOTICE TO THE INDIVIDUAL WHO IS THE SUBJECT OF THIS FILING

Even if you are no longer registered you continue to be subject to the jurisdiction of regulators for at least two years after your registration is terminated and may have to provide information about your activities while associated with this firm. Therefore, you must forward any residential address changes for two years following your termination date or last Form U5 amendment to: CRD Address Changes, P.O. Box 9495, Gaithersburg, MD 20898-9495.

1. GENERAL INFORMATION

FIRST NAME:	MIDDLE NAME:	LAST NAME:	SUFFIX:
FIRM CRD #:	*FIRM* NAME:		*FIRM* NFA#:
INDIVIDUAL CRD #:	INDIVIDUAL SSN:	*INDIVIDUAL* NFA#:	FIRM Billing Code:

Office of Employment Address:

O Registered O Non-Registered	CRD BRANCH #:	NYSE BRANCH CODE#:	FIRM BILLING CODE:	O Located At O Supervised From	START DATE:	END DATE:

OFFICE OF EMPLOYMENT ADDRESS STREET 1:	CITY:	STATE:
OFFICE OF EMPLOYMENT ADDRESS STREET 2:	COUNTRY:	POSTAL CODE:

Private Residence Check Box: If the Office of Employment address is a private residence, check this box. ☐

O Registered O Non-Registered	CRD BRANCH #:	NYSE BRANCH CODE#:	FIRM BILLING CODE:	O Located At O Supervised From	START DATE:	END DATE:

OFFICE OF EMPLOYMENT ADDRESS STREET 1:	CITY:	STATE:
OFFICE OF EMPLOYMENT ADDRESS STREET 2:	COUNTRY:	POSTAL CODE:

Private Residence Check Box: If the Office of Employment address is a private residence, check this box. ☐

O Registered O Non-Registered	CRD BRANCH #:	NYSE BRANCH CODE#:	FIRM BILLING CODE:	O Located At O Supervised From	START DATE:	END DATE:

OFFICE OF EMPLOYMENT ADDRESS STREET 1:	CITY:	STATE:
OFFICE OF EMPLOYMENT ADDRESS STREET 2:	COUNTRY:	POSTAL CODE:

Private Residence Check Box: If the Office of Employment address is a private residence, check this box. ☐

2. CURRENT RESIDENTIAL ADDRESS

NOTICE TO THE FIRM: This is the last reported residential address. If this is not current, please enter the current residential address.	FROM (MM/YYYY):	TO (MM/YYYY):
ADDRESS STREET 1:	CITY:	STATE:
ADDRESS STREET 2:	COUNTRY:	POSTAL CODE:

3. FULL TERMINATION

Is this a *FULL TERMINATION*? O Yes O No
Note: A "Yes" response will terminate ALL registrations with all *SROs* and all *jurisdictions*.

Reason For Termination:

O Discharged O Other O Permitted to Resign O Deceased O Voluntary

Termination Explanation:

If the Reason for Termination entered above is Permitted to Resign, Discharged or Other, provide an explanation below:

If amending the Reason for Termination and/or termination explanation, provide an explanation below:

FORM BD PAGE 1 (Execution Page)	**UNIFORM APPLICATION FOR BROKER-DEALER REGISTRATION** Date:__________ SEC File No: 8- __________ Firm CRD No.: __________	**OFFICIAL USE**	OFFICAL USE ONLY

WARNING: Failure to keep this form current and to file accurate supplementary information on a timely basis, or the failure to keep accurate books and records or otherwise to comply with the provisions of law applying to the conduct of business as a broker-dealer would violate the Federal securities laws and the laws of the *jurisdictions* and may result in disciplinary, administrative, injunctive or criminal action.

INTENTIONAL MISSTATEMENTS OR OMISSIONS OF FACTS MAY CONSTITUTE CRIMINAL VIOLATIONS.

☐ APPLICATION ☐ AMENDMENT

1. Exact name, principal business address, mailing address, if different, and telephone number of *applicant:*

   A. Full name of *applicant* (if sole proprietor, state last, first and middle name):

   ____

   B. IRS Empl. Ident. No.:

   ____

   C. (1) Name under which broker-dealer business primarily is conducted, if different from Item 1A.

   ____

   (2) List on Schedule D, Page1, Section I any other name by which the firm conducts business and where it is used.

   D. If this filing makes a name change on behalf of the *applicant*, enter the new name and specify whether the name change is of the ☐ *applicant* name (1A) or ☐ business name (1C):

   Please check above. ______________________________

   E. Firm main address: (Do not use a P.O. Box)

   ____
   (Number and Street) (City) (State/Country) (Zip+4/Postal Code)

   Branch offices or other business locations must be reported on Schedule E.

   F. Mailing address, if different:

   ____

   G. Business Telephone Number:

   ______ ______________
   (Area Code) (Telephone Number)

   H. Contact Employee:

   ______________ ______ ______________
   (Name and Title) (Area Code) (Telephone Number)

EXECUTION:

For the purposes of complying with the laws of the State(s) designated in Item 2 relating to either the offer or sale of securities or commodities, the undersigned and *applicant* hereby certify that the *applicant* is in compliance with applicable state surety bonding requirements and irrevocably appoint the administrator of each of those State(s) or such other person designated by law, and the successors in such office, attorney for the *applicant* in said State(s), upon whom may be served any notice, process, or pleading in any action or *proceeding* against the *applicant* arising out of or in connection with the offer or sale of securities or commodities, or out of the violation or alleged violation of the laws of those State(s), and the *applicant* hereby consents that any such action or *proceeding* against the *applicant* may be commenced in any court of competent jurisdiction and proper venue within said State(s) by service of process upon said appointee with the same effect as if *applicant* were a resident in said State(s) and had lawfully been served with process in said State(s).

The *applicant* consents that service of any civil action brought by or notice of any *proceeding* before the Securities and Exchange Commission or any *self-regulatory organization* in connection with the *applicant's* broker-dealer activities, or of any application for a protective decree filed by the Securities Investor Protection Corporation, may be given by registered or certified mail or confirmed telegram to the *applicant's* contact employee at the main address, or mailing address if different, given in Items 1E and IF.

The undersigned, being first duly sworn, deposes and says that he/she has executed this form on behalf of, and with the authority of, said *applicant.* The undersigned and *applicant* represent that the information and statements contained herein, including exhibits attached hereto, and other information filed herewith, all of which are made a part hereof, are current, true and complete. The undersigned and *applicant* further represent that to the extent any information previously submitted is not amended such information is currently accurate and complete.

______________ ______________________________
Date (MM/DD/YYYY) Name of Applicant

By: ______________________ ______________________
Signature Print Name and Title

Subscribed and sworn before me this ________ day of ______________________ , ________ by ______________________
Year Notary Public

My Commision expires ______________ County of ______________ State of ______________

This page must always be completed in full with original, manual signature and notarization.
To amend, circle items being amended. Affix notary stamp or seal where applicable.

DO NOT WRITE BELOW THIS LINE - FOR OFFICIAL USE ONLY

FORM BD
PAGE 2

Applicant Name:____________________

Date:__________ Firm CRD No.: __________

OFFICIAL USE | OFFICIAL USE ONLY

2. Indicate by checking the appropriate box(es) each governmental authority, organization, or *jurisdiction* in which the *applicant* is registered or registering as a broker-dealer.

SECURITIES AND EXCHANGE COMMISSION

If *applicant* is registered or registering with the SEC, check here and answer Items 2A through 2D below. ☐

	YES	NO
A. Is *applicant* registered or registering as a broker-dealer under Section 15(b) or Section 15B of the Securities Exchange Act of 1934?	☐	☐
B. Is *applicant* registered or registering as a broker-dealer under Section 15(b) of the Securities Exchange Act of 1934 and also acting or intending to act as a government securities broker or dealer?	☐	☐
C. Is *applicant* registered or registering solely as a government securities broker or dealer under Section 15C of the Securities Exchange Act of 1934? *Do not answer "yes" to Item 2C if applicant answered "yes" to Item 2A or Item 2B.*	☐	☐
D. Is *applicant* ceasing its activities as a government securities broker or dealer?	☐	☐

If applicant answers "yes" to Items 2A and 2D, applicant expressly consents to the withdrawal of its registration as a government securities broker or dealer under Section 15C of the Securities Exchange Act of 1934. See "Instructions."

SRO

☐ AMEX ☐ BSE ☐ CBOE ☐ CHX ☐ NSX ☐ FINRA ☐ NQX ☐ NYSE ☐ PHLX ☐ ARCA ☐ ISE ☐ OTHER *(specify)* ________

JURISDICTION

☐ Alabama	☐ Hawaii	☐ Michigan	☐ North Carolina	☐ Texas
☐ Alaska	☐ Idaho	☐ Minnesota	☐ North Dakota	☐ Utah
☐ Arizona	☐ Illinois	☐ Mississippi	☐ Ohio	☐ Vermont
☐ Arkansas	☐ Indiana	☐ Missouri	☐ Oklahoma	☐ Virgin Islands
☐ California	☐ Iowa	☐ Montana	☐ Oregon	☐ Virginia
☐ Colorado	☐ Kansas	☐ Nebraska	☐ Pennsylvania	☐ Washington
☐ Connecticut	☐ Kentucky	☐ Nevada	☐ Puerto Rico	☐ West Virginia
☐ Delaware	☐ Louisiana	☐ New Hampshire	☐ Rhode Island	☐ Wisconsin
☐ District of Columbia	☐ Maine	☐ New Jersey	☐ South Carolina	☐ Wyoming
☐ Florida	☐ Maryland	☐ New Mexico	☐ South Dakota	
☐ Georgia	☐ Massachusetts	☐ New York	☐ Tennessee	

3. A. Indicate legal status of *applicant*.

☐ Corporation ☐ Sole Proprietorship ☐ Other *(specify)* ________
☐ Partnership ☐ Limited Liability Company

B. Month *applicant's* fiscal year ends: ________

C. If other than a sole proprietor, indicate date and place *applicant* obtained its legal status (i.e., state or country where incorporated, where partnership agreement was filed, or where *applicant* entity was formed):

State/Country of formation: __________ Date of formation: __________
(MM/DD/YYYY)

Schedule A and, if applicable, Schedule B must be completed as part of all initial applications. Amendments to these schedules must be provided on Schedule C.

4. If *applicant* is a sole proprietor, state full residence address and Social Security Number.

Social Security Number: _ _ _ - _ _ _ _ - _ _ _ _ _

____
(Number and Street) (City) (State/Country) (Zip+4/Postal Code)

	YES	NO
5. Is *applicant* at the time of this filing *succeeding* to the business of a currently registered broker-dealer? *Do not report previous successions already reported on Form BD.* *If "Yes," contact CRD prior to submitting form; complete appropriate items on Schedule D, Page 1, Section III.*	☐	☐
6. Does *applicant* hold or maintain any funds or securities or provide clearing services for any other broker or dealer?	☐	☐
7. Does *applicant* refer or introduce customers to any other broker or dealer? *If "Yes," complete appropriate items on Schedule D, Page 1, Section IV.*	☐	☐

FORM BD
PAGE 3

Applicant Name: ____________________

Date: __________ Firm CRD No.: __________

OFFICIAL USE | OFFICIAL USE ONLY

	YES	NO
8. Does *applicant* have any arrangement with any other *person*, firm, or organization under which:		
A. any books or records of *applicant* are kept or maintained by such other *person*, firm or organization?	☐	☐
B. accounts, funds, or securities of the *applicant* are held or maintained by such other *person*, firm, or organization?	☐	☐
C. accounts, funds, or securities of customers of the *applicant* are held or maintained by such other *person*, firm or organization?	☐	☐
For purposes of 8B and 8C, do not include a bank or satisfactory control location as defined in paragraph (c) of Rule 15c3-3 under the Securities Exchange Act of 1934 (17 CFR 240.15c3-3).		
if "Yes" to any part of Item 8, complete appropriate items on Schedule D, Page 1, Section IV.		
9. Does any *person* not named in Item 1 or Schedules A, B, or C, directly or indirectly:		
A. *control* the management or policies of the *applicant* through agreement or otherwise?	☐	☐
B. wholly or partially finance the business of applicant?	☐	☐
Do not answer "Yes" to 9B if the person finances the business of the applicant through: 1) a public offering of securities made pursuant to the Securities Act of 1933; 2) credit extended in the ordinary course of business by suppliers, banks, and others; or 3) a satisfactory subordination agreement, as defined in Rule 15c3-1 under the Securities Exchange Act of 1934 (17 CFR 240.15c3-1).		
If "Yes" to any part of Item 9, complete appropriate items on Schedule D, Page 1, Section IV.		
10. A. Directly or indirectly, does *applicant control*, is *applicant controlled* by, or is *applicant* under common *control* with, any partnership, corporation, or other organization that is engaged in the securities or investment advisory business?	☐	☐
If "Yes" to Item 10A, complete appropriate items on Schedule D, Page 2, Section V.		
B. Directly or indirectly, is *applicant controlled* by any bank holding company, national bank, state member bank of the Federal Reserve System, state non-member bank, savings bank or association, credit union, or foreign bank?	☐	☐
If "Yes" to Item 10B, complete appropriate items on Schedule D, Page 3, Section VI.		
11. Use the appropriate DRP for providing details to "yes" answers to the questions in Item 11. Refer to the Explanation of Terms section of Form BD Instructions for explanations of italicized terms.		
CRIMINAL DISCLOSURE		
A. In the past ten years has the *applicant* or a *control affiliate*:		
(1) been convicted of or pled guilty or nolo contendere ("no contest") in a domestic, foreign or military court to any *felony*?	☐	☐
(2) been *charged* with any *felony*?	☐	☐
B. In the past ten years has the *applicant* or a *control affiliate*:		
(1) been convicted of or pled guilty or nolo contendere ("no contest") in a domestic, foreign or military court to a *misdemeanor involving*: investments or an *investment-related* business, or any fraud, false statements or omissions, wrongful taking of property, bribery, perjury, forgery, counterfeiting, extortion, or a conspiracy to commit any of these offenses?	☐	☐
(2) been *charged* with a *misdemeanor* specified in 11B(1)?	☐	☐
REGULATORY ACTION DISCLOSURE		
C. Has the U.S. Securities and Exchange Commission or the Commodity Futures Trading Commission ever:		
(1) *found* the *applicant* or a *control affiliate* to have made a false statement or omission?	☐	☐
(2) *found* the *applicant* or a *control affiliate* to have been *involved* in a violation of its regulations or statutes?	☐	☐
(3) *found* the *applicant* or a *control affiliate* to have been a cause of an *investment-related* business having its authorization to do business denied, suspended, revoked, or restricted?	☐	☐
(4) entered an *order* against the *applicant* or a *control affiliate* in connection with *investment-related* activity?	☐	☐
(5) imposed a civil money penalty on the *applicant* or a *control affiliate*, or *ordered* the *applicant* or a *control affiliate* to cease and desist from any activity?	☐	☐

Applicant Name: ______________________

Date: ____________ Firm CRD No.: ____________

OFFICIAL USE | OFFICIAL USE ONLY

REGULATORY ACTION DISCLOSURE

	YES	NO
D. Has any other federal regulatory agency, any state regulatory agency, or *foreign financial regulatory authority*:		
(1) ever *found* the *applicant or a control affiliate* to have made a false statement or omission or been dishonest, unfair, or unethical?	☐	☐
(2) ever *found* the *applicant* or a *control affiliate* to have been *involved* in a violation of *investment-related* regulations or statutes?	☐	☐
(3) ever *found* the *applicant* or a *control affiliate* to have been a cause of an *investment-related* business having its authorization to do business denied, suspended, revoked, or restricted?	☐	☐
(4) in the past ten years, entered an *order* against the *applicant* or a *control affiliate* in connection with an *investment-related* activity?	☐	☐
(5) ever denied, suspended, or revoked the *applicant's* or a *control affiliate's* registration or license or otherwise, by *order*, prevented it from associating with an *investment-related* business or restricted its activities?	☐	☐
E. Has any *self-regulatory organization or* commodities exchange ever:		
(1) *found* the *applicant* or a *control affiliate* to have made a false statement or omission?	☐	☐
(2) *found* the *applicant* or a *control affiliate* to have been *involved* in a violation of its rules (other than a violation designated as a *"minor rule violation"* under a plan approved by the U.S. Securities and Exchange Commission)?	☐	☐
(3) *found* the *applicant* or a *control affiliate* to have been the cause of an *investment-related* business having its authorization to do business denied, suspended, revoked, or restricted?	☐	☐
(4) disciplined the *applicant* or a *control affiliate* by expelling or suspending it from membership, barring or suspending its association with other members, or otherwise restricting its activities?	☐	☐
F. Has the *applicant's* or a *control affiliate's* authorization to act as an attorney, accountant, or federal contractor ever been revoked or suspended?	☐	☐
G. Is the *applicant* or a *control affiliate* now the subject of any regulatory *proceeding* that could result in a "yes" answer to any part of 11C, D, or E?	☐	☐

CIVIL JUDICIAL DISCLOSURE

	YES	NO
H. (1) Has any domestic or foreign court:		
(a) in the past ten years, *enjoined* the *applicant* or a *control affiliate* in connection with any *investment-related* activity?	☐	☐
(b) ever *found* that the *applicant* or a *control affiliate* was *involved* in a violation of *investment-related* statutes or regulations?	☐	☐
(c) ever dismissed, pursuant to a settlement agreement, an *investment-related* civil action brought against the *applicant* or *control affiliate* by a state or *foreign financial regulatory authority*?	☐	☐
(2) Is the *applicant* or a *control affiliate* now the subject of any civil *proceeding* that could result in a "yes" answer to any part of 11H(1)?	☐	☐

FINANCIAL DISCLOSURE

	YES	NO
I. In the past ten years has the *applicant* or a *control affiliate* of the *applicant* ever been a securities firm or a *control affiliate* of a securities firm that:		
(1) has been the subject of a bankruptcy petition?	☐	☐
(2) has had a trustee appointed or a direct payment procedure initiated under the Securities Investor Protection Act?	☐	☐
J. Has a bonding company ever denied, paid out on, or revoked a bond for the *applicant*?	☐	☐
K. Does the *applicant* have any unsatisfied judgments or liens against it?	☐	☐

FORM BD **PAGE 5**	*Applicant* Name: ____________ Date: ____________ Firm CRD No.: ____________	**OFFICIAL USE**	OFFICIAL USE ONLY

12. Check types of business engaged in (or to be engaged in, if not yet active) by *applicant.* Do not check any category that accounts for (or is expected to account for) less than 1% of annual revenue from the securities or investment advisory business.

- A. Exchange member engaged in exchange commission business other than floor activities .... ☐ EMC
- B. Exchange member engaged in floor activities .... ☐ EMF
- C. Broker or dealer making inter-dealer markets in corporate securities over-the-counter .... ☐ IDM
- D. Broker or dealer retailing corporate equity securities over-the-counter .... ☐ BDR
- E. Broker or dealer selling corporate debt securities .... ☐ BDD
- F. Underwriter or selling group participant (corporate securities other than mutual funds) .... ☐ USG
- G. Mutual fund underwriter or sponsor .... ☐ MFU
- H. Mutual fund retailer .... ☐ MFR
- I. 1. U.S. government securities dealer .... ☐ GSD
  - 2. U.S. government securities broker .... ☐ GSB
- J. Municipal securities dealer .... ☐ MSD
- K. Municipal securities broker. .... ☐ MSB
- L. Broker or dealer selling variable life insurance or annuities .... ☐ VLA
- M. Solicitor of time deposits in a financial institution .... ☐ SSL
- N. Real estate syndicator. .... ☐ RES
- O. Broker or dealer selling oil and gas interests .... ☐ OGI
- P. Put and call broker or dealer or option writer .... ☐ PCB
- Q. Broker or dealer selling securities of only one issuer or associate issuers (other than mutual funds) .... ☐ BIA
- R. Broker or dealer selling securities of non-profit organizations (e.g., churches, hospitals) .... ☐ NPB
- S. Investment advisory services .... ☐ IAD
- T. 1. Broker or dealer selling tax shelters or limited partnerships in primary distributions .... ☐ TAP
  - 2. Broker or dealer selling tax shelters or limited partnerships in the secondary market .... ☐ TAS
- U. Non-exchange member arranging for transactions in listed securities by exchange member .... ☐ NEX
- V. Trading securities for own account .... ☐ TRA
- W. Private placements of securities .... ☐ PLA
- X. Broker or dealer selling interests in mortgages or other receivables .... ☐ MRI
- Y. Broker or dealer involved in a networking, kiosk or similar arrangement with a:
  - 1. bank, savings bank or association, or credit union .... ☐ BNA
  - 2. insurance company or agency .... ☐ INA
- Z. Other *(give details on Schedule D, Page 1, Section II)* .... ☐ OTH

	YES	NO
13. A. Does *applicant* effect transactions in commodity futures, commodities or commodity options as a broker for others or as a dealer for its own account?	☐	☐
B. Does *applicant* engage in any other non-securities business? .... *If "yes," describe each other business briefly on Schedule D, Page 1, Section II.*	☐	☐

Schedule A of FORM BD

DIRECT OWNERS AND EXECUTIVE OFFICERS

(Answer for Form BD Item 3)

Applicant Name: ______________________

Date: ______________ Firm CRD No.: ____________

OFFICIAL USE

1. Use Schedule A only in new applications to provide information on the **direct o**wners and executive officers of the *applicant*. Use Schedule B in new applications to provide information on **indirect** owners. File all amendments on Schedule C. **Complete each column.**

2. List below the names of:

   (a) each Chief Executive Officer, Chief Financial Officer, Chief Operations Officer, Chief Legal Officer, Chief Compliance Officer, Director, and individuals with similar status or functions;

   (b) in the case of an *applicant* that is a corporation, each shareholder that directly owns 5% or more of a class of a voting security of the *applicant*, unless the *applicant* is a public reporting company (a company subject to Sections 12 or 15(d) of the Securities Exchange Act of 1934);
   Direct owners include any *person* that owns, beneficially owns, has the right to vote, or has the power to sell or direct the sale of, 5% or more of a class of a voting security of the *applicant*. For purposes of this Schedule, a *person* beneficially owns any securities (i) owned by his/her child, stepchild, grandchild, parent, stepparent, grandparent, spouse, sibling, mother-in-law, father-in-law, son-in-law, daughter-in-law, brother-in-law, or sister-in-law, sharing the same residence; or (ii) that he/she has the right to acquire, within 60 days, through the exercise of any option, warrant or right to purchase the security.

   (c) in the case of an *applicant* that is a partnership, **all** general partners and those limited and special partners that have the right to receive upon dissolution, or have contributed, 5% or more of the partnership's capital; and

   (d) in the case of a trust that directly owns 5% or more of a class of a voting security of the *applicant*, or that has the right to receive upon dissolution, or has contributed, 5% or more of the *applicant's* capital, the trust and each trustee.

   (e) in the case of an *applicant* that is a Limited Liability Company ("LLC"), (i) those members that have the right to receive upon dissolution, or have contributed, 5% or more of the LLC's capital, and (ii) if managed by elected managers, all elected managers.

3. Are there any indirect owners of the *applicant* required to be reported on Schedule B? ☐ Yes ☐ No

4. In the "DE/FE/I" column, enter "DE" if the owner is a domestic entity, or enter "FE" if owner is an entity incorporated or domiciled in a foreign country, or enter "I" if the owner is an individual.

5. Complete the "Title or Status" column by entering board/management titles; status as partner, trustee, sole proprietor, or shareholder; and for shareholders, the class of securities owned (if more than one is issued).

6. Ownership codes are: NA - less than 5%; A - 5% but less than 10%; B - 10% but less than 25%; C - 25% but less than 50%; D - 50% but less than 75%; E - 75% or more

7. (a) In the "*Control Person*" column, enter "Yes" if *person* has *"control"* as defined in the instructions to this form, and enter "No" if the *person* does not have *control*. Note that under this definition most executive officers and all 25% owners, general partners, and trustees would be "control persons".

   (b) In the "PR" column, enter "PR" if the owner is a public reporting company under Sections 12 or 15(d) of the Securities Exchange Act of 1934.

FULL LEGAL NAME (Individuals: Last Name, First Name, Middle Name)	DE/FE/I	Title or Status	Date Title or Status Acquired		Ownership Code	Control Person		CRD No. If None: S.S. No., IRS Tax No. or Employer ID.	Official Use Only
			MM	YYYY			PR		

OMB APPROVAL	
OMB Number:	3235-0123
Expires:	March 31, 2016
Estimated average burden hours per response......	12.00

UNITED STATES
SECURITIES AND EXCHANGE COMMISSION
Washington, D.C. 20549

Form X-17A-5

FOCUS REPORT

(Financial and Operational Combined Uniform Single Report)

PART II [11]

(Please read instructions before preparing Form.)

This report is being filed pursuant to (Check Applicable Block(s)):
1) Rule 17a-5(a) [16]   2) Rule 17a-5(b) [17]   3) Rule 17a-11 [18]
4) Special request by designated examining authority [19]   5) Other [26]

NAME OF BROKER-DEALER [13]

SEC FILE NO. [14]

FIRM I.D. NO. [15]

ADDRESS OF PRINCIPAL PLACE OF BUSINESS (Do Not Use P.O. Box No.)

[20]
(No. and Street)

[21] (City)   [22] (State)   [23] (Zip Code)

FOR PERIOD BEGINNING (MM/DD/YY) [24]

AND ENDING (MM/DD/YY) [25]

NAME AND TELEPHONE NUMBER OF PERSON TO CONTACT IN REGARD TO THIS REPORT [30]

(Area Code) — Telephone No. [31]

NAMES OF SUBSIDIARIES OR AFFILIATES CONSOLIDATED IN THIS REPORT:

	OFFICIAL USE
[32]	[33]
[34]	[35]
[36]	[37]
[38]	[39]

DOES RESPONDENT CARRY ITS OWN CUSTOMER ACCOUNTS? YES [40] NO [41]

CHECK HERE IF RESPONDENT IS FILING AN AUDITIED REPORT [42]

EXECUTION:
The registrant/broker or dealer submitting this Form and its attachments and the person(s) by whom it is executed represent hereby that all information contained therein is true, correct and complete. It is understood that all required items, statements, and schedules are considered integral parts of this Form and that the submission of any amendment represents that all unamended items, statements, and schedukes remain true, correct and complete as previously submitted.

Dated the ________________ day of ________________ , ____
Manual signatures of:

1) ______________________________
Principal Executive Officer or Managing Partner

2) ______________________________
Principal Financial Officer or Partner

3) ______________________________
Principal Operations Officer or Partner

ATTENTION — Intentional misstatement or omissions of facts constitute Federal Criminal Violations. (See 18 U.S.C. 1001 and 15 U.S.C. 78:f(a))

Persons who respond to the collection of information contained in this form are not required to respond unless the form displays a currently valid OMB control number.

TO BE COMPLETED WITH THE ANNUAL AUDIT REPORT ONLY:

INDEPENDENT PUBLIC ACCOUNTANT whose opinion is contained in this Report

NAME (If individual, state last, first, middle name)

70

ADDRESS

71	72	73	74
Number and Street	City	State	Zip Code

CHECK ONE

- ☐ Certified Public Accountant 75
- ☐ Public Accountant 76
- ☐ Accountant not resident in United States or any of its possessions 77

FOR SEC USE

DO NOT WRITE UNDER THIS LINE . . . FOR SEC USE ONLY

WORK LOCATION	REPORT DATE MM/DD/YY	DOC. SEQ. NO.	CARD			
50	51	52	53			

FINANCIAL AND OPERATIONAL COMBINED UNIFORM SINGLE REPORT
PART II

BROKER OR DEALER [1] | **N 2** | 100

STATEMENT OF FINANCIAL CONDITION

as of (MM/DD/YY) 99
SEC FILE NO. 98
Consolidated 198
Unconsolidated 199

ASSETS

	Allowable	Non-Allowable	Total
1. Cash [2]	$ 200		$ 750
2. Cash segregated in compliance with federal and other regulations	210		760
3. Receivable from brokers or dealers and clearing organizations:			
A. Failed to deliver:			
1. Includable in "Formula for Reserve Requirements"	220		
2. Other	230		770
B. Securities borrowed:			
1. Includable in"Formula for Reserve Requirements"	240		
2. Other	250		780
C. Omnibus accounts:			
1. Includable in"Formula for Reserve Requirements"	260		
2. Other [3]	270		790
D. Clearing organizations:			
1. Includable in"Formula for Reserve Requirements"	280		
2. Other	290		800
E. Other	300	$ 550 [7]	810
4. Receivables from customers:			
A. Securities accounts:			
1. Cash and fully secured accounts	310		
2. Partly secured accounts	320	560	
3. Unsecured accounts		570	
B. Commodity accounts	330	580	
C. Allowance for doubtful accounts [4]	( ) 335	( ) 590	820
5. Receivables from non-customers:			
A. Cash and fully secured accounts	340		
B. Partly secured and unsecured accounts	350	600	830
6. Securities purchased under agreements to resell	360	[6] 605	840
7. Securities and spot commodities owned, at market value:			
A. Bankers acceptances, certificates of deposit and commercial paper	370		
B. U.S. and Candaian government obligations	380		
C. State and municipal government obligations	390		
D. Corporate obligations [5]	400		

OMIT PENNIES

FINANCIAL AND OPERATIONAL COMBINED UNIFORM SINGLE REPORT
PART II

BROKER OR DEALER as of ____________

STATEMENT OF FINANCIAL CONDITION

ASSETS

		Allowable	Non-Allowable	Total
E. Stocks and warrants .....[9]		$ [410]		
F. Options		[420]		
G. Arbitrage		[422]		
H. Other securities		[424]		
I. Sport commodities		[430]		$ [850]
8. Securities owned not readily marketable:				
A. At Cost ..... [8]	$ [130]	[440]	$ [610]	[860]
9. Other investments not readily marketable:				
A. At Cost	$ [140]			
B. At estimated fair value		[450]	[620]	[870]
10. Securities borrowed under subordination agreements and partners' individual and capital securities accounts, at market value:				
A. Exempted securities ..	$ [150]			
B. Other	$ [160] [10]	[460]	[630]	[880]
11. Secured demand notes-market value of collateral:				
A. Exempted securities ..	$ [170]			
B. Other	$ [180]	[470]	[640]	[890]
12. Memberships in exchanges:				
A. Owned, at market value	$ [190]			
B. Owned at cost			[650]	
C. Contributed for use of company, at market value		[12]	[660]	[900]
13. Investment in and receivables from affiliates, subsidiaries and associated partnerships		[480]	[670] [14]	[910]
14. Property, furniture, equipment, leasehold improvements and rights under lease agreements: At cost (net of accumulated depreciation and amortization)		[490]	[680]	[920]
15. Other Assets:				
A. Dividends and interest receivable		[500]	[690]	
B. Free shipments		[510]	[700]	
C. Loans and advances		[520]	[710]	
D. Miscellaneous .....[11]		[530]	[720]	[930]
16. TOTAL ASSETS	$	[540] [13]	$ [740]	$ [940]

OMIT PENNIES

FINANCIAL AND OPERATIONAL COMBINED UNIFORM SINGLE REPORT
PART II

BROKER OR DEALER   as of ____________

STATEMENT OF FINANCIAL CONDITION

LIABILITIES AND OWNERSHIP EQUITY (continued)

Liabilities	A.I. Liabilities*	Non-A.I. Liabilities*	Total
17. Bank loans payable:			
A. Includable in "Formula for Reserve Requirements"	$ 1030	$ 1240	$ 1460
B. Other	1040	$ 1250	$ 1470
18. Securities sold under repurchase agreement		1260	1480
19. Payable to brokers or dealers and clearing organizations:			
A. Failed to receive:			
1. Includable in "Formula for Reserve Requirements"	1050	1270	1490
2. Other	1060	1280	1500
B. Securities loaned:			
1. Includable in "Formula for Reserve Requirements"	1070		[21] 1510
2. Other	[16] 1080	1290	1520
C. Omnibus accounts:			
1. Includable in "Formula for Reserve Requirements"	1090		1530
2. Other	1095	[19] 1300	1540
D. Clearing organizations:			
1. Includable in "Formula for Reserve Requirements"	1100		1550
2. Other	1105	1310	1560
E. Other:	1110	1320	1570
20. Payable to customers:			
A. Securities accounts-including free credits of .... [15] $ ______ 950	1120		[22] 1580
B. Commodities accounts	[17] 1130	1330	1590
21. Payable to non customers:			
A. Securities accounts	1140	1340	1600
B. Commodities accounts	1150	1350	1610
22. Securities sold not yet purchased at market value-including arbitrage of ....$ ______ 960		1360	1620
23. Accounts payable and accrued liabilities and expenses:			
A. Drafts payable	1160		1630
B. Accounts payable	1170		1640
C. Income taxes payable	1180		[23] 1650
D. Deferred income taxes		[20] 1370	1660
E. Acrued expenses and other liabilities	1190		1670
F. Other	[18] 1200	1380	1680

OMIT PENNIES

*Brokers or Dealers electing the alternative net capital requirement method need not complete these columns.

FINANCIAL AND OPERATIONAL COMBINED UNIFORM SINGLE REPORT
PART II

BROKER OR DEALER as of ____________

STATEMENT OF FINANCIAL CONDITION

LIABILITIES AND OWNERSHIP EQUITY (continued)

Liabilities	A.I. Liabilities*	Non-A.I. Liabilities*	Total
24. Notes and mortgages payable:			
A. Unsecured	$ [1210]		$ [1690]
B. Secured	25 [1211]	$ [1390]	[1700]
25. Liabilities subordinated to claims of general creditors:			
A. Cash borrowings:		[1400]	[1710]
1. from outsiders 24 $ [970]			
2. Includes equity subordination (15c3-1 (d)) of .... $ [980]			
B. Securities borowings, at market value from outsiders $ [990]		[1410]	[1720]
C. Pursuant to secured demand note collateral agreements		[1420]	27 [1730]
1. from outsiders $ [1000]			
2. Includes equity subordination (15c3-1(d)) of .... $ [1010]			
D. Exchange memberships contributed for use of company, at market value		26 [1430]	[1740]
E. Accounts and other borrowings not qualified for net capital purposes	[1220]	[1440]	[1750]
26. TOTAL LIABILITIES	$ [1230]	$ [1450]	$ [1760]
Ownership Equity			
27. Sole Proprietorship			$ [1770]
28. Partnership-limited partners	$ [1020]		$ [1780]
29. Corporation:			
A. Preferred stock			[1791]
B. Common stock			28 [1792]
C. Additional paid-in capital			[1793]
D. Retained earnings			[1794]
E. Total			[1795]
F. Less capital stock in treasury			( ) [1796]
30. TOTAL OWNERSHIP EQUITY			$ [1800]
31. TOTAL LIABILITIES AND OWNERSHIP EQUITY			$ [1810]

OMIT PENNIES

*Brokers or Dealers electing the alternative net capital requirement method need not complete these columns.

FINANCIAL AND OPERATIONAL COMBINED UNIFORM SINGLE REPORT
PART II

BROKER OR DEALER as of ____________

COMPUTATION OF NET CAPITAL

1. Total ownership equity from Statement of Financial Conditon - Item 1800 .... $ ______ 3480
2. Deduct Ownership equity not allowable for Net Capital .... (______) 3490
3. Total ownership equity qualified for Net Capital .... ______ 3500
4. Add:
   A. Liabilities subordinated to claims of general creditors allowable in computation of net capital .... ______ 3520
   B. Other (deductions) or allowable credits (List) .... ▼33 ______ 3525
5. Total capital and allowable subordinated liabilities .... $ ______ 3530
6. Deductions and/or charges:
   A. Total nonallowable assets from Statement of Financial Condition (Notes B and C) .... $ ______ 3540
      1. Additional charges for customers' and non-customers' security accounts .... $ ______ 3550
      2. Additional charges for customers' and non-customers' commodity accounts .... ______ 3560
   B. Aged fail-to-deliver .... ______ 3570
      1. Number of items .... ▼29 ______ 3450
   C. Aged short security differences-less reserve of .... $ ______ 3460 ▼30 ______ 3580
      number of items .... ______ 3470
   D. Secured demand note deficiency .... ______ 3590
   E. Commodity futures contracts and spot commodities - proproetary capital charges .... ______ 3600
   F. Other deductions and/or charges .... ______ 3610
   G. Deductions for accounts carried under Rule 15c3-1(a)(6), (a)(7) and (c)(2)(x) .... ______ 3615
   H. Total deductions and/or charges .... (______) 3620
7. Other additions and/or allowable credits (List) .... ______ 3630
8. Net capital before haircuts on securities positions .... $ ______ 3640
9. Haircuts on securities: (computed, where applicable, pursuant to 15c3-1(f)):
   A. Contractual securities committments .... $ ______ 3660
   B. Subordinated securities borrowings .... ______ 3670
   C. Trading and investment securities:
      1. Bankers' acceptances, certificates of deposit and commercial paper .... ▼31 ______ 3680
      2. U.S. and Canadian government obligations .... ______ 3690
      3. State and municipal government obligations .... ______ 3700
      4. Corporate obligations .... ______ 3710
      5. Stocks and warrants .... ______ 3720
      6. Options .... ______ 3730
      7. Arbitrage .... ______ 3732
      8. Other securities .... ▼32 ______ 3734
   D. Undue Concentration .... ______ 3650
   E. Other (List) .... ______ 3736 (______) 3740
10. Net Capital .... $ ______ 3750

OMIT PENNIES

FINANCIAL AND OPERATIONAL COMBINED UNIFORM SINGLE REPORT
PART II

BROKER OR DEALER as of ____________

COMPUTATION OF BASIC NET CAPITAL REQUIREMENT

Part A

11. Minimum net capital required ($6\frac{2}{3}$% of line 19) .... $ ______ [3756]
12. Minimum dollar net capital requirement of reporting broker or dealer and minimum net capital requirement of subsidiaries computed in accordance with Note (A) .... $ ______ [3758]
13. Net capital requirement (greater of line 11 or 12) .... $ ______ [3760]
14. Excess net capital (line 10 less 13) .... $ ______ [3770]
15. Excess net capital at 1000% (line 10 less 10% of line 19) .... 35 $ ______ [3780]

COMPUTATION OF AGGREGATE INDEBTEDNESS

16. Total A.I. liabilities from Statement of Financial Condition .... $ ______ [3790]
17. Add:
    - A. Drafts for immediate credit .... 34 $ ______ [3800]
    - B. Market value of securities borrowed for which no equivilent value is paid or credited .... $ ______ [3810]
    - C. Other unrecorded amounts (List) .... $ ______ [3820] $ ______ [3830]
18. Deduct: Adjustment based on deposits in Special Reserve Bank Accounts (15c3-1(c)(1)(vii)) .... $ ______ [3838]
19. Total aggregate indebtedness .... $ ______ [3840]
20. Percentage of aggregate indebtedness to net capital (line 19 ÷ by lne 10) .... % ______ [3850]
21. Percentage of aggregate indebtedness to net capital *after* anticipated capital withdrawals (line 19 ÷ by line 10 less Item 4880 page 25) .... % ______ [3853]

COMPUTATION OF ALTERNATE NET CAPITAL REQUIREMENT

Part B

22. 2% of combined aggregate debt items as shown in Formula for Reserve Requirements pursuant to Rule 15c3-3 prepared as of date of the net capital computation including both brokers or dealers and consolidated subsidiaries' debits .... 36 $ ______ [3870]
23. Minimum dollar net capital requirement of reporting broker or dealer and minimum net capital requirement of subsidiaries computed in accordance with Note (A) .... $ ______ [3880]
24. Net capital requirement (greater of line 22 or 23) .... $ ______ [3760]
25. Excess net capital (line 10 less 24) .... $ ______ [3910]
26. Percentage of Net Capital to Aggregate Debits (line 10 ÷ by line17 page 8) .... % ______ [3851]
27. Percentage of Net Capital, *after* anticipated capital withdrawals, to Aggregate Debits (line 10 less item 4880 page 11 ÷ by line 17 page 8) .... % ______ [3854]
28. Net capital in excess of the greater of:
    - A. 5% of combines aggregate debit items or $120,000 .... $ ______ [3920]

OTHER RATIOS

Part C

29. Percentage of debt to debt-equity total computed in accordance with Rule 15c3-1(d) .... % ______ [3860]
30. Options deductions/Net Capital ratio (1000% test) total deductions exclusive of liquidating equity under Rule 15c3-1(a)(6), (a)(7) and (c)(2)(x) ÷ Net Capital .... % ______ [3852]

NOTES:

(A) The minimum net capital requirement should be computed by adding the minimum dollar net capital requirement of the reporting broker dealer and, for each subsidiary to be consolidated, the greater of:
1. Minimum dollar net capital requirement , or
2. $6\frac{2}{3}$% of aggregate indebtedness or 2% of aggregate debits if alternative method is used.

(B) Do not deduct the value of securities borrowed under subordination agrements or secured demand notes covered by subordination agrements not in satisfactory form and the market values of memberships in exchanges contributed for use of company (contra to item 1740) and partners' securities which were included in non-allowable assets.

(C) For reports filed pursuant to paragraph (d) of Rule 17a-5, respondent should provide a list of material non-allowable assets.

Form **4789** (Rev. September 1991) Department of the Treasury Internal Revenue Service

Currency Transaction Report

▶ **File a separate report for each transaction.** ▶ **Please type or print.**
▶ **For Paperwork Reduction Act Notice, see page 3.**
(Complete all applicable parts—See instructions)

OMB No. 1545-0183
Expires: 9-30-94

1 Check appropriate boxes if: a ☐ amends prior report, b ☐ exemption limit exceeded, c ☐ suspicious transaction.

Part I Identity of individual who conducted this transaction with the financial institution

2 If more than one individual is involved, see instructions and check here . . . . . . ▶ ☐

3 Reason items 4–15 below are not fully completed (check all applicable boxes): a ☐ Armored car service (name) ▶ ....
b ☐ Mail deposit/shipment c ☐ Night deposit or ATM transaction d ☐ Multiple transactions (see instructions)

4 Last name	5 First name	6 Middle initial	7 Social security number
8 Address (number, street, and apt. or suite no.)		9 Occupation, profession, or business	

10 City	11 State	12 ZIP code	13 Country (if not U.S.)	14 Date of birth (see instructions)

15 Method used to verify identity: a Describe identification ▶ ....
b Issued by ▶ c Number ▶

Part II Person (see General Instructions) on whose behalf this transaction was conducted

16 If this transaction was conducted on behalf of more than one person, see instructions and check here . . . . . . ▶ ☐

17 This person is an: ☐ individual or ☐ organization 18 If trust, escrow, brokerage, or other 3rd party account, see instructions and check here . ▶ ☐

19 Individual's last name or Organization's name	20 First name	21 Middle initial	22 Social security number
			Employer identification number

23 Alien identification: a Describe identification ▶ ....
b Issued by ▶ c Number ▶

24 Address (number, street, and apt. or suite no.)	25 Occupation, profession, or business

26 City	27 State	28 ZIP code	29 Country (if not U.S.)	30 Date of birth (see instructions)

Part III Types of accounts and numbers affected by transaction (If more than one of the same type, use additional spaces provided below)

31 S ☐ Savings ▶ .... T ☐ Securities ▶ .... H ☐ CD/Money market ▶ ....
C ☐ Checking ▶ .... L ☐ Loan ▶ .... O ☐ Other (specify) ▶ ....
☐ ▶ ☐ ▶ ☐ ▶

Part IV Type of transaction. Check applicable boxes to describe transaction

32 E ☐ Currency exchange (currency for currency)

33 CASH IN:
D ☐ Deposit
G ☐ Security purchased
P ☐ Check purchased
F ☐ CD/Money market purchased
H ☐ For wire transfer
A ☐ Receipt from abroad
K ☐ Other (specify) ▶

34 CASH OUT:
C ☐ Check cashed
T ☐ Security redeemed
W ☐ Withdrawal
R ☐ CD/Money market redeemed
U ☐ From wire transfer
B ☐ Shipment abroad
Y ☐ Other (specify) ▶

35 Total amount of currency transaction (in U.S. dollar equivalent) (always round up)	36 Amount in Item 35 in U.S. $100 bills or higher	37 Date of transaction (see instructions)
Cash in $ .... .00 Cash out $ .00	Cash in $ .... .00 Cash out $ .00 ☐ Unknown	

38 If other than U.S. currency is involved, please furnish the following information: a Exchange made ☐ for or ☐ from U.S. currency
b Country .... c Amount of currency (in U.S. dollar equivalent) $ .... .00
b Country c Amount of currency (in U.S. dollar equivalent) $ .00

39 If a negotiable instrument or wire transfer was involved in this transaction, please furnish the following information and check this box (see instructions) . ▶ ☐
a Number of negotiable instruments involved..........
b Number of wire transfers involved
c Total amount of all negotiable instruments and all wire transfers (in U.S. dollar equivalent) ▶ $ .00

Part V Financial institution where transaction took place

40 a ☐ Bank (enter code number from instructions here) ▶ [ ]
b ☐ Savings and loan association c ☐ Credit union d ☐ Securities broker/dealer e ☐ Other (specify) ▶

41 Name of financial institution	42 Address where the transaction occurred (see instructions)	43 Employer identification number
		Social security number

44 City	45 State	46 ZIP code	47 MICR number

48 If this is a multiple transaction, please indicate: a Number of transactions ▶ .... c ZIP codes ▶
b Number of branches ▶

Sign Here ▶	49 Signature (preparer)		50 Title	51 Date
	52 Type or print preparer's name	53 Approving official (signature)	54 Date	55 Telephone number ( )

Cat. No. 42004W

Multiple Transactions

(Complete applicable parts below if box 2 or 16 on page 1 is checked)

Part I Continued—Complete if box 2 on page 1 is checked

4 Last name | 5 First name | 6 Middle initial | 7 Social security number

8 Address (number, street, and apt. or suite no.) | 9 Occupation, profession, or business

10 City | 11 State | 12 ZIP code | 13 Country (if not U.S.) | 14 Date of birth (see instructions)

15 Method used to verify identity: a Describe identification ▶
b Issued by ▶ c Number ▶

4 Last name | 5 First name | 6 Middle initial | 7 Social security number

8 Address (number, street, and apt. or suite no.) | 9 Occupation, profession, or business

10 City | 11 State | 12 ZIP code | 13 Country (if not U.S.) | 14 Date of birth (see instructions)

15 Method used to verify identity: a Describe identification ▶
b Issued by ▶ c Number ▶

Part II Continued—Complete if box 16 on page 1 is checked

17 This person is an: ☐ individual or ☐ organization | 18 If trust, escrow, brokerage, or other 3rd party account, see instructions and check here . ▶ ☐

19 Individual's last name or Organization's name | 20 First name | 21 Middle initial | 22 Social security number

23 Alien identification: a Describe identification ▶
b Issued by ▶ c Number ▶ | Employer identification number

24 Address (number, street, and apt. or suite no.) | 25 Occupation, profession, or business

26 City | 27 State | 28 ZIP code | 29 Country (if not U.S.) | 30 Date of birth (see instructions)

17 This person is an: ☐ individual or ☐ organization | 18 If trust, escrow, brokerage, or other 3rd party account, see instructions and check here . ▶ ☐

19 Individual's last name or Organization's name | 20 First name | 21 Middle initial | 22 Social security number

23 Alien identification: a Describe identification ▶
b Issued by ▶ c Number ▶ | Employer identification number

24 Address (number, street, and apt. or suite no.) | 25 Occupation, profession, or business

26 City | 27 State | 28 ZIP code | 29 Country (if not U.S.) | 30 Date of birth (see instructions)

FinCEN Form 101

January 2003

Suspicious Activity Report by the Securities and Futures Industries

▶ **Please type or print. Always complete entire report. Items marked with an asterisk * are considered critical. (See instructions).**

OMB No. 1506 - 0019

1 Check the box if this report corrects a prior report (see instructions, page 7) ☐

Part I Subject Information

2 Check box (a) ☐ if multiple subjects box (b) ☐ subject information unavailable

*3 Individual's last name or entity's full name | *4 First name | 5 Middle initial

6 Also known as (AKA - individual), doing business as (DBA - entity) | 7 Occupation or type of business

*8 Address | *9 City

10 State | *11 ZIP code | *12 Country (if not U.S.) | 13 E-mail address (if available)

*14 SSN/ITIN (individual), or EIN (entity) | *15 Account number(s) affected, if any. Indicate if closed.
Acc't #________ yes ☐ Acc't #________ yes ☐
Acc't #________ yes ☐ Acc't #________ yes ☐
| 16 Date of birth ___/___/_____ MM DD YYYY

*17 Government issued identification (If available)

a ☐ Driver's license/state ID b ☐ Passport c ☐ Alien registration d ☐ Corporate/Partnership Resolution

e ☐ Other ________

f ID Number | g Issuing state or country ________

18 Phone number - work ( ) – | 19 Phone number - home ( ) – | 20 Is individual/business associated/affiliated with the reporting institution? (See instructions) a ☐ Yes b ☐ No

Part II Suspicious Activity Information

*21 Date or date range of suspicious activity
From ___/___/_____ To ___/___/_____
MM DD YYYY MM DD YYYY

*22 Total dollar amount involved in suspicious activity
$, , .00

23 Instrument type (Check all that apply)

a ☐ Bonds/Notes
b ☐ Cash or equiv.
c ☐ Commercial paper
d ☐ Commodity futures contract
e ☐ Money Market Mutual Fund
f ☐ Mutual Fund
g ☐ OTC Derivatives
h ☐ Other derivatives
i ☐ Commodity options
j ☐ Security Futures Products
k ☐ Stocks
l ☐ Warrants
m ☐ Other securities
n ☐ Other non-securities
o ☐ Foreign currency futures
p ☐ Foreign currencies
q ☐ Commodity type ________ (Please identify)
r ☐ Instrument description ________
s ☐ Market where traded ________ (Enter approprite three or four-letter code.)
t ☐ Other (Explain in Part IV)

24 CUSIP® number | 25 CUSIP® number | 26 CUSIP® number

27 CUSIP® number | 28 CUSIP® number | 29 CUSIP® number

*30 Type of suspicious activity:

a ☐ Bribery/gratuity
b ☐ Check fraud
c ☐ Computer intrusion
d ☐ Credit/debit card fraud
e ☐ Embezzlement/theft
f ☐ Futures fraud
g ☐ Forgery
h ☐ Identity theft
i ☐ Insider trading
j ☐ Mail fraud
k ☐ Market manipulation
l ☐ Money laundering/Structuring
m ☐ Prearranged or other non-competitive trading
n ☐ Securities fraud
o ☐ Significant wire or other transactions without economic purpose
p ☐ Suspicious documents or ID presented
q ☐ Terrorist financing
r ☐ Wash or other fictitious trading
s ☐ Wire fraud
t ☐ Other (Describe in Part VI)

Nasdaq System/ Participant/ Feature	Key Points	Hours of Operation
ACT	Provides the reporting of completed trades to the tape and submission of trades for matching and clearing. ACT reports trades to NSCC, Nasdaq, third market, OTC BB, and PINK OTC. foreign securities and convertible bonds listed on Nasdaq are also reported to ACT.	8 a.m.–8 p.m.
TRACE	Is used to report trades in dollar denominated corporate debt, agency issues, church bonds, and mortgage backed and asset backed bonds (U.S. Treasuries and foreign federal issues are not reported through TRACE). Both sides report the trade within 15 minutes.	8 a.m.–6:30 p.m.
TRACS	Is used to report trades executed through the ADF including Nasdaq listed, CQS securities, and convertible debt. Reports must be made within 10 seconds. TRACS allows 3 party trades for riskless principal trades. TRACS reports trades to the DTCC.	8 a.m.–6:30 p.m.
TRF	User interface operated on the ACT platform, used to report trades executed in Nasdaq and CQS securities. All reports due in 10 seconds.	8 a.m.–8 p.m.
ORF	The order reporting facility (ORF) is used to report trades in OTC BB, Pink OTC and trades in restricted stock under Rule 144A to the NSCC.	8 a.m.–8 p.m.
FQCS	The Firm Quote Compliance System (FQCS) is used to ensure that market makers honor their quotes and do not back away. Members who feel they are owed an execution should contact FQCS within 5 minutes.	N/A
OATS/CATS	Is used to ensure proper handling and routing of orders. All events in an order must be time stamped. Clocks must be synchronized daily to 1 second of NIST atomic clock and must display time in military time. If firms capture time in milliseconds reports to OATS must include milliseconds (not required if firms do not capture time in milliseconds); all reports on T + 1.	By 8 a.m. including Saturday; all orders must have a unique identifier
ACES	Allows market makers to provide direct access to their books to non market making order entry firms. ACES will send a report back to the order entry firm. The market maker pays ACES fees. Market makers can turn access on and off at any time. There is no maximum size of an order entered.	8 a.m.–6:30 p.m.
ECNs	An electronic trading system that matches buyers and sellers. Linked ECNs may display 1-sided markets in Nasdaq. Unlinked ECNs quote in the ADF. ECNs do not take risk and may enter and exit markets for stocks based on orders.	N/A
Market Makers	Required to display 2-sided markets during normal business hours. All quotes are firm for the greater of 1 round lot or displayed size. Shares in reserve are also firm.	Obligated to quote 9:30 a.m. to 4 p.m. regular trading day
Dark Pools	A dark pool provides an alternative trading system for institutional investors to anonymously buy and sell large blocks of stock without impacting the market for the stock.	N/A

(continued)

Nasdaq System/ Participant/ Feature	Key Points	Hours of Operation
ADF	Provides an alternative quoting facility for unlinked ECNs and other market participants to quote Nasdaq and CQS stocks. The ADF does not provide access to quotes; market participants must provide access.	8 a.m.–6:30 p.m.
Nasdaq Market Center	Computer terminal used to route and execute market orders, and immediately executable limit orders for Nasdaq-listed securities for orders for up to 999,999 may be entered.	N/A
OTC BB	Provides an electronic venue to quote non-listed OTC stocks and real-time reporting of volume. The OTC BB is accessed via the Nasdaq work station. Priced quotes are firm. One-sided quotes as well as non-priced indications of interest such as bid wanted or offer wanted may be displayed. All OTC BB stocks may be quoted in sub-penny prices down to .0001. Securities delisted from Nasdaq or NYSE trade on the OTC BB; all companies must be current with their regulatory filings.	6:00 a.m.–5 p.m.
PINK OTC	Operated by the OTC Markets Group, the PINK OTC market is registered as an ATS with the SEC. Form 211 must be filed by initial firm quoting just like for the OTC BB. The are no listing requirements of any kind for a stock to trade on the PINK OTC market.	6:00 a.m.–5 p.m.
Opening Cross	Provides for initial price discovery for Nasdaq listed stocks. Nasdaq opens quotes for cross at 9:25 a.m. orders may be placed for the opening cross between 7 a.m. and 9:28 a.m. Orders placed after 9:28 a.m. will not participate in the opening cross with the exception of imbalance orders only. Orders may not be modified during this time, unless the modification makes the order more aggressive in price or size. At 9:30 a.m. the clearing price determines the Nasdaq Official Opening Price (NOOP). 9:28 a.m.–9:30 a.m. Net imbalance indicator is sent every 5 seconds.	9:28 a.m.–9:30 a.m.
Closing Cross	Provides for uniform closing price. Orders for the closing cross may be placed from 7 a.m.–3:50 p.m. only. Imbalance only orders may be entered after 3:50 p.m. Imbalance only orders may be entered until the close NOII, sent every 5 seconds from 3:50 p.m. until close.	3:50 p.m.–4:00 p.m.
MOC/LOC Orders	Nasdaq market on close and limit on close orders may be entered from 7 a.m.–3:50 p.m. On the NYSE, MOC and LOC orders may be entered until 3:45 p.m. Orders on close may only be entered on the NYSE after 3:45 p.m. if there is an imbalance of 50,000 shares or greater.	N/A
IO Orders	Imbalance only entered to offset buy side or sell side imbalances during the opening or closing of the market. These orders will only be executed if an imbalance exists.	N/A
Initial Quote Nasdaq	For Nasdaq stocks a request is sent over the Nasdaq workstation. Same day approval to quote. The firm must enter initial quote within 5 days. If not quoted in 5 days, the firm must reapply to quote.	N/A

(continued)

Nasdaq System/ Participant/ Feature	Key Points	Hours of Operation
Initial Quote OTC BB	First firm must file Form 211 three business days prior to quoting. If the initial quote is a priced quote, the broker dealer must provide information as to how the price was determined. If the dealer is not going to enter an initial priced quote (i.e., bid wanted or offer wanted) the reason for the quote is not needed. If a non-priced quote is going to be changed to a priced quote prior to approval, the basis must be provided and it must be sent to FINRA via a supplemental report three business days prior to quoting.	N/A
Piggy-backing a Quote on OTC BB	Once an OTC BB security is active all subsequent broker dealers may enter quotes without filing Form 211, so long as the stock has had quotes open for 12 of the last 30 days and at no point were there more than four consecutive days without a quote.	N/A
Customer Limit Order Protection	Covers Nasdaq, CQS, and OTC BB securities. Customer orders and orders received from another BD are considered to be customer orders. If the market maker trades at a price that would satisfy a customer's limit order, that customer is owed an equal print. Customer limit order must be displayed in 30 seconds.	9:30 a.m.–6:30 p.m.
Securities Information Processor	A SIP is a market data processor that collects and distributes trade data for completed trades or quotes for securities, such as Bloomberg, and the consolidated tape association CTA. SIPs must be registered with the SEC.	N/A
NSDQ	Allows firms to route orders for anonymous display under the MPID NSDQ. The NSDQ function will display the aggregate size entered by all market makers at that price level. Contra party information will not be shown until executed. Parties may request full anonymity under which no contra party details will be disclosed.	N/A
AQR	The auto quote refresh feature can be used by market makers whose quotes have been reduced to less than one round lot (decremented). The AQR can be programed by the firm to match the firm's trading style. If the firm has no size in reserve and has not set the AQR, Nasdaq will zero out the market maker's quote for 30 seconds. If the market maker does not update the quote the AQR will put the marker maker back in the box 1 cent away from the worst quote.	N/A
Preferenced Orders	An order entered by a firm stating which firm it wants to trade with at the inside market. It can access the market maker's displayed size and reserve size. If the firm is not at the inside market the order will be sent back.	N/A
Non-directed Orders	Most orders entered in the Nasdaq system are non-directed orders. The Nasdaq system routes the order to the market maker who was at the inside market first.	N/A
Directed Orders	A directed order is sent by a firm to a market maker's quote and if it is for more than the displayed size, away from the market maker's quote, or AON it is not a liability order.	N/A
AIQ	The anti-internalization qualifier will route the order to the market and will not execute the order against the market maker's own quote.	N/A

(continued)

Action/Event	Taken By	When Taken/Covered Time
Buy-in	A buying broker dealer who has a fail-to-receive from the selling broker dealer.	No earlier than three days after settlement or T + 5
Sellout (broker dealer to broker dealer)	A selling broker dealer who delivers securities to the buying broker dealer who fails to pay.	Any time after settlement/immediately
Sellout customer fails to pay	A broker dealer who has a customer who fails to pay for the trade.	T + 5, one day past Reg T payment date of T + 4
Request an extension for customer to pay for trade	When a broker dealer requests an extension of time for a customer to pay for securities.	Send request to NYSE or FINRA before the end of the fourth business day (payment date)
Termination of accountant	A broker dealer who terminates an accountant.	Within 15 days filed with both FINRA and SEC
Box Count	Broker dealers with custody/clearing firms.	Quarterly, not sooner than 2 months or longer than 4 months from last count
Short securities difference	A clearing firm.	After seven days from discovery, firm must take a haircut equal to 25 percent of market value; after 28 days haircut is 100 percent of market value, must buy in after 45 days
Close out threshold securities	Firms who have an open fail-to-deliver for a security classified as a threshold security by SRO.	After 12 consecutive settlements firms must buy in the securities (10 days past settlement)
Report lost securities non-criminal	Broker dealers.	May try to locate for two business days; if not located report to SIC and transfer agent on third day
Report lost securities criminal	Broker dealers.	Report to SIC transfer agent and FBI in one business day
Lost securities located	Broker dealers.	Report to all parties who were notified within one business day
Filing of subordinated loan	Broker dealer accepting capital.	Two copies of agreement filed at least 10 days prior to effective date
Temporary subordinated loan	Used by a broker dealer to increase net capital, to allow participation in a firm commitment underwriting.	Maximum duration is 45 days, maximum of three temporary subordinated loans allowed in 12 months
Aged fail to deliver	A customer who fails to deliver securities to a broker dealer.	Five days after settlement date, 15 percent haircut on value of securities taken against net capital
Short interest reporting	A clearing firm.	Report short positions for the firm and customers as of the 15th and last settlement day of the month
Trade reported to ACT	The reporting broker dealer who executes a trade not automatically reported to ACT.	Within 10 seconds of trade
Accepting a trade reported to ACT	The contra party in a trade that was reported to ACT manually.	Within 20 minutes of trade

(continued)

Action/Event	Taken By	When Taken/Covered Time
Reporting a bond trade to TRACE	Both parties in a bond trade.	Within 15 minutes of trade
Voluntary withdrawal of quotes Nasdaq listed	Market maker who pulls his quotes.	Cannot requote for 20 days
Voluntary withdrawal of quotes exchange listed CQS	Market maker who pulls his quotes.	Cannot requote for one day
Analyst trading blackout	Analysts and immediate family may not trade stocks during certain time frames before and after the report.	No trading until the intended recipients have had a chances to act on research
Trading blackout additional offerings for actively traded stocks	Syndicate members and issues with ADTV of at least $1 million, float of at least $150 million.	No blackout
Trading blackout additional offerings for tier 2	Syndicate members and issuers for issues with ADTV of $100,000 and float of $25 million.	One business day prior to effective date
Trading blackout additional offerings for tier 3	Syndicate members and issuers for issues with ADTV of less than $100,000 and float of less than $25 million.	Five business day prior to effective date
Covering of short positions with securities purchased through offering	A short seller of securities.	Cannot be used to cover short positions established within five business days of offering
Settlement of syndicate accounts	Syndicate manager.	90 days from the delivery of the securities from the issuer
Research report blackout manager, co-manager, or syndicate member	Manager, co-manager, or syndicate member of an IPO.	Cannot issue research until 10 days have passed
Research report blackout manager or co-manager	Manager or co-manager of a subsequent offering.	Cannot issue research until 3 days have passed
Research report blackout selling group or syndicate member	Selling group or syndicate member of a subsequent offering.	No restriction on issuing research
Prospectus to be delivered to aftermarket purchasers, NYSE or Nasdaq listed IPO	Any broker dealer with a customer who executes an order to buy the security.	25 days from pricing, may be delivered electronically
Prospectus to be delivered to aftermarket purchasers, OTC BB, PINK OTC IPO	Any broker dealer with a customer who executes an order to buy the security.	90 days from pricing, may be delivered electronically
Prospectus to be delivered to aftermarket purchasers, NYSE, or Nasdaq listed additional offerings	Any broker dealer with a customer who executes an order to buy the security.	No requirement

(continued)

Action/Event	Taken By	When Taken/Covered Time
Prospectus to be delivered to aftermarket purchasers, OTC BB, PINK OTC, additional offerings	Any broker dealer with a customer who executes an order to buy the security.	40 days from pricing, may be delivered electronically
Calculation of reserve requirement, (small firm)	A carrying broker dealer who has less than $1 million in customer credits and AI:NC less than 8:1.	Monthly, 105 percent of credits
Calculation of reserve requirement (most firms)	A broker dealer who has more than $1 million in customer credits and AI:NC more than 8:1.	Weekly, 100 percent of credits
Deposit into Special Reserve Account	Carrying broker dealers.	By 10 a.m. Tuesday (two business days after calculation)
Equity withdrawal of more than 30 percent of excess net capital over 30-day period	Owner or lender of or to the broker dealer.	Notification to SEC two business days prior
Computation of Net Asset Value	Investment companies (mutual funds).	Once per business day
Use of a mutual fund prospectus	An agent recommending a mutual fund to a client.	May be used for 16 months from date of the financial information in the prospectus
Updating of a mutual fund prospectus	An investment company (mutual fund).	Should be updated every 12 months; must be updated every 13 months based on the date of the financial information in the prospectus
Dividend distribution	Investment companies (mutual funds).	As often as the fund would like
Capital gain distribution	Investment companies (mutual funds).	Only once per year
Letter of intent	Signed by an investor in a mutual fund.	Good for 13 months; may be backdated up to 90 days to include prior purchase, 13 month window starts from back date
Approval of an annuity application by principal	Principal of the broker dealer.	Seven calendar days from receipt of application

Form	Filed By	Time to File
13 D	Outside investors who acquire 5 percent or more of a company.	Within 10 days of reaching 5 percent ownership
13 G	Investment companies (mutual funds) who acquire 5 percent or more of a company.	Within 45 days of the end of the calendar year during which the position was held
13 F	Investment groups (hedge funds) who manage $100 million or more.	Within 45 days of the end of the calendar quarter
Form 3	Officers and directors who initially report ownership stake in company.	Within 10 days
Form 4	Officers and directors to report a change ownership stake in company.	Within 2 days
S1	Nonexempt issuers going public or offering additional securities.	At least 20 days prior to effective date
S3	Well known seasoned issuers and seasoned issues offering securities to the public.	Effective immediately upon filing
S4	To report mergers and acquisitions.	At least 20 days prior to effective date
F6	To register an ADR.	At least 20 days prior to effective date
20-F	To register foreign securities.	At least 20 days prior to effective date
FOCUS	Carrying firms only.	Within 10 days of month's end
FOCUS 2	Carrying firms only.	Within 17 days of the end of the quarter
FOCUS 2 A	Introducing firms only.	Within 17 days of the end of the quarter
Schedule 1	Firms who have custody must file schedule 1 with the SEC.	Within 17 days of the end of the calendar year
Supplemental Statement of Information	Any broker dealer designated by FINRA to show more detail on revenue and expenses.	Within 20 business days of the end of the calendar quarter
Audited FOCUS	All broker dealers registered with the SEC.	Within 60 days of year end
Early Warning Report	Firms whose AI/NC exceeds 12:1.	Within 24 hours for firms over one year old
Subordinated Loans	Broker dealer receiving loan.	At least 10 days before effective date/with FINRA
10-Q	Reporting companies who report quarterly earnings.	Within 45 days of the end of the calendar quarter
10-K	Reporting companies who report annual earnings.	Within 90 days of the year end
8-K	Reporting companies to disclose a material event.	Within four business days of the event

(continued)

Form	Filed By	Time to File
Form 144	Control persons and insiders owning more than 10 percent who are selling securities.	At the time the order to sell is entered; good for 90 days
Offering Documents	Filed by lead underwriter with FINRA's CFD to review compensation.	Within 1 business day of filing registration statement with the SEC
Settlement of syndicate account	Lead underwriter.	Within 90 days of delivery of securities from issuer to underwriter
Form 211	Market maker who will be the first quoting an OTC BB security.	Three business days prior to quoting
Nondirected Order reports/NMS rule 606	Broker dealers who execute more than 500 orders per month.	Quarterly/upon request of a customer/must notify customers annually of report availability
Market Center Execution Quality Report/Rule 605	Market centers must report effective spreads, price improvement, and how orders are executed for market and immediately marketable limit orders.	Monthly
OATS/CATS reports	Broker dealers must report all events during the life of an order and must sync their clocks to 1 second of the NIST clock in military time.	Daily by 8 a.m., T + 1 including Saturday

Regulation/ Rule	Purpose	Requirement
Regulation AC	To regulate analysts who issue research reports.	Analysts must certify that each report reflects their personal views, as well as certify quarterly within 30 days of the end of the quarter that all reports issued within the previous quarter reflect their own personal views. If the quarterly certification is not made, all reports for the next 120 days must be marked as uncertified.
Regulation FD	To regulate disclosures by public companies.	If a company discloses information to analysts or institutional investors it must disclose the information to the public. Intentional disclosure requires simultaneous release, and an unintentional disclosure must be released before the next trading day. The company may use Form 8-K, a press release, a website, or social media.
Regulation M	Regulates the activities of issuers, syndicate members, and market makers during an offering of additional stock.	When a small company is issuing stock, interested parties may not influence the price of the security during a restricted period. Securities with an ADTV of $100,000 and float of $25 million have a restricted period of one day. Smaller issues have a restricted period of 5 days. Actively traded stocks with an ADTV of at least $1 million and float of $150 million have no restricted period.
Regulation NMS	To ensure orders receive quality executions, to require reports on order routing, and to prohibit quoting in sub-penny pricing.	Broker dealers must disclose their order routing methods for non-directed orders quarterly. Market centers must disclose execution quality monthly. Market makers may not quote in sub-penny prices and may not trade through a protected quote.

(continued)

Regulation/ Rule	Purpose	Requirement
Regulation SP	To protect customer and consumer information.	Broker dealers must provide a privacy notice to customers when accounts are opened and annually thereafter. Customers may opt out of sharing information with unaffiliated parties, but customers may not opt out of sharing information with affiliated parties. Methods of opting out must be reasonable—call an 800 number or click on a link to a website to opt out.
Regulation S-AM	To protect customers from unwanted marketing.	Broker dealers may not use information received from affiliated companies to solicit business unless the potential marketing has been clearly disclosed, and the customer was provided a simple method to opt out and has not opted out.
Regulation SHO	To regulate short sales and locating, borrowing, and delivering securities, as well as order marking.	All orders to sell must be marked long or short. Firms who have independent trading units may allow each unit to determine if it is long or short, and may use the easy to borrow list as long as it is not more than 24 hours old.
Regulation S-K	To regulate forward-looking statements of issuers/ transactions with the related person.	Forward looking statements must be reasonable and based on an appropriate time frame. If a statement has been reviewed by an outside party, the qualifications of the person and the extent of the review must be disclosed. Transactions with related persons over $120,000 must be disclosed.
Regulation MA	To regulate the communications of terms of a merger or acquisition.	Requires that a plain English term sheet be filed relating to the transaction, so that investors may easily understand the proposed transaction.
FINRA Rule 5150	To regulate broker dealers who issue fairness opinions; formerly 2290.	Requires a broker dealer who issues a fairness opinion to disclose all potential conflicts of interest relating to the opinion, such as if the firm was an adviser in the transaction, and any material relationship that has existed in the last two years with the companies. If information was submitted by a party requesting the opinion, it must disclose if the information was verified and all opinions must be conclusive. Member firms must have procedures under which a committee will approve the opinion, and at least one member should have no other involvement with the deal.
Hart-Scott-Rodino Act	To require filings by both parties in a merger or takeover.	Information must be filed by both parties with the DOJ and FTC. The DOJ and FTC will review all-stock and stock and cash deals for 30 days; all-cash transactions will be reviewed for 15 days. To ensure no antitrust laws are broken, deals cannot be closed during the waiting period and filing is only for deals of certain values greater than $70.9 million.
Sarbanes Oxley Act/SOX	To regulate the reporting of financial information by publicly traded companies.	Requires CEOs and CFOs to certify that they have reviewed the financial reports (10Qs and 10Ks), and requires financial reports to disclose all material information. It also prohibits loans to executives, and requires officers, directors, and 10 percent stockholders to notify the SEC within 10 days of ownership. Public companies must publish information on internal controls annually.

(continued)

Regulation/ Rule	Purpose	Requirement
Regulation ATS	To regulate alternative trading systems.	Requires operators of alternative trading systems to register with the SEC as an exchange or as a broker dealer.
The Manning Rule	To protect customer limit orders.	Market makers who accept customer limit orders must protect the customer's order and may not compete with the order. Customer limit orders must be displayed within 30 seconds between 9:30 a.m. and 6:30 p.m.
FINRA Rule 5130	To ensure full offering of securities to public.	Broker dealers may not withhold securities for their accounts or the accounts of restricted persons; they must offer all securities to investors.
Regulation D	To allow for the private offering of securities.	Securities purchasers must be accredited investors or higher max 35 non-accredited investors. No commissions paid on sales to non-accredited investors.
Regulation S	To allow the sale of securities outside of the United States.	Securities issuers may not sell any of the offering to U.S. investors; no resale to U.S. residents for 6 months for a reporting company 40 days in the case of bonds.
Regulation A	To allow the sale of securities offered under a circular, not a prospectus.	Issuer may raise up to $50 million in a 12-month period.
Rule 147	Allows an issuer to sell securities in its home state/ one state.	100 percent of purchasers must be residents of the state and issuers must meet one of the following; 80 percent of the proceeds must be used in the state; 80 percent of the issuer's assets must be located in the state; 80 percent of the issuer's revenue must be generated in that state; there is a 6-month holding period for sales to out-of-state residents. Form 147 must be filed 10 days prior to effective date. If a broker dealer is used to help sell the offering the broker dealer must have an office in the state; all securities sold must be primary/no sales from stockholders.
Rule 137	Allows broker dealers who are not participating in an underwriting to publish research reports.	Firm may not receive compensation for issuing the report and the report must be published in the normal course of business.
Rule 138	Allows broker dealers who are participating in the underwriting to publish research on nonequivalent securities.	Firm may publish research on the company's non-convertible bonds and preferred stock.
Rule 139	Allows broker dealers who are participating in an underwriting to publish research reports.	Report must be part of research that is regularly distributed. Firm cannot upgrade and the company cannot be highlighted more than any other company in the report.
Rule 144	Allows for the sale of restricted securities obtained through a private placement/sets volume limits on sales of control securities by control persons.	Restricted securities must be held for 6 months, fully paid. After 6 months, securities may be sold freely by non-affiliates. Form 144 must be filed at the time the order to sell is entered and the volume limit is 1 percent of the outstanding shares or the average weekly trading volume during the preceding 4 weeks, whichever is greater.

(continued)

Regulation/ Rule	Purpose	Requirement
Rule 144 A	Allows for the sale of restricted equity or debt securities to QIBs.	Allows for the resale of restricted securities to institutional investors (no holding period) with $100 million in assets or more, or broker dealers with $10 million in assets or more. 144A transactions are effected through the portal market and are reported the same business day. Broker dealers must determine if the customer is a QIB.
Rule 415	Allows for the shelf registration of debt securities.	Issuer files with the SEC once effect the issuer who is not a WKSI may sell the securities any time over a 2-year period. A WKSI may sell the securities any time over a 3-year period.
Rule 5110	Requires underwriters to file information regarding an offering with the Corporate Finance Department.	Underwriters must file with the CFD to ensure that compensation is fair. Information to be filed by the syndicate manager includes: the spread, amount of stock options, or warrants received, amount of and description of expense reimbursement, amount of non-accountable expense allowance, any right of first refusal for future offerings, overallotment provisions, and any other consideration of value. The CFD will look at any compensation received by the syndicate within the 180 days preceding the offering. Information must be filed within one business day of the registration statement being filed with the SEC.
Violation of Compensation Rules	The CFD considers any of the items listed to be a violation of compensation rules.	An overallotment/green shoe in excess of 15 percent of offering; options rights or warrants exercisable below the offering price or with a life of greater than 5 years; non accountable expense allowance in excess of 3 percent of spread; freely transferable stock in excess of 1 percent of offering (1 percent or more requires a 6-month lock up); first rights to additional offerings of more than 3 years. Includes a tail or termination fee exceeding 2 years and aggregate stock compensation exceeding 10 percent of offering, including freely transferable shares and the exercise of options, warrants, and rights.
Rule 5121	Regulates member firms going public.	A FINRA member going public must engage an independent underwriter to avoid conflicts of interest. The underwriter must be a qualified underwriter who has been lead or book running manager in at least 3 other offerings of securities and whose participation in the offerings was at least 50 percent in the 3 years prior to the offering. All proceeds of the offering must be placed in escrow, the firm must have no less than 120 percent of its minimum net capital and an AI:NC of no more than 10:1. The proceeds of the issue may be used when calculating net capital.

(continued)

Regulation/ Rule	Purpose	Requirement
Rule 5122	Allows member firms to raise money through a private placement.	The issuer must file the PPM with FINRA before offering, 10 calendar days prior to offering the PPM or term sheet to any investor.
The Securities Act of 1933	Regulates the primary market, requires disclosure.	Requires non-exempt issuers to file a registration statement with the SEC. The registration statement is on review for a minimum of 20 days (cooling off period). During cooling off period no sales may take place; only indications of interest may be accepted via red herring. Due diligence meetings may also be held and tombstone ads may be run. A preliminary prospectus must be received in physical form. No other information may be sent with the preliminary prospectus, including no highlights, business cards, or research. SEC issues an effective date sales may take place. Final prospectus may be accessed electronically, and is considered to be delivered.
The Securities Exchange Act of 1934	Regulates the secondary market.	Created the SEC as the ultimate securities industry regulator. Regulates all exchanges, all broker dealers, and all people who work in the industry. Regulation T gave the FRB the authority to regulate the extension of credit for securities purchases, margin 50% and payment dates 5 days to pay. Requires broker dealers to maintain a minimum net capital and requires agents to be fingerprinted.
The Maloney Act of 1938	An amendment to the Securities Exchange Act of 1934.	Created the NASD as the regulator for the OTC market. Now part of FINRA.
Rules of Fair Practice	FINRA bylaw governing treatment of public.	Ethical treatment is owed to customers of broker dealers. Broker dealers and agents may not misrepresent facts or employ any device to manipulate or defraud customers.
Code of Procedure	Regulates how FINRA investigates complaints and violations.	FINRA investigates complaints and violations through the Code of Procedure. This is not about monetary losses, only about violations of conduct rules. Respondent must reply to FINRA within 25 days. If not, a second notice will be sent providing another 14 days. A second failure to respond will be cause for action being taken and sanctions being imposed.
Code of Arbitration	Provides a forum to settle monetary disputes.	All industry participants must settle disputes in arbitration. Customer must agree in writing. Awards are final and binding with no appeal. Awards must be paid in 30 days. Simplified arbitration is available to anyone for disputes under $50,000. No hearing will be held unless requested by a public customer, and submissions will be read by one arbitrator.
Uniform Practice Code	Regulates how broker dealers do business with other broker dealers.	Sets standards of practice for industry participants. Regulates good delivery, ex dates, settlement dates, DK and reclamation procedures, buy-ins, and sell-outs.

(continued)

Regulation/ Rule	Purpose	Requirement
Penny Stock Cold Call Rule	Regulates the solicitation of penny stocks. Stocks trading under $5 on OTCBB or PINK OTC.	Customers must be sent a Penny Stock Risk Disclosure Document. Customers must sign and return acknowledgment that it was received. They must fill out a suitability statement that includes the customer's financial information and risk profile, and send to the customer for a signature. Once returned, the trade may be executed and a confirmation is sent. The firm must disclose the amount of compensation received by the firm and the rep for executing the order. Customers with penny stocks must be sent monthly statements showing value or estimated value. Exemptions are unsolicited orders, and transactions with established customers who have held assets in the account for 12 months or who have executed three purchases of three different penny stocks on 3 different days, as well as broker dealers who receive less than five percent of revenue from penny stock transactions.

Glossary of Exam Terms

A

AAA/Aaa The highest investment-grade rating for bond issuers awarded by Standard & Poor's and Moody's ratings agencies.

acceptance waiver and consent (AWAC) A process used when a respondent does not contest an allegation made by FINRA. The respondent accepts the findings without admitting any wrongdoing and agrees to accept any penalty for the violation.

account executive (AE) An individual who is duly licensed to represent a broker dealer in securities transactions or investment banking business. Also known as a registered representative.

accredited investor Any individual or institution that meets one or more of the following: (1) a net worth exceeding $1 million, excluding the primary residence, or (2) is single and has an annual income of $200,000 or more or $300,000 jointly with a spouse.

accretion An accounting method used to step up an investor's cost base for a bond purchased at a discount.

accrued interest The portion of a debt securities future interest payment that has been earned by the seller of the security. The purchaser must pay this amount of accrued interest to the seller at the time of the transaction's settlement. Interest accrues from the date of the last interest payment date up to, but not including, the transaction's settlement date.

accumulation stage The period during which an annuitant is making contributions to an annuity contract.

accumulation unit A measure used to determine the annuitant's proportional ownership interest in the insurance company's separate account during the accumulation stage. During the accumulation stage, the number of accumulation units owned by the annuitant changes and their value varies.

acid-test ratio A measure of corporate liquidity found by subtracting inventory from current assets and dividing the result by the current liabilities.

ACT *See* Automated Comparison Transaction (ACT) service.

ad valorem tax A tax based on the value of the subject property.

adjusted basis The value assigned to an asset after all deductions or additions for improvements have been taken into consideration.

adjusted gross income (AGI) An accounting measure employed by the IRS to help determine tax liability. AGI = earned income + investment income (portfolio income) + capital gains + net passive income.

administrator (1) An individual authorized to oversee the liquidation of an intestate decedent's estate. (2) An individual or agency that administers securities' laws within a state.

ADR/ADS *See* American depositary receipt (ADR).

advance/decline line Measures the health of the overall market by calculating advancing issues and subtracting the number of declining issues.

advance refunding The early refinancing of municipal securities. A new issue of bonds is sold to retire the old issue at its first available call date or maturity.

advertisement Any material that is distributed by a broker dealer or issuer for the purpose of increasing business or public awareness for the firm or issuer. The broker dealer or issuer must distribute advertisements to an audience that is not controlled. Advertisements are distributed through any of the following: newspapers/magazines, radio, TV, billboards, telephone.

affiliate An individual who owns 10% or more of the company's voting stock. In the case of a direct participation program (DPP), this is anyone who controls the partnership or is controlled by the partnership.

agency issue A debt security issued by any authorized entity of the U.S. government. The debt security is an obligation of the issuing entity, not an obligation of the U.S. government (with the exception of Ginnie Mae and the Federal Import Export Bank issues).

agency transaction A transaction made by a firm for the benefit of a customer. The firm merely executes a customer's order and charges a fee for the service, which is known as a commission.

agent A firm or an individual who executes securities transactions for customers and charges a service fee known as a commission. Also known as a broker.

aggregate indebtedness The total amount of the firm's customer-related debts.

allied member An owner-director or 5% owner of an NYSE member firm. Allied members may not trade on the floor.

all-or-none (AON) order A non-time-sensitive order that stipulates that the customer wants to buy or sell all of the securities in the order.

all-or-none underwriting A type of underwriting that states that the issuer wants to sell all of the securities being offered or none of the securities being offered. The proceeds from the issue will be held in escrow until all securities are sold.

alpha A measure of the projected change in the security's price as a result of fundamental factors relating only to that company.

alternative minimum tax (AMT) A method used to calculate the tax liability for some high-income earners that adds back the deductions taken for certain tax preference items.

AMBAC Indemnity Corporation Insures the interest and principal payments for municipal bonds.

American depositary receipt (ADR)/ American depositary security (ADS) A receipt representing the beneficial ownership of foreign securities being held in trust overseas by a foreign branch of a U.S. bank. ADRs/ADSs facilitate the trading and ownership of foreign securities and trade in the United States on an exchange or in the over-the-counter markets.

American Stock Exchange (AMEX) An exchange located in New York using the dual-auction method and specialist system to facilitate trading in stocks, options, exchange-traded funds, and portfolios. AMEX was acquired by the NYSE Euronext and is now part of NYSE Alternext.

amortization An accounting method that reduces the value of an asset over its projected useful life. Also the way that loan principal is systematically paid off over the life of a loan.

annual compliance review All firms must hold at least one compliance meeting per year with all of its agents.

annuitant An individual who receives scheduled payments from an annuity contract.

annuitize A process by which an individual converts from the accumulation stage to the payout stage of an annuity contract. This is accomplished by exchanging accumulation units for annuity units. Once a payout option is selected, it cannot be changed.

annuity A contract between an individual and an insurance company that is designed to provide the annuitant with lifetime income in exchange for either a lump sum or periodic deposits into the contract.

annuity unit An accounting measure used to determine an individual's proportionate ownership of the separate account during the payout stage of the contract. The number of annuity units owned by an individual remains constant, and their value, which may vary, is used to determine the amount of the individual's annuity payment.

appreciation An asset's increase in value over time.

arbitrage An investment strategy used to profit from market inefficiencies.

arbitration A forum provided by both the NYSE and FINRA to resolve disputes between two parties. Only a public customer may not be forced to settle a dispute through arbitration. The public customer must agree to arbitration in writing. All industry participants must settle disputes through arbitration.

ask *See* offer.

assessed value A base value assigned to property for the purpose of determining tax liability.

assessment An additional amount of taxes due as a result of a municipal project that the homeowner benefits from. Also an additional call for capital by a direct participation program.

asset Anything of value owned by an individual or a corporation.

asset allocation fund A mutual fund that spreads its investments among different asset classes (i.e., stocks, bonds, and other investments) based on a predetermined formula.

assignee A person to whom the ownership of an asset is being transferred.

assignment (1) The transfer of ownership or rights through a signature. (2) The notification given to investors who are short an option that the option holder has exercised its right and they must now meet their obligations as detailed in the option contract.

associated person Any individual under the control of a broker dealer, issuer, or bank, including employees, officers, and directors, as well as those individuals who control or have common control of a broker dealer, issuer, or bank.

assumed interest rate (AIR) (1) A benchmark used to determine the minimum rate of return that must be realized by a variable annuity's separate account during the payout phase in order to keep the annuitant's payments consistent. (2) In the case of a variable life insurance policy, the minimum rate of return that must be achieved in order to maintain the policy's variable death benefit.

at-the-close order An order that stipulates that the security is to be bought or sold only at the close of the market, or as close to the close as is reasonable, or not at all.

at the money A term used to describe an option when the underlying security price is equal to the exercise price of the option.

at-the-opening order An order that stipulates that the security is to be bought or sold only at the opening of the market, or as close to the opening as is reasonable, or not at all.

auction market The method of trading employed by stock exchanges that allows buyers and sellers to compete with one another in a centralized location.

authorized stock The maximum number of shares that a corporation can sell in an effort to raise capital. The number of authorized shares may only be changed by a vote of the shareholders.

Automated Comparison Transaction (ACT) service ACT is the service that clears and locks Nasdaq trades.

average cost A method used to determine the cost of an investment for an investor who has made multiple purchases of the same security at different times and prices. An investor's average cost may be used to determine a cost base for tax purposes or to evaluate the profitability of an investment program, such as dollar-cost averaging. Average cost is determined by dividing the total dollars invested by the number of shares purchased.

average price A method used to determine the average price paid by an investor for a security that has been purchased at different times and prices, such as through dollar-cost averaging. An investor's average price is determined by dividing the total of the purchase prices by the number of purchases.

B

BBB/Baa The lowest ratings assigned by Standard & Poor's and Moody's for debt in the investment-grade category.

back-end load A mutual fund sales charge that is assessed upon the redemption of the shares. The amount of the sales charge to be assessed upon redemption decreases the longer the shares are held. Also known as a contingent deferred sales charge.

backing away The failure of an over-the-counter market maker to honor firm quotes. It is a violation of FINRA rules.

balanced fund A mutual fund whose investment policy requires that the portfolio's holdings are diversified among asset classes and invested in common and preferred stock, bonds, and other debt instruments. The exact asset distribution among the asset classes will be predetermined by a set formula that is designed to balance out the investment return of the fund.

balance of payments The net balance of all international transactions for a country in a given time.

balance of trade The net flow of goods into or out of a country for a given period. Net exports result in a surplus or credit; net exports result in a deficit or net debit.

balance sheet A corporate report that shows a company's financial condition at the time the balance sheet was created.

balance sheet equation Assets = liabilities + shareholders equity.

balloon maturity A bond maturity schedule that requires the largest portion of the principal to be repaid on the last maturity date.

bankers' acceptance (BA) A letter of credit that facilitates foreign trade. BAs are traded in the money market and have a maximum maturity of 270 days.

basis The cost that is assigned to an asset.

basis book A table used to calculate bond prices for bonds quoted on a yield basis and to calculate yields for bonds quoted on a price basis.

basis point Measures a bond's yield; 1 basis point is equal to 1/100 of 1%.

basis quote A bond quote based on the bond's yield.

bearer bond A bond that is issued without the owner's name being registered on the bond certificate or the books of the issuer. Whoever has possession of (bears) the certificate is deemed to be the rightful owner.

bearish An investor's belief that prices will decline.

bear market A market condition that is characterized by continuing falling prices and a series of lower lows in overall prices.

best efforts underwriting A type of underwriting that does not guarantee the issuer that any of its securities will be sold.

beta A measure of a security's or portfolio's volatility relative to the market as a whole. A security or portfolio whose beta is greater than 1 will experience a greater change in price than overall market prices. A security or portfolio with a beta of less than 1 will experience a price change that is less than the price changes realized by the market as a whole.

bid A price that an investor or broker dealer is willing to pay for a security. It is also a price at which an investor may sell a security immediately and the price at which a market maker will buy a security.

blind pool A type of direct participation program where less than 75% of the assets to be acquired have been identified.

block trade A trade involving 10,000 shares or market value of over $200,000.

blotter A daily record of broker dealer transactions.

blue chip stock Stock of a company whose earnings and dividends are stable regardless of the economy.

Blue List A daily publication of municipal bond offerings and secondary market interest.

blue sky A term used to describe the state registration process for a security offering.

blue-sky laws Term used to describe the state-based laws enacted under the Uniform Securities Act.

board broker *See* order book official.

board of directors A group of directors elected by the stockholders of a corporation to appoint and oversee corporate management.

Board of Governors The governing body of FINRA. The board is made up of 27 members elected by FINRA's membership and the board itself.

bona fide quote *See* firm quote.

bond The legal obligation of a corporation or government to repay the principal amount of debt along with interest at a predetermined schedule.

bond anticipation note Short-term municipal financing sold in anticipation of long-term financing.

bond buyer indexes A group of yield-based municipal bond indexes published daily in the *Daily Bond Buyer.*

bond counsel An attorney for the issuer of municipal securities who renders the legal opinion.

bond fund A fund whose portfolio is made up of debt instruments issued by corporations, governments, and/or their agencies. The fund's investment objective is usually current income.

bond interest coverage ratio A measure of the issuer's liquidity. It demonstrates how many times the issuer's earnings will cover its bond interest expense.

bond quotes Corporate and government bond quotes are based on a percentage of par. Municipal bonds are usually quoted on a yield-to-maturity basis.

bond rating A rating that assesses the financial soundness of issuers and their ability to make interest and principal payments in a timely manner. Standard & Poor's and Moody's are the two largest ratings agencies. Issuers must request and pay for the service to rate their bonds.

bond ratio A measure used to determine how much of the corporation's capitalization was obtained through the issuance of bonds.

bond swap The sale and purchase of two different bonds to allow the investor to claim a loss on the bond being sold without violating wash sale rules.

book entry Securities that are issued in book entry form do not offer any physical certificates as evidence of ownership. The owner's name is registered on the books of the issuer, and the only evidence of ownership is the trade confirmation.

book value A corporation's book value is the theoretical liquidation value of the company. Book value is in theory what someone would be willing to pay for the entire company.

book value per bond A measure used to determine the amount of the corporation's tangible value for each bond issued.

book value per share Used to determine the tangible value of each common share. It is found by subtracting intangible assets and the par value of preferred stock from the corporation's total net worth and dividing that figure by the number of common shares outstanding.

branch office A branch office of a member firm is required to display the name of the member firm and is any office in which the member conducts securities business outside of its main office.

breadth A measure of the broad market's health. It measures how many stocks are increasing and how many are declining.

breakdown A technical term used to describe the price action of a security when it falls below support to a lower level and into a new trading range.

breakeven point The point at which the value of a security or portfolio is exactly equal to the investor's cost for that security or portfolio.

breakout A technical term used to describe the price action of a security when it increases past resistance to a higher level and into a new trading range.

breakpoint sale The practice of selling mutual fund shares in dollar amounts that are just below the point where an investor would be entitled to a sales charge reduction. A breakpoint sale is designed for the purpose of trying to earn a larger commission. This is a violation of the Rules of Fair Practice and should never be done.

breakpoint schedule A breakpoint schedule offers mutual fund investors reduced sales charges for larger dollar investments.

broad-based index An index that represents a large cross-section of the market as a whole. The price movement of the index reflects the price movement of a large portion of the market, such as the S&P 500 or the Wilshire 5000.

broker *See* agent.

broker dealer A person or firm who buys and sells securities for its own account and for the accounts of others. When acting as a broker or agent for a customer, the broker dealer is merely executing the customer's orders and charging the customer a fee known as a commission. When acting as a dealer or principal, the broker dealer is trading for its own account and participating in the customer's transaction by taking the other side of the trade and charging the customer a markup or markdown. A firm also is acting as a principal or dealer when it is trading for its own account and making markets in OTC securities.

broker's broker (1) A municipal bond dealer who specializes in executing orders for other dealers who are not active in the municipal bond market. (2) A specialist on the exchange executing orders for other members or an OTC market.

bullish An investor who believes that the price of a security or prices as a whole will rise is said to be bullish.

bull market A market condition that is characterized by rising prices and a series of higher highs.

business cycle The normal economic pattern that is characterized by four stages: expansion, peak, contraction, and trough. The business cycle constantly repeats itself and the economy is always in flux.

business day The business day in the securities industry is defined as the time when the financial markets are open for trading.

buyer's option A settlement option that allows the buyer to determine when the transaction will settle.

buy in An order executed in the event of a customer's or firm's failure to deliver the securities it sold. The buyer repurchases the securities in the open market and charges the seller for any loss.

buying power The amount of money available to buy securities.

buy stop order A buy stop order is used to protect against a loss or to protect a profit on a short sale of stock.

C

call (1) A type of option that gives the holder the right to purchase a specified amount of the underlying security at a stated price for a specified period of time. (2) The act of exercising a call option.

callable bond A bond that may be called in or retired by the issuer prior to its maturity date.

callable preferred A preferred share issued with a feature allowing the issuing corporation to retire it under certain conditions.

call date A specific date after which the securities in question become callable by the issuer.

call feature A condition attached to some bonds and preferred stocks that allows the issuer to call in or redeem the securities prior to their maturity date and according to certain conditions.

call price The price that will be paid by the issuer to retire the callable securities in question. The call price is usually set at a price above the par value of the bond or preferred stock, which is the subject of the call.

call protection A period of time, usually right after the securities' issuance, when the securities may not be called by the issuer. Call protection usually ranges from 5 to 10 years.

call provision *See* call feature.

call risk The risk borne by the owner of callable securities that may require that the investor accept a lower rate of return once the securities have been called. Callable bonds and preferred stock are more likely to be called when interest rates are low or are falling.

call spread An option position consisting of one long and one short call on the same underlying security with different strike prices, expirations, or both.

call writer An investor who has sold a call.

capital Money and assets available to use in an attempt to earn more money or to accumulate more assets.

capital appreciation An increase in an asset's value over time.

capital assets Tangible assets, including securities, real estate, equipment, and other assets, owned for the long term.

capital gain A profit realized on the sale of an asset at a price that exceeds its cost.

capitalization The composition of a company's financial structure. It is the sum of paid-in capital + paid-in surplus + long-term debt + retained earnings.

capital loss A loss realized on the sale of an asset at a price that is lower than its cost.

capital market The securities markets that deal in equity and debt securities with more than 1 year to maturity.

capital risk The risk that the value of an asset will decline and cause an investor to lose all or part of the invested capital.

capital stock The sum of the par value of all of a corporation's outstanding common and preferred stock.

capital structure *See* capitalization.

capital surplus The amount of money received by an issuer in excess of the par value of the stock at the time of its initial sale to the public.

capped index option An index option that trades like a spread and is automatically exercised if it goes 30 points in the money.

capping A manipulative practice of selling stock to depress the price.

carried interest A sharing arrangement for an oil and gas direct participation program where the general partner shares in the tangible drilling costs with the limited partners.

cash account An account in which the investor must deposit the full purchase price of the securities by the fifth business day after the trade date. The investor is not required by industry regulations to sign anything to open a cash account.

cash assets ratio The most liquid measure of a company's solvency. The cash asset ratio is found by dividing cash and equivalents by current liabilities.

cash dividend The distribution of corporate profits to shareholders of record. Cash dividends must be declared by the company's board of directors.

cash equivalent Short-term liquid securities that can quickly be converted into cash. Money market instruments and funds are the most common examples.

cash flow A company's cash flow equals net income plus depreciation.

cashiering department The department in a brokerage firm that is responsible for the receipt and delivery of cash and securities.

cash management bill Short-term federal financing issued in minimum denominations of $10 million.

cash settlement A transaction that settles for cash requires the delivery of the securities from the seller as well as the delivery of cash from the buyer on the same day of the trade. A trade done for cash settles the same day.

catastrophe call The redemption of a bond by an issuer due to the destruction of the facility that was financed by the issue. Issuers will carry insurance to cover such events and to pay off the bondholders.

certificate of deposit (CD) An unsecured promissory note issued as evidence of ownership of a time deposit that has been guaranteed by the issuing bank.

certificates of accrual on Treasury securities Zero-coupon bonds issued by brokerage firms and collateralized by Treasury securities.

change The difference between the current price and the previous day's closing price.

Chicago Board of Trade (CBOT) A commodity exchange that provides a marketplace for agricultural and financial futures.

Chicago Board Options Exchange (CBOE) The premier option exchange in the United States for listed options.

Chinese wall The physical separation that is required between investment banking and trading and retail divisions of a brokerage firm. Now known as a firewall.

churning Executing transactions that are excessive in their frequency or size in light of the resources of the account for the purpose of generating commissions. Churning is a violation of the Rules of Fair Practice.

class A share A mutual fund share that charges a front-end load.

class B share A mutual fund share that charges a back-end load.

class C share A mutual fund share that charges a level load.

class D share A mutual fund share that charges a level load and a back-end load.

classical economics A theory stating that the economy will do the best when the government does not interfere.

clearing firm A firm that carries its customers' cash and securities and/or provides the service to customers of other firms.

clearinghouse An agency that guarantees and settles futures and option transactions.

close The last price at which a security traded for the day.

closed-end indenture A bond indenture that will not allow additional bonds to be issued with the same claim on the issuer's assets.

closed-end investment company A management company that issues a fixed number of shares to investors in a managed portfolio and whose shares are traded in the secondary market.

closing date The date when sales of interest in a direct participation plan will cease.

closing purchase An order executed to close out a short option position.

Code of Arbitration Procedure The FINRA bylaw that provides for a forum for dispute resolution relating to industry matters. All industry participants must arbitrate in public and the customer must agree to arbitration in writing.

Code of Procedure The FINRA bylaw that sets guidelines for the investigation of trade practice complaints and alleged rule violations.

coincident indicator An economic indicator that moves simultaneously with the movement of the underlying economy.

collateral Assets pledged to a lender. If the borrower defaults, the lender will take possession of the collateral.

collateral trust certificate A bond backed by the pledge of securities the issuer owns in another entity.

collateralized mortgage obligation (CMO) A corporate debt security that is secured by an underlying pool of mortgages.

collection ratio A measure of a municipality's ability to collect the taxes it has assessed.

collect on delivery (COD) A method of trade settlement that requires the physical delivery of the securities to receive payment.

combination An option position with a call and put on the same underlying security with different strike prices and expiration months on both.

combination fund A mutual fund that tries to achieve growth and current income by combining portfolios of common stock with portfolios of high-yielding equities.

combination preferred stock A preferred share with multiple features, such as cumulative and participating.

combination privileges A feature offered by a mutual fund family that allows an investor to combine two simultaneous purchases of different portfolios in order to receive a reduced sales charge on the total amount invested.

combined account A margin account that contains both long and short positions.

commercial paper Short-term unsecured promissory notes issued by large financially stable corporations to obtain short-term financing. Commercial paper does not pay interest and is issued at a discount from its face value. All commercial paper matures in 270 days or less and matures at its face value.

commingling A FINRA violation resulting from the mixing of customer and firm assets in the same account.

commission A fee charged by a broker or agent for executing a securities transaction.

commission house broker A floor broker who executes orders for the firm's account and for the accounts of the firm's customers on an exchange.

common stock A security that represents the ownership of a corporation. Common stockholders vote to elect the board of directors and to institute major corporate policies.

common stock ratio A measure of how much of a company's capitalization was obtained through the sale of common stock. The ratio is found by summing the par value of the common stock, excess paid in capital, and retained earnings, and then dividing that number by the total capitalization.

competitive bid underwriting A method of underwriter selection that solicits bids from multiple underwriters. The underwriter submitting the best terms will be awarded the issue.

compliance department The department of a broker dealer that ensures that the firm adheres to industry rules and regulations.

concession The amount of an underwriting discount that is allocated to a syndicate member or a selling group member for selling new securities.

conduct rules The Rules of Fair Practice.

conduit theory The IRS classification that allows a regulated investment company to avoid paying taxes on investment income it distributes to its shareholders.

confirmation The receipt for a securities transaction that must be sent to all customers either on or before the completion of a transaction. The confirmation must show the trade date, settlement date, and total amount due to or from the customer. A transaction is considered to be complete on settlement date.

consolidated tape The consolidated tape A displays transactions for NYSE securities that take place on the NYSE, all regional exchanges, and the third markets. The consolidated tape B reports transactions for AMEX stocks that take place on the American Stock Exchange, all regional exchanges, and in the third market.

consolidation A chart pattern that results from a narrowing of a security's trading range.

constant dollar plan An investment plan designed to keep a specific amount of money invested in the market regardless of the market's condition. An investor will sell when the value of the account rises and buy when the value of the account falls.

constant ratio plan An investment plan designed to keep the investor's portfolio invested at a constant ratio of equity and debt securities.

construction loan note A short-term municipal note designed to provide financing for construction projects.

constructive receipt The time when the IRS determines that the taxpayer has effectively received payment.

consumer price index (CPI) A price-based index made up of a basket of goods and services that are used by consumers in their daily lives. An increase in the CPI indicates a rise in overall prices, while a decline in the index represents a fall in overall prices.

consumption A term used to describe the purchase of newly produced household goods.

contemporaneous trader A trader who enters an order on the other side of the market at the same time as a trader with inside information enters an order. Contemporaneous traders can sue traders who act on inside information to recover losses.

contingent deferred sales charge *See* back-end load.

contraction A period of declining economic output. Also known as a recession.

contractual plan A mutual fund accumulation plan under which the investor agrees to contribute a fixed sum of money over time. If the investor does not complete or terminates the contract early, the investor may be subject to penalties.

control The ability to influence the actions of an organization or individual.

control person A director or officer of an issuer or broker dealer or a 10% stockholder of a corporation.

control stock Stock that is acquired or owned by an officer, director, or person owning 10% or more of the outstanding stock of a company.

conversion price The set price at which a convertible security may be exchanged for another security.

conversion privilege The right offered to a mutual fund investor that allows the investor to move money between different portfolios offered by the same mutual fund family without paying another sales charge.

conversion ratio The number of shares that can be received by the holder of a convertible security if it were converted into the underlying common stock.

convertible bond A bond that may be converted or exchanged for common shares of the corporation at a predetermined price.

convertible preferred stock A preferred stock that may be converted or exchanged for common shares of the corporation at a predetermined price.

cooling-off period The period of time between the filing of a registration statement and its effective date. During this time, the SEC is reviewing the registration statement and no sales may take place. The cooling-off period is at least 20 days.

coordination A method of securities registration during which a new issue is registered simultaneously at both the federal and state levels.

corporate account An investment account for the benefit of a company that requires a corporate resolution listing the names of individuals who may transact business in the company's name.

corporate bond A legally binding obligation of a corporation to repay a principal amount of debt along with interest at a predetermined rate and schedule.

corporation A perpetual entity that survives after the death of its officers, directors, and stockholders. It is the most common form of business entity.

correspondent broker dealer A broker dealer who introduces customer accounts to a clearing broker dealer.

cost basis The cost of an asset, including any acquisition costs. It is used to determine capital gains and losses.

cost depletion A method used to determine the tax deductions for investors in oil and gas programs.

cost of carry All costs incurred by an investor for maintaining a position in a security, including margin interest and opportunity costs.

coterminous Municipalities that share the same borders and have overlapping debt.

coupon bond *See* bearer bond.

coupon yield *See* nominal yield.

covenant A promise made by an issuer of debt that describes the issuer's obligations and the bondholders' rights.

covered call The sale of a call against a long position in the underlying security.

covered put The sale of a put against a short position in the underlying security or against cash that will allow the person to purchase the security if the put is exercised.

CPI *See* consumer price index (CPI).

credit agreement The portion of the margin agreement that describes the terms and conditions under which credit will be extended to the customer.

credit balance The cash balance in a customer's account.

credit department *See* margin department.

credit risk The risk that the issuer of debt securities will default on its obligation to pay interest or principal on a timely basis.

credit spread An option position that results in a net premium or credit received by the investor from the simultaneous purchase and sale of two calls or two puts on the same security.

crossed market A market condition that results when a broker enters a bid for a stock that exceeds the offering price for that stock. Also a condition that may result when a broker enters an offer that is lower than the bid price for that stock.

crossing stock The pairing off of two offsetting customer orders by the same floor broker. The floor broker executing the cross must first show the order to the crowd for possible price improvement before crossing the orders.

crossover point The point at which all tax credits have been used up by a limited partnership; results in a tax liability for the partners.

cum rights A stock that is the subject of a rights offering and is trading with the rights attached to the common stock.

cumulative preferred stock A preferred stock that entitles the holder to receive unpaid dividends prior to the payment of any dividends to common stockholders. Dividends that accumulate in arrears on cumulative issues are always the first dividends to be paid by a corporation.

cumulative voting A method of voting that allows stockholders to cast all of their votes for one director or to distribute them among the candidates they wish to vote for. Cumulative voting favors smaller investors by allowing them to have a larger say in the election of the board of directors.

current assets Cash, securities, accounts receivable, and other assets that can be converted into cash within 12 months.

current liabilities Corporate obligations, including accounts payable, that must be paid within 12 months.

current market value (CMV)/current market price (CMP) The present value of a marketable security or of a portfolio of marketable securities.

current ratio A measure of a corporation's short-term liquidity found by dividing its current assets by its current liabilities.

current yield A relationship between a securities annual income relative to its current market price. Determined by dividing annual income by the current market price.

CUSIP (Committee on Uniform Securities Identification Procedures) A committee that assigns identification numbers to securities to help identify them.

custodial account An account operated by a custodian for the benefit of a minor.

custodian A party responsible for managing an account for another party. In acting as a custodian, the individual or corporation must adhere to the prudent man rule and only take such actions as a prudent person would do for him- or herself.

customer Any individual or entity that maintains an account with a broker dealer.

customer agreement An agreement signed by a customer at the time the account is opened, detailing the conditions of the customer's relationship with the firm. The customer agreement usually contains a predispute arbitration clause.

customer ledger A ledger that lists all customer cash and margin accounts.

customer protection rule Rule 15C3-3 requires that customer assets be kept segregated from the firm assets.

cyclical industry An industry whose prospects fluctuate with the business cycle.

D

Daily Bond Buyer A daily publication for the municipal securities industry that publishes information related to the municipal bond market and official notices of sales.

dated date The day when interest starts to accrue for bonds.

dealer (1) A person or firm who transacts securities business for its own account. (2) A brokerage firm acting as a principal when executing a customer's transaction or making markets over the counter.

dealer paper Commercial paper sold to the public by a dealer, rather than placed with investors directly by the issuer.

debenture An unsecured promissory note issued by a corporation backed only by the issuer's credit and promise to pay.

debit balance The amount of money a customer owes a broker dealer.

debit spread An option position that results in a net premium paid by the investor from the simultaneous purchase and sale of two calls or two puts on the same security.

debt securities A security that represents a loan to the issuer. The owner of a debt security is a creditor of the issuing entity, be it a corporation or a government.

debt service The scheduled interest payments and repayment of principal for debt securities.

debt service account An account set up by a municipal issuer to pay the debt service of municipal revenue bonds.

debt service ratio Indicates the issuer's ability to pay its interest and principal payments.

debt-to-equity ratio A ratio that shows how highly leveraged the company is. It is found by dividing total long-term debt by total shareholder equity.

declaration date The day chosen by the board of directors of a corporation to pay a dividend to shareholders.

deduction An adjustment taken from gross income to reduce tax liability.

default The failure of an issuer of debt securities to make interest and principal payments when they are due.

default risk *See* credit risk.

defeasance Results in the elimination of the issuer's debt obligations by issuing a new debt instrument to pay off the outstanding issue. The old issue is removed from the issuer's balance sheet and the proceeds of the new issue are placed in an escrow account to pay off the now-defeased issue.

defensive industry A term used to describe a business whose economic prospects are independent from the business cycle. Pharmaceutical companies, utilities, and food producers are examples of defensive industries.

deferred annuity A contract between an individual and an insurance company that delays payments to the annuitant until some future date.

deferred compensation plan A contractual agreement between an employer and an employee under which the employee elects to defer receiving money owed until after retirement. Deferred compensation plans are typically unfunded, and the employee could lose all the money due under the agreement if the company goes out of business.

deficiency letter A letter sent to a corporate issuer by the SEC, requesting additional information regarding the issuer's registration statement.

defined benefit plan A qualified retirement plan established to provide a specific amount of retirement income for the plan participants. Unlike a defined contribution plan, the individual's retirement benefits are known prior to reaching retirement.

defined contribution plan A qualified retirement plan that details the amount of money that the employer will contribute to the plan for the benefit of the employee. This amount is usually expressed as a percentage of the employee's gross annual income. The actual retirement benefits are not known until the employee reaches retirement, and the amount of the retirement benefit is a result of the contributions to the plan, along with the investment experience of the plan.

deflation The economic condition that is characterized by a persistent decline in overall prices.

delivery As used in the settlement process, results in the change of ownership of cash or securities.

delivery vs. payment A type of settlement option that requires that the securities be physically received at the time payment is made.

delta A measure of an option's price change in relation to a price change in the underlying security.

demand deposit A deposit that a customer has with a bank or other financial institution that will allow the customer to withdraw the money at any time or on demand.

Department of Enforcement The FINRA committee that has original jurisdiction over complaints and violations.

depletion A tax deduction taken for the reduction in the amount of natural resources (e.g., gas, gold, oil) available to a business or partnership.

depreciation A tax deduction taken for the reduction of value in a capital asset.

depreciation expense A noncash expense that results in a reduction in taxable income.

depression An economic condition that is characterized by a protracted decline in economic output and a rising level of unemployment.

derivative A security that derives its value in whole or in part based on the price of another security. Options and futures are examples of derivative securities.

designated order An order entered by an institution for a new issue of municipal bonds that states what firm and what agent is going to get the sales credit for the order.

devaluation A significant fall in the value of a country's currency relative to other currencies. Devaluation could be the result of poor economic prospects in the home country. In extreme circumstances, it can be the result of government intervention.

developmental drilling program An oil or gas program that drills for wells in areas of proven reserves.

developmental fee A fee paid to organizers of a direct participation plan for the development of plans, obtaining financing or zoning authorizations, and other services.

diagonal spread A spread that is created through the simultaneous purchase and sale of two calls or two puts on the same underlying security that differ in both strike price and expiration months.

dilution A reduction in a stockholder's proportional ownership of a corporation as a result of the issuance of more shares. Earnings per share may also be diluted as a result of the issuance of additional shares.

direct debt The total amount of a municipality's debt that has been issued by the municipality for its own benefit and for which the municipality is responsible to repay.

direct paper Commercial paper sold to investors directly from the issuer without the use of a dealer.

direct participation program (DPP) An entity that allows all taxable events to be passed through to investors, including limited partnerships and subchapter S corporations.

discount The amount by which the price of a security is lower than its par value.

discount bond A bond that is selling for a price that is lower than its par value.

discount rate The rate that is charged to Federal Reserve member banks on loans directly from the Federal Reserve. This rate is largely symbolic, and member banks only borrow directly from the Federal Reserve as a last resort.

discretion Authorization given to a firm or a representative to determine which securities are to be purchased and sold for the benefit of the customer without the customer's prior knowledge or approval.

discretionary account An account where the owner has given the firm or the representative authority to transact business without the customer's prior knowledge or approval. All discretionary accounts must be approved and monitored closely by a principal of the firm.

disintermediation The flow of money from traditional bank accounts to alternative higher yielding investments. This is more likely to occur as the Federal Reserve tightens monetary policy and interest rates rise.

disposable income The sum of money an individual has left after paying taxes and required expenditures.

disproportional allocation A method used by FINRA to determine if a free-riding violation has occurred with respect to a hot issuer. A firm is only allowed to sell up to 10% of a new issue to conditionally approved purchasers.

disproportionate sharing An oil and gas sharing arrangement where the general partner pays a portion of the cost but receives a larger portion of the program's revenues.

distribution Cash or property sent to shareholders or partners.

distribution stage The period of time during which an annuitant is receiving payments from an annuity contract.

diversification The distribution of investment capital among different investment choices. By purchasing several different investments, investors may be able to reduce their overall risk by minimizing the impact of any one security's adverse performance.

diversified fund/ diversified management company A mutual fund that distributes its investment capital among a wide variety of investments. In order for a mutual fund to market itself as a diversified mutual fund it must meet the 75-5-10 rule: 75% of the fund's assets must be invested in securities issued by other entities, no more than 5% of the fund's assets may be invested in any one issuer, and the fund may own no more than 10% of any one company's outstanding securities.

dividend A distribution of corporate assets to shareholders. A dividend may be paid in cash, stock, or property or product.

dividend department The department in a brokerage firm that is responsible for the collecting of dividends and crediting them to customer accounts.

dividend disbursement agent An agent of the issuer who pays out the dividends to shareholders of record.

dividend payout ratio The amount of a company's earnings that were paid out to shareholders relative to the total earnings that were available to be paid out to shareholders. It can be calculated by dividing dividends per share by earnings per share.

dividend yield Also known as a stock's current yield. It is a relationship between the annual dividends paid to shareholders relative to the stock's current market price. To determine a stock's dividend yield, divide annual dividends by the current market price.

DJIA *See* Dow Jones Industrial Average.

doctrine of mutual reciprocity An agreement that the federal government would not tax interest income received by investors in municipal bonds and that reciprocally the states would not tax interest income received by investors in federal debt obligations.

dollar bonds A term issue of municipal bonds that are quoted as a percentage of par rather than on a yield basis.

dollar-cost averaging A strategy of investing a fixed sum of money on a regular basis into a fluctuating market price. Over time an investor should be able to achieve an average cost per share that is below the average price per share. Dollar-cost averaging is a popular investment strategy with mutual fund investors.

donor A person who gives a gift of cash or securities to another person. Once the gift has been made, the donor no longer has any rights or claim to the security. All gifts to a minor are irrevocable.

do not reduce (DNR) An order qualifier for an order placed under the market that stipulates that the price of the order is not to be reduced for the distribution of ordinary dividends.

don't know (DK) A term used to describe a dealer's response to a confirmation for a trade they "don't know" doing.

Dow Jones Composite Average An index composed of 65 stocks that is used as an indicator of market performance.

Dow Jones Industrial Average (DJIA) An index composed of 30 industrial companies. The Dow Jones is the most widely quoted market index.

Dow Jones Transportation Average An index composed of 20 transportation stocks.

Dow Jones Utility Average An index composed of 15 utility stocks.

Dow theory A theory that believes that the health both of the market and of the economy may be predicted by the performance of the Dow Jones Industrial Average.

dry hole A term used to describe a nonproducing well.

dual-purpose fund A mutual fund that offers two classes of shares to investors. One class is sold to investors seeking income and the other class is sold to investors seeking capital appreciation.

E

early withdrawal penalty A penalty tax charged to an investor for withdrawing money from a qualified retirement plan prior to age 59-1/2, usually 10% on top of ordinary income taxes.

earned income Money received by an individual in return for performing services.

earnings per share The net amount of a corporation's earnings available to common shareholders divided by the number of common shares outstanding.

earnings per share fully diluted The net amount of a corporation's earnings available to common shareholders after taking into consideration the potential conversion of all convertible securities.

eastern account A type of syndicate account that requires all members to be responsible for their own allocation as well as for their proportional share of any member's unsold securities.

economic risk The risk of loss of principal associated with the purchase of securities.

EE savings bonds Nonmarketable U.S. government zero-coupon bonds that must be purchased from the government and redeemed to the government.

effective date The day when a new issue's registration with the SEC becomes effective. Once the issue's registration statement has become effective, the securities may then be sold to investors.

efficient market theory A theory that states that the market operates and processes information efficiently and prices in all information as soon as it becomes known.

Employee Retirement Income Security Act of 1974 (ERISA) The legislation that governs the operation of private-sector pension plans. Corporate pension plans organized under ERISA guidelines qualify for beneficial tax treatment by the IRS.

endorsement The signature on the back of a security that allows its ownership to be transferred.

EPS *See* earnings per share.

equipment leasing limited partnership A limited partnership that is organized to purchase equipment and lease it to corporations to earn lease income and to shelter passive income for investors.

equipment trust certificate A bond backed by a pledge of large equipment, such as airplanes, railroad cars, and ships.

equity A security that represents the ownership in a corporation. Both preferred and common equity holders have an ownership interest in the corporation.

equity financing The sale of common or preferred equity by a corporation in an effort to raise capital.

equity option An option to purchase or sell common stock.

ERISA *See* Employee Retirement Income Security Act of 1974.

erroneous report A report of an execution given in error to a client. The report is not binding on the firm or on the agent.

escrow agreement Evidence of ownership of a security provided to a broker dealer as proof of ownership of the underlying security for covered call writers.

Eurobond A bond issued in domestic currency of the issuer but sold outside of the issuer's country.

Eurodollar A deposit held outside of the United States denominated in U.S. dollars.

Eurodollar bonds A bond issued by a foreign issuer denominated in U.S. dollars.

Euroyen bonds Bonds issued outside of Japan but denominated in yen.

excess equity (EE) The value of an account's equity in excess of Regulation T.

exchange A market, whether physical or electronic, that provides a forum for trading securities through a dual-auction process.

exchange distribution A distribution of a large block of stock on the floor of the exchange that is crossed with offsetting orders.

exchange privilege The right offered by many mutual funds that allows an investor to transfer or move money between different portfolios offered through the same fund company. An investor may redeem shares of the fund, which is being sold at the NAV, and purchase shares of the new portfolio at the NAV without paying another sales charge.

ex date/ex-dividend date The first day when purchasers of a security will no longer be entitled to receive a previously declared dividend.

executor/executrix An individual with the authority to manage the affairs of a decedent's estate.

exempt security A security that is exempt from the registration requirements of the Securities Act of 1933.

exempt transaction A transaction that is not subject to state registration.

exercise An investor's election to take advantage of the rights offered through the terms of an option, a right, or a warrant.

exercise price The price at which an option investor may purchase or sell a security. Also the price at which an investor may purchase a security through a warrant or right.

existing property program A type of real estate direct participation program that purchases existing property for the established rental income.

expansion A period marked by a general increase in business activity and an increase in gross domestic product.

expansionary policy A monetary policy enacted through the Federal Reserve Board that increases money supply and reduces interest rates in an effort to stimulate the economy.

expense ratio The amount of a mutual fund's expenses relative to its assets. The higher the expense ratio, the lower the investor's return. A mutual fund's expense ratio tells an investor how efficiently a mutual fund operates, not how profitable the mutual fund is.

expiration cycle A 4-month cycle for option expiration: January, April, July, and October; February, May, August, and November; or March, June, September, and December.

expiration date The date on which an option ceases to exist.

exploratory drilling program A direct participation program that engages in the drilling for oil or gas in new areas seeking to find new wells.

exploratory well Also known as wildcatting. The drilling for oil or gas in new areas in an effort to find new wells.

ex rights The common stock subject to a rights offering trade without the rights attached.

ex rights date The first day when the common stock is subject to a rights offering trade without the rights attached.

ex warrants Common trading without the warrants attached.

F

face-amount certificate company (FAC) A type of investment company that requires an investor to make fixed payments over time or to deposit a lump sum, and that will return to the investor a stated sum known as the face amount on a specific date.

face amount/face value *See* par.

fail to deliver An event where the broker on the sell side of the transaction fails to deliver the security.

fail to receive An event where the broker on the buy side of the transaction fails to receive the security from the broker on the sell side.

Fannie Mae *See* Federal National Mortgage Association.

Farm Credit Administrator The agency that oversees all of the activities of the banks in the Federal Farm Credit System.

Federal Deposit Insurance Corporation (FDIC) The government insurance agency that provides insurance for bank depositors in case of bank failure.

Federal Farm Credit System An organization of banks that is designed to provide financing to farmers for mortgages, feed and grain, and equipment.

federal funds rate The rate banks charge each other on overnight loans.

Federal Home Loan Mortgage Corporation (FHLMC; Freddie Mac) A publicly traded for-profit corporation that provides liquidity to the secondary mortgage market by purchasing pools of mortgages from lenders and, in turn, issues mortgage-backed securities.

Federal Intermediate Credit Bank Provides short-term financing to farmers for equipment.

Federal National Mortgage Association (FNMA; Fannie Mae) A publicly traded for-profit corporation that provides liquidity to the secondary mortgage market by purchasing pools of mortgages and issuing mortgage-backed securities.

Federal Open Market Committee (FOMC) The committee of the Federal Reserve Board that makes policy decisions relating to the nation's money supply.

Federal Reserve Board A seven-member board that directs the policies of the Federal Reserve System. The members are appointed by the President and approved by Congress.

Federal Reserve System The nation's central banking system, the purpose of which is to regulate money supply and the extension of credit. The Federal Reserve System is composed of 12 central banks and 24 regional banks, along with hundreds of national and state chartered banks.

fictitious quote A quote that is not representative of an actual bid or offer for a security.

fidelity bond A bond that must be posted by all broker dealers to ensure the public against employee dishonesty.

fill or kill (FK) A type of order that requires that all of the securities in the order be purchased or sold immediately or not at all.

final prospectus The official offering document for a security that contains the security's final offering price along with all information required by law for an investor to make an informed decision.

firm commitment underwriting Guarantees the issuer all of the money right away. The underwriters purchase all of the securities from the issuer regardless of whether they can sell the securities to their customers.

firm quote A quote displayed at which the dealer is obligated to buy or sell at least one round lot at the quoted price.

fiscal policy Government policy designed to influence the economy through government tax and spending programs. The President and Congress control fiscal policy.

5% markup policy FINRA's guideline that requires all prices paid by customers to be reasonably related to a security's market price. The 5% policy is a guideline, not a rule, and it does not apply to securities sold through a prospectus.

fixed annuity An insurance contract where the insurance company guarantees fixed payments to the annuitant, usually until the annuitant's death.

fixed assets Assets used by a corporation to conduct its business, such as plant and equipment.

flat A term used to describe a bond that trades without accrued interest, such as a zero-coupon bond or a bond that is in default.

floor broker An individual member of an exchange who may execute orders on the floor.

floor trader Members of the exchange who trade for their own accounts. Members of the NYSE may not trade from the floor for their own accounts.

flow of funds A schedule of expenses and interested parties that prioritizes how payments will be made from the revenue generated by a facility financed by a municipal revenue bond.

forced conversion The calling in of convertible bonds at a price that is less than the market value of the underlying common stock into which the bonds may be converted.

foreign currency Currency of another country.

foreign currency option An option to purchase or sell a specified amount of another country's currency.

Form 10-K An annual report filed by a corporation detailing its financial performance for the year.

Form 10-Q A quarterly report filed by a corporation detailing its financial performance for the quarter.

form letter A letter sent out by a brokerage firm or a registered representative to more than 25 people in a 30-day period. Form letters are subject to approval and recordkeeping requirements.

forward pricing The way in which open-end mutual funds are valued for investors who wish to purchase or redeem shares of the fund. Mutual funds usually price their shares at the end of the business day. The price to be paid or received by the investor will be the price that is next calculated after the fund receives the order.

401K A qualified retirement plan offered by an employer.

403B A qualified retirement plan offered to teachers and employees of nonprofit organizations.

fourth market A transaction between two large institutions without the use of a broker dealer.

fractional share A portion of a whole share that represents ownership of an open-end mutual fund.

fraud Any attempt to gain an unfair advantage over another party through the use of deception, concealment, or misrepresentation.

free credit balance Cash reserves in a customer's account that have not been invested. Customers must be notified of their free credit balances at least quarterly.

free look A privilege offered to purchasers of contractual plans and insurance policies that will allow the individual to cancel the contract within the free-look period, usually 45 days.

freeriding The purchase and sale of a security without depositing the money required to cover the purchase price as required by Regulation T.

freeriding and withholding The withholding of new issue securities offered by a broker dealer for the benefit of the brokerage firm or an employee.

front-end load (1) A sales charge paid by investors in open-end mutual funds that is paid at the time of purchase. (2) A contractual plan that seeks to assess sales charges in the first years of the plan and may charge up to 50% of the first year's payments as sales charges.

frozen account An account where the owner is required to deposit cash or securities up front, prior to any purchase or sale taking place. An account is usually frozen as a result of a customer's failure to pay or deliver securities.

full power of attorney A type of discretionary authority that allows a third party to purchase and sell securities as well as to withdraw cash and securities without the owner's prior consent or knowledge. This type of authority is usually reserved to trustees and attorneys.

fully registered bonds A type of bond issuance where the issuer has a complete record of the owners of the bonds and who is entitled to receive interest and principal payments. The owners of fully registered bonds are not required to clip coupons.

functional allocation An arrangement for oil and gas programs where the general partner pays the tangible drilling costs and the limited partner absorbs the intangible drilling costs.

fundamental analyst A method of valuing the company that takes into consideration the financial performance of the corporation, the value of its assets, and the quality of its management.

funded debt Long-term debt obligations of corporations or municipalities.

fungible Easily exchangeable items with the same conditions.

G

general account An insurance company's account that holds the money and investments for fixed contracts and traditional life insurance policies.

general obligation bond A municipal bond that is backed by the taxing power of the state or municipality.

general partner The partner in a general partnership who manages the business and is responsible for any debt of the program.

general securities principal An individual who has passed the Series 24 exam and may supervise the activities of the firm and its agents.

generic advertising Advertising designed to promote name recognition for a firm and securities as investments, but does not recommend specific securities.

good 'til cancel (GTC) An order that remains on the books until it is executed or canceled.

goodwill An intangible asset of a corporation, such as its name recognition and reputation, that adds to its value.

Government National Mortgage Association (GNMA; Ginnie Mae) A government corporation that provides liquidity to the mortgage markets by purchasing pools of mortgages that have been insured by the Federal Housing Administration and the Veterans Administration. Ginnie Mae issues pass-through certificates to investors backed by the pools of mortgages.

government security A security that is an obligation of the U.S. government and that is backed by the full faith and credit of the U.S. government, such as Treasury bills, notes, and bonds.

grant anticipation note (GAN) Short-term municipal financing issued in anticipation of receiving a grant from the federal government or one of its agencies.

greenshoe option An option given to an underwriter of common stock that will allow it to purchase up to an additional 15% of the offering from the issuer at the original offering price to cover over-allotments for securities that are in high demand.

gross domestic product (GDP) The value of all goods and services produced by a country within a period of time. GDP includes government purchases, investments, and exports minus imports.

gross income All income received by a taxpayer before deductions for taxes.

gross revenue pledge A flow-of-funds pledge for a municipal revenue bond that states that debt service will be paid first.

growth fund A fund whose objective is capital appreciation. Growth funds invest in common stocks to achieve their objective.

growth stock The stock of a company whose earnings grow at a rate that is faster than the growth rate of the economy as a whole. Growth stocks are characterized by increased opportunities for appreciation and little or no dividends.

guardian An individual who has a fiduciary responsibility for another, usually a minor.

H

halt A temporary stop in the trading of a security. If a common stock is halted, all derivatives and convertibles will be halted as well.

head and shoulders A chart pattern that indicates a reversal of a trend. A head-and-shoulders top indicates a reversal of an uptrend and is considered bearish. A head-and-shoulders bottom is the reversal of a downtrend and is considered bullish.

hedge A position taken in a security to offset or reduce the risk associated with the risk of another security.

HH bond A nonmarketable government security that pays semiannual interest. Series HH bonds are issued with a $500 minimum value and may only be purchased by trading matured series EE bonds; they may not be purchased with cash.

high The highest price paid for a security during a trading session or during a 52-week period.

holder An individual or corporation that owns a security. The holder of a security is also known as being long the security.

holding period The length of time during which an investor owns a security. The holding period is important for calculating tax liability.

hold in street name The registration of customer securities in the name of the broker dealer. Most customers register securities in the name of the broker dealer to make the transfer of ownership easier.

horizontal spread Also known as a calendar spread. The simultaneous purchase and sale of two calls or two puts on the same underlying security with the same exercise price but with different expiration months.

hot issue A new issue of securities that trades at an immediate premium to its offering price in the secondary market.

HR 10 plan *See* Keogh plan.

hypothecation The customer's pledge of securities as collateral for a margin loan.

I

immediate annuity An annuity contract purchased with a single payment that entitles the holder to receive immediate payments from the contract. The annuitant purchases annuity units and usually begins receiving payments within 60 days.

immediate family An individual's immediate family includes parents, parents-in-law, children, spouse, and any relative financially dependent upon the individual.

immediate or cancel (IOC) An order that is to be executed as fully as possible immediately and whatever is not executed will be canceled.

income bond A highly speculative bond that is issued at a discount from par and only pays interest if the issuer has enough income to do so. The issuer of the income bond only promises to pay principal at maturity. Income bonds trade flat without accrued interest.

income fund A mutual fund whose investment objective is to achieve current income for its shareholders by investing in bonds and preferred stocks.

income program A type of oil and gas program that purchases producing wells to receive the income received from the sale of the proven reserves.

income statement A financial statement that shows a corporation's revenue and expenses for the time period in question.

indefeasible title A record of ownership that cannot be challenged.

index A representation of the price action of a given group of securities. Indexes are used to measure the condition of the market as a whole, such as with the S&P 500, or can be used to measure the condition of an industry group, such as with the Biotech index.

index option An option on an underlying financial index. Index options settle in cash.

indication of interest An investor's expression of a willingness to purchase a new issue of securities after receiving a preliminary prospectus. The investor's indication of interest is not binding on either the investor or the firm.

Individual Retirement Account (IRA) A self-directed retirement account that allows individuals with earned income to contribute the lesser of 100% of earned income or the annual maximum per year. The contributions may be made with pre- or after-tax dollars, depending on the individual's level of income and whether he or she is eligible to participate in an employer's sponsored plan.

industrial development bond A private-purpose municipal bond whose proceeds are used to build a facility that is leased to a corporation. The debt service on the bonds is supported by the lease payments.

inflation The persistent upward pressure on the price of goods and services over time.

initial margin requirement The initial amount of equity that a customer must deposit to establish a position. The initial margin requirement is set by the Federal Reserve Board under Regulation T.

initial public offering (IPO) The first offering of common stock to the general investing public.

in part call A partial call of a bond issue for redemption.

inside information Information that is not known to people outside of the corporation. Information becomes public only after it is released by the corporation through a recognized media source. Inside information may be both material and immaterial. It is only illegal to trade on inside material information.

inside market The highest bid and the lowest offer for a security.

insider A company's officers, directors, large stockholders of 10% or more of the company, and anyone who is in possession of nonpublic material information, along with the immediate family members of the same.

Insider Trading and Securities Fraud Enforcement Act of 1988 Federal legislation that made the penalties for people trading on material nonpublic information more severe. Penalties for insider traders are up to the greater of 300% of the amount of money made or the loss avoided or $1 million and up to 5 years in prison. People who disseminate inside information may be imprisoned and fined up to $1 million.

INSTINET A computer network that facilitates trading of large blocks of stocks between institutions without the use of a broker dealer.

institutional account An account in the name of an institution but operated for the benefit of others (i.e., banks and mutual funds). There is no minimum size for an institutional account.

institutional communication Any communication that is distributed exclusively to institutional investors. Institutional communication does not require the preapproval of a principal but must be maintained for 3 years by the firm.

institutional investor An investor who trades for its own account or for the accounts of others in large quantities and is covered by fewer protective laws.

insurance covenant The promise of an issuer of revenue bonds to maintain insurance on the financed project.

intangible asset Nonphysical property of a corporation, such as trademarks and copyrights.

intangible drilling cost (IDC) Costs for an oil and gas program that are expensed in the year in which they are incurred for such things as wages, surveys, and well casings.

interbank market An international currency market.

interest The cost for borrowing money, usually charged at an annual percentage rate.

interest rate option An option based on U.S. government securities. The options are either rate-based or priced-based options.

interest rate risk The risk borne by investors in interest-bearing securities, which subjects the holder to a loss of principal should interest rates rise.

interlocking directorate Corporate boards that share one or more directors.

Intermarket Trading System/Computer-Assisted Execution System (ITS/CAES) A computer system that links the third market for securities with the exchanges.

Internal Revenue Code (IRC) The codes that define tax liabilities for U.S. taxpayers.

interpositioning The placing of another broker dealer in between the customer and the best market. Interpositioning is prohibited unless it can be demonstrated that the customer received a better price because of it.

interstate offering A multistate offering of securities that requires that the issuer register with the SEC as well as with the states in which the securities will be sold.

in the money A relationship between the strike price of an option and the underlying security's price. A call is in the money when the strike price is lower than the security's price. A put is in the money when the strike price is higher than the security's price.

intrastate offering *See* Rule 147.

intrinsic value The amount by which an option is in the money.

introducing broker *See* correspondent broker dealer.

inverted yield curve A yield curve where the cost of short-term financing exceeds the cost of long-term financing.

investment adviser Anyone who charges a fee for investment advice or who holds himself out to the public as being in the business of giving investment advice for a fee.

Investment Advisers Act of 1940 The federal legislation that sets forth guidelines for business requirements and activities of investment advisers.

investment banker A financial institution that is in the business of raising capital for companies and municipalities by underwriting securities.

investment company A company that sells undivided interests in a pool of securities and manages the portfolio for the benefit of the investors. Investment companies include management companies, unit investment trusts, and face-amount companies.

Investment Company Act of 1940 Federal legislation that regulates the operation and registration of investment companies.

investment-grade security A security that has been assigned a rating in the highest rating tier by a recognized ratings agency.

investment objective An investor's set of goals as to how he or she is seeking to make money, such as capital appreciation or current income.

investor The purchaser of a security who seeks to realize a profit.

IRA rollover The temporary distribution of assets from an IRA and the subsequent reinvestment of the assets into another IRA within 60 days. An IRA may be rolled over only once per year and is subject to a 10% penalty and ordinary income taxes if the investor is under 59-1/2 and if the assets are not deposited in another qualified account within 60 days.

IRA transfer The movement of assets from one qualified account to another without the account holder taking possession of the assets. Investors may transfer an IRA as often as they like.

issued stock Stock that has actually been sold to the investing public.

issuer Any entity that issues or proposes to issue securities.

J

joint account An account that is owned by two or more parties. Joint accounts allow either party to enter transactions for the account. Both parties must sign a joint account agreement. All joint accounts must be designated as joint tenants in common or with rights of survivorship.

joint tenants in common (JTIC) A joint account where the assets of a party who has died transfer to the decedent's estate, not the other tenant.

joint tenants with rights of survivorship (JTWROS) A joint account where the assets of a party who has died transfer to the surviving party, not the decedent's estate.

joint venture An interest in an operation shared by two or more parties. The parties have no other relationship beyond the joint venture.

junk bond A bond with a high degree of default risk that has been assigned a speculative rating by the ratings agencies.

junk bond fund A speculative bond fund that invests in high-yield bonds in order to achieve a high degree of current income.

K

Keogh plan A qualified retirement account for self-employed individuals. Contributions are limited to the lesser of 20% of their gross income or $51,000.

Keynesian economics An economic theory that states that government intervention in the marketplace helps sustain economic growth.

know-your-customer rule Industry regulation that requires a registered representative to be familiar with the customer's financial objectives and needs prior to making a recommendation; also known as Rule 405.

L

lagging indicator A measurement of economic activity that changes after a change has taken place in economic activity. Lagging indicators are useful confirmation tools when determining the strength of an economic trend. Lagging indicators include corporate profits, average duration of unemployment, and labor costs.

last in, first out (LIFO) An accounting method used that states that the last item that was produced is the first item sold.

leading indicator A measurement of economic activity that changes prior to a change in economic activity. Leading economic indicators are useful in predicting a coming trend in economic activity. Leading economic indicators include housing permits, new orders for durable goods, and the S&P 500.

LEAPS (long-term equity anticipation securities) A long-term option on a security that has an expiration of up to 39 months.

lease rental bonds A municipal bond that is issued to finance the building of a facility that will be rented out. The lease payments on the facility will support the bond's debt service.

legal list A list of securities that have been approved by certain state securities regulators for purchase by fiduciaries.

legal opinion An opinion issued by a bond attorney stating that the issue is a legally binding obligation of the state or municipality. The legal opinion also contains a statement regarding the tax status of the interest payments received by investors.

legislative risk The risk that the government may do something that adversely affects an investment.

letter of intent (LOI) A letter signed by the purchaser of mutual fund shares that states the investor's intention to invest a certain amount of money over a 13-month period. By agreeing to invest this sum, the investor is entitled to receive a lower sales charge on all purchases covered by the letter of intent. The letter of intent may be backdated up to 90 days from an initial purchase. Should the investor fail to invest the stated sum, a sales charge adjustment will be charged.

level load A mutual fund share that charges a flat annual fee, such as a 12B-1 fee.

level one A Nasdaq workstation service that allows the agent to see the inside market only.

level two A Nasdaq workstation service that allows the order-entry firm to see the inside market, to view the quotes entered by all market makers, and to execute orders.

level three A Nasdaq workstation service that allows market-making firms to see the inside market, to view the quotes entered by all market makers, to execute orders, and to enter their own quotes for the security. This is the highest level of Nasdaq service.

leverage The use of borrowed funds to try to obtain a rate of return that exceeds the cost of the funds.

liability A legal obligation to pay a debt either incurred through borrowing or through the normal course of business.

life annuity/straight life An annuity payout option that provides payments over the life of the annuitant.

life annuity with period certain An annuity payout option that provides payments to the annuitant for life or to the annuitant's estate for the period certain, whichever is longer.

life contingency An annuity payout option that provides a death benefit in case the annuitant dies during the accumulation stage.

limit order An order that sets a maximum price that the investor will pay in the case of a buy order or the minimum price the investor will accept in the case of a sell order.

limited liability A protection afforded to investors in securities that limits their liability to the amount of money invested in the securities.

limited partner A passive investor in a direct participation program who has no role in the project's management.

limited partnership (LP) An association of two or more partners with at least one partner being the general partner who is responsible for the management of the partnership.

limited partnership agreement The foundation of all limited partnerships. The agreement is the contract between all partners, and it spells out the authority of the general partner and the rights of all limited partners.

limited power of attorney/limited trading authorization Legal authorization for a representative or a firm to effect purchases and sales for a customer's account without the customer's prior knowledge. The authorization is limited to buying and selling securities and may not be given to another party.

limited principal An individual who has passed the Series 26 exam and may supervise Series 6 limited representatives.

limited representative An individual who has passed the Series 6 exam and may represent a broker dealer in the sale of mutual fund shares and variable contracts.

limited tax bond A type of general obligation bond that is issued by a municipality that may not increase its tax rate to pay the debt service of the issue.

liquidity The ability of an investment to be readily converted into cash.

liquidity risk The risk that an investor may not be able to sell a security when needed or that selling a security when needed will adversely affect the price.

listed option A standardized option contract that is traded on an exchange.

listed security A security that trades on one of the exchanges. Only securities that trade on an exchange are known as listed securities.

loan consent agreement A portion of the margin agreement that allows the broker dealer to loan out the customer's securities to another customer who wishes to borrow them to sell the security short.

locked market A market condition that results when the bid and the offer for a security are equal.

LOI *See* letter of intent.

London Interbank Offered Rate (LIBOR) The interbank rates for dollar-denominated deposits in England.

long A term used to describe an investor who owns a security.

long market value The total long market value of a customer's account.

long-term gain A profit realized through the sale of a security at a price that is higher than its purchase price after a being held for more than 12 months.

long-term loss A loss realized through the sale of a security at a price that is lower than its purchase price after being held for more than 12 months.

loss carry forward A capital loss realized on the sale of an asset in 1 year that is carried forward in whole or part to subsequent tax years.

low The lowest price at which a security has traded in any given period, usually measured during a trading day or for 52 weeks.

M

M1 The most liquid measure of the money supply. It includes all currency and demand and NOW deposits (checking accounts).

M2 A measure of the money supply that includes M1 plus all time deposits, savings accounts, and noninstitutional money market accounts.

M3 A measure of the money supply that includes M2 and large time deposits, institutional money market funds, short-term repurchase agreements, and other large liquid assets.

maintenance call A demand for additional cash or collateral made by a broker dealer when a margin customer's account equity has fallen below the minimum requirement of the NYSE or that is set by the broker dealer.

maintenance covenant A promise made by an issuer of a municipal revenue bond to maintain the facility in good repair.

Major Market Index (XMI) An index created by the Amex to AMEX 15 of the 30 largest stocks in the Dow Jones Industrial Average.

Maloney Act of 1938 An amendment to the Securities Exchange Act of 1934 that gave the NASD (now part of FINRA) the authority to regulate the over-the-counter market.

managed underwriting An underwriting conducted by a syndicate led by the managing underwriter.

management company A type of investment company that actively manages a portfolio of securities in order to meet a stated investment objective. Management companies are also known as mutual funds.

management fee (1) The fee received by the lead or managing underwriter of a syndicate. (2) The fee received by a sponsor of a direct participation program.

managing partner The general partner in a direct participation program.

managing underwriter The lead underwriter in a syndicate who is responsible for negotiating with the issuer, forming the syndicate, and settling the syndicate account.

margin The amount of customer equity that is required to hold a position in a security.

margin account An account that allows the customer to borrow money from the brokerage firm to buy securities.

margin call A demand for cash or collateral mandated by the Federal Reserve Board under Regulation T.

margin department The department in a broker dealer that calculates money owed by the customer or money due the customer.

margin maintenance call *See* maintenance call.

mark to the market The monitoring of a the current value of a position relative to the price at which the trade was executed for securities purchased on margin or on a when-issued basis.

markdown The profit earned by a dealer on a transaction when purchasing securities for its own account from a customer.

marketability The ability of an investment to be exchanged between two investors. A security with an active secondary market has a higher level of marketability than one whose market is not as active.

market arbitrage A type of arbitrage that consists of purchasing a security in one marketplace and selling it in another to take advantage of price inefficiencies.

market letter A regular publication, usually issued by an investment adviser, that offers information and/or advice regarding a security, market conditions, or the economy as a whole.

market maker A Nasdaq firm that is required to quote a continuous two-sided market for the securities in which it trades.

market not held A type of order that gives the floor broker discretion over the time and price of execution.

market on close An order that will be executed at whatever price the market is at, either on the closing print or just prior to the closing print.

market on open An order that will be executed at whatever price the market is at, either on the opening print or just after the opening print.

market order A type of order that will be executed immediately at the best available price once it is presented to the market.

market-out clause A clause in an underwriting agreement that gives the syndicate the ability to cancel the underwriting if it finds a material problem with the information or condition of the issuer.

market risk/ systematic risk The risk inherent in any investment in the market that states an investor may lose money simply because the market is going down.

market value The value of a security that is determined in the marketplace by the investors who enter bids and offers for a security.

markup The compensation paid to a securities dealer for selling a security to a customer from its inventory.

markup policy FINRA's guideline that states that the price that is paid or received by an investor must be reasonably related to the market price for that security. FINRA offers 5% as a guideline for what is reasonable to charge investors when they purchase or sell securities.

material information Information that would affect a company's current or future prospects or an investor's decision to invest in the company.

maturity date The date on which a bond's principal amount becomes payable to its holders.

member A member of FINRA or one of the 1,366 members of the NYSE.

member firm A firm that is a member of the NYSE, FINRA, or another self-regulatory organization.

member order A retail order entered by a member of a municipal bond syndicate for which the member will receive all of the sales credit.

mini maxi underwriting A type of best efforts underwriting that states that the offering will not become effective until a minimum amount is sold and sets a maximum amount that may be sold.

minimum death benefit The minimum guaranteed death benefit that will be paid to the beneficiaries if the holder of a variable life insurance policy dies.

minus tick A trade in an exchange-listed security that is at a price that is lower than the previous trade.

modern portfolio theory An investing approach that looks at the overall return and risk of a portfolio as a whole, not as a collection of single investments.

modified accelerated cost recovery system (MACRS) An accounting method that allows the owner to recover a larger portion of the asset's value in the early years of its life.

monetarist theory A theory that states that the money supply is the driving force in the economy and that a well-managed money supply will benefit the economy.

monetary policy Economic policy that is controlled by the Federal Reserve Board and controls the amount of money in circulation and the level of interest rates.

money market The secondary market where short-term highly liquid securities are traded. Securities traded in the money market include T-bills, negotiable CDs, bankers' acceptances, commercial paper, and other short-term securities with less than 12 months to maturity.

money market mutual fund A mutual fund that invests in money market instruments to generate monthly interest for its shareholders. Money market mutual funds have a stable NAV that is equal to $1, but it is not guaranteed.

money supply The total amount of currency, loans, and credit in the economy. The money supply is measured by M1, M2, M3, and L.

moral obligation bond A type of municipal revenue bond that will allow the state or municipality to vote to cover a shortfall in the debt service.

multiplier effect The ability of the money supply to grow simply through the normal course of banking. When banks and other financial institutions accept deposits and subsequently loan out those deposits to earn interest, the amount of money in the system grows.

municipal bond A bond issued by a state or political subdivision of a state in an effort to finance its operations. Interest earned by investors in municipal bonds is almost always free from federal income taxes.

municipal bond fund A mutual fund that invests in a portfolio of municipal debt in an effort to produce income that is free from federal income taxes for its investors.

Municipal Bond Investors Assurance Corp. (MBIA) An independent insurance company that will, for a fee received from the issuer, insure the interest and principal payments on a municipal bond.

municipal note A short-term municipal issue sold to manage the issuer's cash flow, usually in anticipation of the offering of long-term financing.

Municipal Securities Rulemaking Board (MSRB) The self-regulatory organization that oversees the issuance and trading of municipal bonds. The MSRB's rules are enforced by other industry SROs.

Munifacts A service that provides real-time secondary market quotes. Munifacts is now known as Thomson Muni Market Monitor.

mutual fund An investment company that invests in and manages a portfolio of securities for its shareholders. Open-end mutual funds sell their shares to investors on a continuous basis and must stand ready to redeem their shares upon the shareholder's request.

mutual fund custodian A qualified financial institution that maintains physical custody of a mutual fund's cash and securities. Custodians are usually banks, trust companies, or exchange member firms.

N

naked The sale of a call option without owning the underlying security or the sale of a put option without being short the stock or having cash on deposit that is sufficient to purchase the underlying security.

narrow-based index An index that is based on a market sector or a limited number of securities.

NASD (National Association of Securities Dealers) The industry self-regulatory agency that was authorized by the Maloney Act of 1938 and empowered to regulate the over-the-counter market. The NASD is now part of FINRA.

NASD bylaws The rules that define the operation of the NASD and how it regulates the over-the-counter market. The four major bylaws are the Rules of Fair Practice, the Uniform Practice Code, the Code of Procedure, and the Code of Arbitration. Now known as FINRA bylaws.

NASD Manual An NASD publication that outlines the rules and regulations of NASD membership. Now known as the FINRA Manual.

National Securities Clearing Corporation (NSCC) The clearing intermediary through which clearing member firms reconcile their securities accounts.

NAV (net asset value) The net value of a mutual fund after deducting all its liabilities. A mutual fund must calculate its NAV at least once per business day. To determine NAV per share, simply divide the mutual fund's NAV by the total number of shares outstanding.

negotiability The ability of an investment to be freely exchanged between noninterested parties.

negotiable certificate of deposit A certificate issued by a bank for a time deposit in excess of $100,000 that can be exchanged between parties prior to its maturity date. FDIC insurance only covers the first $250,000 of the principal amount should the bank fail.

NOW (negotiable order of withdrawal) Account A type of demand deposit that allows the holder to write checks against an interest-bearing account.

net change The difference between the previous day's closing price and the price of the most recently reported trade for a security.

net current assets per share A calculation of the value per share that excludes fixed assets and intangibles.

net debt per capita A measure of a municipal issuer's ability to meet its obligations. It measures the debt level of the issuer in relation to the population.

net debt to assessed valuation A measure of the issuer's ability to meet its obligations and to raise additional revenue through property taxes.

net direct debt The total amount of general obligation debt, including notes and short-term financing, issued by a municipality or state.

net interest cost (NIC) A calculation that measures the interest cost of a municipal issue over the life of all bonds. Most competitive underwritings for municipal securities are awarded to the syndicate that submits the bid with the lowest NIC.

net investment income The total sum of investment income derived from dividend and interest income after subtracting expenses.

net revenue pledge A pledge from a revenue bond that pays maintenance and operation expenses first, then debt service.

net total debt The total of a municipality's direct debt plus its overlapping debt.

net worth The value of a corporation after subtracting all of its liabilities. A corporation's net worth is also equal to shareholder's equity.

new account form Paperwork that must be filled out and signed by the representative and a principal of the firm prior to the opening of any account being opened for a customer.

new construction program A real estate program that seeks to achieve capital appreciation by building new properties.

new housing authority (NHA) A municipal bond issued to build low-income housing. NHA bonds are guaranteed by the U.S. government and are considered the safest type of municipal bonds. NHA bonds are not considered to be double-barreled bonds.

new issue *See* initial public offering (IPO).

New York Stock Exchange (NYSE) A membership organization that provides a marketplace for securities to be exchanged in one centralized location through a dual-auction process.

no-load fund A fund that does not charge the investor a sales charge to invest in the fund. Shares of no-load mutual funds are sold directly from the fund company to the investor.

nominal owner An individual or entity registered as the owner of record of securities for the benefit of another party.

nominal quote A quote given for informational purposes only. A trader who identifies a quote as being nominal cannot be held to trading at the prices that were clearly identified as being nominal.

nominal yield The yield that is stated or named on the security. The nominal yield, once it has been set, never changes, regardless of the market price of the security.

noncompetitive bid A bid submitted for Treasury bills where the purchaser agrees to accept the average of all yields accepted at the auction. Noncompetitive tenders are always the first orders filled at the auction.

noncumulative preferred A type of preferred stock whose dividends do not accumulate in arrears if the issuer misses the payment.

nondiscrimination A clause that states that all eligible individuals must be allowed to participate in a qualified retirement plan.

nondiversification An investment strategy that concentrates its investments among a small group of securities or issuers.

nondiversified management company An investment company that concentrates its investments among a few issuers or securities and does not meet the diversification requirements of the Investment Company Act of 1940.

nonfixed UIT A type of UIT that allows changes in the portfolio and traditionally invests in mutual fund shares.

nonqualified retirement plan A retirement plan that does not allow contributions to be made with pre-tax dollars; that is, the retirement plan does not qualify for beneficial tax treatment from the IRS for its contributions.

nonsystematic risk A risk that is specific to an issuer or an industry.

note An intermediate-term interest-bearing security that represents an obligation of its issuer.

not-held (NH) order An order that gives the floor broker discretion as to the time and price of execution.

numbered account An account that has been designated a number for identification purposes in order to maintain anonymity for its owner. The owner must sign a statement acknowledging ownership.

O

odd lot A transaction that is for less than 100 shares of stock or for less than 5 bonds.

odd lot differential An additional fee that may be charged to an investor for the handling of odd lot transactions (usually waived).

odd lot theory A contrarian theory that states that small investors will invariably buy and sell at the wrong time.

offer A price published at which an investor or broker dealer is willing to sell a security.

offering circular The offering document that is prepared by a corporation selling securities under a Regulation A offering.

office of supervisory jurisdiction (OSJ) An office identified by the broker dealer as having supervisory responsibilities for agents. It has final approval of new accounts, makes markets, and structures offerings.

Office of the Comptroller of the Currency An office of the U.S. Treasury that is responsible for regulating the practices of national banks.

official notice of sale The notice of sale published in the *Daily Bond Buyer* by a municipal issuer that is used to obtain an underwriter for municipal bonds.

official statement The offering document for a municipal issuer that must be provided to every purchaser if the issuer prepares one.

oil and gas direct participation program A type of direct participation program designed to invest in oil and gas production or exploration.

oil depletion allowance An accounting method used to reduce the amount of reserves available from a producing well.

omnibus account An account used by an introducing member to execute and clear all of its customers' trades.

open-end covenant A type of bond indenture that allows for the issuance of additional bonds with the same claim on the collateral as the original issue.

open-end investment company *See* mutual fund.

option A contract between two investors to purchase or sell a security at a given price for a certain period of time.

option agreement A form that must be signed and returned by an option investor within 15 days of the account's approval to trade options.

option disclosure document A document that must be furnished to all option investors at the time the account is approved for options trading. It is published by the Options Clearing Corporation (OCC), and it details the risks and features of standardized options.

Options Clearing Corporation (OCC) The organization that issues and guarantees the performance of standardized options.

order book official (OBO) Employees of the CBOE who are responsible for maintaining a fair and orderly market in the options assigned to them and for executing orders that have been left with them.

order department The department of a broker dealer that is responsible for routing orders to the markets for execution.

order memorandum/ order ticket The written document filled out by a registered representative that identifies, among other things, the security, the amount, the customer, and the account number for which the order is being entered.

original issue discount (OID) A bond that has been issued to the public at a discount to its par value. The OID on a corporate bond is taxed as if it was earned annually. The OID on a municipal bond is exempt from taxation.

OTC market *See* over-the-counter (OTC) market.

out of the money The relationship of an option's strike price to the underlying security's price when exercising the option would not make economic sense. A call is out of the money when the security's price is below the option's strike price. A put is out of the money when the security's price is above the option's strike price.

outstanding stock The total amount of a security that has been sold to the investing public and that remains in the hands of the investing public.

overlapping debt The portion of another taxing authority's debt that a municipality is responsible for.

overriding royalty interest A type of sharing arrangement that offers an individual with no risk a portion of the revenue in exchange for something of value, such as the right to drill on the owner's land.

over-the-counter (OTC) market An interdealer market that consists of a computer and phone network through which broker dealers trade securities.

P

par The stated principal amount of a security. Par value is of great importance for fixed-income securities such as bonds or preferred stock. Par value for bonds is traditionally $1,000, whereas par for a preferred stock is normally $100. Par value is of little importance when looking at common stock.

parity A condition that results when the value of an underlying common stock to be received upon conversion equals the value of the convertible security.

partial call A call of a portion of an issuer's callable securities.

participation The code set forth in the Employee Retirement Income Security Act of 1974 that states who is eligible to participate in an employer sponsored retirement plan.

passive income Income received by an individual for which no work was performed, such as rental income received from a rental property.

passive loss A loss realized on an investment in a limited partnership or rental property that can be used to offset passive income.

pass-through certificate A security that passes through income and principal payments made to an underlying portfolio of mortgages. Ginnie Mae is one of the biggest issuers of this type of security.

payment date The day when a dividend will actually be sent to investors. The payment date is set by the corporation's board of directors at the time when they initially declare the dividend.

payout stage The period during which an annuitant receives payments from an annuity contract.

payroll deduction plan A nonqualified retirement plan where employees authorize the employer to take regular deductions from their paychecks to invest in a retirement account.

pension plan A contractual retirement plan between an employee and an employer that is designed to provide regular income for the employee after retirement.

percentage depletion An accounting method that allows for a tax deduction for the reduction of reserves.

periodic payment plan A contract to purchase mutual fund shares over an extended period of time, usually in exchange for the fund company waiving its minimum investment requirement.

person Any individual or entity that can enter into a legally binding contract for the purchase and sale of securities.

personal income Income earned by an individual from providing services and through investments.

phantom income (1) A term used to describe the taxable appreciation on a zero-coupon bond. (2) The term used to describe taxable income generated by a limited partnership that is not producing positive cash flow.

Philadelphia Automated Communication Execution System (PACE) The computerized order-routing system for the Philadelphia Stock Exchange.

pink sheets An electronic quote service containing quotes for unlisted securities that is published by the National Quotation Bureau; operated as the PINK over-the-counter market.

placement ratio A ratio that details the percentage of municipal bonds sold, relative to the number of bonds offered in the last week, published by the *Daily Bond Buyer.*

plus tick A transaction in an exchange-listed security that is higher than the previous transaction.

point An increment of change in the price of a security: 1 bond point equals 1% of par or 1% of $1,000, or $10.

POP *See* public offering price (POP).

portfolio income Interest and dividends earned through investing in securities.

portfolio manager An entity that is hired to manage the investment portfolios of a mutual fund. The portfolio manager is paid a fee that is based on the net assets of the fund.

position The amount of a security in which an investor has an interest by either being long (owning) or short (owing) the security.

power of substitution *See* stock power.

preemptive right The right of a common stockholder to maintain proportional ownership interest in a security. A corporation may not issue additional shares of common stock without first offering those shares to existing stockholders.

preferred stock An equity security issued with a stated dividend rate. Preferred stockholders have a higher claim on a corporation's dividends and assets than common holders.

preferred stock ratio A ratio detailing the amount of an issuer's total capitalization that is made up of preferred stock. The ratio is found by dividing the total par value of preferred stock by the issuer's total capitalization.

preliminary prospectus/red herring A document used to solicit indications of interest during the cooling-off period for a new issue of securities. All of the information in the preliminary prospectus is subject to revision and change. The cover of a preliminary prospectus must have a statement saying that the securities have not yet become registered and that they may not be sold until the registration becomes effective. This statement is written in red ink, and this is where the term *red herring* comes from.

price-earnings ratio (PE) A measure of value used by analysts. It is calculated by dividing the issuer's stock price by its earnings per share.

price spread A term used to describe an option spread where the long and short options differ only in their exercise prices.

primary earnings per share The amount of earnings available per common share prior to the conversion of any outstanding convertible securities.

prime rate The interest rate that banks charge their best corporate customers on loans.

principal (1) The face amount of a bond. (2) A broker dealer trading for its own account. (3) An individual who has successfully completed a principal exam and may supervise representatives.

principal transaction A transaction where a broker dealer participates in a trade by buying or selling securities for its own account.

priority The acceptance of bids and offers for exchange-listed securities on a first-come, first-served (FCFS) basis.

private placement The private sale of securities to a limited number of investors. Also known as a Regulation D offering.

profit sharing plan A plan that allows the employer to distribute a percentage of its profits to its employees at a predetermined rate. The money may be paid directly to the employee or deposited into a retirement account.

progressive tax A tax structure where the tax rate increases as the income level of the individual or entity increases.

project note A municipal bond issued as interim financing in anticipation of the issuance of new housing authority bonds.

prospectus *See* final prospectus.

proxy A limited authority given by stockholders to another party to vote their shares in a corporate election. The stockholder may specify how the votes are cast or may give the party discretion.

proxy department The department in a brokerage firm that is responsible for forwarding proxies and financial information to investors whose stock is held in street name.

prudent man rule A rule that governs investments made by fiduciaries for the benefit of a third party. The rule states that the investments must be similar to those that a prudent person would make for him- or herself.

public offering The sale of securities by an issuer to public investors.

public offering price (POP) The price paid by an investor to purchase open-end mutual fund shares. Also the price set for a security the first time it is sold to the investing public.

put An option contract that allows the buyer to sell a security at a set price for a specific period of time. The seller of a put is obligated to purchase the security at a set price for a specific period of time, should the buyer exercise the option.

put buyer A bearish investor who pays a premium for the right to sell a security at a set price for a certain period of time.

put spread An option position created by the simultaneous purchase and sale of two put options on the same underlying security that differ in strike prices, expiration months, or both.

put writer A bullish investor who sells a put option in order to receive the option premium. The writer is obligated to purchase the security if the buyer exercises the option.

Q

qualified legal opinion A legal opinion containing conditions or reservations relating to the issue. A legal opinion is issued by a bond counsel for a municipal issuer.

qualified retirement plan A retirement plan that qualifies for favorable tax treatment by the IRS for contributions made into the plan.

quick assets A measure of liquidity that subtracts the value of a corporation's unsold inventory from its current assets.

quick ratio *See* acid-test ratio.

quote A bid and offer broadcast from the exchange or through the Nasdaq system that displays the prices at which a security may be purchased and sold and in what quantities.

R

range The price difference between the high and low for a security.

rate covenant A promise in the trust indenture of a municipal revenue bond to keep the user fees high enough to support the debt service.

rating A judgment of an issuer's ability to meet its credit obligations. The higher the credit quality of the issuer is, the higher the credit rating. The lower the credit quality is, the lower the credit rating, and the higher the risk associated with the securities.

rating service Major financial organizations that evaluate the credit quality of issuers. Issuers have to request and pay for the service. Standard and Poor's, Moody's, and Fitch are the most widely followed rating services.

raw land program A type of real estate limited partnership that invests in land for capital appreciation.

real estate investment trust (REIT) An entity that is organized to invest in or manage real estate. REITs offer investors certain tax advantages that are beyond the scope of the exam.

real estate limited partnership A type of direct participation program that invests in real estate projects to produce income or capital appreciation.

real estate mortgage investment conduit (REMIC) An organization that pools investors' capital to purchase portfolios of mortgages.

realized gain A profit earned on the sale of a security at a price that exceeds its purchase price.

realized loss A loss recognized by an investor by selling a security at a price that is less than its purchase price.

reallowance A sales concession available to dealers who sell securities subject to an offering who are not syndicate or selling group members.

recapture An event that causes a tax liability on a previously taken deduction, such as selling an asset above its depreciated cost base.

recession A decline in GDP that lasts for at least 6 months but not longer than 18 months.

reclamation The right of a seller to demand or claim any loss from the buying party due to the buyer's failure to settle the transaction.

record date A date set by a corporation's board of directors that determines which shareholders will be entitled to receive a declared dividend. Shareholders must be owners of record on this date in order to collect the dividend.

recourse loan A loan taken out by a limited partnership that allows the lender to seek payment from the limited partners in the case of the partnership's failure to pay.

redeemable security A security that can be redeemed by the issuer at the investor's request. Open-end mutual funds are an example of redeemable securities.

redemption The return of an investor's capital by an issuer. Open-end mutual funds must redeem their securities within 7 days of an investor's request.

red herring *See* preliminary prospectus.

registered A term that describes the level of owner information that is recorded by the security's issuer.

registered as to principal only A type of bond registration that requires the investor to clip coupons to receive the bond's interest payments. The issuer will automatically send the investor the bond's principal amount at maturity.

registered options principal (ROP) An individual who has passed the Series 4 exam.

registered principal A supervisor of a member firm who has passed the principal examination.

registered representative An individual who has successfully completed a qualified examination to represent a broker dealer or issuer in securities transactions.

registrar An independent organization that accounts for all outstanding stock and bonds of an issuer.

registration statement The full disclosure statement that nonexempt issuers must file with the SEC prior to offering securities for sale to the public. The Securities Act of 1933 requires that a registration statement be filed.

regressive tax A tax that is levied on all parties at the same rate, regardless of their income. An example of a regressive tax is a sales tax. A larger percentage of a low-income earner's income is taken away by the tax.

regular-way settlement The standard number of business days in which a securities transaction is completed and paid for. Corporate securities and municipal bonds settle the, regular way on the second business day after the trade date with payment due on the fourth business day. Government securities settle the next business day.

regulated investment company An investment company that qualifies as a conduit for net investment income under Internal Revenue Code subchapter M, so long as it distributes at least 90% of its net investment income to shareholders.

Regulation A A Regulation A offering allows a company to raise up to 50 million dollars in a tier 2 offering and up to 20 million dollars in a tier 1 offering in any 12-month period.

Regulation D A private placement or sale of securities that allows for an exemption from registration under the Securities Act of 1933. A private placement may be sold to an unlimited number of accredited investors but may only be sold to 35 nonaccredited investors in any 12-month period.

Regulation G Regulates the extension of credit for securities purchases by other commercial lenders.

Regulation T Regulates the extension of credit by broker dealers for securities purchases.

Regulation U Regulates the extension of credit by banks for securities purchases.

Regulation X Regulates the extension of credit by overseas lenders for securities purchases.

Rehypothecation The act of a broker dealer repledging a customer's securities as collateral at a bank to obtain a loan for the customer.

REIT *See* real estate investment trust (REIT).

rejection The act of a buyer of a security refusing delivery.

reorganization department The department in a brokerage firm that handles changes in securities that result from a merger or acquisition or calls.

repurchase agreement (REPO) A fully collateralized loan that results in a sale of securities to the lender, with the borrower agreeing to repurchase them at a higher price in the future. The higher price represents the lender's interest.

reserve maintenance fund An account set up to provide additional funds to maintain a revenue-producing facility financed by a revenue bond.

reserve requirement A deposit required to be placed on account with the Federal Reserve Board by banks. The requirement is a percentage of the bank's customers' deposits.

resistance A price level to which a security appreciates and attracts sellers. The new sellers keep the security's price from rising any higher.

restricted account (1) A long margin account that has less than 50% equity but more than 25%. (2) A customer account that has been subject to a sellout.

restricted stock A nonexempt unregistered security that has been obtained by means other than a public offering.

retail communication Any communication that may be seen in whole or in part by an individual investor. Retail communication must be approved by a principal prior to first use and maintained by the firm for 3 years.

retained earnings The amount of a corporation's net income that has not been paid out to shareholders as dividends.

retention The amount of a new issue that an underwriter allocates to its own clients.

retention requirement The amount of equity that must be left in a restricted margin account when withdrawing securities.

return on equity A measure of performance found by dividing after-tax income by common stockholders' equity.

return on investment (ROI) The profit or loss realized by an investor from holding a security expressed as a percentage of the invested capital.

revenue anticipation note A short-term municipal issue that is sold to manage an issuer's cash flow in anticipation of other revenue in the future.

reverse repurchase agreement A fully collateralized loan that results in the purchase of securities with the intention of reselling them to the borrower at a higher price. The higher price represents the buyer's/lender's interest.

reverse split A stock split that results in fewer shares outstanding, with each share being worth proportionally more.

reversionary working interest A revenue-sharing arrangement where the general partner shares none of the cost and receives none of the revenue until the limited partners have received their payments back, plus any predetermined amount of return.

right A short-term security issued in conjunction with a shareholder's preemptive right. The maximum length of a right is 45 days, and it is issued with a subscription price, which allows the holder to purchase the underlying security at a discount from its market price.

rights agent An independent entity responsible for maintaining the records for rights holders.

rights of accumulation A right offered to mutual fund investors that allows them to calculate all past contributions and growth to reach a breakpoint to receive a sales charge discount on future purchases.

rights offering The offering of new shares by a corporation that is preceded by the offering of the new shares to existing shareholders.

riskless simultaneous transaction The purchase of a security on a principal basis by a brokerage firm for the sole purpose of filling a customer's order that the firm has already received. The markup on riskless principal transactions has to be based on the firm's actual cost for the security.

rollover The distribution of assets from a qualified account to an investor for the purpose of depositing the assets in another qualified account within 60 days. An investor may only roll over an IRA once every 12 months.

round lot A standard trading unit for securities. For common and preferred stock, a round lot is 100 shares. For bonds, it is 5 bonds.

Rule 144 SEC rule that regulates the sale of restricted and control securities requiring the seller to file Form 144 at the time the order is entered to sell. Rule 144 also regulates the number of securities that may be sold.

Rule 145 SEC rule that requires a corporation to provide stockholders with full disclosure relating to reorganizations and to solicit proxies.

Rule 147 An intrastate offering that provides an exemption from SEC registration.

Rule 405 The NYSE rule that requires that all customer recommendations must be suitable and that the representative must "know" the customer.

S

sale *See* sell.

sales charge *See* commission.

sales literature Written material distributed by a firm to a controlled audience for the purpose of increasing business. Sales literature includes market letters, research reports, and form letters sent to more than 25 customers.

sales load The amount of commission charged to investors in open-end mutual funds. The amount of the sales load is added to the net asset value of the fund to determine the public offering price of the fund.

satellite office An office not identified to the public as an office of the member, such as an agent's home office.

savings bond A nonnegotiable U.S. government bond that must be purchased from the government and redeemed to the government. These bonds are generally known as Series EE and HH bonds.

scale A list of maturities and yields for a new serial bond issue.

Schedule 13D A form that must be filed with the SEC by any individual or group of individuals acquiring 5% or more of a corporation's nonexempt equity securities. Form 13D must be filed within 10 days of the acquisition.

scheduled premium policy A variable life insurance policy with fixed premium payments.

SEC *See* Securities and Exchange Commission (SEC).

secondary distribution A distribution of a large number of securities by a large shareholder or group of large shareholders. The distribution may or may not be done under a prospectus.

secondary offering An underwriting of a large block of stock being sold by large shareholders. The proceeds of the issue are received by the selling shareholders, not the corporation.

secondary market A marketplace where securities are exchanged between investors. All transactions that take place on an exchange or on the Nasdaq are secondary market transactions.

sector fund A mutual fund that invests in companies within a specific business area in an effort to maximize gains. Sector funds have larger risk-reward ratios because of the concentration of investments.

Securities Act of 1933 The first major piece of securities industry legislation. It regulates the primary market and requires that nonexempt issuers file a registration statement with the SEC. The act also requires that investors in new issues be given a prospectus.

Securities Act Amendments of 1975 Created the Municipal Securities Rulemaking Board (MSRB).

Securities Exchange Act of 1934 Regulates the secondary market and all broker dealers and industry participants. It created the Securities and Exchange Commission, the industry's ultimate authority. The act gave the authority to the Federal Reserve Board to regulate the extension of credit for securities purchases through Regulation T.

Securities and Exchange Commission The ultimate securities industry authority. The SEC is a direct government body, not a self-regulatory organization. The commissioners are appointed by the U.S. President and must be approved by Congress.

Securities Investor Protection Corporation (SIPC) The industry's nonprofit insurance company that provides protection for investors in case of broker dealer failure. All member firms must pay dues to SIPC based upon their revenue. SIPC provides coverage for each separate customer for up to $500,000, of which a maximum of $250,000 may be cash. The Securities Investor Protection Act of 1970 created SIPC.

security Any investment that can be exchanged for value between two parties that contains risk. Securities include stocks, bonds, mutual funds, notes, rights, warrants, and options, among others.

segregation The physical separation of customer and firm assets.

self-regulatory organization (SRO) An industry authority that regulates its own members. FINRA, the NYSE, and the CBOE are all self-regulatory organizations that regulate their own members.

sell The act of conveying the ownership of a security for value to another party. A sale includes any security that is attached to another security, as well as any security which the security may be converted or exchanged into.

seller's option A type of settlement option that allows the seller to determine when delivery of the securities and final settlement of the trade will occur.

selling away Any recommendation to a customer that involves an investment product that is not offered through the employing firm without the firm's knowledge and consent. This is a violation of industry regulations and may result in action being taken against the representative.

selling concession *See* concession.

selling dividends The act of using a pending dividend to create urgency for the customer to purchase a security. This is a violation and could result in action being taken against the representative.

selling group A group of broker dealers who may sell a new issue of securities but who are not members of the syndicate and who have no liability to the issuer.

sell out A transaction executed by a broker dealer when a customer fails to pay for the securities.

sell-stop order An order placed beneath the current market for a security to protect a profit, to guard against a loss, or to establish a short position.

separate account The account established by an insurance company to invest the pooled funds of variable contract holders in the securities markets. The separate account must register as either an open-end investment company or as a unit investment trust.

separate trading of registered interest and principal securities (STRIPS) A zero-coupon bond issued by the U.S. government. The principal payment due in the future is sold to investors at a discount and appreciates to par at maturity. The interest payment component is sold to other investors who want some current income.

serial bonds A bond issue that has an increasing amount of principal maturing in successive years.

Series EE bond A nonmarketable U.S. government zero-coupon bond that is issued at a discount and matures at its face value. Investors must purchase the bonds from the U.S. government and redeem them to the government at maturity.

Series HH bond A nonmarketable U.S. government interest-bearing bond that can only be purchased by trading in matured Series EE bonds. Series HH bonds may not be purchased with cash and are issued with a $500 minimum denomination.

settlement The completion of a securities transaction. A transaction settles and is completed when the security is delivered to the buyer and the cash is delivered to the seller.

settlement date The date when a securities ownership changes. Settlement dates are set by FINRA's Uniform Practice Code.

75-5-10 diversification The diversification test that must be met by mutual funds under the Investment Company Act of 1940 in order to market themselves as a diversified mutual fund: 75% of the fund's assets must be invested in other issuer's securities, no more than 5% of the fund's assets may be invested in any one company, and the fund may own no more than 10% of an issuer's outstanding securities.

shareholder's equity *See* net worth.

share identification The process of identifying which shares are being sold at the time the sale order is entered in order to minimize an investor's tax liability.

shelf offering A type of securities registration that allows the issuer to sell the securities over a 2-year period.

short A position established by a bearish investor that is created by borrowing the security and selling in the hopes that the price of the security will fall. The investor hopes to be able to repurchase the security at a lower price, thus replacing it cheaply. If the security's price rises, the investor will suffer a loss.

short against the box A short position established against an equal long position in the security to roll tax liabilities forward. Most of the benefits of establishing a short against the box position have been eliminated.

short straddle The simultaneous sale of a call and a put on the same underlying security with the same strike price and expiration. A short straddle would be established by an investor who believes that the security price will move sideways.

simplified arbitration A method of resolving disputes of $50,000 or less. There is no hearing; one arbitrator reads the submissions and renders a final decision.

Simplified Employee Pension (SEP) A qualified retirement plan created for small employers with 25 or fewer employees that allows the employees' money to grow tax-deferred until retirement.

single account An account operated for one individual. The individual has control of the account, and the assets go to the individual's estate in the case of his or her death.

sinking fund An account established by an issuer of debt to place money for the exclusive purpose of paying bond principal.

special assessment bond A municipal bond backed by assessments from the property that benefits from the improvements.

specialist Member of an exchange responsible for maintaining a fair and orderly market in the securities that he or she specializes in and for executing orders left with him or her.

specialist book A book of limit orders left with the specialist for execution.

special situation fund A fund that seeks to take advantage of unusual corporate developments, such as take mergers and restructuring.

special tax bond A type of municipal revenue bond that is supported only by revenue from certain taxes.

speculation An investment objective where the investor is willing to accept a high degree of risk in exchange for the opportunity to realize a high return.

split offering An offering where a portion of the proceeds from the underwriting goes to the issuer and a portion goes to the selling shareholders.

spousal account An IRA opened for a nonworking spouse that allows a full contribution to be made for the nonworking spouse.

spread (1) The difference between the bid and ask for a security. (2) The simultaneous purchase and sale of two calls or two puts on the same underlying security.

spread load plan A contractual plan that seeks to spread the sales charge over a longer period of time, as detailed in the Spread Load Plan Act of 1970. The maximum sales charge over the life of the plan is 9%, while the maximum sales charge in any one year is 20%.

stabilizing The only form of price manipulation allowed by the SEC. The managing underwriter enters a bid at or below the offering price to ensure even distribution of shares.

standby underwriting An underwriting used in connection with a preemptive rights offering. The standby underwriter must purchase any shares not subscribed to by existing shareholders.

statutory disqualification A set of rules that prohibit an individual who has been barred or suspended or convicted of a securities-related crime from becoming registered.

statutory voting A method of voting that requires investors to cast their votes evenly for the directors they wish to elect.

stock ahead A condition that causes an investor's order not to be executed, even though the stock is trading at a price that would satisfy the customer's limit order, because other limit orders have been entered prior to the customer's order.

stock certificate Evidence of equity ownership.

stock or bond power A form that, when signed by the owner and attached to a security, makes the security negotiable.

stock split A change in the number of outstanding shares, the par value, and the number of authorized shares that has been approved through a vote of the shareholders. Forward-stock splits increase the number of shares outstanding and reduce the stock price in order to make the security more attractive to individual investors.

stop limit order An order that becomes a limit order to buy or sell the stock when the stock trades at or through the stop price.

stop order An order that becomes a market order to buy or sell the stock when the stock trades at or through the stop price.

stopping stock A courtesy offered by a specialist to public customers, whereby the specialist guarantees a price but tries to obtain a better price for the customer.

straddle The simultaneous purchase or sale of a call and a put on the same security with the same strike price and expiration.

straight line depreciation An accounting method that allows an owner to take equal tax deductions over the useful life of the asset.

strangle The purchase or sale of a call and a put on either side of the current market price. The options have the same expiration months but different strike prices.

stripped bond A bond that has had its coupons removed by a broker dealer and that is selling at a deep discount to its principal payment in the future.

stripper well An oil well that is in operation just to recover a very limited amount of reserves.

subchapter S corporation A business organization that allows the tax consequences of the organization to flow through to the owners.

subscription agreement An application signed by the purchaser of an interest in a direct participation plan. An investor in a limited partnership does not become an investor until the general partner signs the subscription agreement.

subscription right *See* right.

suitability A determination that the characteristics of a security are in line with an investor's objectives, financial profile, and attitudes.

Super Display Book System (SDBK) The electronic order-routing system used by the NYSE to route orders directly to the trading post.

supervise The actions of a principal that ensure that the actions of a firm and its representatives are in compliance with industry regulations.

support The price to which a security will fall and attract new buyers. As the new buyers enter the market, it keeps the price from falling any lower.

surplus fund An account set up for funds generated by a project financed by a municipal revenue bond to pay a variety of expenses.

syndicate A group of underwriters responsible for underwriting a new issue.

systematic risk A risk inherent in any investment in the market. An investor may lose money simply because the market is going down.

T

takedown The price at which a syndicate purchases a new issue of securities from the issuer.

tax and revenue anticipation note A short-term note sold by a municipal issuer as interim financing in anticipation of tax and other revenue.

tax anticipation note (TAN) A short-term note sold by a municipal issuer as interim financing in anticipation of tax revenue.

tax-deferred annuity A nonqualified retirement account that allows an investor's money to grow tax deferred. A tax-deferred annuity is a contract between an insurance company and an investor.

tax equivalent yield The interest rate that must be offered by a taxable bond of similar quality in order to be equal to the rate that is offered by a municipal bond.

tax-exempt bond fund A bond fund that seeks to produce investment income that is free from federal tax by investing in a portfolio of municipal bonds.

tax liability The amount of money that is owed by an investor after realizing a gain on the sale of an investment or after receiving investment income.

tax preference item An item that receives preferential tax treatment and must be added back into income when calculating an investor's alternative minimum tax.

tax-sheltered annuity (TSA) A qualified retirement plan offered to employees of governments, school systems, or nonprofit organizations. Contributions to TSAs are made with pre-tax dollars.

technical analysis A method of security analysis that uses past price performance to predict the future performance of a security.

Telephone Consumer Protection Act of 1991 Legislation that regulates how potential customers are contacted by phone at home.

tenants in common *See* joint tenants in common.

tender offer An offer to buy all or part of a company's outstanding securities for cash or cash and securities.

term bond A bond issue that has its entire principal due on one date.

term maturity A type of bond maturity that has all principal due on one date.

testimonial The use of a recognized expert or leader to endorse the services of a firm.

third market A transaction in an exchange-listed security executed over the Nasdaq workstation.

third-party account An account that is managed for the benefit of a customer by another party, such as an investment adviser, a trustee, or an attorney.

30-day visible supply The total par value of all new issue municipal bonds coming to market in the next 30 days.

time deposit An account that is established by a bank customer where the customer agrees to leave the funds on deposit for an agreed upon amount of time.

time value The value of an option that exceeds its intrinsic value or its in-the-money amount.

tombstone ad An announcement published in financial papers advertising the offering of securities by a group of underwriters. Only basic information may be contained in the tombstone ad, and all offers must be made through the prospectus only.

top heavy rule The rule that states the maximum salary for which a Keogh contribution may be based. This is in effect to limit the disparity between high- and low-salary employees.

trade confirmation The printed notification of a securities transaction. A confirmation must be sent to a customer on or before the completion of a transaction. The completion of a transaction is considered to be the settlement date.

trade date The day when an investor's order is executed.

tranche A class of collateralized mortgage obligation (CMO) that has a predicted maturity and interest rate.

transfer agent An independent entity that handles name changes, records the names of security holders of record, and ensures that all certificates are properly endorsed.

transfer and hold in safekeeping A request by customers for the brokerage firm to transfer their securities into the firm's name and to hold them in safekeeping at the firm. A brokerage may charge a fee for holding a customer's securities that have been registered in its name.

transfer and ship A request by customers for the brokerage firm to transfer their securities into their name and to ship them to their address of record.

Treasury bill A U.S. government security that is issued at a discount and matures at par in 4, 13, 26, and 52 weeks.

Treasury bond A long-term U.S. government security that pays semiannual interest and matures in 10 to 30 years.

Treasury note An intermediate-term U.S. government security that pays semiannual interest and matures in 1 to 10 years.

Treasury receipt A zero-coupon bond created by a brokerage firm that is backed by U.S. government securities. It is issued at a discount and matures at par.

treasury stock Stock that has been issued by a corporation and that has subsequently been repurchased by the corporation. Treasury stock does not vote or receive dividends. It is not used in the calculation of earnings per share.

trendline A line used to predict the future price movement for a security. Drawing a line under the successive lows or successive highs creates a trendline.

trough The bottoming out of the business cycle just prior to an new upward movement in activity.

true interest cost (TIC) A calculation for the cost of a municipal issuer's interest expense that includes the time value of money.

Trust Indenture Act of 1940 Regulates the issuance of corporate debt in excess of $5 million and with a term exceeding 1 year. It requires an indenture between the issuer and the trustee.

trustee A person who legally acts for the benefit of another party.

12B-1 fee An asset-based distribution fee that is assessed annually and paid out quarterly to cover advertising and distribution costs. All 12B-1 fees must be reasonable.

two-dollar broker An independent exchange member who executes orders for commission house brokers and other customers for a fee.

type A classification method for an option as either a call or a put.

U

uncovered *See* naked.

underlying security A security for which an investor has an option to buy or sell.

underwriting The process of marketing a new issue of securities to the investing public. A broker dealer forwards the proceeds of the sale to the issuer minus its fee for selling the securities.

unearned income Any income received by an individual from an investment, such as dividends and interest income.

uniform delivery ticket A document that must be attached to every security delivered by the seller, making the security "good delivery."

Uniform Gifts to Minors Act (UGMA) Sets forth guidelines for the gifting of cash and securities to minors and for the operation of accounts managed for the benefit of minors. Once a gift is given to a minor, it is irrevocable.

Uniform Practice Code The FINRA bylaw that sets guidelines for how industry members transact business with other members. The Uniform Practice Code establishes such things as settlement dates, rules of good delivery, and ex-dividend dates.

Uniform Securities Act (USA) The framework for state-based securities legislation. The act is a model that can be adapted to each state's particular needs.

Uniform Transfer to Minors Act (UTMA) Legislation that has been adopted in certain states, in lieu of the Uniform Gifts to Minors Act. UTMA allows the custodian to determine the age at which the assets become the property of the minor. The maximum age for transfer of ownership is 25.

unit investment trust (UIT) A type of investment company organized as a trust to invest in a portfolio of securities. The UIT sells redeemable securities to investors in the form of shares or units of beneficial interest.

unit of beneficial interest The redeemable share issued to investors in a unit investment trust.

unit refund annuity An annuity payout option that will make payments to the annuitant for life. If the annuitant dies prior to receiving an amount that is equal to his or her account value, the balance of the account will be paid to the annuitant's beneficiaries.

unqualified legal opinion A legal opinion issued by a bond attorney for the issue where there are no reservations relating to the issue.

unrealized A paper profit or loss on a security that is still owned.

V

variable annuity A contract issued by an insurance company that is both a security and an insurance product. The annuitant's contributions are invested through the separate account into a portfolio of securities. The annuitant's payments depend largely on the investment results of the separate account.

variable death benefit The amount of a death benefit paid to a beneficiary that is based on the investment results of the insurance company's separate account. This amount is over the contract's minimum guaranteed death benefit.

variable life insurance A life insurance policy that provides for a minimum guaranteed death benefit, as well as an additional death benefit, based on the investment results of the separate account.

variable rate municipal security Interim municipal financing issued with a variable rate.

vertical spread The simultaneous purchase and sale of two calls or two puts on the same underlying security that differ only in strike price.

vesting The process by which an employer's contributions to an employee's retirement account become the property of the employee.

visible supply *See* 30-day visible supply.

voluntary accumulation plan A method, such as dollar-cost averaging, by which an investor regularly makes contributions to acquire mutual fund shares.

voting right The right of a corporation's stockholders to cast their votes for the election of the corporation's board of directors as well as for certain major corporate issues.

W

warrant A long-term security that gives the holder the right to purchase the common shares of a corporation for up to 10 years. The warrant's subscription price is always higher than the price of the underlying common shares when the warrant is initially issued.

wash sale The sale of a security at a loss and the subsequent repurchase of that security or of a security that is substantially the same within 30 days of the sale. The repurchase disallows the claim of the loss for tax purposes.

western account A type of municipal security syndicate account where only the member with unsold bonds is responsible for the unsold bonds.

when-issued security A security that has been sold prior to the certificates being available for delivery.

wildcatting An exploratory oil- and gas-drilling program.

wire room *See* order department.

withdrawal plan The systematic removal of funds from a mutual fund account over time. Withdrawal plans vary in type and availability among fund companies.

workable indication An indication of the prices and yields that a municipal securities dealer may be willing to buy or sell bonds.

working capital A measure of a corporation's liquidity that is found by subtracting current liabilities from current assets.

working interest An interest that requires the holder to bear the proportional expenses and allows the holder to share in the revenue produced by an oil or gas project in relation to the interest.

workout quote A nonfirm quote that requires handling and settlement conditions to be worked out between the parties prior to the trade.

writer An investor who sells an option to receive the premium income.

writing the scale The procedure of assigning prospective yields to a new issuer of serial municipal bonds.

Y

Yellow Sheets A daily publication published by the national quotation bureau providing quotes for corporate bonds.

yield The annual amount of income generated by a security relative to its price; expressed as a percentage.

yield-based option An interest rate option that allows the holder to receive the in-the-money amount in cash upon exercise or expiration.

yield curve The rate at which interest rates vary among investments of similar quality with different maturities. Longer-term securities generally offer higher yields.

yield to call An investor's overall return for owning a bond should it be called in prior to maturity by the issuer.

yield to maturity An investor's overall return for owning a bond if the bond is held until maturity.

Z

zero-coupon bond A bond that is issued at a discount from its par value and makes no regular interest payments. An investor's interest is reflected by the security's appreciation toward par at maturity. The appreciation is taxable each year even though it is not actually received by the investor (phantom income).

zero-minus tick A trade in an exchange-listed security that occurs at the same price as the previous transaction, but at a price that is lower than the last transaction that was different.

zero-plus tick A trade in an exchange-listed security that occurs at the same price as the previous transaction, but at a price that is higher than the last transaction that was different.

Index

C

D

M

N

O

Made in the USA
Columbia, SC
09 October 2021